THE NEW GEORGIA ENCYCLOPEDIA COMPANION TO

Georgia Literature

The New Georgia Encyclopedia

COMPANION TO

Georgia Literature

HUGH RUPPERSBURG, Volume Editor

JOHN C. INSCOE, General Editor

A PROJECT OF THE NEW GEORGIA ENCYCLOPEDIA

*Published in association with the Georgia Humanities Council
and the University System of Georgia / GALILEO*

The University of Georgia Press
Athens & London

Publication of this book was made possible in part by a
generous grant from the Watson-Brown Foundation, Inc.

Published in 2007 by the University of Georgia Press
Athens, Georgia 30602
© 2004–7 by the Georgia Humanities Council and
the University of Georgia Press
All rights reserved
Designed by Walton Harris
Set in 10/14 Sabon
Printed and bound by Maple-Vail

The paper in this book meets the guidelines for permanence
and durability of the Committee on Production Guidelines
for Book Longevity of the Council on Library Resources.

Printed in the United States of America

11 10 09 08 07 P 5 4 3 2 1

Library of Congress Cataloging-in-Publication Data

The new Georgia encyclopedia companion to Georgia
literature / Hugh Ruppersburg, volume editor ;
John C. Inscoe, general editor.
    p.   cm.
"A project of the new Georgia encyclopedia."
Includes bibliographical references.
ISBN-13: 978-0-8203-2876-8 (pbk. : alk. paper)
ISBN-10: 0-8203-2876-6 (pbk. : alk. paper)
1. American literature—Georgia—History and criticism.
2. Authors, American—Homes and haunts—Georgia.
3. Georgia—In literature. I. Ruppersburg, Hugh.
II. John C. Inscoe, 1951– .
PS266.G4N48 2007
810.9'975803—dc22   2006021908

British Library Cataloging-in-Publication Data available

CONTENTS

FOREWORD

In his introductory overview, Hugh Ruppersburg notes that, within the South, only Mississippi boasts a stronger fictional output than Georgia. I would suggest that by casting the term *literature* a bit more broadly, as this volume does, Georgia is probably unsurpassed in the impact its writers have had on how the South and the southern experience have been seen and understood by the rest of the nation and the world. By incorporating into that corpus the writings of statesmen and political figures like W. E. B. Du Bois, Martin Luther King Jr., and Jimmy Carter; the texts of journalists like Elias Boudinot, Henry Grady, Ralph McGill, and Lewis Grizzard; and the film adaptations of works like *Gone With the Wind*, *Deliverance*, *The Color Purple*, and *Driving Miss Daisy*, it would be hard to argue that any group of southern writers has had a more substantial and significant literary legacy than have Georgians.

No one knows more about the field or has done as much to collect, catalog, and make accessible this vast array of work than has Hugh Ruppersburg, and *The New Georgia Encyclopedia* was fortunate to acquire his services as the Literature section editor. As a result of his expert guidance and conscientious oversight, that section quickly emerged as one of the most comprehensive sections in the *NGE* and, as such, was an obvious choice to become the first in what we hope will be a series of topical "companions" drawn from the online encyclopedia, thus making the same material accessible in a different format and perhaps to a different audience.

There is probably no scholarly endeavor more collaborative than an encyclopedia, and this is probably even truer of *The New Georgia Encyclopedia* than most. Initiated and guided throughout by Jamil Zainaldin, the president of the Georgia Humanities Council, the *NGE* began in 1998 as a joint project with the

University of Georgia Press. In 1999 the University System of Georgia/GALILEO joined as our vital third partner. Georgia's Office of the Governor provided financial support for the encyclopedia, as did the National Endowment for the Humanities, the Robert W. Woodruff Foundation, and other private foundations and corporate donors. This companion is made possible by a grant from the Watson-Brown Foundation. The first state encyclopedia conceived exclusively for the Internet, the *NGE* went into production in 2000, and the site was publicly "launched" onto the Internet in February 2004, with an initial three hundred articles. Since then, we have continued to commission, edit, and load new material onto the site so that by the end of 2006, when we completed the planned first phase of the project, the site boasted 1,700 articles.

While a host of people have made this possible, including over twenty section editors like Ruppersburg, the core staff of the *NGE* has remained small, with no more than four full-time members at any given time. The original staff consisted of Nancy Grayson, the project's very first full-time editor and staff member, Elisabeth Hughes, and Darby Sanders. Since then, Kelly Caudle, Erin McLeod, Sarah McKee, Mary Koon, Melinda Mullikin, and other staff, past and present, have continued the work begun by the original three. All of these staff members have been closely involved with the articles included here and online, as have a host of copy editors, fact checkers, part-time assistants, media editors, technical advisors, and staff members of the University of Georgia Press, the Georgia Humanities Council, and the University System of Georgia/GALILEO. The project as a whole is the beneficiary of a vast range of expertise, resources, and support from scholars, journalists, educators and students, archivists, museum curators, and government workers throughout the state, whose varied contributions have expanded and enhanced the final product.

What appear in these pages are the full contents of the Literature section of the encyclopedia as of the end of 2006. If this volume is your first exposure to the *NGE*, we hope it will lead you to the Internet to explore our many articles in fourteen broad topical categories. Even if your interest lies primarily with literature, it is well worth exploring the *NGE*'s offerings in related fields, such as the arts, media, and history. The online encyclopedia offers enhanced versions of the articles that appear in this volume beyond what is possible in print — audio and video clips of authors discussing or reading from their work, internal links to related articles and external links to other Web sites, and updated information on those authors still living.

That noted, it is the text itself that has been and always will be the most basic and valuable component of this or any other encyclopedia, and we are grateful to Hugh Ruppersburg and to the Press for making that content so readily available in this comfortable, page-turning form.

JOHN C. INSCOE
General Editor, *The New Georgia Encyclopedia*
www.georgiaencyclopedia.org

LITERATURE: OVERVIEW

Among southern states, only Mississippi, by virtue of William Faulkner, Eudora Welty, Tennessee Williams, and Richard Wright, has produced a richer literature than Georgia. With such authors as Conrad Aiken, Erskine Caldwell, James Dickey, Joel Chandler Harris, Carson McCullers, Flannery O'Connor, and Alice Walker (not to mention Margaret Mitchell), Georgia holds a position of considerable literary prominence.

Georgia writing developed in response to the same events and forces that shaped the national literature: the disappearance of the frontier, the expansion of industry, the growth of cities, the trauma of war and depression, and the tumultuous events of the twentieth century. Yet factors unique to the state also left their marks. The relatively late founding of the Georgia colony in 1733 and the persistence of the frontier well into the nineteenth century significantly influenced the state's literature — especially its penchant for humor and violence — and its emphasis on regional themes and settings. In the twentieth century the explosive growth of Atlanta and its impact on surrounding areas has also played a powerful role.

The first writing in Georgia was not really intended to be literature. It came in the form of letters, diaries, journals, political speeches, and newspaper articles. These provide a valuable record of the state's early history and of the lives of its residents. General James Oglethorpe's journal entries, for instance, report on the early days of the colony's settlement, while Hugh McCall's *History of Georgia* (1811–16) chronicles the colony's development through the end of the eighteenth century.

But the first important literature did not appear until early in the nineteenth century, when the prominence of the frontier in Georgia, and the southeastern United States in general, gave rise to the nation's first native literature. Sometimes called frontier humor or humor of the old Southwest, old southern humor was a rowdy, vital form of writing that vividly described life on the frontier. The men who wrote it usually did not consider themselves "literary" authors. The Georgia humorists were lawyers or doctors or itinerant salesmen who wrote as a hobby or to pass the time while traveling from one town to another. Their humor usually took the form of unpolished short sketches and anecdotes narrated by a relatively educated man describing with condescension and relish the activities of people along the frontier.

The earliest and most popular Georgia humorist was Augustus Baldwin Longstreet, whose 1835 collection, *Georgia Scenes*, helped define the southern humor genre. Like much southern humor, Longstreet's sketches are often brutal; in "The Fight" town rowdies engage in bloody combat, which is described in graphic detail. In "The Horse-Swap" an unsuspecting man is swindled when he trades for a horse with a festering saddle sore (a tale that influenced William Faulkner's novel *The Hamlet*). "The Gander Pulling" describes a small-town contest in which young men on horseback compete to be the first to pull the head off a goose suspended from a tree.

Another Georgia humorist was William Tappan Thompson, whose charming narrator-farmer, Major Jones, writes letters to a city newspaper editor about life in rural Georgia. Thompson's sketches, written mainly during the 1840s, are unusually gentle for the southern humor tradition. Bill Arp (Charles Henry Smith) wrote satirical newspaper columns later in the century (the mid-twentieth-century Piney Woods Pete was his successor). Slave tales preserved by Joel Chandler Harris in the Uncle Remus stories show how African Americans practiced the genre as well.

Readers who found southern humor too vulgar could turn to other kinds of writing. One alternative was the sentimental fiction of Georgia-Alabama novelist Augusta Jane Evans (Wilson). The strong heroines at the center of her novels *Macaria* (1864) and *St. Elmo* (1866) contrasted markedly with the female characters in other works of the time and later influenced Margaret Mitchell's portrayal of Scarlett O'Hara. Evans's fiction is marked by melodrama. In the first thirty-one pages of *St. Elmo* (one of the most popular novels of the nineteenth century), the main character, Edna Earle, sees a man killed in a duel, the man's wife die of paralysis, her own grandfather die of old age, and a baby and others killed in a train wreck.

The end of the Civil War (1861–65) marked a clear point of division in the state's history and literature. Joel Chandler Harris, in the late nineteenth and early twentieth century, wrote an impressive variety of stories, novels, and sketches. He is best known for his Uncle Remus tales. *Uncle Remus: His Songs and His Sayings* appeared in 1880 and was followed over the next twenty-seven years by four more volumes. Some regard these tales as sentimental or racist, but many of them were written with a psychological perceptiveness and a real desire to preserve these remnants of African slave culture.

Another late-nineteenth-century Georgia writer was the realist Will Harben, who focused on poor Georgia whites and who dedicated to Harris one of his best-known books, *Northern Georgia Sketches* (1900). Harris, along with William Tappan Thompson, Bill Arp, Henry W. Grady, and others, worked during the late decades of the nineteenth century at the *Atlanta Constitution*, a newspaper that played an important role in the development of the state's literature.

Georgia's leading nineteenth-century poet was Sidney Lanier, a Civil War veteran and accomplished musician. Lanier's total poetic output amounts to just under 100 poems. Though not often anthologized today, he wrote several poems of considerable merit — especially "The Marshes of Glynn" (1879) and "The Song of the Chattahoochee" (1877). The success of these poems stems from the natural music of Lanier's language and his ability to evoke the emotional impact of landscape.

In "The Song of the Chattahoochee" Lanier playfully manipulates meter, line length, and geographical place-names in a poem that imitates the sound of the rippling waters of the upper Chattahoochee River and recalls the geography of north Georgia. "The Marshes of Glynn" is a more introspective study of coastal landscape, and is considered by many people to be one of the finest poems of the nineteenth century. Written in the tradition of Walt Whitman and the transcendental writers Ralph Waldo Emerson and Henry Thoreau, the poem impressionistically describes the tidal marshes near Brunswick, linking the changing tides and nightfall to human consciousness and the soul. Lanier's poems "Corn" (1875) and "Thar's More in the Man Than Thar Is in the Land" (1869) celebrate the importance of agriculture, and they contributed to the debate between the New South and the agrarian South at the end of the nineteenth century. Lanier also wrote a novel, *Tiger-Lilies* (1867), based partially on his experiences in the Civil War.

Throughout the twentieth century Georgia writers continued to explore their changing region and gradually began to enter into the life of a larger national and world community. Not every Georgia-born writer wrote about Georgia. Conrad Aiken, for example, born in Savannah, and the Harvard University roommate of poet T. S. Eliot, produced distinguished poetry, fiction, and criticism that showed little outward interest in the state. Other writers were directly concerned with Georgia: Margaret Mitchell, Erskine Caldwell, and Byron Herbert Reece are among them. Many writers, such as Carson McCullers and Flannery O'Connor, viewed their state as a microcosm and wrote both as native citizens and as inhabitants of a larger world.

Race was clearly a central issue for twentieth-century Georgia writers. Encouraged by the slow but undeniable progress in Atlanta and other cities, and by the Harlem Renaissance in the North, African Americans in Georgia began to write in every genre. Several public leaders were among them. The educator and philosopher W. E. B. Du Bois, on the faculty of Atlanta University from 1897 to 1910, encouraged the development of a cultural and political identity for blacks in Atlanta and the nation. His 1903 book *The Souls of Black Folk* remains an important study of race and racism in American society. Walter White, a founder and the first executive director of the National

Association for the Advancement of Colored People, wrote two novels, *Fire in the Flint* (1924) and *Flight* (1926), a distinguished autobiography (*A Man Called White*, 1948), and several studies of racism in America.

African American writers faced a complicated set of issues. Foremost among them were the question of identity and the role African Americans should play in the oppressive society in which they lived. Such writers as Jean Toomer, Frank Yerby, Georgia Douglas Johnson, and John Oliver Killens addressed these concerns. Toomer's novel *Cane* (1923) is a powerful celebration of the black folk culture of rural Georgia. Killens in his novel *Youngblood* (1954) examines the forces that confront a young black man in a racist society, and Yerby in his early stories is similarly concerned, though in his later career he became a best-selling romantic novelist. Johnson wrote of these issues from a woman's perspective in poetry and plays that deserve to be better known. More recent writers, such as Alice Walker, Tina McElroy Ansa, John Holman, and Anthony Grooms, have continued to explore similar topics.

Race was also important for white writers. Among them, Lillian Smith gave the issue the most controversial treatment for her time. Her novel *Strange Fruit* (1944) explored racism and interracial love in a small south Georgia town, and her nonfiction work *Killers of the Dream* (1949) graphically described the moral dilemmas posed by life in the pre–civil rights South. Other white writers were still attempting to come to terms with the relationship of whites and blacks in a society predicated on racial separateness. Their struggles, and their ambivalence, could produce powerful literature. Flannery O'Connor's short story "The Artificial Nigger" (1957) is a penetrating study of racial isolation from a white perspective. Byron Herbert Reece's second novel, *The Hawk and the Sun* (1955), and Carson McCullers's novel *The Member of the Wedding* (1946) explore the issue, as do such later novels as Erskine Caldwell's *In Search of Bisco* (1965), Judson Mitcham's *The Sweet Everlasting* (1996), and James Kilgo's *Daughter of My People* (1998).

Among the notable works by Georgians during the 1920s and 1930s were novels by women. Frances Newman, a Georgia Institute of Technology librarian, wrote two highly stylized novels about southern women in a male-dominated society: *The Hard-Boiled Virgin* (1926) and *Dead Lovers Are Faithful Lovers* (1928). Caroline Miller's *Lamb in His Bosom* (1933) records the travails of a young mother in the isolated wiregrass region of south Georgia. It won the Pulitzer Prize.

Three years later another Georgia novel, Margaret Mitchell's *Gone With the Wind* (1936), also won the Pulitzer. This perennially best-selling book was made into a film widely regarded as a classic of its era. Mitchell sought to present a historically accurate account of the nineteenth-century South and the place of women in a male-dominated society defeated in war. Her descriptions of Tara, the plantation home of the O'Hara family, and of the main character, Scarlett O'Hara, have become indistinguishable in the popular imagination from the historical reality of the Old South. Despite a number of brilliant scenes, many critics argue that *Gone With the Wind* is marred by stereotyped characters and a flawed vision of southern history.

Perhaps the best-known Georgia writer during the 1930s was Erskine Caldwell. His novels *Tobacco Road* (1932) and *God's Little Acre* (1933) offered controversial studies of poor whites in eastern Georgia during the depression. In these novels Caldwell combines naturalistic realism with social criticism, dark humor, satire, and graphic sexuality. In its concern with the plight of poor farmers, his novel *Tobacco Road* in particular deserves to stand alongside John Steinbeck's *The Grapes of Wrath* and Faulkner's *As I Lay Dying*. A play based on *Tobacco Road* had a long and controversial run on Broadway. Among Caldwell's other important books are *American Earth* (stories, 1931), *Kneel to the Rising Sun and Other Stories* (1935), *Trouble in July* (novel, 1940), and *You Have Seen Their Faces* (documentary narrative, 1937), a collaboration with the photographer Margaret Bourke-White.

The publication of *The Heart Is a Lonely Hunter* in 1940 by twenty-three-year-old Carson McCullers of Columbus marked the emergence of another major figure. McCullers's wistful, elegiac portraits of isolated, repressed, and psychologically tormented individuals in small southern towns gained her a national reputation. She followed her first novel with *Reflections in a Golden Eye* (1941), *The Member of the Wedding* (1946), and a series of short stories. By the time she published what many consider her best work, *The Ballad of the Sad Café* (1951), her health was failing, and her career was nearly finished.

Less well known, and more traditional in his use of regional subjects and literary forms, was Byron Herbert Reece, a north Georgia mountain poet and novelist. His melancholic, dark lyrics about disappointment in love and emotional and physical suffering also express a strong devotion to the region of his birth. His novels *Better a Dinner of Herbs* (1950) and *The Hawk and the Sun* (1955) are evocative portrayals of modern life and its problems in small-town north Georgia.

With the civil rights movement, the growth of Atlanta into an international city, the crisis in farming, and the dawning of the information age, Georgia plunged headlong into modernity. Writers in the state explore the receding past as a way of understanding their regional identity, examine the difficulties of adjusting to a rapidly changing society, or chronicle those scenes and characters that the modern world threatens to push out of the way. No longer does the state's regional character seem a mark of separateness.

Such writers as Raymond Andrews, Olive Ann Burns, Terry Kay, Ferrol Sams, and Alice Walker turn to the past to recover and define their origins, to place themselves more securely in the modern landscape. Andrews in particular sought to preserve a folk and cultural tradition in his Muskhogean trilogy, a humorous, sweeping chronicle of black life in a small rural county of the state. Olive Ann Burns seemed similarly concerned with recovering the details of life long past in her novel *Cold Sassy Tree* (1984). Donald Windham's stories about Atlanta in *The Warm Country* (1962) and his memoir about growing up in the city, *Emblems of Conduct* (1964), Terry Kay in *The Year the Lights Came On* (1976), Ferrol Sams in *Run with the Horsemen* (1982) and *Whisper of the River* (1984), and Warren Leamon in *Unheard Melodies* (1990) engage in a similar process of preservation.

Four writers have dominated the literary landscape of modern Georgia. Flannery O'Connor, who died in 1964, was a major figure in American writing. Her characters, her use of the grotesque, her fusion of comedy and tragedy, her dark vision of a fallen modern world, and the moral structure of her plots made her one of the century's finest writers of short fiction. She took the change occurring in Georgia and the South as a major theme, though she used it as a metaphor for larger concerns with the human condition. For O'Connor, the South and the modern world had become a place of abandoned faith and lost souls. Alice Walker, Harry Crews, and Marion Montgomery are three of a number of Georgians she influenced. Her short novels, *Wise Blood* (1952) and *The Violent Bear It Away* (1960), and her story collections, *A Good Man Is Hard to Find* (1955) and *Everything That Rises Must Converge* (1965), are remarkable achievements.

James Dickey's poetry, novels, and literary criticism made him a dominating figure in American writing during the 1960s and 1970s. He began publishing in the 1950s, but the appearance of a ten-year retrospective of his poetry in 1967 brought him to the attention of a national audience. For Dickey, intensity of physical and imaginative experience was a source of redemption and identity in the modern world, whether he was writing, sitting in a tree house, floating in a rowboat at night, or contemplating images from his own imagination. Redemption through action is one of his major themes, and it lies at the center of his 1970 novel, *Deliverance* (which considers the ironic links of southern progress and southern traditions), and his final novel, *To the White Sea* (1993).

A third important figure is Alice Walker. She has written from a number of perspectives, exploring the nature of life for black Americans in the modern world and examining the plight of women — especially women of color — in a male-dominated society. Her style is varied, ranging from traditional realism to experimental stream-of-consciousness and postmodern techniques. Her novel *The Color Purple* (1982), for instance, is told through a series of letters. Early in her career she wrote from a traditional southern perspective that values tradition, kinship, and place. In *The Color Purple* her characters find satisfaction by coming to terms with the place of their births, even with those men who have oppressed them. Yet in its concern with Africa, *The Color Purple* showed Walker's growing global perspective. Her later work has ranged widely, covering such subjects as the sexual mutilation of women in Africa to the terrorist attacks on the World Trade Center in September 2001. Among her important books are *Meridian* (novel, 1976), *In Search of Our Mothers' Gardens: Womanist Prose* (essays, 1983), and *The Temple of My Familiar* (novel, 1989).

The career of Harry Crews extends through the last three decades of the twentieth century and includes an impressive list of novels about marginal characters in the nether regions of the modern South. His perspective is darkly comic, and he often focuses on deformed or tormented characters (following in O'Connor's tradition): a paraplegic wrestler in *The Gypsy's Curse* (1974), a female body-builder in *Body* (1990), a failed college athlete who lives in a trailer park near the rattlesnake capital of the world in *A Feast of Snakes* (1976). Crews's fiction advocates stoicism in the face of despair and defeat. His memoir *A Childhood: The Biography of a Place* (1978), about his early life as the son of a south Georgia sharecropper, is considered by many to be his best book.

Contemporary Georgia has produced an impressive group of poets and fiction writers. David Bottoms, Georgia's poet laureate, is one of the leading poets of the last thirty years, along with Edgar Bowers, Alfred Corn, Wyatt Prunty, Charlie Smith, Judith Ortiz Cofer, Kathryn Stripling Byer, Judson Mitcham, and others. In fiction, the novels of Pat Conroy, largely set outside Georgia, have gained a wide following, as have those of Anne Rivers Siddons. Charlie Smith's fiction about torment, sex, and violence in the Deep South has also received national attention. Ferrol Sams gained a popular following with a trilogy of novels about life in early-twentieth-century Fayette County. Pam Durban's stories and novels have established her as a leading writer of southern fiction, as have Mary Hood's two short-story collections, *How Far She Went* (1984) and *And Venus Is Blue* (1986), and her novel, *Familiar Heat* (1995). Other notable contemporary fiction writers in Georgia include Tina McElroy Ansa, Janice Daugharty, Toni Cade Bambara, Frank Manley, Philip Lee Williams, Shay Youngblood, Anthony Grooms (especially his novel *Bombingham*, 2001), Greg Johnson, and others.

In nonfiction, Melissa Fay Greene with *Praying for Sheetrock* (1991) and *The Temple Bombing* (1996), James Kilgo with *Deep Enough for Ivorybills* (1988) and *Inheritance of Horses* (1994), and Janisse Ray with *Ecology of a Cracker Childhood* (1999) gained national followings.

In drama, Margaret Edson's play *Wit* was produced on Broadway, made into an HBO film, and awarded the Pulitzer Prize for drama in 1999. One of the leading contemporary American dramatists has been Atlantan Alfred Uhry, whose plays, including *Driving Miss Daisy* (1987), *The Last Night of Ballyhoo* (1996), and *Parade* (1999), a musical based on the Leo Frank case, were produced on Broadway. His awards include the Pulitzer Prize for drama, a Tony award, and an Academy Award for the film version of *Driving Miss Daisy*. Plays by Pearl Cleage have also been widely performed.

Georgia writers have written about the same subjects that have interested writers across history and throughout the world: family, war, hardship, ambition, love and death, change, the search for knowledge and meaning. But Georgia has provided its writers with a context of history and geography, with social and cultural values, that give their work an identity grounded in time and place, a shared heritage and experience, which out of all the world's literature and history make it distinctive and unique.

HUGH RUPPERSBURG, *University of Georgia*

SUGGESTED READING

Michael E. Price, *Stories with a Moral: Literature and Society in Nineteenth-Century Georgia* (Athens: University of Georgia Press, 2000).

Louis D. Rubin et al., *The History of Southern Literature* (Baton Rouge: Louisiana State University Press, 1985).

Hugh Ruppersburg, ed., *After O'Connor: Stories from Contemporary Georgia* (Athens: University of Georgia Press, 2003).

Hugh Ruppersburg, ed., *Georgia Voices: Fiction* (Athens: University of Georgia Press, 1992).

Hugh Ruppersburg, ed., *Georgia Voices: Nonfiction* (Athens: University of Georgia Press, 1994).

Hugh Ruppersburg, ed., *Georgia Voices: Poetry* (Athens: University of Georgia Press, 2000).

CONRAD AIKEN

(1889–1973)

Over a period of nearly fifty years Conrad Aiken published poems, essays, short stories, novels, and literary criticism. He won a Pulitzer Prize in 1930 for *Selected Poems* (1929) and a National Book Award for *Collected Poems* (1953). His literary autobiography, *Ushant*, reveals the international nature of his complex life and literary career.

Conrad Potter Aiken was born in Savannah, Georgia, on August 5, 1889, the eldest of four children of a prominent doctor from New York, William Aiken. The author's mother, Anna, was the daughter of a prominent Massachusetts Unitarian minister. When Aiken was eleven, Aiken's father killed his wife and then shot himself — without any warning. The young Aiken was sent to live with an aunt in Cambridge, Massachusetts. He later attended Harvard University, where he met the young T. S. Eliot, who became a lifelong friend and literary associate.

Aiken married Jessie McDonald in 1912. They had three children but divorced in the late 1920s, after they had settled in England.

Aiken's earliest poetry was written partly under the influence of a beloved teacher at Harvard, the philosopher George Santayana. This association shaped Aiken as a poet who was deeply musical in his approach and, at the same time, philosophical in seeking answers to his own problems and the problems of the modern world. After 1960, when his work was rediscovered by readers and critics, a new view of Aiken emerged — one that emphasized his psychological problems, along with his continuing study of Sigmund Freud, Carl G. Jung, and other depth psychologists. Two of his five novels deal with depth psychology.

In the 1920s Freud himself knew of Aiken's novels and wanted to psychoanalyze the poet. Aiken actually embarked for Europe on a visit to see Freud. Aboard ship, however, he met one of

Freud's disciples, Erich Fromm, who cautioned against psychoanalysis unless Aiken seriously needed it. Aiken took Fromm's advice and thus never met Freud, the psychologist who influenced him more than any other modern thinker.

Aiken remained private about his psychological problems, which grew largely out of the trauma of his parents' death. Such problems emerge clearly in two of his most famous stories, "Strange Moonlight" and "Silent Snow, Secret Snow." Aiken's second wife, Clarissa M. Lorenz, vividly described in her book *Lorelei Two: My Life with Conrad Aiken* the psychological difficulties the author had in the 1930s, when the couple was living in England. She wrote of having once saved the poet from suicide.

Yet in this same period Aiken was making progress in finding new depths of creativity. He had established himself in a home in Rye, England, and had met and begun to influence the young English writer Malcolm Lowry, who later wrote *Under the Volcano*, a semiautobiographical novel about Aiken and Lowry in Mexico. One of Aiken's best poems, "The Poet in Granada: Homage to Lorca," was inspired by the two poets' visit to Spain during the 1930s.

At the beginning of World War II, Conrad Aiken returned to America to settle in a house on Cape Cod in the small town of West Brewster, Massachusetts. He no longer sought his chief inspiration in Great Britain, Spain, and France, though he continued to have readers in those countries. With new poems about his native country's past and present, he at last gained an American audience.

In 1952 Aiken published a spiritual autobiography describing his destroyed childhood in Savannah, his journey to Europe, and his rediscovery of a new America during and after World War II. Dedicated to his third wife, Mary Hoover, and to a literary friend, Edward Burra, *Ushant* contains the most profound statement Aiken made about himself during a writing career of more than fifty years. The book contains brilliant portraits of the literary scene in Boston, London, and New York during the first half of the century. But essentially it recounts — in prose that often becomes deeply poetic — the poet's literary pilgrimage. *Ushant* and other works that followed brought Aiken into the company of the American literary establishment and earned him the kind of recognition his admirers had always thought he deserved. He received, among other honors, the position of consultant in poetry to the Library of Congress.

Aiken did not, however, become simply another literary figure of the Northeast. In the early 1960s he was offered the opportunity to live free of charge in his parents' house on Oglethorpe Avenue in Savannah — directly across from the Colonial Park Cemetery, where Aiken had often played as a child. He chose instead to live next door at 230 Oglethorpe Avenue.

Aiken and his wife Mary became significant figures in the life of Savannah. They entertained many visitors, including a number of scholars and authors who sought out Aiken and talked with him at great length. When T. S. Eliot died in 1965, Aiken wrote a memorable article in *Life* magazine about his friend's place in modern literature. Aiken's final book, a collection of religious poems entitled *Thee* deals in part with his own literary and religious pilgrimage.

Before he died Aiken had a marble bench erected next to his parents' graves in Savannah's Bonaventure Cemetery. It contained two epitaphs: "Give my love to the world" and "Cosmos Mariner Destination Unknown."

Six months before Aiken's death on August 17, 1973, Governor Jimmy Carter appointed him poet laureate of the state of Georgia. In front of the house on Oglethorpe Avenue, a historical marker describes Conrad Aiken's life and work.

TED R. SPIVEY, *Atlanta*

SUGGESTED READING

Butscher, Edward, *Conrad Aiken: Poet of the White Horse Vale* (Athens: University of Georgia Press, 1988).

Killorin, Joseph, ed., *Selected Letters of Conrad Aiken* (New Haven: Yale University Press, 1978).

Lorenz, Clarissa M., *Lorelei Two: My Life with Conrad Aiken* (Athens: University of Georgia Press, 1983).

Spivey, Ted R., *Revival: Southern Writers in the Modern City* (Gainesville: University of Florida Press, 1986).

Spivey, Ted R., *Time's Stop in Savannah: Conrad Aiken's Inner Journey* (Macon: Mercer University Press, 1997).

RAYMOND ANDREWS
(1934–1991)

Raymond Andrews was a widely acclaimed novelist and chronicler of the African American experience in north central Georgia. His first novel, *Appalachee Red*, won the James Baldwin Prize for fiction in 1979.

The fourth of ten children of sharecropping parents, Andrews was born and reared near Madison. At fifteen he left home for Atlanta, where he worked during the day and attended night classes at Booker T. Washington High School. After graduating from high school he served four years in the U.S. Air Force, including a tour of duty in Korea. On returning he attended Michigan State University and then moved to New York City, where he lived from 1958 until 1984. While there he married, and worked as an airline agent, air courier, and proofreader, among other jobs. His marriage ended in divorce in 1980.

Andrews's first national publication was a description in *Sports Illustrated* of the first time the game of football was played in the rural community of Plainview, where he grew up. In the late 1970s Dial Press began publishing his Muskhogean trilogy, which tells of black life in the Deep South from the end of World War I (1917–18) to the beginning of the 1960s, from the days of mules and white men with bullwhips to the moment the civil rights tide began to change the Georgia Piedmont. The trilogy includes three novels: *Appalachee Red* (1978), *Rosiebelle Lee Wildcat Tennessee* (1980), and *Baby Sweet's* (1983). *Appalachee Red* tells the story of a large, red-skinned black man who changes everything for African Americans in the small town of Appalachee, which is based on the town of Madison. *Rosiebelle Lee Wildcat Tennessee* traces the fortunes of a remarkable black woman and her family through the depression and World War II. Finally, *Baby Sweet's* takes the story into the 1960s, wrapping up story lines begun in *Appalachee Red.* The novels particularly describe the world of those whose background includes both white and African American cultures of the period.

After moving to a home near Athens in 1984, Andrews published a memoir, *The Last Radio Baby* (1990), which described his childhood years when his family lived on the same property with their black grandmother and white grandfather. Noted newsman and author Charles Kuralt called this book "one of the truest and best pieces of writing I've ever come across."

Andrews's last book, *Jessie and Jesus and Cousin Claire* (1991), consists of two novellas. It introduces two powerful African American women who are as unlike as night and day but are similarly determined to have their way. His final manuscript, *Once upon a Time in Atlanta,* was published in a single issue of the Chattahoochee Review in 1998. All of Andrews's books were illustrated by his brother, the nationally known artist Benny Andrews.

An expansive, engaging man who made friends effortlessly, Andrews was known for his encyclopedic knowledge of old movies and sports, especially football and baseball, from the 1940s through the 1970s. His modesty and sense of humor, along with a real warmth, made him one of the most widely loved southern writers of his era. He took his art very seriously and laboriously printed his work on yellow legal pads in the mornings, then rewrote and typed the results in the afternoon. He famously enjoyed literary parties and traveled widely to read from his works.

The books of Raymond Andrews have received considerable critical acclaim from numerous critics and other writers. Novelist Richard Bausch aptly described Andrews's writing as having "a smiling generosity of spirit." The *San Francisco Chronicle* called Andrews's first book "an auspicious beginning for a fine talent," and the *Los Angeles Times* said *Rosiebelle Lee Wildcat Tennessee* had the "infectious exuberance and soul-satisfying warmth of a folk tale."

In 1989 the Robert W. Woodruff Library of Emory University

in Atlanta purchased Andrews's papers. The Raymond Andrews papers are available for research and include correspondence, photographs, clippings, and drafts and manuscripts of his novels.

Andrews died from a self-inflicted gunshot wound in Athens on November 25, 1991.

PHILIP LEE WILLIAMS, *Athens*

SUGGESTED READING

Jeffrey J. Folks, "'Trouble' in Muskhogean County: The Social History of a Southern Community in the Fiction of Raymond Andrews," *Southern Literary Journal* 30 (spring 1998): 66–75.

TINA McELROY ANSA
(b. 1949)

Novelist, journalist, essayist, and short-story writer Tina McElroy Ansa was born in Macon on November 18, 1949. Macon and its historic African American Pleasant Hill district serve as a model for the fictional town of Mulberry, the setting of her first four novels. After graduating from Spelman College in Atlanta in 1971, Ansa began work as editor and writer for the *Atlanta Constitution* and later the *Charlotte Observer* in North Carolina. Since 1982 she has been a freelance writer with work appearing in magazines, newspapers, short-story collections, and nonfiction anthologies. She also contributed the essays "Postcards from Georgia" to the television series *CBS News Sunday Morning* and has taught writing workshops at Spelman, Brunswick College, and Emory University. In 1978 she married Jonée Ansa and moved to St. Simons Island.

Ansa's profound sense of place, strong characters, lively communities, and vivid images appeal to a variety of readers. Sharply contrasting the realistic particulars, however, are ghosts that play crucial roles in her stories. They provide charmed, informative, and often healing inner lives for characters otherwise caught up with ties to family, community, and material possessions. *Baby of the Family* (1989) revolves around a child, Lena McPherson, born with a caul, the membrane that surrounds a fetus and sometimes covers a baby's head at birth. A nurse recognizes the sign, according to folklore, of a child with extraordinary spiritual powers, including the ability to see ghosts. The unfolding of this gift is traumatic, and Lena learns to keep her visions private. As she grows up, a series of spirits, including a slave named Rachel and her grandmother who dies during the story, teach Lena about love and the search for self.

In Ansa's second novel, *Ugly Ways* (1993), three sisters return to Mulberry for their mother's funeral. She had withdrawn from the family when the children were young, leaving them to fend for themselves physically and emotionally. As they reminisce, the mother's ghost defends herself against their resentments. She makes clear that her decision to live for herself has led her daughters to develop self-sufficiency and, in turn, a sense of their own isolation.

Ansa's third novel, *The Hand I Fan With* (1996), again concerns Lena McPherson, now forty-five, a successful café owner with a "dark copper-colored 450 SLK Mercedes," fashionable wardrobe, and other valuable possessions. She is nevertheless agitated, unsatisfied, and lonely because her ability to read minds makes romance difficult and also because her success entails relentless obligations. She conjures a ghost, Herman, who becomes the love of her life but soon withdraws as a physical presence. Through the experience, however, Lena learns to forgive others as well as herself and to take pleasure rather than anger from her dealings with the world.

You Know Better (2002), Ansa's fourth novel, follows three generations of the Pines women, focusing in particular on children's issues in the twenty-first century.

Critical reaction to Ansa's writings has been favorable. *Baby of the Family* was named a Notable Book of the Year by the *New York Times* and also won the Georgia Authors Series Award. *Ugly Ways* was named "best fiction" by the African American Blackboard List in 1994 and 1995, and *The Hand I Fan With* also won the Georgia Authors Series Award, making Ansa the only two-time winner of the award. In 2005 Ansa received the Stanley W. Lindberg Award, which honors a lifetime of significant contributions to Georgia's literary culture.

TED WADLEY, *Georgia Perimeter College*

SUGGESTED READING

Contemporary African American Novelists, ed. Emmanuel S. Nelson (Westport, Conn.: Greenwood Press, 1999), s.v. "Tina McElroy Ansa."

Anthony Grooms, "Big Bad Mudear — *Ugly Ways* by Tina McElroy Ansa," *Callaloo* 17, no. 2 (spring 1994): 653–55.

Sharon Smith Henderson, "An Interview with Tina McElroy Ansa," *Kalliope* 21, no. 2 (1999): 61–68.

Valerie Sayers, "The Girl Who Walked with Ghosts," *New York Times Book Review,* Nov. 26, 1989.

BILL ARP

(Charles Henry Smith, 1826–1903)

In the late nineteenth century Bill Arp's weekly column in the *Atlanta Constitution*, syndicated to hundreds of newspapers, made him the South's most popular writer. Others surpassed him in literary quality, but in numbers of regular readers, no one exceeded Bill Arp.

Bill Arp was born Charles Henry Smith in Lawrenceville on June 15, 1826. He married Mary Octavia Hutchins, the daughter of a wealthy lawyer and plantation owner, and started a family that would eventually include ten surviving children. Smith studied law with his father-in-law and then moved to Rome in 1851.

Smith took his famous pen name in April 1861 when, after the Confederate attack on Fort Sumter, President Abraham Lincoln issued a proclamation ordering the Southern rebels "to disperse and retire peaceably." Smith wrote a satiric response to the president in the dialect favored by humorists of the day ("I tried my darnd'st yesterday to disperse and retire, but it was no go") and signed it "Bill Arp," in honor of a local "cracker" named Bill Arp. The letter to "Mr. Lincoln, Sir" was reprinted across the South and made Bill Arp a household name. During the war Smith wrote almost thirty more Arp letters for southern newspapers, attacking Union policies, praising the Confederacy, and describing in a humorous fashion his family's experiences as refugees ("runagees," he called them) while fleeing from advancing Federal troops in 1864. Arp later criticized the nation's Reconstruction policies in letters that often expressed a good bit of frustration, even anger. The Arp letters ended in the early 1870s, as Reconstruction came to a close in Georgia.

In 1877 Smith and his family moved to a farm in Bartow County, just outside of Cartersville. A year later the *Atlanta Constitution* printed a new letter from Bill Arp, his first in half a dozen years and the beginning of a twenty-five-year series of weekly columns called "The Country Philosopher." The letter, on the joys of farming, was in many ways different from the Bill Arp of the war and Reconstruction. Gone was most of the dialect (it would never completely disappear), but more important, the subject matter had changed: Arp now wrote delightful epistles of the pleasures of rural life, the comfort of home and family, the independence and strength of Georgia's common folk, and the bright memories of the days of his youth. Arp still wrote occasionally on political, economic, and social issues, including a number of pro-lynching columns in the 1890s, but it was his "homely philosophy," as it was called — his writings on the farm and fireside, the past, and various pastoral topics — that made him so popular.

The message of Arp's *Constitution* columns was ambiguous. On one hand he promoted the economic growth of Henry W. Grady's New South program; on the other hand he criticized many aspects of New South society, and one can read his homely philosophy as implicit criticism of the new age. Perhaps this explains his popularity: he reflected the ambiguous feelings of many other New Southerners.

Smith died on August 24, 1903, and is buried in Oak Hill Cemetery in Cartersville.

DAVID B. PARKER, *Kennesaw State University*

SUGGESTED READING

James C. Austin, *Bill Arp* (New York: Twayne, 1969).

David B. Parker, *Alias Bill Arp: Charles Henry Smith and the South's "Goodly Heritage"* (Athens: University of Georgia Press, 1991).

COLEMAN BARKS

(b. 1937)

Coleman Barks, a poet and professor emeritus at the University of Georgia (UGA) in Athens, has gained world renown for his translations of Near Eastern poets, especially Jalal al-Din Rumi. He is also an accomplished poet, whose interest in Near Eastern mysticism infuses his observations of southern landscape and life. Barks has published six collections of his own poetry and numerous poetry translations, and his work has appeared in a wide array of anthologies, textbooks, and journals, including the *Ann Arbor Review*, *Chattahoochee Review*, *Georgia Review*, *Kenyon Review*, *New England Review*, *Plainsong*, *Rolling Stone*, and *Southern Poetry Review*.

Coleman Bryan Barks was born on April 23, 1937, in Chattanooga, Tennessee, to Elizabeth Bryan and Herbert Bernard Barks. His sister, Elizabeth, also became a writer, and her fiction has been published under the name Elizabeth Cox. Barks attended Baylor School, where his father served as headmaster for thirty-five years, and later received his Ph.D. in English from the University of North Carolina at Chapel Hill. In 1962 he married Kittsu Greenwood. The couple had two children, Benjamin and Cole, before they divorced. After teaching for two years at the University of Southern California in Los Angeles, California, Barks joined the faculty of the UGA English department. For the next thirty years he taught creative writing, American literature, and twentieth-century literature. Since his retirement from UGA in 1997, Barks has lived in Athens, where he works on his poetry and translations and operates the Maypop Press, which publishes translations of Rumi and other Near Eastern religious poets.

Barks's first poetry collection, *The Juice* (1972), reflects the range of styles and subjects he developed more fully later in his career. Considerable whimsy, a common feature in Barks's poetry, occurs alongside a tendency toward the meditative, an appreciation of the natural world, and an interest in people and relationships. The poems in the book's first section, "Body Poems," describe parts of the human body in sensual, imagistic, sometimes enigmatic ways. In the poem "Spine," for example, the backbone,

> a curl of rainwater
> down the windshield
> moves around
> like it's hearing
> the radio.

The second section, "Choosing," contains longer narrative poems. Many seem autobiographical, describing people or experiences from Barks's life. Poems in the third section, "The Swim," tend to be shorter; many of them are about animals. In form some of these poems, consisting of couplets or three-line stanzas, at first seem more conventional than the free-flowing narrative style Barks would later favor. But even at this relatively early point in his career, Barks has mostly abandoned rhyme and conventional meter for a more relaxed, improvisational, even musical approach to language. An example is "The Coyote Cage at the Athens (Ga.) Zoo," which is composed of four three-line stanzas using irregular three-foot lines. The poem comments on the unnatural state of a coyote living in a small-town zoo and imagines its release from captivity:

> Nobody could live
> like you do, you dumb
>
> beast. Come out of there
> and lie down in the grass
> with me. Easy. Good boy.

Barks's work continued to appear in journals and anthologies, and in the mid-1970s he published two chapbooks of poetry, *New Words* (1976) and *We're Laughing at the Damage* (1977). In 1993 Barks published his second major collection of poetry,

Gourd Seed. The poems in this volume reflect the work of a poet with wide-ranging interests. His preferred style in *Gourd Seed* is narrative, with an emphasis on description and meditation. He writes about his family, experiences in the natural world, old friends, the 1990 Persian Gulf War, and other subjects. Some poems verge on the comic and nonsensical: in "Summer Food" he delights in recounting the names of vegetables ("O, to put the whole pod / of Okra in the mouth"), while in "W R F C" he recounts the forty-nine entries he submitted to a contest inviting listeners to name the call letters of a radio station ("WITHOUT REASON FISH CHANGE / WE RADIATE FLIRTATIOUS CHARM / WOP-SIDED RED FOLDING CHAIRS") — these entries he compares to the random connections he has made with people in his life. Other short poems describe objects and moments of curiosity or won-der — flowers, animals, encounters with strangers, an attempt to repair a door, or memories. One humorous poem describes an encounter with a strange child in a grocery store parking lot.

Barks is especially effective in longer narrative poems, which he typically begins by focusing on a specific subject or theme that he then extends into wider speculations. The influence of Rumi and other mystic poets Barks has translated is evident in the longer poems. An example is "A Section of the Oconee near Watkinsville," which begins with a description of his difficulties navigating a canoe down a shallow stream and ends with rumi-nations on trying to lead a balanced life, of trying to follow a teacher whose

> example is everywhere open,
> like a boat never tied up, no one in it,
> that drifts day and night, metallic dragonfly
> above the sunken log.

In "Hymenoptera" an encounter with angry yellow jackets be-comes a subtle meditation on life's randomness and the poet's power or powerlessness to influence his own future. One of the finest poems in *Gourd Seed* is "New Year's Day Nap," in which the sight of his son sleeping on a sofa leads Barks to ponder his role as a parent and the lives of his sons, now grown. Interspersed through this poem are excerpts from a hymn, printed in shape-note form. When Barks reads the poem out loud (an experience the printed version cannot convey), he sings the hymn.

Club, a collection of poems written with and about his grand-daughter, followed *Gourd Seed* in 2001. The light and playful verse in this volume allows full expression of the humor and whimsy typical of many poems written throughout Barks's career. Poems about children, especially about what children do and say, occur frequently not only in *Club* but also in *Tentmaking* (2002), Barks's third major collection. These poems build on the styles and themes of *Gourd Seed*. Most are written in three-line stanzas. Still contemplative and inclined toward narratives, these later poems are tinged with concerns about mortality and about his fellow writers — Robert Bly, Emily Dickinson, Allen Ginsberg, Donald Hall, Seamus Heaney, William Matthews, Mary Oliver, James Wright, and others — as if Barks is assessing his own place among poets. Love, sex, dreams, his parents, animals, and strange encounters are also frequent subjects. Especially noteworthy are the title poem, "Tentmaking"; "Black Rubber Ball"; and "Elegy for John Seawright," written in honor of a deceased friend. There are other equally compelling poems. "Hyssop" considers the pertinence of Jesus' remonstrance to the Pharisees and suggests that only those without sin should cast the first stone at the sex scandal involving U.S. president Bill Clinton. "1971 and 1942" wistfully remembers his parents and their continuing effect on him: "What does it mean to me, *The heart grows old.*" "The Final Final" recounts with humor and sadness the day of his retirement, when Barks sleeps through the last final examination he would give and misses the chance to thank and say good-bye to his students:

> I'm unrepentently, sufficiently, some would say terribly, alone. Look
> at me and be frightened of not pouring the last of the love and

wakefulness you're given, which is every moment, but
more so some
than others. Emptying out is the point. In time, over time,
be early.

Tentmaking contains some of the best poetry Barks has written. His more recent work reflects his continuing proficiency with narrative. The poem "Just This Once," a letter to U.S. president George W. Bush arguing for alternatives to war in Iraq, was widely distributed on the World Wide Web prior to the start of the conflict in 2002.

Barks is internationally known for his translations of Islamic poetry. In 1976 the poet Robert Bly showed him some academic translations of Jalal al-Din Rumi, a thirteenth-century Islamic poet. Following Bly's suggestion that "these poems need to be released from their cages," Barks began translating the thousands of poems by Rumi. To date, he has published fourteen volumes of Rumi translations, including *The Essential Rumi* (1995), in collaboration with other translators. He has been interviewed by Bill Moyers as part of two Public Broadcasting Service television series on poetry, *The Language of Life* and *Fooling with Words*, and his translations of Rumi appear in the *Norton Anthology of World Masterpieces*. *The Essential Rumi* has even appeared on nonfiction best-seller lists around the United States.

In rendering seven-hundred-year-old poems for today's readers, Barks claims "to make what I am given — which is literal, scholarly transcriptions of poems — into what I hope are valid poems in American English." Persian poetry is highly structured, and Barks feels that reproducing the same sound patterns found in its rhyming syllables would produce a trivial effect in English. Instead, he has attempted "to connect these poems with a strong American line of free-verse spiritual poetry," such as that of Theodore Roethke, Gary Snyder, Walt Whitman, and James Wright.

Rumi's poetry can be seen as having influenced Barks's own work. Rumi's work often puts religious concerns into concrete images, for this mystic poet often uses fables, compares earthly love to sacred love, and puts the daily concerns of living in the context of spiritual challenges. "Don't let your throat tighten / with fear," Barks translates in the *Essential Rumi.* "Take sips of breath / all day and night, before death / closes your mouth." The same concerns of essential love and daily life often can be seen in Barks's own poetry, as in "New Year's Day Nap":

> Some songs don't ever get completely sung.
> They're sung by the blood,
> inside creeks and rocks and air,
> in some cellular Beulah land,
> the harmonizing water sings them.

"Poetry became one of my ways," Barks writes in "These Things, Hereafter." The "way" that Barks indicates in all of his work — whether in the translations of centuries-old poems or in his own work — is that of a journey that will never be finished. Instead, it is one embarked upon because of the joys found in the journey itself.

BRIAN C. FERGUSON-AVERY, *Georgia Southwestern State University*
HUGH RUPPERSBURG, *University of Georgia*

SUGGESTED READING

Coleman Barks, *Gourd Seed* (Athens, Ga.: Maypop Press, 1993).
Coleman Barks, *The Juice* (New York: Harper and Row, 1972).
Coleman Barks, *Tentmaking* (Athens, Ga.: Maypop Press, 2002).
"Coleman Barks," in *The Language of Life: A Festival of Poets,* ed. James Haba (New York: Doubleday, 1995).
Maulana Jalal al-Din Rumi, *The Essential Rumi,* trans. Coleman Barks, with John Moyne, A. J. Arberry, and Reynold Nicholson (New York: HarperCollins, 1995).

VEREEN BELL
(1911–1944)

Vereen McNeill Bell wrote fiction and magazine articles set in the southern outdoors, and he achieved popular success with *Swamp Water*, a coming-of-age novel set in the Okefenokee Swamp. A World War II naval officer, Bell was killed during the Battle for Leyte Gulf.

The son of Jennie Vereen and Reason Chesnutt Bell, a prominent Georgia judge, Bell was born in Cairo on October 5, 1911. After graduating from North Carolina's Davidson College in 1932, he began his career under the tutelage of Frederic Litten in Lake Charles, Louisiana, writing for "Sunday school" and juvenile magazines. In 1934 Bell married Florence Eleanor Daniel of Thomasville, Georgia. They settled near Bell's family home in Cairo and had two sons, Vereen McNeill and Frederic Daniel.

Bell worked briefly as an editor at the Detroit-based *American Boy/Youth's Companion*, but he preferred to write as a freelancer from his south Georgia home. In the late 1930s his outdoor stories and wildlife photography routinely sold to *Collier's* and the *Saturday Evening Post*. His two novels, *Swamp Water* and *Two of a Kind*, first appeared serially in the *Post*.

Swamp Water (1940) follows a defiant young man into the wild Okefenokee, where his friendship with a fugitive ignites a struggle within his backwoods community. The story inspired a 1942 Hollywood movie and a 1952 remake. *Two of a Kind* (1943) tells a similar story of a young man's conflicting loyalties against a backdrop of sporting dogs and field trials. Several of his stories about hunting dogs were published in a posthumous Armed Services Edition compilation, *Brag Dog and Other Stories*, which was republished (2000) in an expanded form.

In World War II, Bell volunteered for Navy air combat intelligence duty. He was a lieutenant assigned to the escort carrier USS

Gambier Bay when the ship was sunk October 25, 1944, near Samar in the Philippines.

In 1947 his college roommate, Mr. D. Grier Martin, established the Vereen Bell Award for creative writing at Davidson College in memory of Bell.

KEITH HULETT, *University of Georgia Libraries*

SUGGESTED READING

Vereen M. Bell Jr., foreword to *Swamp Water* (Athens: University of Georgia Press, 1981).

National Cyclopedia of American Biography, vol. 39 (New York: J. T. White, 1954), s.v. "Vereen McNeill Bell."

Obituary, *Publishers Weekly*, December 30, 1944.

Alexander Sesonske, "Jean Renoir in Georgia: *Swamp Water*," *Georgia Review* 36 (spring 1982): 24–66.

ROY BLOUNT JR.

(b. 1941)

From the "ring-tailed roarers" of Augustus Baldwin Longstreet's antebellum satire to the "rednecks" of Jeff Foxworthy's New South schtick, Georgia has long been a fertile ground for humorists. A leading modern practitioner in this tradition is Roy Alton Blount Jr. — humorist, journalist, sportswriter, poet, novelist, performer, editor, lyricist, lecturer, screenwriter, dramatist, and philologist. Like many of the southwestern humorists more than a century before him, Blount seems a true Renaissance man — multitalented, highly educated, and capable of sophisticated wit, yet not so removed from his roots that he cannot appreciate the comedic possibilities of the southern, and national, landscape.

Born to southern parents in Indianapolis, Indiana, in 1941, Roy Blount grew up in Decatur, Georgia. His professional writing career began in Georgia, where he worked as a reporter and sports columnist for the *Decatur-DeKalb News* from 1958 to 1959; he then worked two summers as a cub reporter for the *Morning Telegraph* in New York City (1961–62) and for the *Times-Picayune* (1963) in New Orleans, Louisiana. After receiving degrees from Vanderbilt University (B.A., 1963) and Harvard University (M.A., 1964), Blount served in the U.S. Army for two years (1964–66), achieving the rank of first lieutenant. He then returned to Georgia, where he worked for the *Atlanta Journal* as a reporter, editorial writer, and columnist and as a part-time instructor at Georgia State College in English from 1966 to 1968.

After his stint as a journalist in Atlanta, Blount returned to New York City as a staff writer and editor for *Sports Illustrated* from 1968 to 1975. Utilizing his classic and often raucous humor, he gathered comic material during his time at *Sports Illustrated*. In 1974 he published his first book, *About Three Bricks Shy of a Load: A Highly Irregular Lowdown on the Year the Pittsburgh*

Steelers Were Super but Missed the Bowl, still widely recognized as one of the most insightful and hilarious treatments of professional football. Blount left his staff position at *Sports Illustrated* in 1975 to become a freelance writer, a career move that proved to be auspicious. His second book, *Crackers: This Whole Many-Angled Thing of Jimmy, More Carters, Ominous Little Animals, Sad-Singing Women, My Daddy and Me* (1980), cemented his reputation as a humorist. Chronicling the Carter administration, Blount delved into the presidency of his fellow Georgian and offered political commentary both erudite and entertaining. The book was a critical success, garnering praise from northern and southern critics alike.

Having established himself as a columnist, a sportswriter, an editor, and a humorist, Blount, with his boundless energy, felt compelled to tackle other challenges. In the past twenty years he has also written poetry and screenplays; published thirteen books, ranging from the novel *First Hubby* (1990) to his memoir *Be Sweet: A Conditional Love Story* (1998); contributed to some 100 periodicals, including the *Atlantic Monthly*, *Esquire*, the *Oxford American*, *Playboy*, and *Rolling Stone*; performed on television, stage, and radio; and played with an authors' rock band, the Rock Bottom Remainders, along with Dave Barry and Stephen King. He lives in New York City and serves as a contributing editor to the *Atlantic Monthly*.

LESA C. SHAUL, *University of Alabama, Tuscaloosa*

SUGGESTED READING

Jerry Elijah Brown, *Roy Blount, Jr.* (Boston: Twayne, 1990).

ADRIENNE BOND
(1933–1996)

Adrienne Moore Bond, poet, fiction writer, scholar, and mentor to other writers, was a native of Macon County. She was born in 1933 to Violet Moore, a writer, and Sidney L. Moore Sr., an attorney. She earned her B.A. and M.F.A. from Mercer University (1954, 1971) and studied for the Ph.D. at Georgia State University. She taught in the English department at Mercer from 1965 until her death in 1996.

Bond's main body of work is centered in three books. In *The Voice of the Poet: The Shape and Sound of Southern Poetry Today* (1989), she focused on a variety of poets in her discussion of the important themes of traditional southern poetry, such as the land, hunting, and storytelling. By the time the book appeared, she was already gaining attention through her own poems, which appeared in such prominent journals and magazines as the *Southern Review*, the *Georgia Review*, and the *New Yorker*.

Sugarcane House and Other Stories about Mr. Fat, published posthumously in 1997, is a book of children's stories, although adults find them entertaining as well. These stories are reminiscent of the folk/fantasy method of narration practiced by Morgan County's Raymond Andrews, especially in his book *Appalachee Red*. They have been compared as well to the Brer Rabbit stories of Joel Chandler Harris.

Bond's selected poems were published in 1996 under the title *Time Was, She Declares*. Her poems are eclectic in setting and subject. They include scenes from Georgia's rural past in Macon County and draw from the concrete realities of Norway and Switzerland, and Macon as well. Characterizing southern poets in her first chapter to *The Voice of the Poet*, she could have been describing her own style: southern poets, she wrote, "tend to focus on place, and they often see place as informed by time, by history and memory. They write about family members and family events. Southern poets tend to use concrete details and to approach abstraction cautiously through explorations of the natural world. . . . southern poets love folklore and tall tales, and have a gift for story telling and character portrayal, as well as a fine ear for the spoken language."

One of Bond's best-known poems, "Time Was, She Declares," whimsically speculates on the nature of time and memory by musing over the Big Bang:

> She's heard (and entertains
> the possibility it's true)
> a point in time will come, taut
> between bang, and crunch, all silvery quiver
> and in perfect tune, when reach
> will momentarily equal grab,
> and we will see the things we thought we'd lost
> all pause, turn, and come avalanching
> back — coins, lovers, kites and luggage,
> teeth and keys and jobs,
> umbrellas and the dead.

"Christmas Basket: 1943," her recollection of a childhood trip with her grandmother to visit an infirm black friend, becomes a meditation on personal responsibility, race, and the southern past. Another poem, "Blues," is about the musical tradition Bond was researching when she became ill in 1995. It reveals her characteristic terseness, humor, and perceptiveness:

> Woke up this morning, saw
> my feet way down at the end of the bed,
> toes bent that went to market; I
> closed my eyes, willed to lie
> sprawled, still, new in cool grass,
> hear Miss Minnie's sprinkler whip the sidewalk,

smell wet mint, see zinnias, gold, orange, red,
as rough as cats' tongues, glow
in their stiff, starched rows,
and couldn't.

Bond was advisor and mentor to a wide range of Georgia poets, including those in the "Macon Poetry Group" — Michael
Cass, Judith Ortiz Cofer, George Espy III (George Muhammed),
Anthony Grooms, Anna Holloway, Seaborn Jones, Anthony
Kellman, Robert Kelly, and Judson Mitcham. She brought many
of the nation's poets to numerous Georgia colleges and communities through the Georgia Poetry Circuit (funded in part by
the Georgia Humanities Council), which she founded and directed. She also served as associate vice president for development and director of the university grants program at Mercer
University. Among her many honors was the Governor's Award
in Humanities in 1996. Married for a time to Alpha M. Bond,
she was the mother of three sons: Alpha, Ernest, and Thomas.

ANNA R. HOLLOWAY, *Fort Valley State University*

DAVID BOTTOMS

(b. 1949)

When David Bottoms was twenty-nine, his first book, *Shooting Rats at the Bibb County Dump*, was chosen by Pulitzer Prize–winning novelist and poet Robert Penn Warren from more than thirteen hundred submissions as winner of the 1979 Walt Whitman Award of the Academy of American Poets. In 2000, at age fifty, Bottoms was appointed by Governor Roy Barnes as Georgia's Poet Laureate. His many awards and publications over the past two decades attest to his stature as one of the South's leading writers.

Bottoms was born on September 11, 1949, in Canton, the only child of David H. Bottoms, a funeral director, and Louise Ashe Bottoms, a registered nurse. He graduated from Cherokee High School in 1967 and entered Mercer University in Macon, where he received his B.A. in English in 1971. He worked for a year as a guitar salesman before marrying Margaret Lynn Bensel, an elementary school art teacher, and enrolling in the graduate English program at West Georgia College. He received his M.A. in 1973, and from 1974 to 1978 he taught high school English and worked part-time in the Georgia Poets-in-the-Schools Program. In 1979, when he received the Whitman Award, he resigned his teaching position and accepted a graduate fellowship at Florida State University, where he received his Ph.D. in American poetry and creative writing in 1982. That same year he took a teaching position at Georgia State University (GSU) in Atlanta, where he became professor of creative writing and a founding coeditor, along with Pam Durban, of the literary magazine *Five Points*.

In 1986 Bottoms accepted a visiting appointment as Richard Hugo Poet-in-Residence at the University of Montana; a year later he and his wife divorced. At the University of Montana he met Kelly Jean Beard, a law student. They were married in 1989 and moved to Billings, where she practiced law and he finished his second novel. The following year they moved to Atlanta, and Bottoms returned to GSU. They have one child, Rachel, born in 1991.

Bottoms serves as the Associate Dean of Fine Arts and holds the John B. and Elena Diaz-Verson Amos Distinguished Chair in English Letters at GSU.

Over the years Bottoms has received many awards for his work, including the Levinson Prize from *Poetry* magazine, an Ingram Merrill Award, fellowships from the National Endowment for the Arts and the John Simon Guggenheim Foundation, and an Award in Literature from the American Academy and Institute of Arts and Letters. He has been published widely in such publications as the *Atlantic*, the *New Yorker*, *Harper's*, *Poetry*, and the *Paris Review*, as well as in some two dozen anthologies and textbooks.

Although Bottoms published a chapbook of ten poems, *Jamming with the Band at the VFW*, in 1978, it was his first full-length book, *Shooting Rats at the Bibb County Dump*, that brought him national attention in 1980. In these early poems, in a landscape of southern woods and honky-tonks, "good old boys" and semioutlaws reveal the purposelessness and boredom of their lives. These poems are graphic and violent, and Bottoms's narratives of death and religion draw a link between the human and the animal as he searches for meaning below the surface of our everyday lives.

This book was followed closely by *In a U-Haul North of Damascus* (1983), a collection of thirty-one poems written largely in Florida. They show a kinship to the poetry of James Dickey and rely on more domestic settings. Lyrics that are sensitive and spiritual often contrast with violence. The connection between the animal and the human continues to fascinate Bottoms, and he begins to explore the relationship between danger and beauty, speaking in what James Dickey called his "compassionate countryman's voice."

The thirty poems in Bottoms's third collection, *Under the*

Vulture-Tree (1987), continue to join the lyrical and the narrative. Though some critics saw these new poems as still paying homage to old mentors, Bottoms had outgrown his literary influences. He continued to explore his interests in violence and beauty and displayed his skills as a superb nature poet. The collection also includes solid poems built around scenes from childhood and family life.

In the same year Bottoms published his first novel, *Any Cold Jordan* (1987), set in Florida and reflecting many of the themes in his poetry. Billy Parker is a thirty-three-year-old guitar player whose childless wife feels like a failure. Their lives change when he meets Jack Giddens, a professional soldier, and adventures ensue. This is a narrative about people adrift, and Bottoms uses his poetic gift of language to craft a novel about values, sacrifice, and compromise.

Bottoms finished his second novel, *Easter Weekend* (1990), while living in Montana. Set in Macon, the book covers three days in the life of Connie Holtzclaw, a twenty-something ex-boxer and small-time loser. A plot to kidnap a wealthy college student to pay off Connie's brother's gambling debts goes awry when gangsters move in on the game. This is a violent novel of desperation, loss, and redemption. In the end, after a double murder and betrayal, Connie is found hiding in an open grave on Easter Sunday morning.

Armored Hearts: Selected and New Poems (1995) includes poems from the first three collections and introduces new poems that are darker in tone and more overtly religious; Bottoms's earlier controversial style has grown more intense and evocative. Nine of the new poems are set in Montana, and Bottoms explores more deeply the complex world of rural and suburban values.

In *Vagrant Grace* (1999), Bottoms focuses intensely on the mystical aspects of beauty. Here, even death becomes lovely. Southern life and history are infused not only with moments of intense anxiety, but of grace and transcendence:

memory becomes portentous
like some newfound gospel
promising, finally, the whole fantastic story.

In several longer poems, Bottoms also experiments with a new style, achieving what critic David Baker has called a masterful blend of narrative and meditation. His latest collection of poems, *Waltzing through the Endtime*, was published in 2004.

Bottoms has confirmed the promise of Robert Penn Warren's early praise. Out of the natural world of rats, snakes, buzzards, and snapping turtles, and out of the deepest concerns of the human heart, Bottoms has made a spiritually charged but highly accessible poetry. The critic Ernest Suarez writes, "Bottoms has generated a complex body of poetry that often confronts the darkest dimensions of human nature."

GARY KERLEY, *North Hall High School*

SUGGESTED READING

Contemporary Poets, Dramatists, Essayists, and Novelists of the South, ed. Robert Bain and Joseph M. Flora (Westport, Conn.: Greenwood Press, 1994), s.v. "David Bottoms."

Contemporary Southern Writers, ed. Roger Matuz (Detroit: St. James Press, 1999), s.v. "Bottoms, David."

Benjamin Griffith, "A Retrospective Look at Poems by David Bottoms," *Southern Review* 32 (autumn 1996): 812–19.

Jane Hill, "To Own My Father's Name: Not Hiding the Masculine in the Poems of David Bottoms," *Studies in the Literary Imagination* 37 (spring 2002): 25–59.

Robert W. Hill, "Warbling with TV in the Background: David Bottoms in the Suburbs," *Southern Quarterly* 37 (spring–summer 1999): 80–84.

The Oxford Companion to Twentieth Century Poetry in English, ed. Ian Hamilton (Oxford: Oxford University Press, 1994), s.v. "David Bottoms."

Don Russ, "'Up toward Light': Resurrection, Transfiguration, Metamorphosis, and Evolution in David Bottoms's *Armored Hearts*," *Southern Quarterly* 37 (spring–summer 1999): 66–72.

Ernest Suarez, "A Deceptive Simplicity: The Poetry of David Bottoms," *Southern Quarterly* 37 (spring–summer 1999): 73–79.

ELIAS BOUDINOT
(ca. 1804–1839)

Elias Boudinot was a formally educated Cherokee who became the editor of the *Cherokee Phoenix*, the first Native American newspaper in the United States. In the mid-1820s the Cherokee Nation was under enormous pressure from surrounding states, especially Georgia, to move to a territory west of the Mississippi River. Ultimately, the Cherokee Nation was divided, with the majority opposing removal, and a small but influential minority, including Boudinot, favoring removal. As an educator, an advocate of Cherokee acculturation, and editor of the *Phoenix*, Boudinot played a crucial role in Cherokee history during the decades preceding the Nation's forced removal, often referred to as the Trail of Tears.

Elias Boudinot was born in Oothcaloga, in northwest Georgia, about 1804. He was called Gallegina, or the Buck, and was the eldest of nine children. His father, Oo-watie, was considered a progressive Cherokee. Oo-watie enrolled Gallegina and a younger son, Stand Watie, later a Confederate general, in a Moravian missionary school at Spring Place, in northwest Georgia. In 1817 young Gallegina was invited to attend the American Board of Commissioners for Foreign Missions school in Cornwall, Connecticut. On his journey there, Gallegina was introduced to Elias Boudinot, the aged president of the American Bible Society, and adopted his name in deference and tribute.

Boudinot spent several successful years at the American Board school, and in 1820 he converted to Christianity. Four years later he became engaged to a white woman, Harriet Ruggles Gold, the daughter of a Cornwall physician. Their engagement ignited a firestorm of racial prejudice, and the betrothed couple was burned in effigy. Labeled a breeding ground for mixed couples, the American Board school was forced to close immediately.

Boudinot and Harriet Gold married in 1826, then returned to High Tower in the Cherokee Nation to work in a mission. Earlier in the spring of 1826 Boudinot had embarked on a national speaking tour to elicit financial, spiritual, and political support for the Cherokee Nation's continuing progress in the "arts of civilization." His pamphlet, "An Address to the Whites" (1826), was based on a speech he made in Philadelphia. Boudinot proved remarkably effective at fund-raising. By 1827 the General Council of the Cherokee Nation was able to purchase a printing press and Cherokee typeface for the publication of a national newspaper, with Elias Boudinot as its editor. The groundbreaking first issue of the bilingual periodical, known as the *Cherokee Phoenix*, appeared on February 21, 1828. Boudinot pledged to print the official documents of the Nation and tracts on religion and temperance, as well as local and international news.

In the years following the Indian Removal Act (1830) Boudinot also began to publish editorials in favor of the voluntary removal of the Cherokees to a territory west of the Mississippi River. But his opinions were at odds with those held by the majority of the Nation, including the General Council. He resigned as editor of the *Phoenix* in August 1832 but continued to take an active role in the removal crisis and even printed a pamphlet attacking antiremoval chief John Ross. He ultimately signed the New Echota Treaty (1835), which required the Cherokees to relinquish all remaining land east of the Mississippi River and led to their forced removal to a territory in present-day Oklahoma. Soon after moving west with his family in 1839, Boudinot and two other treaty signers (his uncle Major Ridge and cousin John Ridge) were attacked and stabbed to death by a group of Ross supporters.

Boudinot was inducted into the Georgia Writers Hall of Fame in 2005.

ANGELA F. PULLEY, *Yale University, New Haven, Connecticut*

SUGGESTED READING

Cherokee Cavaliers: Forty Years of Cherokee History as Told in the Correspondence of the Ridge-Watie-Boudinot Family, ed. Edward Everett Dale and Gaston Litton (Norman: University of Oklahoma Press, 1995).

Theda Perdue, ed., *Cherokee Editor: The Writings of Elias Boudinot* (Athens: University of Georgia Press, 1996).

EDGAR BOWERS

(1924–2000)

When Edgar Bowers published his *Collected Poems* in 1997, literary critic Harold Bloom called him "one of the best living American poets these past forty years." Although Bowers had received the prestigious Bollingen Prize for Poetry, as well as two Guggenheim Fellowships, and though his work was admired and praised by such writers as Yvor Winters, Donald Justice, Richard Howard, Thomas Gunn, and Ted Hughes, he was largely unknown among readers of contemporary poetry. His modest productivity and, according to poet Leon Driskell, compact and rigorous formalism may account for his neglect in a time when confessionalism and poetic informalism were popular.

Bowers was born in 1924 in Rome, Georgia, the son of Grace and William E. Bowers. Although he spent his childhood in various parts of the state, he lived in Decatur during his high school years and graduated from Boys High School in 1941. Bowers earned his B.A. from the University of North Carolina at Chapel Hill, and his M.A. and Ph.D. degrees at Stanford University in California, where he studied under the critic and poet Yvor Winters. His education at Stanford was interrupted by service in World War II, however, and his experiences in Germany during the war and in the months following are said to have had a significant impact on him.

After returning to America and finishing his degree, Bowers taught at Duke University in Durham, North Carolina, and Harpur College (now the State University of New York at Binghamton) before settling in at the University of California at Santa Barbara in 1958, where he spent the remainder of his teaching career as a faculty member in the English department. He was named Professor of English in 1967. He retired from teaching in 1991 and moved to San Francisco, where he lived the rest of his life. Bowers's first book of poems was *The Form of Loss* (1956), followed by *The Astronomers* (1965), *Living Together: New and Selected Poems* (1973), *For Louis Pasteur* (1989), and *Collected Poems* (1997).

Bowers's experience in World War II apparently marked for him the dividing point between the cruel horrors of the modern world and the more humane, less forbidding past, an idea he explored fully in his long poem "John," which introduces *Collected Poems*. Bowers's poems can be described as inward, private meditations on life. He returns repeatedly through his career to a small number of subjects: love, art (especially music), childhood, and World War II. He often draws images from science, especially astronomy, and from nature. His Georgia roots play only a small part in his poetry, though in a few poems he addresses them at length, as in "Elegy: Walking the Line" and "The Mountain Cemetery". But Bowers does not write regional poetry. His landscape is his own self-consciousness, reveries and meditations on his life, people he has known, places traveled, and deeds accomplished.

Pervasive in Bowers's work is loss — of the past, of friends, of values, of humanity. He explores this topic in a number of ways and settings. In "Elegy: Walking the Line," from his 1989 collection *For Louis Pasteur*, he remembers walking the line of the family property with his father, a nurseryman whose plantings the poem vividly describes. With the exception of his mother, all the family members he names in the poem (reminiscent of poet John Greenleaf Whittier's "Snow-Bound") are dead, lost to the past. Their memories, he writes, are "presences like muses, prompting me / In my small study, all listening to the sea, / All of one mind, the true posterity." In "Ice Ages" he notes the extreme changes brought about by geologic time, which cast all human concerns into a paltry insignificance:

> Lonely at night, I read the book of science.
> It tells that what seems permanent will change
> Slowly or by catastrophe, that warm

Savannahs kind to trusting birds and trees,
Grasses and beasts, will build a house of ice,
Ice leave behind it crevice, stone, and waste.

Another poem, "In Defense of Poetry," focuses more narrowly on changes in the sensibilities of a younger generation, contrasting their superficial lives of material affluence (they "Drive Camrys, drink good wines, play Shostakovich / Or TV news before they go to bed") against life's darker realities, such as the German Holocaust.

One of his longest poems, "Autumn Shade," from his second collection, *The Astronomers*, may be his best, though in some ways it is not wholly representative of his work. "Autumn Shade" is a sequence of ten brief lyrics that meditate, from the poet's perspective as he lies awake at night, on the meaning and direction of his life. Bowers contrasts his own deeds with those of such mythic heroes as Odysseus and Hercules and contrasts his own aspirations with the realities that have determined and confined his life. Although he understands to an extent the people and the events that have helped make him the person he is, he is uncertain what it all means:

My image of myself, apart, informed
By many deaths, resists me, and I stay
Almost as I have been, intact, aware,
Alive, though proud and cautious, even afraid.

Self-consciously aware of his mortal transience, this fearful uncertainty is the burden of his self-awareness.

Bowers was homosexual, but his poetry does not call direct attention to the fact. Many of his poems are about love and often seem concerned with individuals from his life; but without knowledge of his sexual preference, readers would be as likely to identify these figures as women as they would men. Moreover, the concise, carefully worded lines of his poetry tend to conceal references to sexuality. Reading more deeply, one notes how Bowers avoids referring to gender. Some poems reflect more openly on issues of sexuality, such as the late poem "John," with its references to New Orleans, Louisiana, bathhouses, and a friend's death from (presumably) AIDS. Bowers's poetry does not hide his sexuality, but it is, as in all things, circumspect.

The complexity of Bowers's poems lies in their stylistic concision. When his language grows abstract, his poems increase in difficulty. His occasional tendency to allude to people and events from his own experience without identifying them creates in the reader a sense of detachment, as if, rather than opening himself up, he is holding the reader at a distance, allowing the reader to observe his meditations and thoughts without really sharing them. Most of his poems are relatively short. In his first volume, *The Form of Loss*, he wrote as a strict formalist, using rhymed lines divided into orderly four- and five-line stanzas. In later volumes he writes in a more open-ended blank-verse style, and he varies the lengths of his poems as well. The emotional tone of his poems grows increasingly less formal, even relaxed, though never lacking in an inward intensity. In his best poems, whether brief lyrics such as "The Astronomers of Mont Blanc," longer narrative meditations such as "Elegy: Walking the Line," or lyric sequences such as "Autumn Shade," he is an unappreciated master of formalist poetry in its most eloquent mode.

HUGH RUPPERSBURG, *University of Georgia*

SUGGESTED READING

Leon Driskell, "Edgar Bowers," in *The Dictionary of Literary Biography*, vol. 5, *American Poets since World War II*, 1st ser., ed. Donald J. Greiner (Detroit: Gale, 1980).

Richard Howard, "What Seems Won Paid for as in Defeat," in *Alone with America: Essays on the Art of Poetry in the United States since 1950* (New York: Atheneum, 1969).

Douglas L. Peterson, "The Early Poems of Edgar Bowers," *Centennial Review* 42 (winter 1998): 51–84.

Helen P. Trimpi, "The Theme of Loss in the Earlier Poems of Catherine Davis and Edgar Bowers," *Southern Review* 9, no. 3 (1973): 595–616.

VAN K. BROCK
(b. 1932)

As a poet who craved a connection with language from an early age, Van K. Brock began to contemplate a career in poetry while studying as an undergraduate at Emory University in Atlanta. Since his days there as both a student and a teacher, Brock has published several books of poetry.

Vandall Kline Brock was born on October 31, 1932, near Boston in Thomas County to Gladys Lewis, a teacher, and William Arthur Brock, a farmer. He first encountered poetry when his mother read it to him on a regular basis. He also began reading a great deal for himself. As a child, he told his mother that he wanted to be a poet.

At sixteen Brock entered Florida State University in Tallahassee as an engineering major. He soon transferred to the Georgia Institute of Technology in Atlanta, where a humanities course caused him to change directions. He transferred to Emory University in the winter of 1952 to major in humanities and graduated two years later.

After attending Garrett Theological Institute at Northwestern University in Evanston, Illinois, from 1954 to 1956, Brock returned to Atlanta and began working in the Medical Records Department at Emory. While this job consumed his nights, he spent the rest of his time reading major contemporary poets and experimenting with his craft. After transferring to a job working the door control desk at the Emory library, he found more opportunity to read and write.

During this time Brock met Paul Engle, the director of the Iowa Writers' Workshop, who asked him to enter the graduate program at the University of Iowa in Iowa City. Brock accepted and graduated with an M.A. in English in 1963 and an M.F.A. in poetry in 1964. He returned to Atlanta in 1964 and took a job teaching English, creative writing, and humanities courses at

Oglethorpe University from 1964 to 1968. He then moved back to Iowa to complete his Ph.D. in modern letters, which he earned in 1970.

In 1970 Brock joined the faculty at Florida State University, where he helped found a new writing program. He served as both teacher and codirector for the program, which eventually achieved a national reputation. Brock also founded Anhinga Press in 1972. Based in Tallahassee, Anhinga began as a small organization that sought to bring writers together. It also gave the young, aspiring poets whom Brock was teaching the opportunity to experience what he called "a sense of literary presence." Anhinga Press began by publishing chapbooks (small books or pamphlets containing poems, ballads, or stories), and in 1980 it published its first full-length poetry collection, by nationally renowned poet Michael Mott. Anhinga continues to thrive and holds an annual competition for poetry, a tradition that began in 1983.

Brock's personal publishing career also met with success. Beginning in the summer of 1961 his poems appeared in anthologies and in such publications as the *New Yorker*, *Georgia Review*, and *Yale Review*. He also published several chapbooks. In 1977 the periodical *Poets in the South* published a forty-two-page feature on Brock that included a critical essay on his poetry and a selection of his work.

Along with his work with Anhinga Press, Brock also served as the poetry editor of *National Forum: The Journal of the Phi Kappa Phi Honor Society* from 1978 to 1984. In the 1990s he founded and became the editor of *International Quarterly*.

Following his teaching and publishing house successes, Brock published a series of full-length collections, including *Spelunking* (1978), *The Hard Essential Landscape* (1979), *The Window* (1981), and *Unspeakable Strangers: Descents into the Dark Self, Ascents into Light* (1995). *Unspeakable Strangers*, perhaps Brock's most powerful work, deals with the Holocaust. Brock released a new collection of poetry called *Lightered: New and Selected Poems* in 2005.

Brock retired from Florida State University in 1999. He lives in Tucson, Arizona, with his second wife, Flavia Maria Da Silveira Lobo, a Brazilian writer and translator, and two sons.

M. BLAIR SPIVA, *University of Georgia*

OLIVE ANN BURNS

(1924–1990)

Olive Ann Burns was a professional writer, journalist, and columnist for most of her life. She published two novels, one posthumously, and for many years was a staff writer for Atlanta newspapers and the *Atlanta Journal Magazine*. Her most notable achievement was *Cold Sassy Tree*, a novel that describes rural southern life and a young boy's coming-of-age at the turn of the century.

Olive Ann Burns was born in Banks County on July 17, 1924, to Ruby Celestia Hight and William Arnold Burns. The youngest of four children, she grew up during the 1930s in her father's hometown of Commerce and attended high school in Macon. She then continued her education at Mercer University in Macon, where she studied for two years before transferring to the University of North Carolina at Chapel Hill. Shortly after graduating with a journalism degree in 1946, she was hired as a staff writer for the *Atlanta Journal and Constitution Magazine* (later *Atlanta Journal Magazine*) under the editorship of Angus Perkerson.

Burns wrote for the magazine for ten years. During that time she became acquainted with fellow journalist Andrew Sparks, and the two married in 1956. They had a daughter in 1957 and a son in 1960. Burns continued working as a freelance writer, serving as advice columnist "Amy Larkin" for the *Atlanta Journal Magazine* and the *Atlanta Constitution* until 1967.

Burns once stated, "Being a journalist, I never expected to get around to fiction," but in 1975 a cancer diagnosis altered her plans. Even before she left the doctor's office, she had decided to write a novel, a decision that "surprised me more than the diagnosis." Her preparations for the writing of the novel actually began somewhat earlier, when her mother was diagnosed with cancer in 1971. This diagnosis prompted Burns to begin a family history shortly thereafter. After her mother died in 1972, Burns relied on her father's recollections to help her write the history. One of his favorite family stories was about Grandpa Power, a practical man who remarried three weeks after the death of his first wife, in part because he needed a housekeeper. Although Burns thought that the story of Grandpa Power's quick marriage and its scandalous impact in a small town like Commerce would make an excellent premise for a book, she had never anticipated writing a novel until her own cancer diagnosis.

Burns worked on *Cold Sassy Tree* for eight-and-a-half years. Drawing from her family history, she continued to gather material about people and events at the turn of the century from relatives and friends, books, and newspapers. She transformed their vivid memories into the coming-of-age story of Will Tweedy, the novel's main character and narrator, and his life in fictional Cold Sassy, Georgia, in 1906. The fourteen-year-old Tweedy was inspired by Burns's father; his "adolescent" counterpart, the newly married Grandpa Blakeslee, was a reincarnated Grandpa Power. Inhabited by irreverent characters, the idyllic town of Cold Sassy provides the setting for a poignant and funny story about southern life at the turn of the century.

Cold Sassy Tree was published in 1984, when Burns was sixty. The novel became an instant success and was chosen as a Book-of-the-Month Club alternate selection. In 1985 it was added to the list of books recommended for teenagers by the American Library Association and the New York Public Library.

Burns began work on a sequel to *Cold Sassy Tree* before her relapse into cancer. In 1987 chemotherapy resulted in congestive heart failure, and Burns was prescribed bed rest. She turned for assistance to her neighbor Norma Duncan, who transcribed the author's words, enabling her to finish the second novel, which was initially called *Time, Dirt, and Money*. After battling cancer for fifteen years, and being confined to bed for the last three, Burns died on July 4, 1990. Her second novel, renamed *Leaving Cold Sassy*, was published in 1992.

KIM PURCELL, *Georgia Center for the Book*

SUGGESTED READING

Olive Ann Burns, "Boy Howdy, Ma'am, You Have Sent Us a Fine Book," *English Journal* 78 (December 1989): 16–20.

Marsha A. Stithem, "Olive Ann Burns and *Cold Sassy Tree* in the High School Classroom," *English Journal* 83 (December 1994): 81–84.

KATHRYN STRIPLING BYER
(b. 1944)

Poet and essayist Kathryn Stripling Byer is a native of Georgia but has set most of her poems in the mountains of North Carolina. Creating an identity that is both distinct and in line with the concerns of southern culture, Byer reclaims in her poetry the traditions, customs, and voices of past Appalachian women. In doing so, she defines herself as an artist and, at the same time, addresses the concerns of women in today's South.

Byer was born in Camilla, Georgia, in 1944 to C. M. Stripling, a farmer, and Bernice Campbell Stripling, a homemaker. She attended Wesleyan College in Macon, Georgia, and attained an M.F.A. from the University of North Carolina at Greensboro. There Byer studied with Allen Tate, Fred Chappell, and Robert Watson and won the Academy of American Poets Student Prize. While at UNC-G, Byer decided to make the North Carolina mountains her home, in large part, she says, because the mountains were "the place my grandmother had wanted to be when she died."

Byer has served as poet-in-residence at Western Carolina University (1988–98), UNC-G (1995), and Lenoir-Rhyne College (1999). Her work has appeared in prestigious poetry and scholarly journals, including *Poetry*, *Georgia Review*, *Southern Review*, and *Hudson Review*. She has published numerous essays, including the autobiographical "Deep Water" in *Bloodroot: Reflections on Place by Appalachian Women Writers* (1998) and "Turning the Windlass at the Well: Fred Chappell's Early Poetry," which was published in *Dream Garden: The Poetic Vision of Fred Chappell* (1997). She has received numerous awards, including fellowships from the National Endowment for the Arts and the North Carolina Arts Council. Her second volume, *Wildwood Flower* (1992), received the Lamont Prize for the best second book by an American poet. In 2005 Byer was named poet laureate of North Carolina.

Byer focuses on the power and liabilities of the solitude she finds in the mountains. In her essay "Deep Water," she addresses that solitude and what it has meant, historically, to women:

> To the women living in these mountains years ago, singing must have seemed the only way they could travel. . . . [T]hey remained. They knew their place. They knew its jump-offs, its laurel hells, its little graves grown over with honeysuckle and blackberry briars. They knew the lay of cloud shadows rolling down one ridge and up another. And their place knew them. Out of that reciprocal knowing, they were able to sing their way through their solitude and into a larger web of voices.

It is this "larger web of voices" that Byer works to recover. *Girl in the Midst of the Harvest* (1986), her first volume of poetry and her only collection set in rural Georgia, describes the difficult, often ambivalent relationship of a modern woman to the culture of the past. As she explains in "Wide Open, These Gates":

> . . . I've come a long way
> from what's been described as a mean and starved
> corner of backwoods America. That has a ring
> to it. Rhythm, like my grandmother's hands
> in the bread dough.

Byer's attempts to connect with her cultural past dominate this volume. It is in *Wildwood Flower* that she begins her exploration of Appalachian culture, a theme identified in the introductory poem, "At Kanati Fork," in which the narrator encounters a ruined homestead and addresses its ghost, "a lone woman haunting the trail":

> *"Who are you?" I asked the shade*
> *where her milk bucket rusted to nothing*

but rim. I saw, half-buried
under the leaf mold, a spoon catch the sun.

In her basin
a mirror of water.

Byer intensifies and extends the theme of identification and reclamation in *Black Shawl*, her third volume. In this book the distinction between the present and past fades away; the narrators who speak are often ghosts or local women, and often the difference between them is indiscernible. The continuity of their concerns, the sense of the presentness of the past, and the illusory quality of the present informs each woman's perspective. All these women have, Byer suggests, is the sense of continuity, their crafts, their collective life experiences and life wisdom to sustain them. In the light of that wisdom, many of them mistrust or refuse outside influences. As Delphia, one of *Black Shawl*'s many personae, tells us:

Don't ask me the big questions
none but a fool tries to answer
straight. All I can tell you of why
you were born is to take your own time
once the needle's been threaded,
the stray thimble fetched from the cloth bag.

The strengths of these volumes are progressive, and each bespeaks the growth and vision of the poet.

Byer's fourth volume of poetry, *Catching Light* (2002), deals with the experience of aging from a woman's perspective. In 2003 she published *Wake*, a chapbook reflecting on the events of September 11, 2001. *Coming to Rest* (2006), her fifth volume of poetry, investigates the experience of homecoming.

Byer lives in Cullowhee, North Carolina, and is married to Jim Byer, a professor of nineteenth-century literature at Western Carolina University. They have one daughter, Corinna Lynette.

SAM PRESTRIDGE, *Gainesville State College*

ERSKINE CALDWELL
(1903–1987)

Over the course of a long career, Erskine Caldwell wrote twelve books of nonfiction, twenty-five novels, and nearly 150 short stories. Profoundly influenced by his father, a minister and social reformer, he was intent on depicting life among the lowly in Georgia and the rest of the South. His concern for the less fortunate — poor whites and blacks — shines in his great novels and short stories of the 1930s. This concern also permeates the strongest writing of his later years, his nonfiction works of the 1960s.

Born December 17, 1903, in Coweta County, Caldwell was the only child of Caroline "Carrie" Bell, a schoolteacher, and Ira Sylvester Caldwell, a minister in the Associate Reformed Presbyterian (ARP) Church. Ira's work led the family to move frequently. By the time Erskine was fifteen, he and his parents had lived in Georgia, Florida, the Carolinas, Virginia, and Tennessee. In the summer of 1919 they moved back to Georgia and settled in Wrens, a small town about thirty miles south of Augusta. His parents lived there until Ira's death in 1944.

Erskine was profoundly influenced by his father, a social reformer in a deeply conservative denomination. As a teenager, Erskine helped Ira provide assistance to desperately poor people in east central Georgia. His experiences with his father shaped much of his writing.

Following high school, Caldwell attended Erskine College, an ARP school in South Carolina, and the University of Virginia, among other institutions. He never received a degree, but at the University of Virginia a professor encouraged him to be a writer. Outside class, he met fellow student Helen Lannigan, whom he married early in 1925. During their thirteen-year marriage, they had three children: Erskine Jr., Dabney, and Janet.

Caldwell broke into print as a student at the University of

Virginia with an essay entitled "The Georgia Cracker" (1926), which contained many of the themes that he later treated in fiction: political demagoguery, racial injustice, orgiastic religion, cultural sterility, and social irresponsibility. Most of his early fiction was published in little magazines. In spite of their shoestring budgets and small circulations, these magazines exerted an important influence on American literature by encouraging experimentation in form and content.

Two of Caldwell's early stories caught the attention of a major figure in the literary establishment, Maxwell Perkins, senior editor at Charles Scribner's Sons. Perkins read Caldwell's work at the suggestion of F. Scott Fitzgerald. In 1931 Scribner's published *American Earth*, Caldwell's first significant book. Among the stories in the collection are "Joe Craddock's Old Woman," a poignant vignette of the hardships of farming; "Savannah River Payday," a telling example of Caldwell's ability to weave humor and horror; and "Saturday Afternoon," a gut-wrenching story of a lynching. Introducing his work to a wider audience, *American Earth* ushered in an extraordinarily productive decade. By 1940 Caldwell had written, among other works, the novels *Tobacco Road*, *God's Little Acre*, and *Trouble in July*; the short-story collection *Kneel to the Rising Sun*; and the documentary *You Have Seen Their Faces*.

Included by experts among the one hundred most significant novels in English of the twentieth century, *Tobacco Road* (1932) describes the body-breaking and soul-numbing effects of poverty among Georgia's tenant farmers during the Great Depression, a description leavened by Caldwell's dark humor. *God's Little Acre* (1933) portrays the abuse of southern industrial workers and the disintegration of a family, both of which are emphasized by a raw rendition of sex. *Trouble in July* (1940) is a gripping tale of white southerners' fear of interracial sex and a searing indictment of a brutal, violent, racist society.

The short-story collection *Kneel to the Rising Sun* (1935) contains the writing of an author who was at the height of his powers. Caldwell's mastery of the short-story form, together with his outrage over social injustice and his great talent, enabled him to write such unforgettable pieces as "The Growing Season," which poignantly portrays a cotton farmer's travail, and "Candy-Man Beechum" and "Kneel to the Rising Sun," both burning condemnations of racism.

In addition to his fiction from the 1930s, Caldwell collaborated in the production of an overwhelmingly powerful work of nonfiction. In the summer of 1936 and again early in 1937 he traveled over the South with the noted photographer Margaret Bourke-White, interviewing people as she took their pictures. The result was *You Have Seen Their Faces* (1937), a combination of forceful writing and memorable photographs. It is a graphic depiction of life among the region's country people during the Great Depression. Over the course of their travels, Caldwell and Bourke-White fell in love and were married after Caldwell's wife divorced him.

The marriage lasted only three years. Both Caldwell and Bourke-White were more committed to their work than to their union, and they divorced in 1942. Thereafter, Caldwell married June Johnson, a college student half his age. During their rocky twelve-year marriage, they had one child, a son named Jay. Following his divorce from June, Caldwell married Virginia Fletcher. Their marriage lasted thirty years until his death and equaled the total time of his previous marriages.

After the great work of the 1930s, Caldwell's fiction declined significantly. The beginning of the decline coincided with the death of his father, who had been a steady and enthusiastic source of support and encouragement. The turmoil of his personal life also took its toll. Moreover, he believed that the optimal powers of a creative writer lasted only ten years.

Millions of readers in the late 1940s and the 1950s paid much more attention to Caldwell's work of the 1930s than to his postwar writing. The paperback revolution in American publishing that began right after World War II exponentially increased the sales of *Tobacco Road*, *God's Little Acre*, and others of Caldwell's 1930s books by packaging those works in ways that obscured their full meaning. Their covers, featuring scantily clad, alluring young women, suggested that sex was the primary focus of the works. Caldwell made a good deal of money from his paperback publishers — at least $200,000 between 1945 and 1951 without writing a word — but his cooperation with them adversely affected his reputation within the literary establishment and helped ensure that his work would be neglected by scholars.

The best work of the latter part of Caldwell's career is his nonfiction, especially his travel writing. Journeying over the South in the 1960s with his wife, Virginia, he wrote *In Search of Bisco* (1965) and *Deep South* (1968). The former deals with race and shows his disappointment with the white South's opposition to integration. The latter, which explores religion, illustrates his ongoing frustration with white Christians who use their faith to oppose social reform — whether they are holy-rollers in the country or corporate executives in the city.

Considering the great volume of Erskine Caldwell's work, the quality might be expected to be uneven. Much of his early writing is among the best in American literature. That writing lodges in the reader's memory. One does not forget the characters and circumstances described in *Tobacco Road*, *God's Little Acre*, and many of the short stories.

Caldwell's focus on the issues of class and race was more intense than that of any other white southern writer of his generation. What distinguishes his best fiction dealing with class is his ability to evoke emotion while avoiding sentimentality. For example, if Jeeter Lester of *Tobacco Road* were only pitiable, then the reader, after feeling sorry for him, could forget him. But because his behavior is so outrageous, it is disturbing and unforgettable.

Notwithstanding the artistic power with which Caldwell invested his delineation of the effects of poverty, his anger and agony over the poison that racism injected into southern life called forth his best work. No rational person, not even a white southerner in the 1930s, could contend that the black protagonists in such stories as "Saturday Afternoon," "Candy-Man Beechum," and "Kneel to the Rising Sun" deserved their terrible fate. Their self-respect and good habits, coupled with white jealousy, got them killed.

Caldwell's harsh criticism of social injustice in his native region brought forth equally sharp criticism by some white southerners who accused him of being a communist, a corrupter of morals, and a traitor to the South. At the same time, other southerners commended his artistic skill and his social conscience. Controversy over his writings stalked his career and extended beyond the grave.

Although Caldwell settled outside of Georgia shortly before he was twenty-five, he paid extended visits to his parents in Wrens for as long as they lived there. Later, he returned to Georgia and other southern states on numerous occasions. Though he lived much of his life outside the South, the region stayed on his mind and figured prominently in most of his writing. Nostalgia for his native Georgia found expression when he reached his sixties. As he wrote Governor Lester Maddox with an ironic twist in 1967, "I like to think that I am as much a Georgian as Brer Rabbit." Nostalgia did not diminish the social concern, however. In his seventies, he asked an old friend at the *Atlanta Journal* to help with arrangements for a proposed volume that would update *You Have Seen Their Faces*.

A month before his death on April 11, 1987, Peachtree Publishers in Atlanta issued his final book, an autobiography entitled *With All My Might*. It is supremely fitting that his farewell was published in his native Georgia, a place that had supplied such rich material about the poor people whose lives he sought to improve.

WAYNE MIXON, *Augusta State University*

Colin Campbell, "Hall of Fame Panel Sorts Out Best of Georgia Literature," *Atlanta Journal-Constitution*, April 2, 2000.

Sylvia Jenkins Cook, *Erskine Caldwell and the Fiction of Poverty: The Flesh and the Spirit* (Baton Rouge: Louisiana State University Press, 1991).

Sylvia Jenkins Cook, *From Tobacco Road to Route 66: The Southern Poor White in Fiction* (Chapel Hill: University of North Carolina Press, 1976).

Harvey L. Klevar, *Erskine Caldwell: A Biography* (Knoxville: University of Tennessee Press, 1993).

James Korges, *Erskine Caldwell* (Minneapolis: University of Minnesota Press, 1969).

Scott MacDonald, ed., *Critical Essays on Erskine Caldwell* (Boston: G. K. Hall, 1981).

Robert L. McDonald, ed., *The Critical Response to Erskine Caldwell* (Westport, Conn.: Greenwood Press, 1997).

Shields McIlwaine, *The Southern Poor-White from Lubberland to Tobacco Road* (Norman: University of Oklahoma Press, 1939).

Dan B. Miller, *Erskine Caldwell: The Journey from Tobacco Road* (New York: Knopf, 1994).

Wayne Mixon, *The People's Writer: Erskine Caldwell and the South* (Charlottesville: University Press of Virginia, 1995).

The generative force behind Jean Toomer's great work *Cane* was Georgia. Toomer grew up amid the African American elite in Washington, D.C., and attended the University of Wisconsin, the Massachusetts College of Agriculture, the American College of Physical Training in Chicago, the University of Chicago, and City College of New York. In 1920 he decided to become a writer, filled a trunk with manuscripts, and the next fall, at the age of twenty-six, took a position in Sparta, Georgia, as the substitute head of a small industrial school for blacks. On the train home to Washington just three months later, in November 1921, he began writing the first of the segments that would become part of the Modernist masterpiece published in 1923 as *Cane*.

"Things are so immediate in Georgia," remarks the narrator in explaining the agony of Toomer's alter ego, Kabnis, in the final section of the work. "God Almighty, dear God, dear Jesus, do not torture me with beauty," Kabnis beseeches. "Take it away. Give me an ugly world. Ha, ugly. . . . Dear Jesus, do not chain me to myself and set these hills and valleys heaving with folksongs. So close to me that I cannot reach them. There is a radiant beauty in the night that touches and . . . tortures me. Ugh. Hell. Get up you damn fool. Look around. Whats beautiful there? Hog pens and chicken yards. Dirty red mud. Stinking outhouse. Whats beauty anyway but ugliness if it hurts you?"

Georgia forced the mixed-race Toomer (and Kabnis) to confront the African American past — the mixture of agrarian beauty, spiritual yearning, violence, and oppression — and to ponder his own place within the races and within the race to which society assigned him. Toomer responded with a mixture of poetry, lyrical sketches, short stories, vignettes, and finally, in the work's third and final section, the genre-bending "Kabnis," which mixes the lyric, the narrative, and the dramatic modes. The resulting composite, *Cane*, evokes powerful feelings of aesthetic pleasure, despair, confusion, and longing for mystical transcendence.

The first section, set in Georgia, is a collection of sketches and stories interspersed with poems, both imagist lyrics and verse inspired by African American spirituals. Focused upon women who are allied with nature and promise to serve as mediums to mystical fulfillment, the prose pieces finally document failure and alienation. The haunting beauty of the landscape and the prose that captures it are, in the end, overwhelmed by the horror of racial injustice and oppression. The second section, set in the North, is dominated by images of enclosure. Cut off from spirituality, spontaneity, and history, the focal characters are southern migrants who feel thwarted, conflicted, and finally confused even about their place within the race. The third section is a return to Georgia, where the Toomer figure, the northern man Kabnis, is both drawn to and tortured by the South and the racial past. Through its characters the Kabnis section presents an entire gallery of African American response, and then in the end a symbolic descent into the womb of time, where a blind prophet brings the word that the only sin is that against the soul. At the conclusion, as Kabnis climbs up into the dawn, Toomer achieves an ambiguity as rich as that of the poet T. S. Eliot at the end of *The Waste Land*.

The white literary avant garde responded to *Cane* with enthusiasm. The African American reaction was divided, it seems, among generational lines. The educator W. E. B. Du Bois saw in the work real talent but found it needlessly confusing and opaque. The writer Langston Hughes, on the other hand, greeted it as the finest prose by an African American.

Toomer was to comment that the writing of *Cane* was probably the most painful event in his life. "Never again in life," he said, "do I want a repetition of those conditions." But the rich and strange work stands as the literary pinnacle of his career. Never again did he write anything matching its quality and power as he went on to immerse himself in mystic cults, Eastern religions, Quakerism, and psychoanalysis.

Nothing touched Toomer so profoundly as the few months he spent in Georgia. As he enunciates in the poem "Song of the Son" from *Cane*, in Georgia he had returned to the past just before it vanished:

> O land and soil, red soil and sweet-gum tree,
> So scant of grass, so profligate of pines,
> Now just before an epoch's sun declines
> Thy son, in time, I have returned to thee,
> Thy son, I have in time returned to thee.
> In time, for though the sun is setting on
> A song-lit race of slaves, it has not set;
> Though late, O soil, it is not too late yet
> To catch thy plaintive soul, leaving, soon gone,
> Leaving, to catch thy plaintive soul soon gone.

When Toomer turned his back on the pain caused by his own return to the roots of African American life and ceased trying to come to terms with his own racial identity, he lost the great subject for his art.

HUBERT H. McALEXANDER, *University of Georgia*

SUGGESTED READING

Barbara Foley, "'In the Land of Cotton': Economics and Violence in Jean Toomer's *Cane*," *African American Review* 32 (summer 1998).

Barbara Foley, "Jean Toomer's Sparta," *American Literature* 67 (December 1995).

Nellie Y. McKay, *Jean Toomer, Artist: A Study of His Literary Life and Work, 1894–1936* (Chapel Hill: University of North Carolina Press, 1984).

JIMMY CARTER
(b. 1924)

Jimmy Carter, the only Georgian elected president of the United States, held the office for one term, 1977–81. His previous public service included a stint in the U.S. Navy, two senate terms in the Georgia General Assembly, and one term as governor of Georgia (1971–75). After being defeated in the presidential election of 1980, he founded the Carter Center, a nonpartisan public policy center in Atlanta.

During his years of public service at the local, state, and federal levels, Carter's policies contained a unique blend of liberal social values and fiscal conservatism. He emphasized comprehensive reform and stressed efficiency and economy, advance planning, and rational organization. He also championed equal rights for all Americans, especially women and minorities, and basic human rights for all people. In 2002 Carter won the prestigious Nobel Peace Prize for his humanitarian efforts.

Jimmy Carter's journey to the nation's highest office began in the small Sumter County town of Plains. Born on October 1, 1924, James Earl Carter Jr. later adopted the more informal "Jimmy" as his official designation. His father, a farmer and small-town merchant, was one of the area's leading citizens.

After attending public school in Plains, Carter matriculated at Georgia Southwestern College in Americus and the Georgia Institute of Technology in Atlanta before receiving a coveted appointment to the U.S. Naval Academy in Annapolis, Maryland. He graduated with a baccalaureate degree and a naval commission in 1946 and eventually became senior officer of the precommissioning crew of the *Seawolf*, the second nuclear submarine.

Shortly after leaving the Naval Academy, Carter married Rosalynn Smith, also from Plains. They had three sons, John William, James Earl III, and Donnel Jeffrey, and a daughter, Amy Lynn. After the death of Carter Sr. in 1953, the younger Carter resigned his naval commission, forgoing a promising military career, and returned to Plains. He spent the next several years reviving the family-owned peanut warehouse business, farming, and generally assuming the patriarchal and paternalistic responsibilities previously exercised by his father.

The family businesses thrived under Jimmy and Rosalynn Carter's adroit management. Consequently, with more time to devote to community affairs, politics increasingly attracted Carter's attention. His father had represented Sumter County in the state legislature at the time of his death, and now Carter prepared to make his own entry into state politics. In 1962, he overcame the unlawful machinations of a political boss in Quitman County to win election to the state senate from the Fourteenth District. During his two senate terms, Carter devoted much time and attention to educational affairs. While serving on the Sumter County School Board, he vigorously promoted efficiency and educational opportunity through school reorganization and consolidation. But fearing such reforms would be the first step in school integration, a predominantly white county electorate voted them down in a referendum election. Later, as chair of the Senate Education Committee, Carter continued to advocate such policies on a statewide level.

After briefly flirting with a run for the U.S. Congress in 1966, Carter instead joined the race for the Democratic gubernatorial nomination. For a little-known state senator, he ran a surprisingly strong race but missed the runoff, finishing third. During his second gubernatorial campaign Carter subtly appealed to class antagonisms, running as the representative of the ordinary people. It was a successful strategy wherein Carter projected himself as a traditional southern conservative.

After easily defeating his Republican opponent, Carter surprised most of his Georgia supporters and attracted national attention during a short, twelve-minute inaugural address when he proclaimed that the time for segregation had ended. "No poor, rural, weak, or black person," he declared, "should ever have to bear the additional burden of being deprived of the opportunity of an education, a job, or simple justice." He soon revealed himself as a moderate business progressive with an extensive reform agenda designed to make state government operate more efficiently and to be more responsive to the needs of its citizens.

The reorganization of state government served as the cornerstone of Carter's gubernatorial program. This massive reform effort, which continued through much of his four-year term, produced large-scale structural reform. Carter also took a variety of actions, both substantive and symbolic, to promote civil rights and equal opportunity for women and minorities. The governor reflected his commitment to fairness and justice most obviously in his appointment policy. He appointed more women and minorities to his own staff, to major state policy boards and agencies, and to the judiciary than all of his predecessors combined.

Still a relatively young man of fifty at the end of his term and ineligible to run for reelection under the state constitution (later changed), Carter began to explore possibilities for higher office well before leaving the gubernatorial office. This led him to pursue the presidency. In 1976, Carter prevailed during the presidential primaries and won the Democratic Party presidential nomination. He then narrowly defeated Republican president Gerald R. Ford in the general election. In office Carter emphasized high moral standards, ethical behavior, and democratic principles. He often projected himself in populist terms, dressed casually, and sharply reduced the level of pomp and ceremony that had come to be associated with the modern American presidency.

An unpretentious, egalitarian demeanor, however, did little to offset the severity of the national and international problems that Carter inherited. In 1973 the Arab oil-producing nations of the Organization of Petroleum Exporting Countries (OPEC) had sharply reduced oil production, driving up prices and creating selective gasoline shortages. In addition to higher fuel costs, escalating health and food prices spurred a tenacious inflationary surge. The Carter administration sought to slow inflation by raising interest rates and restraining federal spending.

Along with other measures, the program of federal fiscal austerity that Carter followed eventually brought inflation under control but at considerable political cost. Wage workers, a core Democratic Party constituency, fared poorly under Carter's economic prescriptions. In the battle to control inflation, administration policies encouraged reduced employment, and for those employed, it advocated pay restraints that had the effect of decreasing real wages. Disillusioned, many traditional Democratic supporters either deserted the party or abandoned politics altogether.

In addition to continuing domestic problems, international crises, over which Carter had little control, further undermined his leadership. Two events that occurred late in Carter's term proved particularly ill-starred: the Soviet Union's invasion of Afghanistan and the seizure of the American embassy in Tehran, Iran, following the expulsion of the Shah by the followers of the Ayatollah Khomeini, a fundamentalist Muslim cleric. Ultimately, Carter managed these two crises judiciously, but the incidents embarrassed the nation, and Carter's measured response to them won him little public applause. In 1980 Carter decisively lost his bid for reelection to Republican nominee Ronald Reagan.

Although at the time he departed office his presidency was widely perceived as a failure, Jimmy Carter left behind a solid record of accomplishment in both domestic and international affairs. On the domestic front, Carter created two new cabinet-level departments (Energy and Education), developed a national energy policy, deregulated the trucking and airline industries, and — continuing the practice he had followed in the Georgia governor's mansion — appointed a record number of women and minorities to federal government offices. In the international arena, he firmly established human rights as an essential component of foreign policy, opened diplomatic relations with China, and helped to negotiate the Panama Canal Treaties, the Camp David Accords between Israel and Egypt, and SALT II (Strategic Arms Limitation Treaty) with the Soviet Union.

Shortly after returning to Georgia following his reelection defeat, the former president founded the Carter Center in Atlanta and became the University Distinguished Professor at Emory University. Under Carter's direction, center associates have not only examined and analyzed national and international policy issues but also actively engaged in efforts to promote democratic practices, advance human rights, and resolve conflicts. The Carter Center has monitored more than forty elections in twenty-one countries, including Venezuela, Mozambique, Nicaragua, and the Dominican Republic. It worked to resolve conflicts in Haiti, Bosnia, Ethiopia, North Korea, Sudan, and other countries.

Through its Global 2000 programs, the center has sought to eradicate or control such debilitating diseases as river blindness, guinea worm, and trachoma, which have devastated the populations of many poorer countries. It also has striven to relieve hunger through agricultural reform, especially in drought-plagued sub-Saharan Africa. Along with his support of Carter Center projects, Carter continues to champion Habitat for Humanity, a Georgia-based philanthropy that helps needy people build new homes or renovate older ones.

In 2002 Carter was awarded the Nobel Peace Prize for his continuing effort to find peaceful solutions to international conflicts and to advance democracy and human rights. Carter is the third American president to win the Nobel Peace Prize. Theodore Roosevelt and Woodrow Wilson both received the prize while still in office. Carter shares with Martin Luther King Jr. the distinction of being the only native Georgians to be so honored.

At the time of his presidential candidacy, Carter published *Why Not the Best?* (1975), a biographical introduction of his political stance and viability as a candidate. In his postpresidential career, Carter has written seventeen books, including one he cowrote with his wife, Rosalynn, and a children's book (illustrated by daughter Amy). Covering a variety of topics, from postpresidency activity to aging/retirement, faith, human rights, and even fiction and poetry, Carter has made a point in his publications to be not only informative but also forthright about his life and political philosophy.

In *A Government as Good as Its People* (1977), Carter discusses government policy on crime, poverty, nuclear energy, foreign policy, and human rights, and with *The Blood of Abraham: Insights into the Middle East* (1993) he breaks down the history of that region. In 2005 Carter's collection of essays entitled *Endangered Values: America's Moral Crisis* spent several weeks at the top of the *New York Times* best-seller list. A sharp critique of the religious right and the administration of U.S. president George W. Bush, the book addresses a wide range of topics, including global warming, gun control, human rights abuses, and the war in Iraq.

In a book coauthored with his wife, *Everything to Gain: Making the Most of the Rest of Your Life* (1987), Carter discusses their experiences with Habitat for Humanity and the Carter Center. In *Turning Point: A Candidate, a State, and a Nation Come of Age* (1992), Carter relates the story of his first campaign for public office, a seat in the Georgia state senate in 1962. He recounts the difficulties of resisting segregationist groups in the wake of the Supreme Court ruling that stated "one man, one vote."

In addition to two memoirs published in 2001, *Christmas in Plains: Memories* and *An Hour before Daylight: Memories of a Rural Boyhood*, Carter has written an autobiography, *Living Faith* (1996), which focuses on his spiritual faith in service to the country. His semiautobiographical poetry appears in *Always a Reckoning, and Other Poems* (1995). With the 2003 publication of *The Hornet's Nest*, a work of historical fiction about the Revolutionary War in the South, Carter became the first U.S. president to write a novel.

GARY M. FINK, *Georgia State University*

Peter G. Bourne, *Jimmy Carter: A Comprehensive Biography from Plains to Post-Presidency* (New York: Scribner, 1997).

Douglas Brinkley, *The Unfinished Presidency: Jimmy Carter's Journey beyond the White House* (New York: Viking, 1998).

Kenneth E. Morris, *Jimmy Carter, American Moralist* (Athens: University of Georgia Press, 1996).

TURNER CASSITY
(b. 1929)

Poet, playwright, and short-story writer Turner Cassity has earned fame with the fine formal poetry he has published prolifically for forty years. Cassity's poetry shares the sentiments of the New Formalist movement that matured in the 1980s: for example, the tendency to eschew the autobiographical, the preference for meter and rhyme over free verse, a stylized language, a taste for clarity, and the unfolding of a poem through narrative. Cassity's wit, humor, stringent satire, and iconoclastic views as well as the musicality of his verse make of this southern writer a venerated poet.

Allen Turner Cassity was born in January 1929, in Jackson, Mississippi, to Dorothy and Allen Cassity. Raised a Calvinist, he grew up in Jackson and Forest, Mississippi. His grandparents on both maternal and paternal sides were in the sawmill business. His mother, a violinist, and his grandmother, a pianist, were silent-movie musicians. Cassity's father died when he was four, and at the age of sixteen, he began managing his own inheritance. He attended Millsaps College in Jackson, graduating in 1951, and then enrolled at Stanford University in Stanford, California, earning a master's degree in English in 1952.

Toward the end of the Korean War, Cassity was drafted and stationed near San Juan and in Cayey, Puerto Rico, from 1952 to 1954. After leaving the military, Cassity attended Columbia University in New York on the GI Bill and received a master's degree in library science in 1956. After graduation he worked for the Jackson Public Library and then moved to South Africa, where he worked from 1958 to 1960 as a librarian in Pretoria and then near Johannesburg. After this he returned to work for the Jackson Public Library for one year and then spent four months in Europe.

In 1962 Cassity accepted the position of librarian in the Robert W. Woodruff Library at Emory University, from which he retired in 1991. He cofounded the Callanwolde Readings Program, which highlights poets and writers, with poet Michael Mott.

Cassity started writing poetry at the age of fifteen. His books include *Watchboy, What of the Night?* (1966), *Steeplejacks in Babel* (1973), a verse play *Silver Out of Shanghai* (1973), *Yellow for Peril, Black for Beautiful* (1975), *The Defense of the Sugar Islands* (1979), *Phaëthon unter den Linden* (1979), *Keys to Mayerling* (1983), *The Airship Boys in Africa* (1984), a verse play *The Book of Alna* (1985), *Hurricane Lamp* (1986), *Lessons* (1987), a book-length poem *To the Lost City, or, the Sins of Nineveh* (1989), *Between the Chains* (1991), *The Destructive Element: New and Selected Poems* (1998), and *No Second Eden* (2002). Cassity has been awarded the Levinson Prize for Poetry, the Broude Award of the American Academy of Arts and Letters, and the Ingram Merrill Foundation Award.

Cassity writes with a voice that is impersonal, sober, and gritty and a language that is at once "clear and mysterious," as critic J. D. McClatchy has observed. From Yvor Winters, his teacher at Stanford, Cassity acquired a penchant both for moralism and for rigor in metrics. A typical Cassity line runs in couplets and sometimes in tercets, quartets, blank verse, and other variations. "In Sydney by the Bridge," commonly regarded as Cassity's *ars poetica*, compares verse to the ferry and vers libre to the cruise ship, and hints that "the scheduled ferry, not the cruise ship, [is] precious" for the former is free from detours. Another poem, "The Metrist at the Operetta," indicates that formal verse allows enough freedom for creation since "in the arts / [i]t is the tricks that are the trade."

Cassity's views of the South are iconoclastic, despite his use of traditional literary forms. Though he is a poet from the Bible Belt, he asserts that a poet should be more than a mere teller of oracles. In "By the waters of Lexington Avenue," Cassity likens a poet to a steeplejack who builds the modern tower of Babel, a symbol of humanity's "will to power" erected to conquer "the quotidian." To Cassity a poet sings the "[t]wanging sound" of "the elevator cables" sending people up nearer to God.

Moreover, in Cassity's opinion, the meaning of "the South" has broadened and transformed as southerners have traveled, colonized, and suffused new lands with southern regionalism. His poem "Cartography Is an Inexact Science" accentuates his idea of the syndication of culture, suggesting that geography is defined more by people's interrelationships and less by space: "We thrive a little, one the other's climate, / Our two backs / A sort of landfall." Cassity's poetry depicts a postcolonial South whose sin, avarice, pride, and morality unveil themselves in exotic outposts, in the interplay of colonial forces of the past and postcolonial lives of the present.

Cassity considers himself a southerner yet disagrees with the notion that southernness is merely a "literary convention," since the latter can no longer describe modern southern life. Other than continuing the myths of a "tragic" and "guilt-ridden" South evoked by Faulkner and other writers, Cassity's poetry implies that southern writers can and should reinvent their language and subject matter. Considered by Dana Gioia to be the "most brilliantly eccentric poet in America," Cassity is now in his seventies and continues to deploy a complex and exotic imagination, all the while using traditional literary form.

He lives in Decatur.

YI-HSUAN TSO, *National Taiwan Ocean University, Keelung, Taiwan*

SUGGESTED READING

Donald Davie, "On Turner Cassity," *Chicago Review* 34, no. 1 (1983).

John Griffin Jones, "Turner Cassity," in *Mississippi Writers Talking*, vol. 2 (Jackson: University Press of Mississippi, 1983).

Keith Tuma, "Turner Cassity," in *Dictionary of Literary Biography*, vol. 105 (Detroit: Gale, 1991).

The *Chattahoochee Review* is a literary journal published four times a year by Georgia Perimeter College. It features fiction, poetry, and essays by regional and national writers. The journal was founded in 1981 by Lamar York, a professor of English. In 1997 Lawrence Hetrick succeeded York as editor.

The *Chattahoochee Review* has achieved a national reputation for publishing both new writers and established writers. Recently published authors include Michael Bishop, Nicole Cooley, Walter Griffin, Anthony Grooms, Seaborn Jones, Terry Kay, Marjorie Kemper, Marion Montgomery, Ron Rash, and Virgil Suarez. The *Review* has taken as one of its missions advocacy for writers from the Southeast, specifically from Georgia. The publication's staff not only cosponsors the Townsend Prize for Fiction but also works to foster a literary community centered in Atlanta and north Georgia. Despite its regional emphasis, inclusiveness is an important principle of the *Review*, which features writers from all over the nation and the world.

In 2003 the *Review* received the Governor's Award in the Humanities. In her letter of nomination, Wanda Yancey Rodwell, a member of the Board of Regents of the University System of Georgia, observed that the *Chattahoochee Review* "is more than a nationally ranked literary quarterly. It is a cultural organization based on the idea of building community in Georgia among established and emerging writers, as well as educating the public about their work and literary values. . . . The *Review*'s inclusive approach in its sponsorship of literary readings, symposia, and cultural programs has built a sense of trust in which diverse groups participate in discussion and debate."

The *Review* has published several single-author issues highlighting the work of important regional writers. A 1988 issue was devoted to the work of southern author and Agrarian Andrew

Lytle. In the same year another issue was devoted to publishing *Once upon a Time in Atlanta*, a memoir written by Georgia native Raymond Andrews and illustrated by his brother Benny Andrews. Entire issues have also been devoted to poetry, fiction, or nonfiction. A more typical issue includes a collection of stories, poetry, essays, and reviews.

Works first published in the *Review* have been reprinted in *New Stories from the South*, *Pushcart Prize Anthology*, *Anthology of Magazine Verse and Yearbook of American Poetry*, *Best American Mystery Stories*, and *Utne Reader*.

HUGH RUPPERSBURG, *University of Georgia*

BRAINARD CHENEY

(1900–1990)

Brainard Cheney was a twentieth-century novelist, political speechwriter, and essayist from the wiregrass region of south Georgia. During a writing career that spanned four decades, Cheney published four novels — *Lightwood* (1939), *River Rogue* (1942), *This Is Adam* (1958), and *Devil's Elbow* (1969) — that depict the social transformation of south Georgia between 1870 and 1960. These novels contain accounts of Cheney's own coming of age (*Devil's Elbow*) as well as land feuds (*Lightwood*), timber rafting (*River Rogue*), and race relations (*This Is Adam*) in the area where he grew up. Along with his wife, Frances Neel Cheney, he was a member of a community of writers that included Caroline Gordon, Allen Tate, Andrew Lytle, Robert Penn Warren, and Flannery O'Connor.

Born in Fitzgerald on June 3, 1900, to a family with considerable land holdings in the area, Brainard Bartwell Cheney moved with his family to Lumber City, in Telfair County, when he was six years old. His father died when he was eight, and his mother reared him and his two sisters on their farm near Lumber City. Cheney attended Vanderbilt University in Nashville, Tennessee, sporadically between 1920 and 1925, becoming friends with many of the Fugitive and Agrarian writers associated with the Vanderbilt English department in the 1920s and 1930s. After leaving school he worked for the *Nashville Banner* from 1925 to 1942, serving as reporter, editor, feature writer, and editorialist. After a series of political appointments and public relations positions, he served as public relations director for Tennessee governor Frank Clement from 1952 to 1958.

Throughout his newspaper and political careers Cheney continued to work on his own novels and maintained a voluminous correspondence with his literary friends, especially Tate, Gordon, Lytle, and Warren. In 1953, through the sponsorship of Tate and

Gordon, he and his wife became members of the Roman Catholic Church. Living primarily in Nashville and at their home, "Idler's Retreat," in Smyrna, Tennessee, the Cheneys (Lon and Fannie to their friends) remained for many years at the center of a lively literary circle. Cheney died in 1990 at the age of eighty-nine; his wife died in 1996, also at the age of eighty-nine.

Cheney's published novels reveal his sympathy with the Agrarian themes of individualism, tradition, anti-industrialism, and harmony with nature. They express the romance of a return to the land, and his authorial character, Marcellus Hightower, indicates his support of a patriarchal social system. Yet as a political pragmatist, Cheney differed from his Agrarian counterparts in significant ways. He supported New Deal programs like the Tennessee Valley Authority, and his novels reflect a more liberal attitude toward racial integration and social change. The protagonist of *River Rogue*, an independent, alienated young white man, lives and works openly with a black family in the swamps of south Georgia. In *This Is Adam* Cheney makes his title character the mixed-race overseer of a farm much like the one on which he grew up. In all of his novels Cheney's acute political ear and his awareness of the complexities of a changing society create a graphic and memorable portrait of a region.

MICHAEL E. PRICE, *Armstrong Atlantic State University*
CAROL M. ANDREWS, *Armstrong Atlantic State University*

SUGGESTED READING

Wilton Irving Beauchamp Jr., "Look a-Yonder, I See Sunday: A Critical Study of the Novels of Brainard Cheney" (Ph.D. diss., Emory University, 1977).

James Edwin Young, "The Search for a Hero: A Literary Biography of Brainard Cheney, Southern Novelist, Reporter, and Polemicist" (Ph. D. diss., George Peabody College for Teachers / Vanderbilt University, 1979).

THOMAS HOLLEY CHIVERS

(1809–1858)

Thomas Holley Chivers, poet and physician, published eleven volumes of poetry, plays, and pamphlets. He also contributed to leading antebellum literary periodicals and newspapers, especially the *Georgia Citizen*, and wrote a biography of Edgar Allan Poe, his friend and kindred spirit. Nevertheless, the eccentric Georgia writer never achieved the critical acclaim that he craved. Unfortunately, his famous legacy — the Poe-Chivers plagiarism controversy — has overshadowed his talent as a mystical poet.

Born and reared near Washington, Georgia, Chivers left Wilkes County after a failed youthful marriage. In 1830 he earned a medical degree from Transylvania University in Lexington, Kentucky, but rarely practiced medicine. With his inheritance he was free to write, travel, live intermittently in the Northeast, and pay to publish his books. In the early 1830s he traveled widely throughout the western frontier and the North.

Before his 1835 return to Georgia, Chivers published *The Path of Sorrow*, mostly autobiographical poems, and *Conrad and Eudora*, a play about a notorious Kentucky murder trial. The title poem of *Nacoochee* (1837) celebrates a Cherokee legend. In 1837 Chivers married Harriette Hunt; of their seven children, four died in youth. In *The Lost Pleiad* (1845) the grieving father eulogizes his beloved daughter Allegra Florence (1839–42), the eldest of his children with Harriette and the first to die. His most memorable poetry appeared in *Eonchs of Ruby* (1851) and *Virginalia* (1853).

His traditional Baptist heritage notwithstanding, the tormented romantic visionary embraced the beliefs of the Transcendentalists and Swedenborgians, the latter based on a Swedish mystic's writings on spiritualism and immortality. The deep but troubled friendship between Chivers and Edgar Allan Poe was founded on a mutual fascination with metaphysical speculations, as well as on shared literary interests. The close association between the two poets, however, ended in bitterness when each began to regard the other's artistic borrowings as plagiarism.

Convinced that he was a divinely inspired poet, Chivers passionately devoted his life to composing musical, euphonious verse. An innovative experimenter, he excelled in capturing the rhythms and dialect of slave songs. A number of his poems and plays also reflect his ideaized views of American Indians and their plight, inspired in part by his contacts with Cherokees during his frontier travels.

Chivers spent his last years in Decatur, Georgia, where he died on December 19, 1858, and is buried.

JOY HUGHES MALLARD, *Atlanta*

SUGGESTED READING

S. Foster Damon, *Thomas Holley Chivers, Friend of Poe* (New York: Harper and Bros., 1930).

Charles M. Lombard, *Thomas Holley Chivers* (Boston: Twayne, 1979).

Edd Winfield Parks, *Ante-bellum Southern Literary Critics* (Athens: University of Georgia Press, 1962).

Charles Henry Watts II, *Thomas Holley Chivers: His Literary Career and His Poetry* (Athens: University of Georgia Press, 1956).

PEARL CLEAGE
(b. 1948)

Pearl Cleage is a fiction writer, playwright, poet, essayist, and journalist who has lived in Atlanta for more than thirty years. In her writing, Cleage draws on her experiences as an activist for AIDS and women's rights, and she cites the rhythms of black life as her muse. Cleage's first novel, *What Looks Like Crazy on an Ordinary Day*, was an Oprah Book Club selection in 1998 and appeared on the *New York Times* best-seller list for nine weeks.

Cleage (pronounced "cleg") was born on December 7, 1948, in Springfield, Massachusetts, the younger daughter of Doris Graham and Albert B. Cleage Jr. She grew up in Detroit, Michigan, where her father was a church pastor and played a prominent role in the civil rights movement. Many leaders of the movement passed through the Cleage house on their way to rallies and demonstrations in other cities in the Midwest and Northeast.

After graduating from the Detroit public schools in 1966, Cleage enrolled at Howard University in Washington, D.C., where she majored in playwriting and dramatic literature. In 1969 she moved to Atlanta and enrolled at Spelman College, graduating in 1971 with a bachelor's degree in drama. She later joined the Spelman faculty as a writer and playwright in residence and as a creative director. Also in 1969 she married Michael Lomax, an Atlanta politician and educator and the current president of Dillard University in New Orleans, Louisiana. They have one daughter, Deignan Njeri. The marriage ended in divorce in 1979. Cleage married Zaron W. Burnett Jr., writer and director for the Just Us Theater Company, in 1994.

In her writing Cleage is zealous about those issues of black life she feels need a forum for discussion, and she promotes practical education with regard to these issues whenever possible. In the essay collection *Deals with the Devil and Other Reasons to Riot*

(1993), she discusses sexism and domestic abuse. Of particular interest in this nonfiction volume is a section entitled "Mad at Miles" (which previously appeared in a self-published volume, *Mad at Miles: A Blackwoman's Guide to Truth*, in 1990) in which she criticizes jazz musician Miles Davis for brutality to women and draws parallels to abusive male behavior in everyday relationships. Among other topics, she also writes about the controversial hearings for Clarence Thomas's nomination to the U.S. Supreme Court as well as the controversies sparked by the film director Spike Lee and his work.

Throughout her career Cleage has often been in the public eye. She worked as press secretary and speech writer in the 1970s for Maynard Jackson, the first black mayor of Atlanta. Since then, her contribution to the Atlanta community has been steady and intense, finding expression through her columns in the *Atlanta Journal-Constitution* and the *Atlanta Tribune*; in the pages of *Catalyst*, a literary journal she cofounded and edited; and in her work as a faculty member at Spelman. Noted for her willingness to address difficult issues, Cleage explains her purpose for writing in the introduction to *Mad at Miles*:

> "I am writing to expose and explore the point where racism and sexism meet. I am writing to help understand the full effects of being black and female in a culture that is both racist and sexist. I am writing to try and communicate that information to my sisters first and then to any brothers of good will and honest intent who will take the time to listen. . . . I am writing to allow myself to feel the anger. I am writing to keep from running toward it or away from it or into anybody's arms. . . . I am writing, writing, writing, for my life."

The novel *What Looks Like Crazy on an Ordinary Day* (1997) deals with the ins and outs of living a truthful life, or as Cleage puts it, "getting to what the truth is." After television personality Oprah Winfrey chose Cleage's first novel for her TV book club in September 1998, Cleage's work became known to a huge national audience. In particular Cleage focuses on the issues of sex, drugs, and pregnancy, aiming to keep her message centered on black youth while presenting mature perspectives on coming to grips with good and bad life choices. In *I Wish I Had a Red Dress* (2001) Cleage returns to the characters from *What Looks Like Crazy* to focus on the challenges that modern-day black women face. In *I Wish I Had a Red Dress*, Joyce, a minor character in Cleage's first novel, confronts the tragic elements of her past squarely with the hardness of her present relationships.

Set in southwest Atlanta, Cleage's third novel, *Some Things I Thought I'd Never Do* (2003), portrays utopian black Atlanta neighborhoods in pragmatic terms. Her trademark — a highly readable style that imparts a sense of immediacy — is in evidence, and her flawed yet generous characters share their Atlanta community's hopes and desires. In the novel Cleage highlights such Atlanta landmarks as Paschal's Restaurant, Lenox Square Mall, and Stone Mountain, as well as coastal Tybee Island. Using political themes Cleage addresses some of the same issues found in earlier works while grappling with newer ones, including reactions to the September 11, 2001, attacks on the World Trade Center in New York City. Continuing the inspirational, idealistic, and spiritual themes she explored in *Red Dress*, Cleage weaves in the themes of mysticism and reincarnation in *Some Things*.

Cleage's fourth novel, *Babylon Sisters,* appeared in 2004.

Cleage's theatrical works include *Bourbon at the Border*, a full-length drama commissioned and premiered at the Alliance Theatre in 1997 under the direction of Kenny Leon, her frequent collaborator who was then the artistic director of the Alliance. Their previous collaborations include *Blues for an Alabama Sky* (1995) and *Flyin' West* (1992), both of which were also commissioned for and first performed at the Alliance Theatre. An anthology of her plays, *Flyin' West and Other Plays* (1999), offers a penetrating look at the African American experience over the past hundred years.

Blues for an Alabama Sky was performed in Atlanta as part of the 1996 Cultural Olympiad in conjunction with the 1996 Olympic Games. Since its opening, *Flyin' West* has had more than a dozen productions across the country, including one at the Kennedy Center in Washington, D.C. Cleage's work has also appeared in such anthologies as *Double Stitch, Black Drama in America, New Plays from the Women's Project,* and *Contemporary Plays by Women of Color.* Cleage has received numerous awards in recognition of her work, including the Bronze Jubilee Award for Literature in 1983 and the outstanding columnist award from the Atlanta Association of Black Journalists in 1991.

JUNE AKERS SEESE, *Atlanta*

JUDITH ORTIZ COFER
(b. 1952)

Judith Ortiz Cofer is one of a number of Latina writers who rose to prominence during the 1980s and 1990s. Her stories about coming-of-age experiences in Puerto Rican communities outside of New York City and her poems and essays about cultural conflicts of immigrants to the U.S. mainland have made Ortiz Cofer a leading literary interpreter of the U.S.–Puerto Rican experience.

Ortiz Cofer was born in 1952 in the small town of Hormigueros, Puerto Rico, a semiurban municipality in the western part of the island. The author's parents came to the United States in 1956 and settled in Paterson, New Jersey. As the daughter of a frequently absent military father stationed at Brooklyn's Navy Yard and an uprooted mother nostalgic for her beloved island, Ortiz Cofer spent portions of her childhood commuting between Hormigueros and Paterson. Even though most of her schooling was in Paterson, she lived for extended periods at her grandmother's house in Puerto Rico and attended the local schools. This back-and-forth movement between her two cultures became a vital part of her poetry and fiction. There is a strong island presence in her narratives, and the authenticity with which she captures life on the island is as powerful as her descriptions of the harsh realities of the Paterson community.

When she was fifteen years old, Ortiz Cofer moved with her family to Augusta, Georgia. She attended college and received an undergraduate degree in English from Augusta College. A few years later she moved to Florida and received an M.A. from Florida Atlantic University. In 1984 she joined the faculty of the University of Georgia in Athens, where she is now Regents and Franklin Professor of English and Creative Writing.

The author's first literary expressions were in poetry. One of her early chapbooks, *Peregrina* (1986), won the Riverstone

International Chapbook Competition. Two years later her poetry collection *Terms of Survival* (1987) was published, but it was not until the publication of her first major work of prose fiction, *The Line of the Sun* (1989), a novel nominated for the Pulitzer Prize, that the author began to receive more critical attention. After this successful debut as a fiction writer, she continued to demonstrate her abilities in storytelling through short stories and personal essays. However, she also kept writing poetry, which she declares "contains the essence of language," and published two more collections, *Reaching for the Mainland* (1995) and *A Love Story Beginning in Spanish* (2005).

Ortiz Cofer claims to have inherited the art of storytelling from her *abuelita* ("grandmother"), a fact suggested in the powerful attributes of the grandmother character who appears in *The Line of the Sun* and many of her other narratives. "When my abuela sat us down to tell a story, we learned something from it, even though we always laughed. That was her way of teaching. So early on I instinctively knew storytelling was a form of empowerment, that the women in my family were passing on power from one generation to another through fables and stories. They were teaching each other to cope with life in a world where women led restricted lives." Cofer's most powerful characters are Puerto Rican women who try to break away from restrictive cultural and social conventions or who develop survival strategies to deal with the sexism in their own culture.

Silent Dancing: A Partial Remembrance of a Puerto Rican Childhood (1990) is a book of memories described as "stellar stories patterned after oral tradition." The volume also includes poems that highlight the narratives' major themes. *Silent Dancing* received the 1991 PEN / Martha Albrand Special Citation in Nonfiction and was awarded a Pushcart Prize. It was followed by *The Latin Deli* (1993), a combination of poetry, short fiction, and personal narrative. In these collections, as in her subsequent volumes, *An Island Like You* (1995), *The Year of Our Revolution* (1998), and *Woman in Front of the Sun: On Becoming a Writer* (2000), Ortiz Cofer continues to recall and explore through different genres the memories of her formative years. *Woman in Front of the Sun*, especially, provides invaluable insights into the inner world of the author, what motivates her writing, and where she places herself in terms of the American mainstream and U.S. Latino literature. In her novel *The Meaning of Consuelo* (2003) Cofer explores language and communication: communication between the title character and her schizophrenic sister, between men and women, English and Spanish.

Many of Ortiz Cofer's stories, poems, and personal essays describe the lives of Puerto Rican youths, straddling the Puerto Rican culture of their parents and a mainland culture consumed by its own prejudices, while asserting their own dignity and creative potential. *An Island Like You* received the 1995 Reforma Pura Belpré Medal and was listed among the best books for young adults by the American Library Association. *Call Me María* (2004) is a young adult novel chronicling a teenage girl's move from Puerto Rico to New York City.

Due to a growing interest in her work in Puerto Rico and in other Spanish-speaking countries, the University of Puerto Rico published *La linea del sol* (1996), a Spanish translation of her acclaimed novel *The Line of the Sun*. The Fondo del Cultura Económica in Mexico published *Una isla como tú* (1997), a translation of *An Island Like You*. The same year Arte Público Press released *Bailando en silencio: Escenas de una niñez puertorriqueña* (1997), a translation of *Silent Dancing*. Several of the author's stories are also available in other languages.

EDNA ACOSTA-BELÉN, *State University of New York, Albany*

SUGGESTED READING

Edna Acosta-Belén, "A *MELUS* Interview: Judith Ortiz Cofer," *MELUS* 18, no. 3 (1993): 83–97.

THE COLOR PURPLE

The *Color Purple* is the international best-selling novel by Alice Walker, an African American writer from Eatonton. Published in 1982, Walker's epistolary tale chronicles the startling tragedy and triumph of a poor black woman named Celie in her struggle for self-empowerment, sexual freedom, and spiritual growth in rural Georgia in the early twentieth century. The novel has received numerous awards, including the Pulitzer Prize for Fiction and the National Book Award, and was nominated for the National Book Critics Circle Award. As a film directed by Steven Spielberg and produced by Quincy Jones in 1985, *The Color Purple* was nominated for eleven Academy Awards.

The Color Purple opens just after the turn of the century, when Celie is fourteen years old. She has been raped and impregnated by the man she believes is her father (but who is really, she later discovers, her stepfather). Afterward he warns, "You better not never tell nobody but God. It'd kill your mammy." This chilling preface initiates the journal entries that Celie writes and addresses as letters to God. The act of writing becomes a crucial medium of self-discovery for Celie, allowing her to divulge her secret humiliation and pain while charting a growing awareness of the world around her. Critics have often praised Walker's forthright depiction of taboo subjects in the novel and her clear rendering of folk idiom and dialect through Celie's written voice.

When Celie gives birth to a second child by her stepfather, the infant boy is taken from her and presumably killed. She is then forced to marry a widowed farmer named "Mr. —— " in order to care for his home and his four children. Her letters detail the cruel emotional and physical abuse she receives from her husband. Further intensifying her loneliness is the fact that her prearranged marriage requires her to separate from her beloved sister, Nettie.

Yet Celie forges an unusual kinship with her husband's former mistress, the blues singer Shug Avery. Their relationship features both erotic and spiritual dimensions that not only defy social conventions but also culminate in a more self-affirming vision of existence. Shug encourages Celie to honor her own desires and to praise God through admiration. Indeed, it is Shug who states, "I think it pisses God off if you walk by the color purple in a field somewhere and don't notice it."

Together the two women also discover letters from Celie's sister that Mr. —— kept hidden in a locked trunk. Years of correspondence from Nettie detail her experience as a Christian missionary in West Africa. Through the letters Celie learns that her two children, Adam and Olivia, are alive and have been adopted by Nettie's benefactors, a preacher and his wife. Empowered by the existence of Nettie and her children, and strengthened by Shug's love, Celie finds the courage to leave her oppressive household. She moves briefly to Shug's residence in Memphis, Tennessee, and opens her own sewing business. After the death of her step-father, Celie returns to Georgia to live in her newly inherited house. There she achieves a satisfying measure of financial security and independence, and even makes a tenuous reconciliation with Mr. —— . At the conclusion of the novel, Nettie returns to America, and Celie is reunited not only with her sister but with her grown son and daughter as well.

In 1984 music producer Quincy Jones bought the film rights to the novel, although Walker initially doubted whether it should be made into a movie. The film director Steven Spielberg, who had been given the book by his collaborator, Kathleen Kennedy, saw it as a chance to demonstrate that he could make a serious drama and thus overcome a reputation established by his action and fantasy films, such as *Jaws*, *E.T.*, and the *Indiana Jones* series. He met with Walker in San Francisco, where she lived, and convinced her that he shared her vision for the characters and the story. She agreed to allow him to direct the film, and she served as a consultant on the set. She wrote a screenplay as well, though Spielberg rejected it in favor of an adaptation by Dutch-born screenwriter Menno Meyjes.

Walker was also instrumental in casting Whoopi Goldberg as Celie. Goldberg was at the time a stand-up comedienne performing in the San Francisco area, and even though she had never acted, she wrote to Walker, asking to be considered for the role of Celie if the book was ever filmed. Also appearing for the first time onscreen was Oprah Winfrey, then a popular local talk-show host in Chicago, who played the strong-willed Sofia, the wife of Celie's stepson. The part of Shug Avery was portrayed by another unknown actress, Margaret Avery, although such well-known entertainers as Tina Turner and Diana Ross had been considered for the part. All three actresses were nominated for Academy Awards for their performances. Danny Glover, a more established star, played the central male role of "Mister."

Location filming for *The Color Purple* took place in the summer of 1985 near Monroe, North Carolina, after it was determined that modern development in Eatonton, Walker's hometown, rendered it unsuitable.

The film, which cost nearly $15 million to make, generated about $142 million in box-office sales after its release in December 1985, and it quickly became the subject of much critical praise and controversy. While some reviewers criticized as unjustly negative Walker's portrayal of black men, such organizations as the Coalition against Black Exploitation expressed concerns that the story promoted the lesbian relationship of Celie and Shug as a remedy to the difficulties between black men and women. Other reviewers noted that the film was a "Spielbergized" version — far more upbeat, affirmative, and prettified — of a world that Walker portrayed as harsh, impoverished, and bleak. Despite eleven Academy Award nominations, the film won no Oscars, perhaps because of these controversies.

Ten years after the film's release, however, Walker expressed her satisfaction with the production and addressed her harshest critics in a 1996 book entitled *The Same River Twice: Honoring the Difficult*. The book features Walker's rejected screenplay of *The Color Purple*. Essays in the collection discuss the author's personal struggles during the making of the film, from her mother's declining health and a troubled romantic relationship to her own battle against Lyme disease. *The Same River Twice* also includes articles about the film's production and numerous letters from supportive fans.

A two-disc DVD rerelease of *The Color Purple* debuted in early 2003. In addition to behind-the-scenes footage, the special edition features background information on the novel, interviews with Walker and the film's actors and actresses, and a documentary tribute to the original songs composed by Quincy Jones.

In September 2004 the Alliance Theatre in Atlanta produced a musical stage version of *The Color Purple*. Once Walker overcame her initial reluctance to see her novel adapted for the theater, the Pulitzer Prize-winning playwright Marsha Norman (who won a Pulitzer for drama in 1983, the same year Walker won hers for fiction) was commissioned to write the script. Composers Brenda Russell, Allee Willis, and Stephen Bray provided a varied musical score consisting of blues, jazz, gospel, swing, and African music. With Walker's endorsement, the Atlanta production opened to generally positive reviews. In 2005 the musical, produced by Oprah Winfrey, premiered on Broadway.

QIANA WHITTED, *Yale University, New Haven, Connecticut*

SUGGESTED READING

Harold Bloom, *Alice Walker's "The Color Purple"* (New York: Chelsea House, 2000).

Douglas Brode, *The Films of Steven Spielberg* (New York: Carol Publishing Group, 1995).

Henry Louis Gates and K. A. Appiah, eds., *Alice Walker: Critical Perspectives Past and Present* (New York: Amistad Press, 1993).

Alice Walker, *The Same River Twice: Honoring the Difficult* (New York: Washington Square Press, 1997).

PAT CONROY
(b. 1945)

Contemporary southern author Pat Conroy has written a number of highly popular books, including *The Water Is Wide, The Great Santini, The Lords of Discipline, The Prince of Tides,* and *Beach Music.* Conroy also has achieved considerable success as a screenwriter. He is the author or coauthor of several Hollywood and television scripts, most notably the film adaptation of his own novel *The Prince of Tides.*

Donald Patrick Conroy was born in Atlanta on October 26, 1945, the eldest of seven children of Donald Conroy, a career U.S. Marine Corps pilot from Chicago, and Frances "Peggy" Peek Conroy, described by her son as "a north-Georgia beauty full of love and beauty." Conroy credits his mother for instilling in him a love of language and literature.

Another early literary influence on Conroy was Eugene Norris, a high school English teacher who gave Conroy a copy of Thomas Wolfe's *Look Homeward, Angel* and also drove the young student to Asheville, North Carolina, to visit Wolfe's home. From that time on Wolfe served as the literary model for Conroy. Like Wolfe's, Conroy's fiction is characterized by a lyrical, emotionally charged prose, a heavy reliance on personal and family experiences, and a strong sense of place.

A "military brat," Conroy moved with his family numerous times during his childhood and youth — by his count twenty-three times before he turned fifteen. During his last two years of high school, however, the family settled in Beaufort, South Carolina, the town and state that figure so prominently in the settings of his novels. Nevertheless the constant moves, along with the abusive behavior of his father, produced a degree of uncertainty and insecurity in the young boy that undoubtedly contributed to the search for acceptance and belonging that is a dominant theme in his fiction.

At the encouragement (even insistence) of his father, after high school Conroy enrolled in the Citadel, the military school located in Charleston, South Carolina. There he enjoyed considerable success both academically and athletically (he was a starting guard on the school's basketball team), but he also developed a strong ambivalence toward the school's rigid code of military discipline and harassment. Seeing the domineering and abusive actions of his father now repeated at an institutional level, Conroy developed a heightened awareness and concern for individuality and personal freedom.

The Citadel experience also led Conroy to his first serious writing attempt. Three years after his graduation, while working as a schoolteacher in Beaufort, Conroy decided to record his fond recollections of the assistant commandant of cadets, Lieutenant Colonel Thomas Nugent Courvoisie, in a volume entitled *The Boo* (1970). Conroy published that amateurish effort at his own expense. Although today copies of the first printing bring high prices on the collectors' market, the author himself has called it "a book without a single strength." He inscribed one copy to an English teacher with the note, "Teach them not to write like this." Still, *The Boo* helped Conroy discover that writing was to be both his passion and his vocation.

Beginning with the publication of *The Water Is Wide* in 1972, Conroy produced a succession of critically acclaimed works, many of which have been adapted into popular and commercially successful motion pictures. In 1999 Conroy was presented with the inaugural Stanley W. Lindberg Award for significant contributions to the literary heritage of Georgia. He was inducted into the Georgia Writers Hall of Fame in 2005. These literary and film successes, however, have not always been accompanied by personal happiness. His life has been marked by conflicts with his parents and siblings, as well as by two divorces.

Conroy and his third wife, Sandra, also a writer, maintain residences in South Carolina and San Francisco.

In his memoir *The Water Is Wide* Conroy draws upon his sad and comical experiences as an elementary teacher of underprivileged black children on Daufuskie Island, just off the South Carolina coast. He dramatizes the conflict between a young, idealistic teacher and a cumbersome, outmoded, and racist educational system on this isolated island. In 1974 the book was successfully adapted as the Twentieth Century Fox film *Conrack*, starring Jon Voight. It received further adaptation as the musical play *Conrack*, first produced at New York's AMAS Repertory Theater in 1987.

Conroy's first novel, *The Great Santini* (1976), depicts a chaotic household ruled by the egotistical and despotic Bull Meecham, a highly decorated Marine fighter pilot known to his family and others as "the Great Santini." A mixture of harsh realism and outlandish comedy, the novel traces the growing resentment and rebellion of Ben, the teenage son who both hates and loves his abusive father. Judged to be too confessional by members of the Conroy family, *The Great Santini* led to a protracted estrangement between Conroy and his father — an estrangement that did not end until Robert Duvall's portrayal of Bull Meecham in the 1979 film version of the novel made Colonel Conroy into a national celebrity.

Will McLean, the protagonist of *The Lords of Discipline* (1980), is a student cadet at a military institution much like the Citadel. In Conroy's prefatory note it is identified more generally as "the military school as it has evolved in America." A staunch individualist like other Conroy heroes, McLean finds himself in fierce opposition to "The Ten," a conspiratorial group of fellow cadets appointed to enforce and perpetuate the institute's policy of intimidation, prejudice, and harassment.

In what is generally considered his most artistic novel, *The Prince of Tides* (1986), Conroy places the midlife crisis of Tom Wingo, an unemployed teacher/coach who is estranged from his wife, within the larger story of the dysfunctional but heroic Wingo family that must cope with the death of a beloved brother, the violent rape of both Tom and his mother, and the nervous breakdown and attempted suicide of Tom's twin sister, Savannah. The 1991 movie version of *The Prince of Tides*, produced and directed by Barbra Streisand and featuring Nick Nolte and Streisand in the leading roles, was a tremendous financial and critical success. It was nominated for several Academy Awards, including one for Conroy as screenwriter.

Beach Music (1995) is based in part on the breakup of Conroy's first marriage. The novel presents the struggle of middle-aged Jack McCall in coping with the suicide of his wife, the schizophrenia of his brother, and the impending death of his mother. Interwoven into this personal drama, making it representative of a wider historical and cultural tragedy, are the devastating legacies of the Holocaust and the Vietnam War. While continuing to demonstrate Conroy's masterful skills in storytelling and characterization, this book, unlike his previous ones, fails to pull the various subplots into a satisfying whole.

Conroy's second work of nonfiction, *My Losing Season* (2002), focuses on his senior year at the Citadel in Charleston, South Carolina, and the basketball season of 1966–67, in which he and his college teammates lost 13 of 21 games played. Inspired by renewed acquaintances with several members of that team, Conroy came to realize that the experience had been as important to them as it had been to him. Conroy draws on aspects of his youth laid out in his earlier work, most notably his strained relationship with his father.

Pat Conroy's novels are essentially "coming of age" or "initiation" stories in which the male protagonists undergo long and perilous quests in search of maturity and wholeness. His heroes are survivors who have been horribly wounded, both physically and psychologically, by various types of victimization — abusive fathers, overly possessive mothers, violent criminals, bungling bureaucrats, corrupt institutions, oppressive social mores, psychic disorders. The conflicts typically revolve around issues of gender, race, personal identity, and freedom. Male-dominated institutions (such as the military and sports) and prejudicial social codes (such as those in the American South or Nazi Germany) insist on clear lines between sexes and races and on an unswerving loyalty to established authority and the status quo. Hence

Conroy's heroes are also rebels. Their ultimate goal, never fully realized, is expressed by Will McLean toward the end of *The Lords of Discipline*: "I wanted to live life passionately, in luxurious free form, without squads, without uniforms or ranks. Freedom was the only thing I had ever known, and it was time to walk with abandon, immune from the battalions, answerable only to myself. I would make my own way now, conscious of my singularity, proud of it." Because one of the major obstacles to the achievement of individual freedom is the traditional definition of masculinity, Conroy's males must frequently depend upon females (loving mothers, sympathetic sisters, understanding lovers) as saviors who assist the males in discovering and developing the feminine side of their personalities.

ROBERT W. HAMBLIN, *Southeast Missouri State University, Cape Girardeau*

SUGGESTED READING

John Berendt, "The Conroy Saga," *Vanity Fair*, July 1995.
Landon C. Burns, *Pat Conroy: A Critical Companion* (Westport, Conn.: Greenwood Press, 1996).
Robert Hamblin, "Sports Imagery in Pat Conroy's Novels," *Aethlon: The Journal of Sport Literature* 11, no. 1 (1993): 49–59.
David Toolan, "The Unfinished Boy and His Pain: Rescuing the Young Hero with Pat Conroy," *Commonweal* 118, no. 4 (February 1991): 127–31.
Lamar York, "Pat Conroy's Portrait of the Artist as a Young Southerner," *Southern Literary Journal* 19, no. 2 (1987): 34–46.

STEPHEN COREY
(b. 1948)

Poet, essayist, and editor Stephen Corey has lived and worked in Athens, Georgia, since 1983. As assistant, associate, and finally acting editor of the *Georgia Review*, he has helped shape the literary landscape in this country for the past two decades. He has also gained national recognition for his own poems and essays.

Corey was born on August 30, 1948, in Buffalo, New York, to Dale B. Corey, a certified public accountant, and Julienne Holmes, a nurse and homemaker. Educated at the State University of New York at Binghamton, Corey received a B.A. in 1971 and an M.A. in 1974. Corey then headed south, where he received a Ph.D. in English from the University of Florida in 1979. While at the University of Florida, Corey began *The Devil's Millhopper*, a literary journal he coedited until 1981, when he became sole editor. In 1983 he joined the staff of the *Georgia Review*, serving first as assistant editor (1983–86) and then as associate editor (1986–98). In November 1998 Corey was appointed acting editor of the *Georgia Review*, a position he held until July 2001, when T. R. Hummer assumed editorship.

Corey is one of the more influential literary figures in the state. His editorial contributions to the *Georgia Review* alone ought to secure that ranking, but he has also been a prolific poet, essayist, and reviewer. He has published nine volumes of poetry, beginning with *The Last Magician* (1981, rev. ed. 1987) and extending to *There Is No Finished World* (2003), as well as more than 150 poems in the country's leading periodicals and journals. He has edited three anthologies of essays, poems, and fiction: *Necessary Fictions: Selected Stories from the Georgia Review* (1986) and *Keener Sounds: Selected Poems from the Georgia Review* (1987), both coedited with Stanley Lindberg, and *Spreading the Word: Editors on Poetry* (2001).

In his poetry the paradox of the one and the many remains Corey's thematic bedrock. On the one hand, the individual knows only himself; on the other, knowledge of self is shaped, refined, and redirected by our knowledge of others and the world around us. The narrators in Corey's poetry explore this paradox, often walking the fine line between communion and isolation. He begins this exploration in his first book, *The Last Magician*, in a remarkable section called "Crafts." Assuming the personae of artists and craftsmen, Corey examines the paradox of creation. The artisan makes, but not for himself, because the utility of his or her work informs his connection to those around him and to the physical world. For instance, in "Smith" a blacksmith boasts of his centrality in his village's life — even as he maintains his exclusivity:

> I go to church on the rims of carriage wheels,
> into the chest on the scalpel.
> I am hinged and latched to every village home,
> hammered deep into my own hammer
> . . . .
> What non-living things re-create themselves?
> Tools. Tools the others must have to begin.
> What can I do that lovers only dream?
> Fuse two things into one, forever.

The curious contradiction in the smith's boast is an excellent point of entry to Corey's work, for his narrators refuse, with varying degrees of politeness, to be assimilated into a world of paradox and disunity. Even the titles of Corey's books offer readers the fundamental contradictions of our existence: *The Last Magician* (if magic *is* magic, how can there be a *last* magician?); *Fighting Death* (death is losing the fight, not the fight itself); *Synchronized Swimming* (the ultimate oxymoron — a sanctioned sport that meets no requirement of any sport Americans understand); and *All These Lands You Call One Country* (again, the illusion of the one made of the many).

This is a difficult theme, and a measure of Corey's artistic determination is how consistently he explores it. Even when one of his poems fails, its failure underscores the urgency that fuels it. As he tells us in "Condition: Pachyderm," his aim is to "consider all possibilities, / presume no conclusions."

Arguably, these two imperatives are mirror images, not opposites, but certainly irreconcilable: to consider *is* to presume, and to presume limits, if only for a time, other considerations. The ongoing compulsion to do both creates an irresolvable tension in which Corey explores the situation of contemporary man.

In *All These Lands You Call One Country* Corey explores the complexities of time, possession, and perception through a remarkable variety of personae, including two ancient Chinese poets, Li Po and Tu Fu; Lurleen Wallace, wife of Alabama governor George Wallace; and Lazlo Toth, the vandal responsible for the 1972 desecration of Michelangelo's *Pietà*. What emerges is a sense of multiplicity, of contrasting, often conflicting personalities coming to terms with the diversity of America. Consider, for instance, Li Po's assessment of American excess in "Li Po Enters New York City":

> I have been accepting all
> These lands you call one country.
> Sometimes I have had to say *dream*,
> Softly to myself, even when sober;
> Yet I have gotten along
> Watching the faces and horizons,
> Touching the coarse leaves and barks,
> Lifting curious objects from countless shelves.

Li Po reacts to his New York experience by quoting Socrates: "*I never knew there could be so many things / I did not want.*"

In such moments of rejection, however, Corey remains open to documenting the richness of experience in a world that beckons, outrages, and captivates his imagination. Corey's fascination with the phenomenon of consciousness remains a driving force in his poetry. And if he cannot come to terms with the reality that entices and eludes, he can at least document his experience. For this reason, Corey's Li Po can conclude "The Last Journey" with a statement of recognition rather than frustration:

> I saw I could love each place I stood,
> Each person I met or passed,
> With baffled, baffling energy.

SAM PRESTRIDGE, *Gainesville State College*

ALFRED CORN
(b. 1943)

Since the appearance of his first book of poems in 1976, Alfred Corn has distinguished himself as one of the most original poets writing in the United States. Known primarily as the author of nine volumes of poetry to date, Corn has also published one novel, a highly praised manual of prosody, a collection of essays, translations of poetry and drama, and critical writing on art, music, and the theater, as well as an edited collection of essays on the New Testament. Corn's poetry is in the visionary mode of earlier American poets like Walt Whitman and Hart Crane, but at the same time it is the work of a poet's poet, full of craft and the keen, urbane sensibility of mid-century poets like Elizabeth Bishop and James Merrill.

Born August 14, 1943, in Bainbridge, Georgia, Alfred DeWitt Corn III was the youngest of three children and the only son born to Grace Lahey Corn and Alfred DeWitt Corn Jr. Shortly after the boy's birth, his father was mustered into the army, assigned to the Army Corps of Engineers, and stationed in the Philippines. In 1945, on the day of Alfred's second birthday, his mother died of complications following a burst appendix. The children were then cared for by family friends and later by their aunt Jon and her husband, Fred Schroer, who lived on a farm near Ray City in southern Georgia, until the children's father's army discharge in 1946. From there, the family moved to Valdosta, living at first with the father's parents. In 1948 Alfred Jr. married Virginia Whitaker Macmillan, a young war widow fourteen years his junior. Five years later, the couple had a daughter, but she died within a year from meningitis.

Young Alfred Corn distinguished himself academically early on in grammar school, attending public schools and eventually graduating as salutatorian from his junior high school before entering Valdosta High School. Exceptional SAT scores helped him gain acceptances from Columbia, Emory, Harvard, Princeton, and Yale, and in 1961 he began studies at Emory as a French major, traveling abroad through a summer program during his junior year. While flying to France in 1964, he met Ann Jones, whom he would marry three years later. (The marriage lasted until 1972, when the couple divorced amicably.) Corn graduated from Emory with highest honors and chose Columbia for graduate study, in part because of its location in New York City.

Corn's first book of poems, *All Roads at Once* (1976), drew high praise from the literary critic Harold Bloom, and his second book, *A Call in the Midst of the Crowd* (1978), with a long, accomplished poem about New York City, put Corn on the literary map. By the time of his third and fourth collections, *The Various Light* (1980) and *Notes from a Child of Paradise* (1984), Corn was writing highly original, innovative poetry. For instance, *Notes*, while structurally modeled on Dante's *Divine Comedy*, is an autobiographical piece that stands as the only long poem in American literature to record a history of intellectual life and the counterculture in America during the turbulent 1960s. This volume points the way to later work by Corn that demonstrates great social empathy and awareness.

By the 1980s Corn was writing poignantly about the AIDS pandemic and began to be recognized as a major voice in gay literature. One of his most striking later works is an innovative long poem titled "1992," from his volume *Autobiographies* (1992), a poem that chronicles several American lives over a period of more than twenty years. With the publication of *Stake: Poems, 1972–1992* (1999), readers can reencounter the variety of Corn's work. Corn's most recent collection of poems is *Contradictions* (2002).

Corn has received two fellowships from the National Endowment for the Arts as well as fellowships from the Guggenheim Foundation, the Academy and Institute of Arts and Letters, and the Academy of American Poets. He won the 1982 Levinson Prize from *Poetry* magazine. He has taught at such schools as City University of New York, Yale University, UCLA, Ohio State

University, Oklahoma State University, and the University of
Tulsa. An extensive traveler, he currently lives in Rhode Island.

ERNEST SMITH, *University of Central Florida*

SUGGESTED READING

Alfred Corn, *Autobiographies* (New York: Viking, 1992).
Alfred Corn, *Notes from a Child of Paradise* (New York: Viking,
1984).
Alfred Corn, *Stake: Poems, 1972–1992* (Washington: Counterpoint,
1999).
Alfred Corn, *The Various Light* (New York: Viking, 1980).

HARRY CREWS
(b. 1935)

Harry Crews is a prolific novelist whose often freakish characters populate a strange, violent, and darkly humorous South. He is also the author of a widely lauded memoir, *A Childhood: The Biography of a Place*, about growing up poor in rural south Georgia. Crews has focused much of his work on the poor white South, influencing a growing number of younger writers to do the same, including Larry Brown and Tim McLaurin.

Harry Eugene Crews was born in Bacon County on June 7, 1935, the second of two sons. His parents, Myrtice and Ray Crews, were poor farmers barely scratching out a living. After his father died of a heart attack in the middle of the night with Crews, just twenty-two months old, asleep beside him, Myrtice soon married Ray's brother Pascal. Her decision would prove fateful, as Pascal revealed himself to be a violent and dangerous drunk. In his memoir Crews describes the tenuous situation of his early family life: "The world that circumscribed the people I come from had so little margin for error, for bad luck, that when something went wrong, it almost always brought something else down with it. It was a world in which survival depended on raw courage, a courage born out of desperation and sustained by a lack of alternatives."

Raw courage was needed early, as Crews experienced two major physical setbacks as a child. At the age of five, he was struck with a fever followed by leg cramps so severe that his heels drew up to the backs of his thighs. He was bedridden for more than six weeks before he could be carried around the farm. He then gradually began to walk again by hauling himself along a fence. Later in life Crews would blame psychological stress from his increasingly volatile home life as the cause.

When he was six, an accident during a children's game called "pop-the-whip" caused him to be thrown into a cast-iron boiler being used to scald pigs. With burns covering more than two-thirds of his body, Crews survived, doctors told him, only because his head had stayed above water. He describes the ordeal in his memoir: "Then hands were on me, taking off my clothes, and the pain turned into something words cannot touch, or at least my words cannot touch. There is no way for me to talk about it because when my shirt was taken off, my back came off with it. When my overalls were pulled down, my cooked and glowing skin came down."

Crews joined the marines when he was seventeen, while his brother was away fighting in the Korean War. During his time in the service, Crews began to read seriously. When his term ended, he enrolled at the University of Florida on the GI Bill, with the intention of becoming a writer. The Agrarian writer Andrew Lytle, who had once taught Flannery O'Connor and James Dickey, was Crews's undergraduate writing teacher.

The years leading up to his first publication were hard both personally and professionally. Crews married in 1960 and had two sons, but the marriage did not last. In 1964 tragedy struck when his older son drowned. Crews began teaching in 1962, and after years of rejection his first novel, *The Gospel Singer*, was published in 1968 and garnered good reviews. Its publication earned Crews a new teaching job at the University of Florida and paved the way for the publication of seven more novels over the next eight years, including *Naked in Garden Hills* (1969); *Car* (1972); *The Hawk Is Dying* (1973), which was adapted into a film released in 2006); *The Gypsy's Curse* (1974); and the widely acclaimed *A Feast of Snakes* (1976).

Crews's reputation as a bold and daring new voice in southern writing grew during this time. The well-known writer Norman Mailer said, "Harry Crews has a talent all his own. He begins where James Dickey left off." His writing is rooted in the Southern Gothic tradition, but Crews has claimed other influences, notably the British novelist Graham Greene. Most of his books are set in modern-day Florida or Georgia and are often edgy in their exploration of such extremities as blood sports, the limits of sanity, and bizarre compulsions and obsessions.

Crews, like Flannery O'Connor, has an affinity for the grotesque in his characters. He explains this fascination as being rooted in a specific childhood experience — waking up in a carnival trailer one morning, Crews witnessed a bearded lady and a man with a cleft face talking about their dinner plans and kissing. Crews claims, "And I, lying at the back of the trailer, was never the same again."

After 1976 Crews didn't publish another novel for roughly ten years. During this time his persona would increasingly become a source of interest to critics and readers. He was frank in interviews about his drinking and drug use and often changed his appearance by wearing a Mohawk, shaving his head, or getting tattoos. One tattoo features a skull under which is written, "How do you like your blue-eyed boy, Mr. Death?"

Crews continued to teach during these years, and he wrote screenplays, plays, and nonfiction pieces, some of which are collected in *Florida Frenzy* (1982). He also became a regular contributor to *Esquire, Playboy, Sport*, and other magazines. A column he wrote for *Esquire* called "Grits" laid the groundwork for what many critics consider his best book, *A Childhood: The Biography of a Place* (1978). In *A Childhood* Crews's style is honest and unflinching as he describes the violence and desperation surrounding him as a young boy, yet he is also nonjudgmental and shows an affection and respect for people despite their flaws. This poignant account of life in rural Georgia among the very poor earned Crews wide praise from critics. The *New York Times Book Review* said of the work, "It's easy to despise poor folks. *A Childhood* makes it more difficult. It raises almost to a level of heroism these people who seem of a different century. . . . *A Childhood* is not about a forgotten America; it is about a part of America that has rarely, except in books like this, been properly discovered."

Crews resumed publishing novels with *All We Need of Hell*

(1987) and went on to publish *The Knockout Artist* (1988), *Body* (1990), *Scar Lover* (1992), *The Mulching of America* (1995), *Celebration* (1998), and *An American Family: The Baby with the Curious Markings* (2006). In 1997 he retired from his teaching career and continued to write. Published in France, Italy, Holland, Israel, and the United Kingdom, Crews was inducted into the Georgia Writers Hall of Fame in 2001. He is featured in the documentary *Searching for the Wrong-Eyed Jesus* (2005), which chronicles the road trip of a country musician through the South.

Crews lives in Gainesville, Florida.

JOHN McLEOD, *University of Georgia Press*

SUGGESTED READING

Erik Bledsoe, ed., *Getting Naked with Harry Crews: Interviews* (Gainesville: University Press of Florida, 1999).

Erik Bledsoe, ed., *Perspectives on Harry Crews* (Jackson: University Press of Mississippi, 2001).

David K. Jeffrey, ed., *A Grit's Triumph: Essays on the Works of Harry Crews* (Port Washington, N.Y.: Associated Faculty Press, 1983).

Southern Quarterly 37 (fall 1998), special issue on Harry Crews.

ADDITIONAL RESOURCES

Harry Crews: Blood and Words, dir. Wayne Schowalter (Wayne Schowalter Productions, 1983), film.

Harry Crews: Guilty as Charged, dir. and prod. Tom Thurman and Chris Iovenko (Fly by Noir Films, 1993), film.

The Rough South of Harry Crews, dir. Gary Hawkins (Chapel Hill: University of North Carolina Center for Public Television, 1992), film.

ROSEMARY DANIELL
(b. 1935)

A writer and a teacher of writing, Rosemary Daniell is known for her provocative poems and memoirs. Her works testify to the power of lived experience to supply rich material for writing and for the new forms of writing, especially confessional poetry and personal memoir, prevalent in women's and ethnic literatures since the 1970s. In her stories of growing up female in the South, Daniell defies the implicit southern edict against women who publicly discuss their sexuality and anger, explores the psychology behind southern ideals of womanhood, and challenges the traditional gender and sexual roles of southern women.

Rosemary Hughes was born in Atlanta on November 29, 1935, to Melissa Ruth Connell and Parker McDonald Hughes, a tire salesman. She was the older of two daughters. After dropping out of Tucker High School in Tucker at age sixteen, she married Larry Ramos, an army cook with whom she had a son, David. Ramos was abusive, and the marriage soon broke up. She married Sidney Daniell, an architect, in 1956, and they had two daughters, Laura and Darcy. They divorced in 1968, and in 1969 she married Jonathan Coppelman, also a writer. She and Coppelman divorced in 1976.

In the late 1950s or early 1960s Daniell took a continuing education class at Emory University and fell in love with modern poetry. She began writing poetry herself. While participating in a writers' group in Atlanta, Daniell met the poet James Dickey, who influenced her early work. Though Dickey encouraged her to write, he was not sympathetic to the poetry of Sylvia Plath and Anne Sexton, whom Daniell greatly admired.

In 1975 Daniell's mother committed suicide, and her father, an alcoholic, also died. The same year she published her first book of poetry, *A Sexual Tour of the Deep South*. The following year her second poetry book, *The Feathered Trees*, was published. During this time Daniell became involved in activities that encouraged the appreciation of writers and writing. From 1971 to 1972 she served as the director of Georgia's Poetry in the Schools Program, a national program that gives students the opportunity to work with published poets. In 1974 Daniell received a grant for poetry from the National Endowment for the Arts; she was awarded another for fiction in 1981, the same year in which she founded a creative writing workshop for women in Savannah. Similar workshops soon opened in Atlanta and in Charleston, South Carolina. Two years later Daniell named the workshop Zona Rosa, Spanish for "pink zone." The workshops, which she still teaches, have been a critical part of her writing career. In 1987 Daniell received a grant in fiction from the Georgia Council for the Arts. Over the course of her career, she has also been granted residencies with the Ossabaw Island Project, the Ucross Foundation in Wyoming, the Writers' Colony at Dairy Hollow in Arkansas, and Yaddo in New York.

Daniell's other publications are a book of poetry, *Fort Bragg and Other Points South* (1988); two memoirs, *Fatal Flowers: On Sin, Sex, and Suicide in the Deep South* (1980), which won the 1999 Palimpsest Prize, and *Sleeping with Soldiers: In Search of the Macho Man* (1985); a novel, *The Hurricane Season* (1992), about a female painter in New Orleans; two guidebooks for writers, *The Woman Who Spilled Words All Over Herself: Writing and Living the Zona Rosa Way* (1997) and *Secrets of the Zona Rosa: How Writing (and Sisterhood) Can Change Women's Lives* (2006); and a collection of essays, *Confessions of a (Female) Chauvinist* (2001).

In *Fatal Flowers* Daniell examines southern womanhood and its mythology: the ideal female as materialistic woman, wife of a powerful man, perfect hostess, and dame loyal to her land. She argues that these stereotypes inhibit women's freedom, stultify their personal growth, and stymie the creativity of an emerging female writer.

In *The Woman Who Spilled Words All Over Herself*, Daniell recommends writing as a cathartic process in which the writer can distance herself from her traumas and thus vanquish the demons in her mind. Daniell seeks to reestablish her relationship with men in *Sleeping with Soldiers*, which draws upon her experiences working as one of two women on an oil rig off the coast of Savannah in 1979, and continues to explore this theme in *Confessions of a (Female) Chauvinist*. In these two books she defines "macho men," who inveterately attract her, as men who take risks, hold fast to their opinions and prejudices, and in physical strength, mettle, and prowess embody the southern ideal of masculinity.

In keeping with her prose, Daniell's poetry expresses her anger with candor and little sublimation; for Daniell, the latter is an unsuitable mode for poets wishing to achieve authenticity. *The Feathered Tree* collects the most subdued of her lyrical verse. These poems are written in a tone far removed from the emotion-laden poems of *A Sexual Tour* and *Fort Bragg*, books in which she shifts her focus to women's experiences of writing.

Daniell's writings attack not the South in general but those southern aspects that stifle women and their emotions. While supplying a reinterpretation of the South, Daniell's efforts to break the silence around women's private lives consolidate the myth of the South as a region of moral degeneration and libido, a rich reservoir of the American unconscious.

Daniell lives in Savannah with her fourth husband, Timothy Zane Ward, whom she married in 1987.

YI-HSUAN TSO, *National Taiwan Ocean University, Keelung, Taiwan*

Contemporary Authors: New Revision Series, vol. 44 (Detroit: Gale, 1994), s.v. "Daniell, Rosemary."

Contemporary Authors, vol. 118 (Detroit: Gale, 1986), s.v. "Daniell, Rosemary."

Diane O'Donnell, "A Missionary of Sorts: An Interview with Rosemary Daniell," *New Orleans Review* 5, no. 2 (1976).

Jack Stewart, "Interview with Rosemary Daniell," *Kalliope* 18, no. 3 (1996).

JANICE DAUGHARTY
(b. 1944)

Since 1994 Janice Staten Daugharty has published a volume of short fiction, six novels, and numerous short stories and essays. She has built a national reputation as a chronicler of life and people in south Georgia and is one of the state's most popular and prolific contemporary authors.

Janice Staten grew up in Echols County, the second of seven children of Frances and G. F. Staten. She married her high school sweetheart, Seward Daugharty, in 1963. She attended Valdosta State College for two years, performed the duties of a devoted wife and mother until her children were grown, and at the age of thirty-nine began to write. She credits Joyce Carol Oates, whom she calls her "fairy godmother," with her initial success in the publishing world. Oates bought the first short story Daugharty sold, and Oates and her husband, Ray Smith, published a collection of Daugharty's short stories, *Going Through the Change*, in 1994 under the Ontario Review Press imprint. In the same year Baskerville Publishers printed a hardback edition of the novel *Dark of the Moon* and HarperCollins issued the paperback edition. In the following five years HarperCollins published both hardback and paperback copies of five other Daugharty novels: *Necessary Lies* (1995), *Pawpaw Patch* (1996), *Earl in the Yellow Shirt* (1997), *Whistle* (1998), and *Like a Sister* (1999).

Daugharty uses the fictional community of Cornerville, a typical south Georgia town, as the setting for most of her works. She models her characters after people in Echols County, where she has lived all her life. Most characters are composites of people she has known, but some are fictional recreations of specific people. Daugharty says she based Alamand in *Earl in the Yellow Shirt* on her late brother and Willa in *Like a Sister* on her mother. She claims that she patterned the dead woman who appears at the beginning of *Whistle* after herself.

Daugharty published her first historical fiction in 2004. That novel, *Just Doll*, is a romance set on a plantation in the wiregrass region of southeast Georgia in the 1880s. It is the first of what Daugharty plans as "the Stanton Bay trilogy."

Though Daugharty writes primarily to entertain, she often deals with such social issues as religious hypocrisy, rigid class structure, and racial prejudice. She explains, "I look around me at all the evil and ignorance and feel that niggling to preach again, to try to make us all look inside at who we are and what we are in danger of becoming."

The theme of art and its redemptive power underlies much of Daugharty's writing. Her fictional artists include musicians (Merdie in *Dark of the Moon*) and visual artists (Alamand in *Earl in the Yellow Shirt*). Other characters are lovers of the written word — for example, Archie Wall, the small-town attorney who appears in several works, and Loujean in *Earl in the Yellow Shirt*. Often misunderstood and isolated, these characters find happiness in art and come to terms with reality through the creative process.

Janice Daugharty claims that she "can't quit writing." She is currently writer-in-residence at Valdosta State University.

CHARLOTTE PFEIFFER, *Abraham Baldwin Agricultural College*

SUGGESTED READING

Lisa Alther, "If the Shoe Fits . . . ," *Washington Post Book World*, March 22, 1998.

Greg Johnson, "'Sister' of the South: Daugharty Tells a Hardscrabble Tale," *Atlanta Journal-Constitution*, December 2, 2000.

Bret Lott, "The Literature of Blame: Four Recent Novels," *Southern Review* 31 (autumn 1995): 974.

Chris Solomon, "Pass the Collards," *New York Times Book Review*, December 19, 1999.

DELIVERANCE

James Dickey's first novel, *Deliverance*, is an adventure story of a three-day canoe trip in the rugged wilderness of southern Appalachia, in which four suburbanites are brutalized both by the sheer force of the river and by violent and degenerate mountain men. Although James Dickey, an Atlanta native, never identified Georgia as the book's setting, the city from which the four men come was widely assumed to have been Atlanta. The river where most of the book's action takes place, the Cahulawassee, closely resembles the Chattooga River, which forms the border between Georgia and South Carolina in the former's northeasternmost corner in Rabun County.

Only a few months after the book's publication in March 1970, a film adaptation confirmed its Georgia setting by filming on location in Rabun County and on the Chattooga. Released in 1972, the film became one of the most popular of the year. Both book and movie had much to do with confirming to a national audience the hillbilly stereotypes that had long plagued southern Appalachia. The film, in particular, stands as the most degrading depiction of southern mountaineers ever put on film and led to strong protests both by north Georgians and by Appalachian scholars.

Dickey, already a well-regarded poet, conceived the idea for the book after his involvement in a traumatic canoe accident on the Coosawattee River in the early 1960s. His story centers on four middle-aged suburbanites who head north for a weekend of whitewater canoeing on a wild river shortly before the completion of a new dam that would make it inaccessible. Three of the men, including Ed Gentry, who is the narrator and Dickey's alter ego, are inexperienced in the ways of the wilderness, and they defer to Lewis Medlock, a seasoned outdoorsman and survivalist, who plans the trip and leads the group. Once underway the novice adventurers encounter not only a far more physically challenging and dangerous river than they were prepared for but also some equally threatening local inhabitants. The novel's centerpiece is an attack and sexual assault by two mountaineers on the banks of the river that leads to a series of murders, including that of one of the four Atlantans. Their ever-escalating struggle for survival becomes a moral dilemma as well, as the would-be adventurers find themselves forced to cover up their ordeal when they reach the town of Aintry at the river's end.

The novel has been interpreted in a variety of ways, most of which focus on the tensions wrought when the sensibilities of modern suburbia are pitted against the more elemental values of the natural world or the primitivism of rural mountain life. The four men bring to their adventure different attitudes and assumptions. For Lewis and Ed, in particular, the challenges they face in defending themselves, individually and collectively, serve as a deliverance not only from the hostile forces of man and nature but also from their own mental and psychological shortcomings as the products of a soft, comfortable, materialistic culture.

The book faced a mixed reception initially. *Deliverance* was widely acknowledged as a compelling adventure story, but some critics found its violence excessive and its stereotypical portrayal of mountain people demeaning and simplistic. It was an unqualified success commercially and became a best-seller.

Dickey anticipated a film adaptation of his book well before it was finished, and he did not have to wait long for that process to begin. Warner Brothers purchased the rights before the book's publication, and production began in the summer of 1971. Directed by British director John Boorman, who cowrote the script with Dickey, the film starred Burt Reynolds and Jon Voight, both established stars, as Lewis and Ed respectively. Ronny Cox and Ned Beatty were cast as the other two adventurers, and Dickey himself played the small role of the skeptical sheriff investigating the canoers' story in Aintry. During the filming in Rabun County tensions developed between the Hollywood film crew and local residents and between Dickey and Boorman. Two versions of those encounters have been published: that of local residents interviewed by Foxfire students, fully described by J. W. Williamson in his book *Hillbillyland* (1995), and that of Dickey's son, Christopher, in his memoir about his relationship with his father, *Summer of Deliverance* (1998).

Fueled by Burt Reynolds's box-office drawing power and the novel's recent popularity, the film was an immediate hit, both commercially and critically, with Rabun County residents among the few who were offended by its depictions of demented mountaineers, which were even more graphic than those conveyed in Dickey's prose. The movie's theme song, "Dueling Banjos," became a hit, although the albino boy playing half of the duet further accentuated the degeneracy of Georgia mountaineers. The film was nominated for an Academy Award as the year's best picture, and Boorman was nominated as best director, though in a year dominated by *The Godfather* and *Cabaret*, none of the actors were recognized, nor was Dickey as screenwriter.

JOHN C. INSCOE, *University of Georgia*

SUGGESTED READING

Keen Butterworth, "The Savage Mind: James Dickey's *Deliverance*," *Southern Literary Journal* 28 (spring 1996): 69–78.

John Lane, *Chattooga: Descending into the Myth of Deliverance River* (Athens: University of Georgia Press, 2004).

Lance Morrow, "The Sins of the Father," *Time*, August 24, 1998, p. 80.

Terry Thompson, "Cahulawassee: The Bend Sinister River in *Deliverance*," *English Language Notes* 36 (December 1998): 44–48.

James Dickey ranks, along with Conrad Aiken, as one of the two most important Georgia poets in the twentieth century. His strongly visceral, sensory-laden descriptions and a poetic style that deviated from the intellectualism of such high modernist poets as T. S. Eliot, Ezra Pound, and Gertrude Stein made him a distinctive figure in contemporary American writing. He began to reach artistic maturity in the 1950s, and his work is typically considered alongside that of a number of other well known mid-century poets, including Allen Ginsberg, Robert Lowell, and John Berryman. His poetry is intensely confessional, largely apolitical, and directly focused on the interactions of the individual with the natural as well as the technologically transformed modern world. Dickey's most important work was as a poet, but he wrote criticism, screenplays, essays, and three novels, one of which, *Deliverance*, was a best-seller and the basis of a widely praised film. As an artist, critic, and public celebrator of poetry, Dickey was a highly visible literary figure during the last half of the century. His misbehavior at public events, his disorderly personal life, and his self-destructive alcoholism only enhanced his public image as a masculine, burly poet and man of American letters.

Dickey was born in Atlanta on February 2, 1923, the son of Maibelle Swift and Eugene Dickey. He spent his first eighteen years in Atlanta and attended North Fulton High School. His poem "Looking for the Buckhead Boys" recalls some of the friends he knew during those years. He enrolled at Clemson University in 1942 (then known as Clemson College) but dropped out after a semester to join the Army Air Corps. Although he spent thirteen months training to be a bomber pilot, he failed flight school and became a navigator instead (for most of his life, however, he claimed to have been a bomber pilot). In 1945 he joined the 418th Night Fighter Squadron in the Philippines, subsequently flying missions in Okinawa and Japan. He earned a promotion to second lieutenant and five bronze stars for his service.

After the war Dickey enrolled at Vanderbilt University in Nashville, Tennessee, where he completed his undergraduate studies in English in 1949 and his M.A. degree the next year. Among his teachers were Donald Davidson and Andrew Lytle, the latter of whom became an early mentor. It was at Vanderbilt that Dickey began trying his hand at poetry. In 1948 Dickey married Maxine Syerson, and they became the parents of two children, Christopher, born in 1951, and Kevin, born in 1958. In 1950 Dickey began teaching as an English instructor at Rice University in Houston, Texas, but was recalled to active service when the Korean War began (his Korean War service was all state-side). He returned to Rice in 1952 and moved to the University of Florida in 1955 but resigned his position there a year later after reading a controversial poem at a women's poetry circle.

For the next five years Dickey wrote advertising copy for McCann-Erickson in Atlanta, and at the same time worked in earnest to develop his skills as a poet. Following the publication of poems in such journals as *Poetry*, the *Sewanee Review*, and the *Virginia Quarterly Review* and the publication of his first poetry volume *Into the Stone and Other Poems* in 1960, he left the advertising firm and returned full time to teaching and writing. He also began touring the country, reading his poems and arguing for the importance of poetry. In 1968 he was named poet-in-residence and professor of English at the University of South Carolina, where he remained for the rest of his career.

Dickey's personal life was hardly conventional. Maxine Dickey died after a long illness in late October 1976. Two months later Dickey married a former student, Deborah Dodson. Their daughter, Bronwen, was born in 1981. This was a tumultuous marriage, difficult for both partners and for all of Dickey's children, and it did not contribute to a stable lifestyle for the poet.

The South and Georgia are often present in Dickey's work both as a setting and a theme. But in his temperament, his interests, and the range of writers he admired, Dickey is not a regionalist, and he devotes himself to the exploration of themes and topics that are equally non-regional. Dickey is a southern poet and a Georgia poet more because of his place of birth and the settings of his poem than for the "southern" attitudes they express. Dickey's poetic topics cover a wide and varied range. He writes of personal experiences, memories, specific places, and situations. Almost always the poet occupies the center of his poems, usually as an actor, less often as an observer, in the scene he describes. An example is the poem "Springer Mountain," wherein Dickey imagines himself hunting a deer in the early winter morning air and entering into a ritualistic sense of oneness with his intended prey:

> The world catches fire.
> I put an unbearable light
> Into breath skinned alive of its garments:
> I think, beginning with laurel,
> Like a beast loving
> With the whole god bone of his horns:
> The green of excess is upon me.

The typical Dickey poem is one of meditation on memory or experience. Poems built around memories may concern places Dickey has visited ("Slave Quarters," "Near Darien") or people he has known ("The Performance," "Mary Sheffield," "Looking for the Buckhead Boys"). Poems about experience are numerous and vary widely. They may concern things Dickey has actually done ("The Firebombing") or that he imagines wholly or partially ("May Day Sermon," "Cherrylog Road," "The Sheep Child"). Some of his most successful poems are about experiences had by others that he reconceives and imagines for himself ("Falling" is a notable example). In all of these poems, the goal is always to experience and to understand and often to consecrate or to celebrate. Dickey's basic subject is the individual as he struggles to negotiate his relationship with others and with the natural world. His poems often end with affirmations of unity or mystic comprehension, as at the end of "For the Last Wolverine," where he pleads, " *Lord, let me die / but not die Out*," or in "Cherrylog Road," where he drives away down Highway 106 on his motorcycle, "Drunk on the wind in my mouth, / Wringing the handlebar for speed, / Wild to be wreckage forever." His poems largely avoid literary allusions and intellectual references and rely instead on sensory images to convey the intensity of experience.

Dickey's best work came in the first fifteen years of his career, and most of it is presented in his collection *Poems: 1957–1967*. His novel *Deliverance*, published in 1970, brought him popular success and a degree of notoriety, and it was clearly a turning point for him both personally and artistically. With the publication of *The Eye-Beaters, Blood, Victory, Madness, Buckhead, and Mercy* in 1970 his poetry became more experimental and abstract, less spontaneous and effective. Alcoholism, the dissolution of his first marriage, followed by Maxine's death in 1976 and his second marriage later the same year became drains on his energy and attention. His son Christopher, in his memoir *Summer of Deliverance*, marks 1972 — the year in which *Deliverance* was made into a movie — as the point when Dickey began to lose focus as an individual, a father, and an artist. In the years that followed, Dickey was much caught up in his own cult of celebrity, one in which he fervently believed. *The Zodiac* (1976), *The Strength of Fields* (1979), *Puella* (1982), and *The Eagle's Mile* (1990) showed a genuine struggle to forge a new poetic voice, but these later poems, with a few exceptions, fell short of the lyric ferocity of the earlier work.

For many readers Dickey's name is closely linked to the novel *Deliverance*. This tale of four businessmen from Atlanta, whose weekend canoe trip in the hills of north Georgia ends in death and disaster, cemented the public persona that Dickey had been building throughout his career. A number of critics have faulted the novel for its stereotypical portrayal of north Georgia hillbillies, ignorance, inbreeding, and violence. An accurate portrayal was probably not Dickey's intention (he does camouflage place names). Rather, he explores several of his basic themes: the collision of civilized and uncivilized worlds, the struggle of the modern individual to maintain, or recover, connections with his primal nature, and the retreat of nature against the advances of science and technology. The book to which the novel has often been compared is the one with which it shows the closest affinity: Joseph Conrad's *Heart of Darkness*, in which a civilized man discovers, and must learn to live with, the savagery of his essential nature. John Boorman's film of *Deliverance*, based on Dickey's screenplay and featuring him in a small role as a sheriff, perpetuated the stereotypes in the novel and boosted its notoriety and popularity. Jon Voight and Burt Reynolds were featured actors in the film, which was nominated for three Academy and five Golden Globe awards.

As early as the 1950s Dickey began mentioning ideas for a story about a blind man named Cahill, an aviator whose son dies mysteriously in a military plane crash. This idea eventually developed into the novel *Alnilam* (1987), which uses parallel columns of text to narrate from both a blind and a sighted man's point of view. *Alnilam* was a serious and ambitious effort that was widely if unenthusiastically reviewed. Oddly, the vitality that Dickey seemed unable to achieve in his last major book of poetry, *The Eagle's Mile*, clearly left a mark on his last novel, *To the White Sea* (1993), about a tail gunner's struggle for survival after his B-29 is shot down over Tokyo during a bombing mission in 1945. The novel is marked with violence and a kind of deliberate brutality as the man flees the soldiers who pursue him. The novel is penetrated with images and language from the poetry, and the main character himself can be taken as an image of Dickey in old age, fighting illness and unsympathetic critics, demanding his place in a world that seeks to erase him.

Dickey's last years were sad ones. He continued teaching at the University of South Carolina, but he no longer held the place of national prominence he had once occupied. Afflicted with alcoholism and the collapse of his second marriage, he kept at his writing, convinced that he was doing, or on the verge of doing, his best work ever. He grew seriously estranged from his wife, Deborah. He reconciled with his son Christopher in 1994 and stopped drinking, but liver disease and fibrosis of the lungs drained his energies. He died in January 1997, three days after his last class, leaving a novel unfinished.

HUGH RUPPERSBURG, *University of Georgia*

SUGGESTED READING

Ron Baughman, *Understanding James Dickey* (Columbia: University of South Carolina Press, 1985).

Matthew Bruccoli and Judith Baughman, eds., *Crux: The Letters of James Dickey* (New York: Knopf, 1999).

Christopher Dickey, *Summer of Deliverance: A Memoir of Father and Son* (New York: Simon and Schuster, 1998).

Henry Hart, *The World as a Lie: James Dickey* (New York: Picador, 2000).

Robert Kirschten, *James Dickey and the Gentle Ecstasy of Earth: A Reading of the Poems* (Baton Rouge: Louisiana State University Press, 1988).

John Lane, *Chattooga: Decending into the Myth of Deliverance River* (Athens: University of Georgia Press, 2004).

Ernest Suarez, *James Dickey and the Politics of Canon: Assessing the Savage Ideal* (Columbia: University of Missouri Press, 1993).

The play *Driving Miss Daisy* had its New York premiere on April 15, 1987, off Broadway at the Studio Theatre at Playwrights Horizons. Written by Alfred Uhry and directed by Ron Lagomarsino, the original theatrical production featured a cast including Atlanta native Dana Ivey as Miss Daisy, Morgan Freeman as Hoke, and Ray Gill as Boolie. The play received a Pulitzer Prize in 1988, and in 1989 it was adapted into a film directed by Bruce Beresford and starring Jessica Tandy, Morgan Freeman, and Dan Aykroyd. The film received nine Academy Award nominations and won for Best Picture, Best Actress, Best Makeup, and Best Screenplay.

Driving Miss Daisy is set in Atlanta, Uhry's hometown. Spanning a quarter of a century, from 1948 to 1973, the action takes place before, during, and after the civil rights movement. The plot centers on two characters, an elderly Jewish widow named Miss Daisy Werthan and her African American driver, Hoke Colburn. Although the story was inspired by Uhry's grandmother Lena Fox and her chauffeur, Will Coleman, the characters are universal figures that appeal to a wide audience.

At the beginning of the play, Hoke is hired by Miss Daisy's son, Boolie, who has become concerned about his aging mother's driving abilities. The proud Miss Daisy resents Hoke's presence, as she believes that he will do nothing but sit around, take up space, eat her food, and run up her phone bill. Concerned about appearances, Miss Daisy is also terrified that her neighbors will consider her a snob because she has a chauffeur to drive her around town. Hoke persists, however, and soon Miss Daisy is not only tolerating the kindly man but also accepting him as a friend. By the end, the proud, elderly, and frail woman, confined to a nursing home, tells Hoke that he is her best friend, and she allows him to spoon-feed her when she is unable to eat on her own.

Both the theatrical and film versions of *Driving Miss Daisy* were written by Uhry and are similar, but some differences are evident. The play includes only three characters, Miss Daisy, Hoke, and Boolie, and the set is very simple, utilizing two stools to represent the car in which much of the dramatic action takes place. The play consists of a series of vignettes, with the passage of time revealed in the actors' mannerisms and by topical references, as well as by set and costume changes. The movie, by contrast, was filmed in and around Atlanta and features such locations as Druid Hills, Lullwater Road, Agnes Scott College, and The Temple. Characters who are only mentioned in the play, including Boolie's wife and Miss Daisy's cook, were given roles in the film, and all of the characters were enhanced and expanded to allow for more insight into their lives and environment.

The personal and social conflicts of its characters are at the heart of *Driving Miss Daisy*. These conflicts result mainly from the mixture of southern and Jewish cultures, a theme about which Uhry, himself a southern Jew, often writes. The play is cast against the background of the civil rights movement in Atlanta, and many of the tensions that mark the developing relationship between Hoke and Miss Daisy reflect the world that is changing around them. As Hoke begins to test and push the boundaries of his social and working relationship with Miss Daisy, she begins to realize not only her own prejudices but also those of the mainstream Christian community in which she lives.

Miss Daisy also experiences conflicts with Boolie that further illustrate the theme of change within the South. As a representative of the "Old South" and its traditions, Miss Daisy is highly resistant to change. Boolie, by contrast, is a shrewd businessman who, along with his wife, exemplifies the transformation of the South from an agrarian to an industrial culture. He owns all of the latest technology, including intercom systems in his store, decorative Christmas lights at his house, and a hi-fi stereo system from which he blasts music that the whole neighborhood hears. Boolie constantly tries to push this newer, more technologically advanced way of life on his mother, who refuses it all.

The critical reception of *Driving Miss Daisy* has been mixed. While some reviewers found the work a "touching tribute to friendship and human dignity" and praised its subtle and subversive portrayal of the civil rights movement and racial prejudice, others criticized its romanticized and overly simplistic portrayal of a relationship between a rich white woman and her black employee. Nonetheless, the play and the film have both been popular with audiences, and the story is prominently identified with the South and its culture.

MIRIAM TERRY, *Macon*

SUGGESTED READING

Beverly Branch, "Southern Society in *Driving Miss Daisy*," in *Motion Pictures and Society*, ed. Douglas Radcliff-Umstead (Kent, Ohio: Department of Romance Languages, Kent State University, 1990).

Angela J. Mason and Timothy J. Viator, "*Driving Miss Daisy*: A Sociosemiotic Analysis," *Southern Quarterly* 33, no. 1 (1994).

Don Shewey, "Ballyhoo and Daisy, Too," *American Theatre* 14, no. 4 (1997).

Helene Vann and Jane Caputi, "*Driving Miss Daisy*: A New 'Song of the South,'" *Journal of Popular Film and Television* 18, no. 2 (1990): 80–82.

W. E. B. DU BOIS IN GEORGIA

William Edward Burghardt Du Bois (1868–1963) was an African American educator, historian, sociologist, and social activist who poignantly addressed the issues of racial discrimination, black social problems, and world peace during the first half of the twentieth century. During two extended stints in Atlanta, 1897–1910 and 1934–44, Du Bois contributed immensely to the black intellectual and activist community and produced a number of studies that explored the social, economic, and political conditions of African Americans in Georgia and across the United States.

In Georgia, Du Bois wrote some of his best-known works, including *The Souls of Black Folk, Dusk of Dawn,* and *Black Reconstruction,* and established a journal dealing with the African American experience called *Phylon,* which has recently resumed publication. His life and work in Georgia improved the lives of blacks in the state and across the country while educating all races about the contributions of African Americans to American society.

Du Bois was born in the small New England hamlet of Great Barrington, Massachusetts. His mother, Mary Burghardt, was a descendent of the Burghardt clan, and her family had deep roots in the Great Barrington community. With the support of his mother, extended family, school principal, and the local community, Du Bois enjoyed a relatively comfortable childhood and succeeded in school.

In 1885 Du Bois attended Fisk University in Nashville, Tennessee. There he was exposed to the harsh realities of Jim Crow segregation and the social and economic residuals of slavery that continued to keep most blacks in a squalid state of poverty and impotence in the South. At Fisk, Du Bois immersed himself in his studies, focusing on philosophy, history, and law. It was at this point that he began to form his idea of the "talented tenth" — a cadre of college-educated blacks that would break down the institutional structures of American racism while elevating their race to a pinnacle of respect in the world community. Du Bois graduated from Fisk in 1888 with a B.A. and set his sights on Harvard University in Cambridge, Massachusetts.

Du Bois enrolled in Harvard in the fall of 1888. He entered as a junior because Harvard would not accept all of his Fisk credits. He graduated cum laude in 1890, receiving a B.A. degree. In 1891 he received an M.A. in history from Harvard, and between 1892 and 1894 he studied at the University of Berlin. After returning to the United States in 1894, Du Bois accepted a professorship at Wilberforce University in Ohio and completed his dissertation on the African slave trade, receiving a Ph.D. from Harvard in 1896.

Du Bois left Wilberforce in 1896 and accepted a position as an assistant instructor at the University of Pennsylvania, where he embarked on a sociohistorical urban study on African Americans in the Seventh Ward of Philadelphia, *The Philadelphia Negro* (1899). This study remains a pioneering work in urban sociology.

Before publishing *The Philadelphia Negro*, Du Bois accepted a faculty position at Atlanta University (later Clark Atlanta University) in 1897. Atlanta University (AU) president Horace Bumstead brought Du Bois to Atlanta to establish a sociology program and to develop the university's curriculum. Du Bois's major work to come out of this relationship was his famous series of conferences and studies on black social conditions called the Atlanta University Studies.

The first years Du Bois and his wife, Nina, spent in Atlanta were not happy ones. In the spring of 1899 their two-year-old son, Burghardt, died of diphtheria. The Du Boises later believed that Burghardt might have lived had appropriate medical facilities and services been available for blacks in Atlanta. Du Bois paid tribute to Burghardt in *The Souls of Black Folk* in a chapter entitled "The Passing of the First Born." In this soliloquy to his son, Du Bois's emotional turmoil and his feelings about Georgia are expressed. "I held him in my arms, after we sped far away from our Southern home, — held him, and glanced at the hot red soil of Georgia and the breathless city of a hundred hills, and felt a vague unrest."

In that same year a black man named Sam Hose was lynched in Newnan after he was accused of killing his landlord's wife. On his walk to the *Atlanta Constitution* office to submit a statement on the brutal lynching, Du Bois heard that Hose's knuckles were on display in a local Atlanta store. Du Bois then turned around and headed back to AU. It was after this event that Du Bois questioned his methods of scientific research as the sole method of agitation for equality. He stated, "Two considerations thereafter broke in upon my work and eventually disrupted it: first, one could not be a calm, cool, and detached scientist while Negroes were lynched, murdered, and starved; and secondly, there was no such definite demand for scientific work of the sort I was doing."

During his early years at AU, Du Bois published significant studies that examined black conditions in the state. In 1901, under the auspices of the U.S. Department of Labor, he published *The Negro Landholder of Georgia*, in which he examined how in only a generation after slavery, blacks had accumulated more than a million acres of land. In 1904 he published *Some Notes on Negro Crime, Particularly in Georgia*. Du Bois and his team of researchers concluded that Georgia's prison industrial complex was financed by the incarceration of black males and that laws were applied to blacks in blatantly discriminatory ways. They also argued that while black crime decreased between 1895 and 1903, lengthy sentences for blacks made it appear that blacks committed more crimes.

The years from 1905 to 1910 were eventful for Du Bois. In 1905 he founded and served as the general secretary of the Niagara Movement, a group of black intellectuals, and in 1909 he helped found the National Association for the Advancement of Colored People (NAACP). During these years Du Bois also wrote *The Souls of Black Folk* (1903) and *John Brown* (1909) and founded two literary magazines, *The Moon* (1906) and *Horizon* (1907). In 1906 Du Bois penned "A Litany of Atlanta" in response to what he saw and felt when he witnessed the Atlanta race riots of that year. Afterward he kept a double-barreled shotgun in his home for protection against the white mobs. In 1910 Du Bois left Atlanta University to become director of publications and research of the NAACP in New York and later that year he founded its monthly magazine, *The Crisis*. He remained connected to Georgia and affiliated with the AU Studies until 1914.

In 1934 AU president John Hope invited Du Bois back to chair the university's sociology department. During the next decade Du Bois published his seminal *Black Reconstruction* (1935), which challenged the dominant historiography of the time by arguing that Reconstruction was not a total failure and that blacks played an important role in democratizing America. While at AU, Du Bois also published the black history treatise *Black Folk Then and Now* (1939) and the autobiographical *Dusk of Dawn* (1940) and founded a scholarly journal, *Phylon* (1940). After Hope's death in 1936, Du Bois found himself at odds with AU's power structure. In 1944 he resigned from his position to work again in New York as the director of special research at the NAACP.

Du Bois's years in Georgia were some of the most productive in his seventy-plus years of scholarship and activism. While he has most often been associated with New England, it was in Georgia and other parts of the South that Du Bois focused much of his studies on black social conditions.

DERRICK P. ALRIDGE, *University of Georgia*

SUGGESTED READING

David Levering Lewis, *W.E.B. Du Bois: Biography of a Race, 1868–1919* (New York: Henry Holt, 1993).

Manning Marable, *W.E.B. Du Bois: Black Radical Democrat* (Boston: Twayne, 1986).

PAM DURBAN

(b. 1947)

A southern writer who has received much recognition for her gripping, insightful fiction, Pam Durban was professor of creative writing at Georgia State University from 1986 until 2001, when she moved to the University of North Carolina at Chapel Hill. Some of her earliest fiction bears the imprint of the time she spent as a textile worker in Atlanta in the early 1970s and of her interviews with residents of the community.

Durban has written several highly acclaimed short-story collections and novels, including *All Set About with Fever Trees and Other Stories* (1985), *The Laughing Place* (1993), and *So Far Back* (2000). During the course of her career she has won numerous literary awards and honors, including the Townsend Prize for Fiction (1994), the Whiting Writer Award (1988), and the Rinehart Award for Fiction (1984). Her work has appeared in numerous literary journals such as *Tri-Quarterly*, *Crazyhorse*, and the *Georgia Review*.

Rosa Pam Durban was born March 4, 1947, in Aiken, South Carolina, to Frampton Durban, a real estate appraiser, and his wife, Maria. Her educational background includes a B.A. degree from the University of North Carolina at Greensboro (1969) and an M.F.A. from the University of Iowa (1979).

From 1974 to 1975 Durban was affiliated with the *Atlanta Gazette* as an editor and writer. She later began an academic career, teaching creative writing at the State University of New York at Geneseo, Murray State University, Ohio University, and Georgia State University. Durban was also founding coeditor (along with David Bottoms) of the prize-winning literary journal *Five Points*. In 2001 she joined the faculty of the University of North Carolina at Chapel Hill as Doris Betts Professor of Creative Writing.

Of her experience as a textile worker in Atlanta, Durban says,

"One of my first published stories, 'This Heat,' came out of this experience, and I believe that the time I spent in that place helped me see that I was most interested in who people are and how they got to be that way, and what makes them or allows them to go on living in the face of everything that happens to them."

Much of Durban's fiction has a southern setting, and her writing is infused with an understanding of the customs and traditions unique to southern culture. Her first short-story collection, *All Set About with Fever Trees and Other Stories* (1985), consists of seven stories that deal with family relationships and the struggles for love, understanding, and rebirth in the face of hardships and tragedies. The characters in this collection come from a wide spectrum of southern society, including a country singer seeking elusive stardom, a mill worker dealing with the sudden death of her teenage son, a young boy caught in the throes of first love, and a father psychologically distanced from his family because of war trauma. *The Laughing Place* (1993) deals with the struggle of Annie Vess, a young woman who must come to terms with the deaths of her husband and father, redefine her relationship with a domineering mother, and map out a new life for herself. *So Far Back* (2000), chronicles the inner growth of Louisa Hillard, a Charleston society woman who, through the discovery of an antebellum journal written by a slaveholding ancestor, comes to a greater understanding of her family history and race relations in the South.

VALERIE FRAZIER, *College of Charleston and The Citadel, Charleston, South Carolina*

SUGGESTED READING

Contemporary Literary Criticism Yearbook 1985 (Detroit: Gale, 1986), s.v. "Pam Durban."

Contemporary Southern Writers, ed. Roger Matuz (Detroit: St. James Press, 1998), s.v. "Durban, Pam."

MARGARET EDSON

(b. 1961)

Margaret Edson, a playwright and kindergarten teacher in Atlanta, is best known for *Wit*, a play about a literary scholar diagnosed with terminal ovarian cancer. Although Edson considers herself first an educator and then a playwright, her play has won many prestigious awards, including the Pulitzer Prize for Drama in 1999.

Edson was born in Washington, D.C., on July 4, 1961. Her father, Peter Edson, was a newspaper columnist, and her mother, Joyce Edson, was a medical social worker. Edson briefly pursued her interest in drama during high school at Sidwell Friends School in Washington, D.C.

After majoring in Renaissance history and graduating magna cum laude in 1983 from Smith College in Northampton, Massachusetts, Edson worked in a series of odd jobs. She returned to graduate school at Georgetown University in Washington, D.C., in 1991. Between degrees, Edson spent two years working as a unit clerk at an AIDS-oncology research hospital in the D.C. area. Drawing on her experiences there, she began to write *Wit* in the summer of 1991, a year before receiving her master's degree in English literature from Georgetown.

Wit's main character, Vivian Bearing, is a fifty-year-old renowned literary scholar of John Donne's seventeenth-century metaphysical poetry. The play concerns Bearing's attempts to put her life together as it comes to an end.

By combining concepts of metaphysical poetry and human mortality within the complex mind of a dying scholar, Edson creates an extraordinary character of fortitude and wit. Edson's use of *wit*, referring to intelligence and wisdom, develops this multilayered work into a play about grace and redemption. An uncompromising look at cancer, the play shows how language has the power both to complicate and to ameliorate understanding. "The play is not about doctors or even cancer. It's about kindness, but it shows arrogance. It's about compassion, but it shows insensitivity," Edson explains. By showing the opposite of kindness, Edson's play effectively leaves the audience "yearning for kindness."

Producing an "unfriendly" play proved to be a considerable challenge. Edson searched for four years before finding a theater company that would produce it. The play finally premiered at the South Coast Repertory in 1995 in Costa Mesa, California. In 1997 it continued its run at the Long Wharf Theater in New Haven, Connecticut, under the direction of Edson's childhood friend Derek Anson Jones. In 1998 the play made its off-Broadway debut in the MCC Theatre, where Kathleen Chalfont played Vivian Bearing. Chalfont remained in the role when the play moved to Union Square Theatre in 1999. Judith Light replaced Chalfont in the fall of 1999.

Edson was awarded the Pulitzer Prize for Drama in 1999. The play has since received numerous other awards, including the New York Drama Critics Circle Award, the Lucille Lortel Award, the Outer Critics Circle Award, the Oppenheimer Award, and the Drama Desk Award. Hundreds of productions have been staged, in national and international theaters, in dozens of languages. An HBO production of the play, directed by Mike Nichols and featuring Emma Thompson as the main character, won an Emmy Award in 2001 for Outstanding Made for Television Movie of the year. Nichols also received an Emmy for directing, and in 2002 the television production of *Wit* won a prestigious Peabody Award.

Edson's teaching career progressed along with the success of her play. Despite her newfound fame as a playwright, she continued teaching elementary school in Washington, D.C. — English as a second language for five years and first grade for one year — until she moved to Atlanta in 1998 and began teaching kindergarten.

Fully dedicated to teaching elementary school in her adopted town of Atlanta, Edson does not intend to write another play.

She lives with her partner, Linda Merrill, and their two sons, Timmy and Pete.

KIM PURCELL, *Georgia Center for the Book*

SUGGESTED READING

Adrienne Martini, "The Playwright in Spite of Herself," *American Theatre* 16 (October 1999).

AUGUSTA JANE EVANS (WILSON)

(1835–1909)

Augusta Jane Evans wrote nine novels about southern women that were among the most popular fiction in nineteenth-century America. Her most successful novel, *St. Elmo* (1866), sold a million copies within four months of its appearance and remained in print well into the twentieth century. The sexual tensions between the book's cynical Byronic hero, St. Elmo, and its beautiful Christian heroine, self-made writer Edna Earl, inspired the christening of villages, plantations, steamboats, railway carriages, male infants, a punch, a cigar, and one infamous parody, *St. Twel'mo, or the Cuneiform Cyclopedist of Chattanooga* (1867). Edna Earl also later became the namesake of Eudora Welty's heroine Edna Earle Ponder in *The Ponder Heart* (1954).

Evans was born in Columbus in 1835 and died in Alabama in 1909, buried among the Confederate soldiers she loved. She became a writer partially to recuperate the family fortune. Her father, Matthew Evans, lost palatial Sherwood Hall — dubbed "Matt's Folly" by Columbus citizens — after he was bankrupted in the 1840s. His family of ten migrated to Texas. However, the dangers of a frontier border town and the Mexican-American War caused them to resettle in Mobile, Alabama. There Evans penned her anonymous first novel, *Inez: A Tale of the Alamo* (1855), an anti-Catholic diatribe, followed by the much more popular *Beulah* (1859). *Beulah* began the theme of female education that persisted in her novels. Although Evans never returned to Columbus, she made it the setting for *St. Elmo.*

Slavery remained in the background of Evans's novels, but she supported the Confederacy zealously in her life and fiction. She broke off her engagement to New York journalist James Reed Spaulding in 1860 because he supported Abraham Lincoln.

During the Civil War, Evans sewed sandbags for community

defense, wrote patriotic addresses, and set up a hospital dubbed "Camp Beulah" near her home. She worked as a hospital nurse yet wrote General P. G. T. Beauregard in mid-1862 that she still felt marginal to war efforts. Her novel *Macaria* (1864) attempts to remedy that situation by showing how Southern women can sacrifice their lives for the Confederacy. *Macaria* penetrated the Northern blockade with five thousand bootlegged copies sold in the North. So effective was *Macaria* as pro-Southern propoganda that General G. H. Thomas, commander of the Union Army in Tennessee, banned it among his troops and confiscated and burned those copies that existed.

Evans and her family faced serious financial problems at the war's end, with the loss of their slaves and other property. She accompanied her brother Howard to New York City seeking a medical specialist to treat a paralyzed arm resulting from a war wound. In meeting with her publisher there, she discovered that he had been holding for her a substantial sum of money from northern sales of *Macaria*. Realizing just how profitable her writing could be, she quickly completed *St. Elmo* and ended any future financial worries for herself and her family.

In 1868 Evans married Colonel Lorenzo Madison Wilson, a wealthy planter twenty-eight years her senior who had been widowed in 1862. She moved to his estate, Ashland, next door to the Evans home and spent much of the rest of her life making it and its surrounding gardens one of Mobile's most beautiful showplaces. She continued to write, though more sporadically. She published three novels over the course of her married life at Ashland, one of which, a murder mystery entitled *At the Mercy of Tiberius* (1887), she declared her favorite.

When Colonel Wilson died in 1891, Evans Wilson left Ashland and moved into her brother Howard's home in Mobile. Despite deteriorating health and eyesight, she wrote two more romantic novels, *A Speckled Bird* (1902) and *Devota* (1907). She died of a heart attack in 1909, a day after her seventy-fourth birthday.

Recent feminist critics have read past the marriage themes in

Evans's novels to show how her women characters are as intellectually capable as men and how they gain personal and public power in their world.

JANET GABLER-HOVER, *Georgia State University*

SUGGESTED READING

Drew Gilpin Faust, introduction to *Macaria* (Baton Rouge: Louisiana State University Press, 1992).

William Perry Fidler, *Augusta Evans Wilson, 1835–1909: A Biography* (University, Ala.: University of Alabama Press, 1951).

Susan K. Harris, "Introduction to the Exploratory Text: Subversions of the Narrative Design," in *St. Elmo* (Cambridge, England: Cambridge University Press, 1990).

Anne Goodwyn Jones, "Augusta Jane Evans: Paradise Regained," in *Tomorrow Is Another Day: The Woman Writer in the South, 1859–1936* (Baton Rouge: Louisiana State University Press, 1981).

Elizabeth Moss, *Domestic Novelists in the Old South: Defenders of Southern Culture* (Baton Rouge: Louisiana State University Press, 1992).

Rebecca Grant Sexton ed., *A Southern Woman of Letters: The Correspondence of Augusta Jane Evans Wilson* (Columbia: University of South Carolina, 2002).

FIVE POINTS

Founded in 1996, *Five Points* has achieved an international following and attracted some of today's most distinguished poets and fiction writers. Published three times yearly by Georgia State University's Department of English and its creative writing program, the magazine has established a reputation for the diversity and quality of the writers, artists, essayists, and interviewers it publishes. "We always say that our only standard is excellence," says Megan Sexton, *Five Points* executive editor. Poet Phillip Levine calls the journal a "refreshing combination of the old and the new. The best literary magazine I've read in ages!"

Founded by poet and novelist David Bottoms and fiction writer Pam Durban and named after a historic Atlanta intersection, *Five Points* offers artists and writers a forum, its editors say, for "the convergence of ideas and genres, photographs and text, north and south, east and west, young and old." Sexton says that such a convergence creates a sense of each genre's potential, often by juxtaposition as much as by variety. "One of the major impacts a literary magazine can have," she says, "is the way in which it illuminates genre. When a story runs next to a poem and an essay runs next to a story . . . questions of form are raised — how one form may offer different challenges for the language and various experiences for the reader."

At its inception, *Five Points* was available only in print editions. However, since 1998, an online edition has made available selections from the print edition and provides information about the magazine. The online presence also underscores *Five Points*'s commitment to being more than a regional publication, an aspiration reflected in the diversity of writers it publishes. The journal is named for an intersection in downtown Atlanta that marks the traditional center of the city.

Five Points has garnered considerable critical attention, especially given its relatively brief existence. It has received a Best New Journal Award (1998) from the Council of Literary Magazines. Additionally, work first published in *Five Points* has reappeared in *Best American Short Stories*, *Pushcart Best of the Small Presses*, *New Stories from the South*, *Utne Reader*, *Harper's Poetry Daily*, and Norton's *In Short*. Recent contributors include Richard Bausch, Ann Beattie, Barbara Hamby, Edward Hirsch, Philip Levine, W. S. Merwin, Naomi Shihab Nye, Joyce Carol Oates, Christine Stewart, Ellen Bryant Voigt, Martin Walls, and Charles Wright.

SAM PRESTRIDGE, *Gainesville State College*

BERRY FLEMING

(1899–1989)

Publishers Weekly magazine once called Berry Fleming "the quintessential Southern writer; funny, wise and like the best of those from the South, an incredibly good storyteller." His long career began in 1927 with the publication of *The Conqueror's Stone*, an adventure story about a bloodthirsty pirate off the South Carolina coast. Fleming is best known for his novel *Colonel Effingham's Raid*, published in 1943. Among his other books are *Siesta* (1935), *The Lightwood Tree* (1947), *The Fortune Tellers* (1951), *Carnival* (1953), *The Winter Rider* (1960), *Lucinderella* (1967), *The Acrobats* (1969), *The Make-Believers* (1972), *The Affair at Honey Hill* (1981), and *The Bookman's Tale and Others* (1986).

Fleming grew up in Augusta, the son of Daisy and Porter Fleming. His father was in the cotton and fertilizer businesses. He graduated in 1922 from Harvard University. One year earlier he had sold his first article to the *New York Evening Post*. He began his writing career in New York, where he met Anne Shirley Molloy of Lexington, Kentucky. They married in 1925 and remained married until her death in 1973.

When Fleming moved back to Augusta in 1940 after living in New York for more than a decade, he became disturbed by "political shenanigans" there: the arrest of a printer named Bridges Evans, who had openly criticized the Cracker Party, prompted him to write *Colonel Effingham's Raid*, a thinly veiled story of political corruption in Richmond County. This was the most popular novel Fleming ever wrote, a best-selling Book-of-the-Month Club selection. It describes a thinly disguised Cracker Party, a small group of political bosses who controlled the Augusta and Richmond County governments. In the novel Augusta is disguised as Fredericksville, as it is in Fleming's later novel *The Make-Believers*. Partially as a result of the novel and of Fleming's own activism, the Crackers were defeated at the polls in 1946. Earlier that year Twentieth Century Fox released a film version of *Colonel Effingham's Raid*, starring Savannah-born actor Charles Coburn in the title role. Fleming's later novels did not fare as well. He blamed his decision to serve as his own agent for the relative neglect of his books in later years.

Along with writing, painting was a lifelong passion for Fleming. He studied in 1946 at the Gertrude Herbert Institute of Art in Augusta, with Lamar Dodd at the University of Georgia, and at the University of Wisconsin. In June 1973, he became one of the first winners of the Governor's Awards in the Arts program with the award presented by then Governor Jimmy Carter.

Fleming died in 1989 at the age of ninety, shortly after the republication of several of his novels brought increased attention to his work. In 1988 North Carolina poet and novelist Fred Chappell wrote in the *Los Angeles Times* that Fleming "is a Southern novelist who is able to treat his material with humor and detachment. . . . He shows a gift for wit as well as for broader humor, a delicate eye for detail, a keen eye for nuance of manners."

DON RHODES, *Morris Communications*

SUGGESTED READING

Fred Chappell, "The Afternoon-ness of the Civilized South: *Colonel Effingham's Raid* by Berry Fleming," *Los Angeles Times*, January 31, 1988.

Shirley K. Sullivan, "A Writer Reminisces: When Berry Fleming Returned to Georgia He Didn't Plan to Stay," *Atlanta Journal-Constitution Magazine*, February 25, 1973.

Bob Summer, "Berry Fleming," *Publishers Weekly*, January 22, 1988.

FRANCIS FONTAINE

(1845–1901)

Francis Fontaine, an aristocrat possessed of a cultivated mind and brilliant conversational abilities, was a Renaissance man of nineteenth-century Georgia. A fearless Confederate soldier, a newspaper editor, Georgia's representative to the Paris Exposition, a delegate to the state constitutional convention of 1877, and a force in Atlanta real estate and lending concerns, he is best remembered for his literary endeavors.

Born May 7, 1845, in Columbus to John Fontaine, first mayor of that city and one of Georgia's leading entrepreneurs, and his wife, Mary Ann Stewart, Francis Fontaine was a student at the Georgia Military Institute in Marietta when the Civil War began. Though only a boy, he enlisted in the Confederate army and served throughout the war as a private and aide-de-camp, even after suffering serious hearing loss in the field. He distinguished himself in a number of battles, most notably at the Battle of Peachtree Creek. There he took the flag from the wounded standard bearer and spurred his horse in advance of his comrades toward the enemy line, rallying the dazed, retreating Confederate force as his horse was shot from under him. After the defeat of the Confederacy at Appomattox, Virginia, Fontaine returned home to Columbus and managed his father's vast planting interests.

In 1874 he and an associate founded the *Columbus Times*. And although Fontaine had no previous political experience, in 1877 he was elected to represent his district at the convention to draw a new state constitution.

The following year G. P. Putnam's Sons in New York published his narrative poem *The Exile: A Tale of St. Augustine*, treating the Florida massacre of Huguenots by the Spanish in 1565. Before publication Fontaine sought the advice and approval of Henry Wadsworth Longfellow, whose own long poems had provided Fontaine a model. Both Longfellow and reviewers in the *New*

York Times and the *Evening Post* found little merit in the work, and subsequently Fontaine turned his attention to prose.

His next publication, *The State of Georgia: What It Offers to Immigrants, Capitalists, Producers and Manufacturers, and Those Desiring to Better Their Condition* (1881) grew out of his position as immigration emissary to Europe. Six years later he published his best-known work, *Etowah: A Romance of the Confederacy*, privately printed in Atlanta. Set in the South during wartime and Reconstruction, the novel is anything but a romance. Exhibiting definite Confederate sympathies but presenting a humane vision embracing sectional reconciliation, expressing the hope of the American dream, and arguing for any number of worthy causes (from opposition to convict labor to the medical treatment of alcoholism), *Etowah* is curiously lifeless, closer to a series of essays than a novel. It was, however, widely and favorably reviewed, especially in the North. Fontaine published one more novel, which appeared in 1891 as *Amanda, the Octoroon: A Novel* (published in Atlanta by J. P. Harrison) and in 1892 as *The Modern Pariah: A Story of the South* (privately printed in Atlanta). In many ways more interesting and more novelistic than *Etowah*, it too has its share of essay-like passages, and its moral focus is ambiguous, seeming to be both an attack on racial prejudice and an endorsement of it.

Fontaine was twice married, first in 1870 to Mary Flournoy of Columbus, by whom he had two children (Francis Maury, a graduate of the University of Georgia, who died young, and Mary Flournoy). His second marriage, in 1885, to Nathalie Hamilton of Athens produced no offspring. Fontaine died on May 3, 1901, at his home in Atlanta. He is buried in the Fontaine plot in Columbus.

HUBERT H. McALEXANDER, *University of Georgia*

GEORGIA CENTER FOR THE BOOK

The Georgia Center for the Book is the state affiliate of the Center for the Book at the Library of Congress in Washington, D.C. Based at the DeKalb County Public Library in Decatur, the Georgia Center provides collaborative support and focus for the state's literary community of libraries, authors, educators, publishers, booksellers, and readers, with a particular emphasis on promoting the rich literary heritage of Georgia. Since receiving its affiliate charter in 1997, the center has presented dozens of well-known authors in public forums around the state; inaugurated two statewide literary programs for students; created an "All Georgia Reading the Same Book" program in 2002, which brought thousands of readers to a discussion of one book; developed a "Georgia Top Twenty-Five" reading list; and assisted with the debut of a biannual state literary award.

The Georgia Center for the Book — one of fifty-one centers hosted by an academic or public institution in each state and Washington, D.C. — was the brainchild of Darro C. Willey, the director of the DeKalb County Public Library. The center was formally named an affiliate of the Center for the Book in 1997 and held its first meeting at the DeKalb library in early 1998. It is overseen by an executive director and an advisory council consisting of fifteen members from the worlds of academe, publishing, and libraries, along with three notable Georgia authors: Terry Kay, Tina McElroy Ansa, and Janisse Ray.

The center's most widely known activity is the "All Georgia Reading the Same Book" program, which was held in 2002. A panel of literary authorities, with public input, selected a list of twenty-five books that every resident should know by Georgia authors. From that list Janisse Ray's 1999 memoir *Ecology of a Cracker Childhood* was chosen to be read statewide. Bookstores provided support for the program, and Ray made appearances in half a dozen cities during the year. In 1999 the center cosponsored the first Lindberg Award at the University of Georgia, which was presented to Pat Conroy, a native of Atlanta. The award, named for poet and *Georgia Review* editor Stanley Lindberg, recognizes the distinguished literary accomplishments of Georgia authors.

Through its first six years, the center has collaborated on literary programs with a number of regional libraries and organizations as diverse as the Margaret Mitchell House in Atlanta, the Little White House in Warm Springs, the University of Georgia at Athens, and the DeKalb History Center in Decatur. It sponsors two literary competitions for middle and high school students: "Letters about Literature," in which students write essays to their favorite author describing the impact of the author's work on their lives, and "River of Words," an environmental essay contest developed with the Georgia Department of Natural Resources. Future projects include the creation of a literary map of Georgia and sponsorship of the annual Georgia Literary Festival.

WILLIAM W. STARR, *Georgia Center for the Book*

GEORGIA HUMORISTS

The Georgia humorists were early-nineteenth-century writers who published satiric sketches about the lawlessness and debauchery of frontier conditions in antebellum Georgia. Mostly lawyers, newspaper editors, and other professional men, they included Augustus Baldwin Longstreet (1790–1870), William Tappan Thompson (1812–82), and John Basil Lamar (1812–62). Lesser-known writers were T. A. Burke, T. W. Lane, and Francis James Robinson. More conservative than the later writers who followed the southwestern expansion of the frontier toward the Mississippi River (such Southwest humorists as Johnson Jones Hooper of Alabama, Thomas Bangs Thorpe of Louisiana, and George Washington Harris of Tennessee), the Georgia humorists strove to protect plantation society from further erosion by satirizing the earthiness, deceit, and violence of the frontier.

Drawing their topics from the events of everyday life, including hunts, fights, courtship and marriage, dances, horse races and other contests, militia drills, elections, the law and courts, religion, gambling, practical jokes, illness, drinking bouts, and the treatment of country bumpkins in the city, the Georgia humorists used the literary device of the frame to distance themselves and their readers from the harshness of life on the frontier. Longstreet, for example, created the narrators Abraham Baldwin and Lyman Hall, naming them in honor of two Yale-educated men who had provided Georgia with outstanding leadership in the more virtuous days of the early republic. Thompson, in his epistolary sketches and stories, used the first-person voice of his character Major Jones, a rustic farmer and homely philosopher, to comment on the customs and quirks of rural life in middle Georgia. Although Major Jones is not as refined as Longstreet's narrators, he represents the simple virtues of rural life, symbolizing the promise of social mobility through hard work and a good marriage.

Born in Augusta in 1790, Augustus Baldwin Longstreet was the dean of the Georgia humorists. Admitted to the Georgia bar in 1815, he settled into a successful life as a lawyer-farmer. After he was elected to the state legislature and named judge of the Superior Court of the Ocmulgee District, he stood for Congress in 1824, but the deaths of his eldest son and mother-in-law led him to abandon further efforts to win political office. After a long period of melancholy that culminated in a religious conversion, he returned to Augusta in 1827 and joined a prosperous legal practice. Drawing on his experiences of riding the circuit, he published several humor sketches in the Milledgeville *Southern Recorder*. He then purchased the Augusta newspaper *North American Gazette*, changed its name to the *State Rights Sentinel*, and began publishing additional sketches in 1834. The next year he published his collected sketches under the title of *Georgia Scenes* (1835); the book made his literary reputation.

Underlying all of the sketches of *Georgia Scenes* is the tension between town and country and the gradual emergence of social and moral controls over the violence and unrestrained behavior of the frontier. Law and order prevail, but it is a tenuous victory at best. Longstreet's comedic talents are most evident in his often-anthologized sketches "The Gander Pulling," "The Fight," and "The Horse-Swap." His patrician narrators are scandalized by such country recreations as pulling the head off a greased gander while riding by at a canter; settling differences of honor with a no-holds-barred, nose-biting, dirt-grinding fist fight; and hiding a horse's huge saddle sore so he can be offered up for trade. But the moralizing of the narrators does little to undermine the humor of the sketches, in which a character like Ransy Sniffle, a poor white dirt-eater who loves fights, listens in "breathless delight" as a local champion calls the wife of another a "sassy heifer," or a horse trader boasts that he can "outswap any live man, woman, or child that ever walked these hills" and gets a horse that is both "blind and *deef*" for his trouble.

Although his talent for comic exaggeration did not equal that of his mentor Longstreet, William Tappan Thompson's epistolary sketches and stories paint a realistic picture of southern rural life. Born in Ohio in 1812, Thompson moved to Augusta in 1834 or 1835 and studied law while managing Longstreet's printing establishment. When the Second Seminole War erupted (1835), Thompson enlisted in the Richmond Blues, a local militia unit. His militia experiences inspired two sketches, which he published in his literary periodical, the *Augusta Mirror*. When the *Mirror* merged with a Macon periodical Thompson served briefly as co-editor before moving to Madison to edit a weekly entitled the *Southern Miscellany*. Within two years he had established his reputation as a humorist with his character Major Jones. A collection of his Major Jones letters appeared in 1843, and an expanded edition was published the following year under the title *Major Jones's Courtship*. A revised edition in 1872 added two Major Jones letters and a series of sketches Thompson had published in periodicals in the late 1840s and early 1850s.

Most of the Major Jones letters deal with such topics as a coon hunt, a ride on a new railroad, the food at the Planter's Hotel in Madison, the trouble and confusion caused by the move into town from the plantation each winter, and the joys of hog-killing time, pulling "lasses" candy, and Christmas. Rustic, uneducated, and unfamiliar with the manners of polite society, Thompson's spokesman Major Jones is nevertheless generous, good-hearted, and sensible. Whiggish in his political sympathies, this uncommon common man communicates through his marriage to the polished Mary Stallins that the best hope of the South is unity among planters, small slaveholders, and yeoman farmers rather than an alliance with the commercial North.

Several other Georgia humorists are included in the anthology *Polly Peablossom's Wedding* (1851), edited by T. A. Burke. The author of the title sketch, John Basil Lamar, is the best known of these writers. Born in Milledgeville in 1812, Lamar was a substantial planter who lived near Macon. He owned holdings in thirteen Georgia counties and in Florida. Highly literate and well traveled, Lamar supported secession, joined the Confederate army, and was killed in the Battle of Crampton's Gap in Maryland in September 1862. His known literary canon consists of six sketches. "Polly Peablossom's Wedding" is a brief tale of a comic wedding that celebrates egalitarianism on the Georgia frontier. Another sketch by Lamar, "The 'Experience' of the Blacksmith of the Mountain Pass," recounts the conversion of a proud, free-thinking mountain artisan who is beaten in a fair fight by a Methodist circuit rider.

Burke's own contribution to the anthology, "A Losing Game of Poker; or, The Gambler Outwitted," follows the form of the moral disclaimer established by Longstreet: while the subject of the tale is gambling, drinking, and swindling, the narrator makes it clear that such behavior is no longer the social norm. Burke's anthology also includes a sketch by the Augusta author T. W. Lane, "The Thimble Game," about a country bumpkin in the city who is conned out of four hundred dollars by a "Gimbletman" (cotton buyer) in a shell game.

A final writer of interest is Francis James Robinson, who published a collection of seven humor sketches entitled *Kups of Kauphy: A Georgia Book in Warp and Woof* (1853). Little is known about Robinson except that he was a country doctor and newspaper writer who was born around 1820. Fiercely partisan toward the South before the Civil War, Robinson supported the Republican Party during Reconstruction and apparently died in Oglethorpe County in 1870. Several of the sketches in *Kups of Kauphy* show the influence of Longstreet and Thompson in theme, setting, and dialect. Robinson also incorporated a lengthy proslavery argument into the frame of one sketch that reveals the impact of the sectional crisis on the Georgia humor tradition.

Spokesmen for a social system that rejected the free labor assumptions of the North, the Georgia humorists initially dedicated many of their literary efforts to the cause of moral reform. The escalation of sectional conflict in the 1850s, however, made life more difficult for literary reformers in Georgia. Every agency of cultural expression was enlisted in the defense of plantation slavery as the secession crisis drew near.

MICHAEL E. PRICE, *Armstrong Atlantic State University*
CAROL M. ANDREWS, *Armstrong Atlantic State University*

SUGGESTED READING

Hennig Cohen and William B. Dillingham, eds., *Humor of the Old Southwest,* 3d ed. (1964; reprint, Athens: University of Georgia Press, 1994).

Robert L. Phillips Jr., "The Novel and the Romance in Middle Georgia Humor and Local Color: A Study of Narrative Method in the Works of Augustus Baldwin Longstreet, William Tappan Thompson, Richard Malcolm Johnston, and Joel Chandler Harris" (Ph.D. diss., University of North Carolina, 1971).

Michael E. Price, *Stories with a Moral: Literature and Society in Nineteenth-Century Georgia* (Athens: University of Georgia Press, 2000).

David Rachels, ed., *Augustus Baldwin Longstreet's Georgia Scenes Completed* (Athens: University of Georgia Press, 1998).

Hugh Ruppersburg, ed., *Georgia Voices: Fiction,* vol. 1 (Athens: University of Georgia Press, 1992).

GEORGIA LITERATURE COMMISSION

Georgia launched its first major campaign against obscene literature in 1953, when the General Assembly unanimously voted to establish the Georgia Literature Commission. The onset of the paperback book revolution in the years after World War II, the rising popularity of adult magazines, and the introduction of *Playboy* magazine in the United States led the legislature to create the commission, consisting of three members who would meet monthly to investigate literature that they suspected to be "detrimental to the morals of the citizens of Georgia." If the commission determined something to be obscene, it had the power to inhibit distribution by notifying the distributor and then, thirty days later, recommending prosecution by the proper prosecuting attorney. Governor Herman Talmadge appointed Atlanta minister James P. Wesberry, Royston newspaper publisher Hubert L. Dyar, and Greensboro theater owner William R. Boswell to serve four-year terms.

Most of the commission's early work was through a program of mutual cooperation with publishers, distributors, and retailers, although the commission became increasingly ineffective in its dealing with magazines, as it could prohibit distribution of a particular issue it found to be obscene but not any future issue. In late 1956 four out-of-state publishing companies sued the commission in federal district court on the grounds that the statute establishing the commission was unconstitutional. A special three-judge appellate panel ruled that the statute as correctly construed did not raise a constitutional question. Because the court concluded that the commission did not have any powers of censorship — the commission could only recommend to distributors that a publication not be sold or to prosecuting attorneys that a distributor be prosecuted — the suit was subsequently dismissed.

Through 1967 the commission was required to take legal action in only six instances. The beginning of the end of the commission's efforts came on August 19, 1966, when the commission sought and received a declaratory judgment in Muscogee County Superior Court that Alan Marshall's *Sin Whisper* (1965) was obscene. The Georgia Supreme Court also sided with the commission, concluding that the book was "filthy and disgusting." The unanimous opinion continued, "Further description is not necessary, and we do not wish to sully the pages of the reported opinions of this court with it." The U.S. Supreme Court, however, reversed the judgment without comment in a memorandum decision without any explanation of why the book was not obscene, without any comment about the standards applied by Georgia courts determining it to be obscene, and without any ruling on the constitutionality of the commission itself. Other books chosen for review by the commission were Erskine Caldwell's *God's Little Acre* (1933), J. D. Salinger's *Catcher in the Rye* (1951), Norman Mailer's *The Naked and the Dead* (1948), George H. Smith's *Strip Artist* (1964), and John Dexter's *Lust Avenger* (1965).

The commission ceased operations sometime after 1973, a victim of Governor Jimmy Carter's zero-based budgeting system, which required state agencies to justify their existence each fiscal year. Coupled with his and successive governors' failure to appoint replacements for the two commission members who died that year, the agency was thereafter unable to conduct business.

GREGORY C. LISBY, *Georgia State University*

SUGGESTED READING

Gregory C. Lisby, "'Trying to Define What May Be Indefinable': The Georgia Literature Commission, 1953–1973," *Georgia Historical Quarterly* 84 (spring 2000): 72–97.

In 1932 the radical journalist John Spivak published *Georgia Nigger*, a thinly fictionalized condemnation of Georgia's penal system that unveiled the harsh working conditions and brutal treatment suffered by African Americans in the state's convict camps. Walter White, the executive secretary of the National Association for the Advancement of Colored People (NAACP), described Spivak's novel as "the most devastating exposé of the treatment of Negroes in the Georgia chaingang that has ever been written." Nevertheless, *Georgia Nigger* was ultimately overshadowed by Robert Elliot Burns's *I Am a Fugitive from a Georgia Chain Gang!*, which was published the same year.

In 1930, when visiting the Georgia Prison Commission office in Atlanta, Spivak, a documentary reporter known for his investigative journalism during the Great Depression, surreptitiously photographed the "whipping reports" that detailed the punishment of convict labor on the road gangs. In response to a letter of introduction he obtained from the commission, camp wardens allowed him to document their skill in torturing recalcitrant prisoners. By 1930 Georgia had more than 8,000 convicts scattered in chain gangs that worked on the roads in 116 counties; three-quarters of these prisoners were black. Failure to meet the demands of hard labor resulted in a whipping with a strap, the stretching of arms with a rope tied to a post, or confinement in a "sweat box." Spivak documented these torments with photographs that accompany his novel. "America would not believe what I would say unless I could prove it with visual evidence," he later wrote in his autobiography.

Fiction it may have been, but the *New York Times* found *Georgia Nigger* to have "the weight and authority of a sociological investigation." During the 1920s Spivak had supported himself by writing for pulp-fiction magazines, learning in the process to embellish single facts into gripping stories. In *Georgia Nigger* he combined the style of pulp fiction with the radical documentary journalism of the 1930s, a form of writing he would use again in works like *America Faces the Barricades* (1935), which dealt with unions and labor relations.

Like many other works of "proletarian fiction" about the South in the 1930s, *Georgia Nigger* focuses on "the tenant farmer, hard working, but doomed to poverty," in the words of the poet Sterling Brown. The fatalistic novel tells the story of David Jackson, a black sharecropper's son who finds himself caught between serving a chain-gang sentence and working in peonage for a planter willing to pay his fine. Returning home after a six-month stint on the chain gang, Jackson is caught on a Saturday night in a sheriff's dragnet launched at the behest of Jim Deering, the most powerful planter in the fictional Ochlockonee County. Faced with a long wait in jail before the next court session, Jackson accepts Deering's offer to pay his fine as an advance against wages. But after witnessing Deering murder another peon, Jackson flees. He is instantly picked up as a vagrant in the neighboring county and hauled into court; this time he chooses to work the roads for the county rather than return to the peon farm. The book ends with another failed escape attempt; Jackson is sentenced to a cruel spell in the "sweat box," which confined convicts for a full day in an enclosed space under the blazing Georgia sun.

Georgia Nigger found an audience among both left-wing activists and mainstream readers. Spivak serialized his story in the Communist Party's newspaper, the *Daily Worker*, and it also appeared in the *Des Moines* (Iowa) *Tribune* and the *Milwaukee* (Wisc.) *Journal*. Published in England and translated into French, German, and Russian, *Georgia Nigger* won Spivak renown in international left-wing circles in the 1930s. The book, along with the Atlanta trial of the African American communist Angelo Herndon in 1933, helped make the Georgia chain gang an often-cited example of southern racial injustice during the Great Depression.

Despite widespread serialization, favorable reviews, endorsement by the NAACP, and Spivak's efforts to promote the book through the black press, the black church, and bookstore and lecture appearances, *Georgia Nigger* was eclipsed by Burns's *I Am a Fugitive from a Georgia Chain Gang!* Burns's story became the basis of a movie, and it was Hollywood's popular version of social injustice that cast a national spotlight on the abuses of Georgia's chain gangs, not Spivak's more realistic documentary account. Unlike *I Am a Fugitive*, Spivak's exposé asked Americans to confront the racial caste system that made the brutalities of the chain gang possible, something all too few were willing to do at the time.

ALEX LICHTENSTEIN, *Rice University, Houston, Texas*

SUGGESTED READING

Alex Lichtenstein, "Georgia History in Fiction: Chain Gangs, Communism, and the 'Negro Question,'" *Georgia Historical Quarterly* 79 (fall 1995).

Jeanne Perreault, "Chain Gang Narratives and the Politics of 'Speaking For,'" *Biography* 24 (winter 2001).

John L. Spivak, *A Man in His Time* (New York: Horizon, 1967).

GEORGIA POETRY SOCIETY

The Georgia State Poetry Society was founded by Edward Davin Vickers and Charles J. Bruehler on August 30, 1979, in Atlanta. Its objectives were to stimulate the reading and writing of poetry. The society was incorporated in 1981 and later changed its name to the Georgia Poetry Society.

The society is a member of the National Federation of State Poetry Societies (NFSPS). The NFSPS is a nonprofit educational and literary organization that seeks to recognize the importance of poetry in America's cultural heritage, to further the appreciation of poetry on a national level, and to unite poets in the bond of fellowship. Both the NFSPS and the Georgia Poetry Society are nonprofit, nonpolitical, nonsectarian organizations open for membership to anyone who is interested. The national convention was hosted by the Georgia chapter in June 1999 in Atlanta.

Georgia Poetry Society membership meetings are held in the months of January, April, July, and October in cities throughout the state. Agenda items include readings by members and distinguished guests, workshops, guest speakers, book reviews, publishers' panels, networking, and recognition of contest winners. National Poetry Day and National Poetry Month are celebrated each year. Speakers have included Evan Boland, Bettie Sellers, Ha Jin, Donna Harper, Beverly Head, Phebe Davidson, Thelma Hall, Memye Tucker, Janice Moore, Judith Ortiz Cofer, and Ron Colombe, among others.

The society sponsors several poetry contests each year. The Byron Herbert Reece International Award is the most important among them. Regular publications of the society include *The Reach of Song*, an anthology of society members' poetry, and *Georgia Poetry News*, a newsletter. The winning manuscript in the Dickson Chapbook Contest is also published. The Poetry in the Schools Program is a major Georgia Poetry Society outreach effort. The program sponsors poetry reading and writing workshops for students and teachers in public, private, and parochial schools.

HERBERT W. DENMARK, *Georgia Poetry Society*

SUGGESTED READING

Georgia State Poetry Society, *The Reach of Song* (Atlanta: Georgia State Poetry Society, annual).

Poetry in Motion: Award Winning Poems in the Coca-Cola 1996 Centennial Olympic Games Poetry Contest (Atlanta: Georgia State Poetry Society, 1996).

THE GEORGIA REVIEW

The *Georgia Review* is an internationally distributed quarterly journal of arts and letters featuring general interest and interdisciplinary essays as well as short stories, poems, book reviews, and full-color visual art. First published in 1947 at the University of Georgia (UGA) and based there to the present day, this highly regarded literary periodical has published such notable past and current authors as Conrad Aiken, Harry Crews, Rita Dove, William Faulkner, Robert Frost, Ernest J. Gaines, Joyce Carol Oates, Anne Sexton, Robert Penn Warren, and Eudora Welty. At the same time, the *Review* has earned a reputation for being open and encouraging to lesser-known and even unpublished writers.

Founded by UGA English professor John Donald Wade, the *Georgia Review* was initially intended to be confined "to topics that bear somewhat closely upon the history, literature, art, education and social activities" of the state. Wade maintained this editorial perspective throughout his tenure as editor (1947–50), as did his two immediate successors, John Olin Eidson (1950–57) and William Wallace Davidson (1957–68). Although the journal's scope and reach inevitably broadened somewhat over its first two decades, James Colvert (1968–72) was the editor who purposefully set his sights on moving the *Review* toward national recognition in its field, and his larger ambitions were taken to heart by all the subsequent editors: Edward Krickel (1972–74), John T. Irwin (1974–77), Stanley Lindberg (1977–99), Stephen Corey (2000–2001), and T. R. Hummer (2002–present).

Since the 1980s, the *Georgia Review* has been widely considered to be among the finest literary publications in the United States, with work from its pages regularly reprinted in such leading annuals as *The Best American Short Stories* and *The Pushcart Prize*. Perhaps even more impressive are the nearly twenty finalist nominations the *Review* has received in the National Magazine

Awards competition, where the journal competes against not only other literary publications but also such large-circulation magazines as the *New Yorker*, the *Atlantic Monthly*, and *Harper's*.

In 1986 the *Review* marked its fortieth anniversary of continuous publication with two oversized retrospective issues featuring the best short stories (spring) and the best poems (fall) from the journal's first four decades. These gatherings, edited by Lindberg and Corey, subsequently came out in book form from the University of Georgia Press as *Necessary Fictions: Selected Stories from the Georgia Review* (1986) and *Keener Sounds: Selected Poems from the Georgia Review* (1987). Also in 1986, the *Review* won the National Magazine Award in Fiction with stories by Lee K. Abbott, Gary Gildner, and Mary Hood.

A double issue (winter 2001 / spring 2002) offered a retrospective of essays from the *Georgia Review*'s first half century, including work from Jacques Barzun (1952), Robert Graves (1962), Harold Bloom (1975), Raymond Carver (1983), Donald Barthelme (1985), Eavan Boland (1990), Albert Goldbarth (1992), Barry Lopez and Louise Erdrich (both 1993), and N. Scott Momaday (1996), as well as a posthumous offering from Randall Jarrell (1996).

During Lindberg's years as editor, the *Georgia Review* initiated several major literary conferences: in 1985 "Roots in Georgia" brought nearly two dozen Georgia-born writers to Athens for several days of readings, talks, and panel discussions. Among those on the program were Erskine Caldwell, James Dickey, Mary Hood, James Kilgo, and John Oliver Killens. In 1995, at Lindberg's suggestion and in conjunction with the 1996 Olympic Games, the Carter Center in Atlanta hosted "The Nobel Laureates of Literature: An Olympic Gathering." This landmark event brought onto one stage eight Nobel laureates of literature — more than had ever before been together. In 1997 the *Review* celebrated its fiftieth anniversary in Athens with a festival that invited all past contributors to visit and participate. Across three days, nearly fifty writers took the podium of the UGA Chapel.

The *Georgia Review* continues to publish outstanding writing in several genres by both established and new literary artists, and its long-standing national and international reputations seem secure.

STEPHEN D. COREY, *The Georgia Review*

GEORGIA WRITERS ASSOCIATION

The Georgia Writers Association formed in 1994 as a nonprofit support and advocacy group for writers in the state. As its mission, "The Georgia Writers Association seeks to improve the quality of life for writers by providing information about the literary industry and skills-building knowledge; fostering ongoing communication among writers of diverse literacy, genres, geographies, ethnicities, and backgrounds; increasing public awareness of the lives and works of contemporary Georgia writers; encouraging the imagination and integrity of the written word; and organizing activities that celebrate the achievements of writers across the state of Georgia." The association sponsors conferences, seminars, monthly meetings in several cities, writing contests, and a Web-based bimonthly journal, the *Georgia Writers News/Mag* (http://www.georgiawriters.org/NewsMag.html).

Especially noteworthy among the association's activities are the annual Georgia Author of the Year awards, first given in 1964 by the Dixie Council of Authors and Journalists. The Georgia Writers Association assumed responsibility for the awards shortly after its founding. According to the association's Web site the awards are presented to "recognize and acknowledge Georgia's wealth of outstanding writers and to acquaint them with the public and one another, thus continuing our literary heritage." Commercially as well as independently published authors are eligible. Awards are presented in a variety of categories, including poetry, fiction, biography, memoir, history, essay, self-help, first novel, and children's literature. Judges select award winners from a list of nominees on the basis of such criteria as creativity, style, craft, and enduring value.

Awards are announced and presented at a banquet each spring at the Georgia Institute of Technology. Winners of the awards for works published in 2005 included Bruce Feiler for *Where God*

Was Born: Journey by Land to the Roots of Religion (creative nonfiction), Steve Suitts for *Hugo Black of Alabama* (biography), Jimmy Carter for *Our Endangered Values: America's Moral Crisis* (essay), James C. Cobb for *The Brown Decision, Jim Crow, and Southern Identity* (history), David Fulmer for *Jass* (fiction), and Brian Jay Corrigan for *The Poet of Loch Ness* (first novel).

Among the activities recently sponsored by the association was the Sixth Annual Spring Festival for Writers and Readers, held in Smyrna. Workshops taught by writers, publishers, teachers, and editors covered a variety of topics.

The Georgia Writers Association is sponsored by and housed at Kennesaw State University.

HUGH RUPPERSBURG, *University of Georgia*

GEORGIA WRITERS HALL OF FAME

As part of the University of Georgia's Year 2000 millennial celebration, the University Libraries established the Georgia Writers Hall of Fame — a public awards program and a permanent Internet exhibit honoring Georgia's most influential writers.

The mission of the Georgia Writers Hall of Fame is "to recognize Georgia writers, past and present, whose work reflects the character of the state — its land and its people. Although there are a few award programs in the state that recognize specific books, the Georgia Writers Hall of Fame is the first to honor Georgia writers for their overall contribution to our culture."

The organizers also conceived the Hall of Fame as a library reference, or "gateway," program. The annual induction process and the corresponding Internet Hall of Fame exhibit are designed to introduce interested groups to the university's unparalleled collections of Georgia literature and literary source materials.

The Hall of Fame online presence includes a virtual pantheon or "cyberhall" of digital portraits, capsule biographies, and bibliographies of the authors' published works. These lists of published works are compiled from the catalogs of the Hargrett Rare Book and Manuscript Library. The staff manages the nomination process of the Georgia Writers Hall of Fame awards program.

The program annually solicits nominations from the public and turns the eligible nominations over to a board of volunteer judges, which consists of twelve to twenty academics, civic leaders, librarians, and publishing professionals selected for rotating three-year terms by the director of the University of Georgia Libraries, who also chairs the board. To be eligible for nomination a writer "must have been either a native of Georgia or have produced a significant work during or subsequent to a substantial time of work and/or residence in Georgia."

The Hall of Fame officially opened in April 2000. At that time the board of judges selected a charter membership of twelve famous writers from Georgia's history. Since then, judges have convened annually to select two new members from among the nominations.

As of 2006 the Georgia Writers Hall of Fame includes Conrad Aiken (1889–1973), Elias Boudinot (ca. 1804–39), Erskine Caldwell (1903–87), Jimmy Carter (b. 1924), Pat Conroy (b. 1945), Harry Crews (b. 1935), James Dickey (1923–97), W. E. B. Du Bois (1868–1963), Henry W. Grady (1850–89), Joel Chandler Harris (1845–1908), Terry Kay (b. 1938), John Oliver Killens (1916–87), Martin Luther King Jr. (1929–68), Sidney Lanier (1842–81), Augustus Baldwin Longstreet (1790–1870), Carson McCullers (1917–67), Ralph McGill (1898–1969), Margaret Mitchell (1900–1949), Flannery O'Connor (1925–64), Byron Herbert Reece (1917–58), Lillian Smith (1897–1966), Jean Toomer (1894–1967), Alice Walker (b. 1944), and Frank Yerby (1916–1991).

From the time of their selection, all living writers are invited to serve three-year terms as ex officio members of the board of judges.

KEITH HULETT, *University of Georgia Libraries*

SUGGESTED READING

Hugh Ruppersburg, ed., *Georgia Voices*, 3 vols. (Athens: University of Georgia Press, 1992–2000).

Although Erskine Caldwell wrote more than sixty books, twenty-five novels among them, he is best known for two works of long fiction, *Tobacco Road* (1932) and *God's Little Acre* (1933). *God's Little Acre* remains Caldwell's single most popular work, having sold more than ten million copies. Along with the less well-known *Journeyman* (1935), these books make up a seriocomic trilogy of Georgia life in the first half of the twentieth century. They detail the ruination of the land, the growth of textile mills, and the abiding influence of fundamentalist religion in the South. They present a radical contrast to the traditionally genteel and romantic views of the region, popularized most notably by Margaret Mitchell in *Gone With the Wind* (1936).

God's Little Acre was published by Viking Press in 1933, one year after *Tobacco Road*, which focused on the plight of poor white farmers during the Depression. In *God's Little Acre*, Caldwell shifts his sights to the industrialized South. Influenced in part by the textile mill strikes in Gastonia, North Carolina, he considered this work to be a "proletarian" novel dealing with the plight of workers deprived of union protection. It was intended to support these mill hands, or "lintheads," as they were sometimes called. Will Thompson, who leads the strike, represents both the inherent power and the frustration of the working class. When Thompson is killed by guards as he attempts to reopen the mill shut down by its ruthless owners, his death becomes a rallying cry; and his corpse is borne through the streets, but the mills remain closed.

The book also examines the misuse of the land and other natural resources. Ty Ty Walden, who (unlike Jeeter Lester) still owns his farm, spends his time digging for gold instead of farming the rich soil. His delusion and the tragedy it brings to his family again illustrate the waste Caldwell saw in southern attitudes toward the land.

Like *Tobacco Road*, *God's Little Acre* contains scenes of explicit sexuality. In April 1933 the New York Society for the Suppression of Vice took Caldwell and Viking Press to court for dissemination of pornography. More than sixty authors, editors, and literary critics rallied in support of the book, and Judge Benjamin Greenspan of the New York Magistrates Court ruled in its favor. The court case is still considered a major decision in the establishment of artists' First Amendment rights in freedom of expression. The book became a worldwide best-seller and remains today one of the most popular novels ever published.

In 1958 director Anthony Mann and screenwriter Phillip Yordan, in collaboration with Caldwell, made the film version of *God's Little Acre*, starring Robert Ryan as Ty Ty Walden and Aldo Ray as Will Thompson. The film, like the book, was considered scandalous and became one of the top-grossing movies for that year. Truer to its source than John Ford's *Tobacco Road* had been, *God's Little Acre* remains the best representation of Caldwell on film.

EDWIN T. ARNOLD, *Appalachian State University, Boone, North Carolina*

SUGGESTED READING

Edwin T. Arnold, ed., *Conversations with Erskine Caldwell* (Jackson: University Press of Mississippi, 1988).

Sylvia Jenkins Cook, *Erskine Caldwell and the Fiction of Poverty: The Flesh and the Spirit* (Baton Rouge: Louisiana State University Press, 1991).

Robert L. McDonald, ed., *The Critical Response to Erskine Caldwell* (Westport, Conn.: Greenwood Press, 1997).

Dan B. Miller, *Erskine Caldwell: The Journey from Tobacco Road. A Biography* (New York: Knopf, 1995).

Wayne Mixon, *The People's Writer: Erskine Caldwell and the South* (Charlottesville: University Press of Virginia, 1995).

GONE WITH THE WIND

Atlantan Margaret Mitchell's 1936 novel of the Civil War and Reconstruction in Georgia, *Gone With the Wind*, occupies an important place in any history of twentieth-century American literature. Dismissed by most academic literary critics for being uneven, flawed, and conventionally written in an age marked by literary experimentation, and attacked by some cultural commentators as promulgating racist myths and undermining the very foundations of its basically feminist paradigm, the bestselling novel of the twentieth century continues to withstand its detractors.

Upon its publication, reviewers drew comparisons with William Makepeace Thackeray's *Vanity Fair* and Leo Tolstoy's *War and Peace*. Margaret Mitchell claimed not to have read Thackeray's novel until after she had completed her Civil War saga and confessed her inability ever to get very far in Tolstoy's monumental work. She did admit her saturation in Charles Dickens and her sense that her work was a "'Victorian' type novel." Mitchell chose an epic moment in American history and never flinched in bringing it to life on a grand scale; a creative energy reminiscent of the nineteenth century drives the work. From the memorable first sentence through the Twelve Oaks barbecue on the eve of the war, the fall of Atlanta, Scarlett O'Hara's unforgettable journey back home to Tara, and her beginning struggles during Reconstruction, Mitchell's narrative power (at the very top of its form) propels the reader through the limning of a culture (its grace and color and folly and weakness), a vivid evocation of the cauldron of war, and a bitter picture of the devastation following.

The author spoke often of her research in accounts and memoirs of the period, but probably more important was her knowing people who had lived through the era. A child naturally drawn to old people and to the great drama of her region, Mitchell had gone horseback riding with Confederate veterans, sat listening in the parlors of faded belles, and taken every literary advantage of her exposure to the past. The result is a Balzacian sense of the texture of the period — Scarlett O'Hara's green morocco slippers, the bright rag rugs in her bedroom at Tara, Melanie Hamilton's black lace mittens — that leads to the capturing of color and movement in great scenes like the Twelve Oaks barbecue and the ball in Atlanta. Alternating with such scenes are remarkably evocative descriptions of the languorous beauty of the landscape.

Though her four major characters have now become stereotypes, when she drew them, with the exception of the Byronic Rhett Butler, they were not. Scarlett is a full-blooded woman, selfish, deluded, conflicted, but driven by her own strength of will. Melanie is far from the foolishly duped Amelia of Thackeray's novel; underlying her sweetness and Christian charity is enormous strength and purpose. And the Hamlet-like Ashley Wilkes is not the beau ideal of the southern planter or Confederate stalwart.

Mitchell's upland Georgia is also not the dreamy land of a Thomas Nelson Page plantation novel. She is insightful on the social structure, its closeness to pioneer days, and its mixture of old blood lines and new men. She is astute about the violence lying not far submerged beneath the surface of all classes. She is unsentimental about the Lost Cause, tracing its origins to unreconstructed women, not to the men who fought the war. And she is remarkably good as a novelist of manners, understanding the mores and shibboleths of the culture she is examining and bringing them skillfully into play.

Like many of the omnibus novels of the nineteenth century that influenced it, *Gone With the Wind* is a powerful, flawed, uneven, and sometimes disturbing novel that explores diverse facets of the human experience.

The novel also contains the stuff of great romance. Two great loves — one a misplaced, deluded infatuation, and the other a thwarted union of two passionate spirits — share equal focus with the story of people swept along by the forces of history. Additionally, the novel is sexually charged. Scarlett's Bovaristic attraction to Ashley could not be sustained were she not given proof at two significant points in the novel that he responds to her sexually, that he wants, in his own phrase, to "take" her. The powerful sexual chemistry dramatized between Scarlett and Rhett provides a running tension of the novel, countered as it is by Scarlett's incredibly dogged and willful attachment to her first romantic ideal. It is testimony to Mitchell's skill that these basic sexual and emotional tensions could be sustained for 1,037 pages in the original Macmillan edition.

Mitchell's *Gone With the Wind* is one of the great novels of survival, and therein lies much of its appeal. In chapter 43 Mitchell gives to Rhett Butler a version of the speech that we know now her own mother had given her when she was a child. He is speaking, in the war's aftermath, about Ashley Wilkes: "Whenever the world up-ends, his kind is the first to perish. And why not? They don't deserve to survive because they won't fight — don't know how to fight. This isn't the first time the world's been upside down and it won't be the last. . . . But there are always a hardy few who come through and, given time, they are right back where they were before the world turned over." The Darwinian message is made flesh in Scarlett O'Hara. But Mitchell is clear-sighted enough to see that a moral and emotional price is often paid for survival against great odds. That fact is borne out in a number of ways in the novel's conclusion.

Mitchell also wrote a distinctly feminist novel. She sounds the note early with the narrator's comment that "at no time, before or since, had so low a premium been placed on feminine naturalness," and she mercilessly exposes a southern patriarchy that requires that women be flatteringly subservient to males, no matter how much less intelligent and capable. But even more telling than its overtly repeated feminist message, it is a novel dominated by strong women — Scarlett, Melanie, Ellen O'Hara, Mrs. Tarleton, Grandma Fontaine, Mrs. Meade, and Mammy. Mitchell takes

pains to show the spine of a southern matriarchy secretly underlying a patriarchy.

Some critics have argued that Scarlett's feminist success story
is undercut by a sexual desire to be engulfed and dominated.
Mitchell does problematize human sexuality. Ashley Wilkes's
own fear of being passionately released but then engulfed and
dominated by Scarlett is a case in point. "You would want all of
a man," he laments. In Mitchell's failure to bend sexual desire
to some clinically theorized, balanced, emotionally healthy paradigm, she is a modern.

The inherent racism of the novel is more difficult to defend.
Characteristic of her generation of southerners is Mitchell's un-
questioning acceptance of the essential inferiority of African
Americans, whom she presents, in a few distasteful instances, in
nonhuman terms. Melded with that prejudice, contradictorily,
comes great respect for some members of the race. Such a bifur-
cated vision is the very dilemma that Mississippi author William
Faulkner wrestled with his entire writing career. In the novel
Mitchell merely accepts the institution of slavery and fails to recognize the strength and courage of those who rebelled against
their status as slaves.

What she presents well is an array of portraits of an unlettered
African American peasantry, ranging from the nobility, shrewd-
ness, loyalty, and affection of Mammy to the foolishness of Prissy.
Like William Shakespeare, Mitchell has her fools among all
classes. No one has yet criticized her portrayal of Honey Wilkes.
Margaret Mitchell was proud of the fact that she had tried to
convey accurately the speech of the old African Americans of her
acquaintance without resorting to the entangled dialect of Joel
Chandler Harris, and she reacted against all the stock figures,
white and black, of the sentimental plantation novels that preceded *Gone With the Wind*.

Mitchell is most open to criticism in the last third of the novel.
The narrative drive diminishes, returning only in fits and starts.
Historical background is too often telegraphed, rather than
blended, into the fabric of the novel. And Mitchell appears to

succumb to a nightmare vision of white female purity under attack by black bestiality only to be saved by the Ku Klux Klan. The model here, which Mitchell halfway acknowledges in a letter, is Thomas Dixon's racist novel *The Clansman* (1905), made into what is often regarded as the first masterpiece of American cinema, *The Birth of a Nation*, in 1915 — both works lying solidly behind the reemergence of the Klan in the twentieth century.

Mitchell's conflicted sensibility is apparent when she has Scarlett comment about one such incident, "Probably the girl hadn't been raped after all. Probably she'd just been frightened silly." And she has Scarlett deliberately and foolishly expose herself to danger, against all advice, by her stubborn drive through Shantytown, where the homeless and desperate have collected. And even though the black man's assault upon her seems closer to a robbery than a rape attempt — still by introducing the situation of the imperiled white female threatened by the powerful black man and the resulting Klan vengeance, Mitchell's novel invites the same criticism heaped on Dixon's work.

With its richly detailed evocation of a former age, its narrative engagement, its compelling portrait of the archetypal human instinct for survival, and its reflection of the contrariness of romantic dreams, *Gone With the Wind* continues to capture entertain, excite, and sometimes exasperate readers. As well as being a gripping novel of epic proportions, it is valuable as a historical document — though one that must be carefully read. A vivid record of a segment of life in the nineteenth-century South, the novel is also the record of a twentieth-century sensibility's engagement with the region's past.

HUBERT H. McALEXANDER, *University of Georgia*

Richard Harwell, ed., *Margaret Mitchell's "Gone With the Wind" Letters, 1936–1949* (New York: Macmillan, 1976).

Anne Goodwyn Jones, *Tomorrow Is Another Day: The Woman Writer in the South, 1859–1936* (Baton Rouge: Louisiana State University Press, 1981).

Claudia Roth Pierpont, "A Critic at Large: A Study in Scarlett," *New Yorker*, August 31, 1992, 87–103.

Darden Asbury Pyron, *Southern Daughter: The Life of Margaret Mitchell* (New York: Oxford University Press, 1991).

HENRY W. GRADY

(1850–1889)

Henry W. Grady, the "Spokesman of the New South," served as managing editor for the *Atlanta Constitution* in the 1880s. A member of the Atlanta Ring of Democratic political leaders, Grady used his office and influence to promote a New South program of northern investment, southern industrial growth, diversified farming, and white supremacy.

Henry Woodfin Grady was born on May 24, 1850, in Athens. His father, William S. Grady, a successful merchant who served as a major in the Confederate army, died in the fall of 1864 from wounds received at the siege of Petersburg. Brought up after his father's death by his mother, Anne Gartrell Grady, young Grady showed talent as a writer and debater. After graduating from the University of Georgia, he briefly studied literature and history at the University of Virginia in Charlottesville before returning to Georgia in 1869 to pursue a career in journalism.

Grady first wrote for the *Rome Courier* before its bankruptcy in 1871. After marrying Julia King of Athens, he shared ownership with Robert Alston and Alexander St. Clair Adams of the *Atlanta Daily Herald*. On March 14, 1874, Grady published an editorial in the *Herald* entitled "The New South," in which he advocated industrial development as a solution to the postwar South's economic and social troubles. His aggressive, no-nonsense writing style and promotion of railroad development in Atlanta brought him to the attention of Evan P. Howell and W. A. Hemphill, major stockholders of the *Atlanta Constitution*. Howell offered Grady one-fourth ownership of the newspaper for the price of twenty thousand dollars, along with the position of managing editor. Grady enthusiastically accepted both offers.

As managing editor Grady quickly turned the *Constitution* into a platform for endorsing his own political views. He wrote in support of antiliquor laws, the construction of a new library, and care for Confederate veterans. Between 1880 and 1886 the *Constitution* also became the primary instrument of the Atlanta Ring, a loosely connected group of urban, proindustry Democrats that included Howell and Grady. Grady became the group's leader and dominant political force, helping to arrange the legislature's election of a fellow Ring member, Joseph E. Brown, to the U.S. Senate in 1880.

In 1883 Grady orchestrated the throwing of party votes toward Henry D. McDaniel's nomination for governor. When McDaniel refused to run again in 1886, challenges emerged from rival Democrats centered in Macon. Grady supported Ring member John B. Gordon for the party's nomination, using the *Constitution* to coax voters with promotional articles and speeches. Despite the Macon coalition's support from local newspapers, Grady's politicking won Gordon's election as governor.

With the Atlanta Ring's influence in Georgia politics firmly established, Grady turned his attention toward promoting the city's economic development. Invited to speak at the 1886 meeting of the New England Society in New York City, Grady preached the promises of a New South. Though the idea was not original with Grady, his advocacy of unity and trust between the North and South helped to spur northern investment in Atlanta industries.

Upon returning to Atlanta, Grady published in the *Constitution* numerous articles proclaiming the superiority of Atlanta for its diversified small industry and "willing" labor force. Grady infuriated competitors in Augusta, Macon, and Athens with these claims, but his promotional efforts brought results. In 1887 he successfully lobbied for the establishment in Atlanta of the Georgia Institute of Technology, a state school devoted to vocational and industrial education. In 1881 and 1887 Atlanta hosted the International Cotton Exposition, an industrial fair that attracted millions of investment dollars and provided new jobs to the city's growing population.

Despite such achievements, Grady's New South was not universally accepted. Agrarian pundit Thomas E. Watson criticized Grady for allegedly submitting Georgia to northern interests and oppressing farmers. Farmers likewise ignored Grady's advice to raise other crops alongside cotton for additional revenue and higher cotton prices. Grady also struggled to portray a benign racial climate for northerners interested in southern industrial investment but troubled by the region's oppressive racial order. In numerous *Constitution* editorials Grady claimed that African Americans enjoyed "fair treatment" in Georgia and throughout the South. Though such rhetoric pleased white southern readers, few northern reformers looked past the region's record of black disfranchisement, exploitation, and violence.

Grady's attempts to affix northern interests to the city he loved were cut short by his sudden death in Atlanta on December 23, 1889. Nevertheless, his influence as the spokesman of the New South was extensive, providing both the political framework and the rhetorical motivation for Atlanta as a burgeoning symbol of the New South.

Grady was inducted into the Georgia Writers Hall of Fame in 2005.

DARREN GREM, *University of Georgia*

SUGGESTED READING

Ferald J. Bryan, *Henry Grady or Tom Watson? The Rhetorical Struggle for the New South, 1880–1890* (Macon, Ga.: Mercer University Press, 1994).

Harold E. Davis, *Henry Grady's New South: Atlanta, a Brave Beautiful City* (Tuscaloosa: University of Alabama Press, 1990).

Joel Chandler Harris, *Joel Chandler Harris's Life of Henry W. Grady Including His Writings and Speeches* (New York: Cassell, 1890).

Raymond B. Nixon, *Henry W. Grady: Spokesman of the New South* (New York: Russell and Russell, 1943).

JULIEN GREEN
(1900–1998)

J ulien Green, novelist, autobiographer, dramatist, critic, and first non-French national elected to the Académie Française (1971), was greatly attached to his American nationality and to his roots in Georgia. A large section of his writing constitutes a quest for identity by an American living abroad in France.

Green was born in Paris of American parents; his mother was from Savannah, Georgia, his father from Virginia. He was baptized Julien Hartridge Green in honor of his maternal grandfather, Georgia Congressman Julian Hartridge. His paternal grandfather, Charles Green, from Halesowen, England, attained great wealth in the cotton industry in Savannah, where his magnificent Tudor-style mansion, the Green-Meldrim House, was completed in 1861.

Green's father, Edward, had a bent for speculation that led to financial losses and the acceptance of a post with a cotton agency in Le Havre, France, where he already had business contacts. The family left for Le Havre in 1893 and moved in 1897 to Paris, where their eighth child, Julien, was born on September 6, 1900. Julien's childhood was imbued with his mother's Civil War stories and her regret that the South had lost the war. This created in Green a nostalgia for his Georgian roots and a sense of exile, a prominent theme in his novels. His mother died when he was fourteen, and he was converted to Catholicism at sixteen. In 1919 he thought of becoming a Benedictine monk but later abandoned the idea.

During World War I, Green enlisted in the American Field Service in 1917 and later transferred to the French Foreign Legion and then to the regular French army. After the war, in 1919, he left for America to enroll at the University of Virginia, where he studied Latin, Greek, English literature, history, German, and elementary Spanish.

This was a significant period in his career. On the level of his quest for identity, he became acquainted with various family relatives in Savannah and elsewhere. On a personal level there was his encounter with a man whom he called Mark. This platonic relationship left Green burdened with his inability to express his love for Mark. Many of Green's characters share this trait. He also discovered his homosexuality, which intensified his inner religious struggle between flesh and spirit, sin and grace. This conflict constitutes the central drama of his main works. Ultimately, Green's homosexuality led him to reject Catholicism, and he did not rejoin the church until 1939.

Green published his first literary work, a short story, "The Apprentice Psychiatrist," in the *University of Virginia Magazine* in May 1920. In the 1920s he continued to write short stories, some of them set in Savannah. He also wrote an important article on Joyce's *Ulysses* that was published in the review *Philosophies* in May 1924. It was around this time that he began the writing of his journal, an activity that was to engage him all his life. The entries written in Virginia contain the embryo of his novels of the 1940s. Green returned to France in 1922, but he visited America again in the 1930s and spent the World War II years there as well.

Green's first novel, *Mont-Cinère* (1926; published in English as Avarice House), occurs in Virginia on the property of Kinloch, owned by one of Green's relatives. Set twenty-three years after the end of the Civil War, the novel focuses on a mother and daughter who live in an atmosphere of tension, resentment, and greed. His novels of the 1930s and 1940s deal with family relationships, violence, the quest for identity, and escape into the fantastic and the world of dreams. The main novels of these years are *Epaves* (1932; *The Strange River*), *Le visionnaire* (1934; *The Dreamer*), *Minuit* (1936; *Midnight*), and *Si j'étais vous* (1947; *If I Were You*). Green's interest in eastern mysticism, which developed during the 1930s, is especially evident in such novels of the 1940s as *Varouna* (1940; *Then Shall the Dust Return*) and *Si j'étais vous*, both of which, according to critic John M. Dunaway, concern the migration of souls.

Green's masterpiece is undoubtedly *Moïra* (1950; published in English under the same title), an autobiographical novel set at the University of Virginia and dominated by the conflict between flesh and spirit, sin and grace. His next novel, *Chaque homme dans sa nuit* (1960; *Each in His Darkness*), is partly set in the Wormsloe Historic Site near Savannah and presents a more positive vision of Catholicism.

The culmination of Green's quest for his Georgian roots is his series of novels on the Civil War, "the Dixie trilogy," written in the 1980s and 1990s. Here Green gives full vent to his passion for the South in a vivid and sometimes sentimental evocation of life in Savannah before and during the Civil War.

Green's journal stretches from 1928 to 1996 and deals with a wide variety of topics, including the problems of creative writing, religion, travel, and his conversations with leading twentieth-century French writers. It gives an interesting and moving analysis of his childhood, of his involvement in World War I, and of his study in Virginia. Green also wrote plays, the most important of which, *Sud* (1953; *South*), explores a homosexual drama on the eve of the Civil War. In 1983 he published a biography of St. Francis of Assisi entitled *Frère François* (*God's Fool: The Life and Times of Francis of Assisi*).

Julien Green died on August 13, 1998, and is buried in Klagenfurt, Austria, where he frequently spent his holidays.

MICHAEL O'DWYER, *National University of Ireland, Maynooth*

SUGGESTED READING

Glenn S. Burne, *Julien Green* (New York: Twayne, 1972).
Dictionary of Literary Biography, vol. 72, *French Novelists, 1930–1960*, ed. Catharine Savage Brosman (Detroit: Gale, 1988), s.v. "Julien Green."

John M. Dunaway, *The Metamorphoses of the Self: The Mystic, the Sensualist, and the Artist in the Works of Julien Green* (Lexington: University Press of Kentucky, 1978).

Michael O'Dwyer, *Julien Green: A Critical Study* (Dublin: Four Courts Press, 1997).

Jean-Pierre Piriou, *Sexualité, religion, et art chez Julien Green* (Paris: Nizet, 1976).

Michèle Raclot, *Le sens du mystère dans l'oeuvre romanesque de Julien Green*, 2 vols. (Paris: Aux Amateurs de Livres, 1988).

Kathryn Eberle Wildgen, *Julien Green: The Great Themes* (Birmingham, Ala.: Summa, 1993).

MELISSA FAY GREENE
(b. 1952)

Melissa Fay Greene's award-winning books *Praying for Sheetrock* and *The Temple Bombing* chronicle dramatic episodes in the civil rights movement in Georgia. Focusing on individuals who played important roles in these events, Greene vividly illuminates issues and conflicts that shaped the state in the latter half of the twentieth century.

Melissa Fay Greene, the daughter of Rosalyn Pollock and Gerald A. Greene, was born on December 30, 1952, in Macon. In 1959 the family moved to Dayton, Ohio, where she grew up and attended school. In 1975 she received her B.A. degree with high honors from Oberlin College and subsequently returned to Georgia to work with her husband for the Savannah office of the Georgia Legal Services Program. In the course of that job she began research for what would become her first book. Greene's husband, Donald Franklin Samuel, is an Atlanta criminal defense attorney; they are the parents of five children.

Greene is one of a growing number of authors who write literary nonfiction. She uses the basic elements of fiction — themes, eloquent prose, characterization, plot development — to tell the story of important episodes in the state's and the nation's recent history. Although her articles in the *New Yorker*, *Newsweek*, the *New York Times*, the *Washington Post*, the *Atlantic Monthly*, *Ms.*, and other publications demonstrate her gifts as a journalist, she excels in longer works.

In her work, Greene has explained, "I have tried to combine serious and honorable journalistic and historical research with love of language; to create works of literary richness, pleasing to the senses, gripping to the intellect, yet reliable and true. I believe in the power of words to penetrate deeply and subtly into real past worlds and events; I disdain the use of words to distort, conceal, or rearrange when performed in the name of nonfiction."

Greene's vivid prose style, understanding of the complexity of human character and historical event, sense of drama, and moral convictions enable her to write works of nonfiction that have all the virtues of the best literature.

Greene's first book, *Praying for Sheetrock* (1991), chronicles the coming of the civil rights movement to McIntosh County in coastal Georgia in the 1970s. It narrates the power struggle between the black and white citizens of the county, focusing on the white sheriff, who has run the county for thirty-one years, and the young African American who becomes the spokesman for his disenfranchised community. By describing the rise and fall of both men, and telling a story that does not conclude with the usual happy victory for truth and justice, Greene shows that her real interests are the vagaries of human character.

Praying for Sheetrock was a finalist for both the National Book Award and the National Book Critics Circle Award. It won the Robert F. Kennedy Book Award and the Lillian Smith Book Award, among others. A panel of judges under the aegis of New York University cited the book as one of the top 100 works of American journalism in the twentieth century. It was also adapted as a play and performed in the spring of 1997 by Lifeline Theater in Chicago.

Similar interests are clearly evident in Greene's second book, *The Temple Bombing* (1996). Here she focuses on Jacob Rothschild, rabbi of the Hebrew Benevolent Congregation in Atlanta, whose temple was bombed by still-unidentified individuals in October 1958; a group of white racists whom many thought responsible for the bombing, though they were ultimately acquitted of the crime; and the lawyers who both defended and tried to prosecute them, the flamboyant Reuben Garland among them. Greene treats this bombing as a symbolic moment in the history of Atlanta: until the bombing, the city "too busy to hate" had avoided much of the strife experienced by other southern cities during the backlash against court-ordered integration that shook the region in the 1950s and 1960s. Greene illuminates Rabbi Rothschild's campaign to convince his congregation of the moral necessity of the civil rights movement, in which they became a leading force. She describes as well negotiations between black and white leaders as they sought peaceful racial coexistence and a climate welcoming to business.

Writing in the *Washington Post*, Julius Lester calls *The Temple Bombing* "an important book that brings to life a pivotal time and place in Southern history. Rabbi Jacob Rothschild's story deserves, as Greene puts it, 'to be rescued from the collective historical amnesia.'" The book was also a National Book Award finalist and won several awards, including the Southern Book Critics Circle Award.

Last Man Out: The Story of the Springhill Mine Disaster (2003) at first seems to depart from Greene's earlier interest in Georgia's social history. The book narrates the Nova Scotia mine disaster that gripped the nation's attention in 1958, in which dozens of men were given up for dead before nineteen were unexpectedly rescued after more than a week trapped underground. Written as a kind of documentary novel — relying on meticulous research and including numerous interviews and oral accounts — the book examines the lives of the miners and their families, the causes of the disaster, the plight of the men who lay trapped in the darkness underground, and the aftermath, during which the rescued miners became victims of a different type.

Greene's interest in the civil rights movement becomes evident in her attention to one of the miners, Maurice Ruddick, who is African American, and to Georgia governor Marvin Griffin, who as a publicity stunt invites the miners to vacation at a segregated Jekyll Island resort after their rescue, before discovering that one of them is black. The book thus manages to illuminate and examine the links between various aspects of twentieth-century culture: the coal miners of Nova Scotia, segregated Georgia in the 1950s, the civil rights movement, and the rise of the mass media in modern society.

In 2006 Greene published her fourth book, *There Is No Me without You*. In yet another departure from her Georgia-based histories, the book offers a poignant portrait of Haregewoin

Teferra, an Ethiopian widow who lost her daughter to AIDS and soon thereafter adopted a teenaged girl whose own parents had died of the disease. This, in turn, led to the adoption of other children, so that Teferra's home soon became an orphanage and day-care center for dozens of children who had lost their parents to the epidemic. Greene herself has adopted two Ethiopian children and is in the process of adopting others.

HUGH RUPPERSBURG, *University of Georgia*

SUGGESTED READING

Contemporary Southern Writers, ed. Roger Matuz (Detroit: St. James, 1999), s.v. "Melissa Fay Greene."

Don O'Briant, "A Writer's Recognition," *Atlanta Journal-Constitution*, October 8, 1991, F1.

Poet, teacher, and founder of the Atlanta Poets Workshop, Walter Griffin has spent his career identifying with and celebrating what he calls "the Blue Glass Charlies": the transients, the losers, and the outsiders down on their luck whose lives go unnoticed in the boardinghouses, cheap hotels, and bus stations of middle America.

Griffin was born on August 1, 1937, in Wilmington, Delaware, the only child of Nina Blalock and William Samuel Griffin. A year after Griffin was born, his father abandoned the family, and Griffin and his mother relocated to Florida. He spent his childhood in Florida and South Carolina, and from 1951 to 1954 he attended Gordon Military College in Barnesville, Georgia. His mother remarried, and Griffin spent a year living in Europe with her and his stepfather. To avoid being drafted into the French army, he joined the U.S. Army in Germany in 1955 and served in the infantry for three years. In 1956 Griffin was stationed at Fort Benning, Georgia. Married and divorced, Griffin has one son, Paul Anthony, who teaches high school German in Decatur and also writes poetry.

In 1972 Griffin founded the Atlanta Poets Workshop for aspiring and published poets. The group met in various locations around Atlanta until 1998, when health problems caused Griffin to end the workshop.

Although this award-winning poet has more than four hundred national and international publications to his credit, Griffin has struggled for wider recognition. His early work was published in numerous small-press quarterlies and journals, and after the 1972 publication of his poetry in *Harper's* magazine, Griffin's work began to appear in such major publications as *Atlantic Monthly, Kenyon Review, New England Review, New Yorker, Paris Review, Poetry, Sewanee Review,* and *Southern Review.*

At the same time his poetry was being published in magazines, anthologies, and small-press publications, Griffin taught in the Poetry in the Schools Program, a national program that gives students the opportunity to work with published poets. From 1972 to 1983 he was the visiting writer-in-residence at more than 110 secondary and elementary schools, colleges, and penal institutions in Georgia, South Carolina, and Tennessee. His poetry earned him the Author of the Year Award in 1976 from the Southeastern Regional Council of Authors and Journalists, and in 1978 the Georgia Council for the Arts and Humanities named him master poet-in-residence.

As Griffin told *Contemporary Authors*, "In my poems, I attempt to deal with middle America and isolation, the inherent loneliness of the human spirit." He sees himself as an outsider looking in, one who brings to his poetry his own childhood hurts and adolescent rootlessness. The speaker in a Griffin poem often longs to be elsewhere, hidden from the rest of the world, and is aware of his physical self and mortality. Griffin is adept at creating in his poetry a presence who watches as others move and who is isolated in the world he portrays. For example, the speaker in "Vagrant" identifies himself as "the brother of all mad men, / in bus station lobbies and rented rooms, / the lover of all my waitress sisters." In "At the All Night Cafeteria" the speaker reviews the ghostlike photographs of his past:

I take them out on the counter,
decide which ones to have dinner with.
Their cracked and folded smiles
lie amid the crumbs.

Alone with the photographs, he will "crawl inside the circled edges and / hold their faded white hands."

Griffin's poetry collections are *Leaving for New York* (1968), *Other Cities* (1971), *Bloodlines* (1972), *Ice Garden* (1973), *Night Music* (1974), *Port Authority: Selected Poems, 1965–1976* (1976), and *Machineworks* (1976). *Machineworks* was published in the Sweetwater Southern Poetry Series, for which Georgia poet

David Bottoms served as series editor. *Night Music* won both the International Small Press Book Award and Georgia Poet of the Year Award from the Dixie Council of Authors and Journalists. More recent publications include *Western Flyers* (1990), which won the University of West Florida's Panhandler Series competition, and *Nights of Noise and Light* (1999).

Griffin lives in East Point, Georgia.

GARY KERLEY, *North Hall High School*

SUGGESTED READING

Contemporary Authors, vols. 73–76 (Detroit: Gale, 1978), s.v. "Griffin, Walter."

Hugh Ruppersburg, ed., *Georgia Voices: Poetry* (Athens: University of Georgia Press, 2000).

LEWIS GRIZZARD

(1946–1994)

Georgia-born humorist and best-selling author Lewis Grizzard conveyed the ambivalence of many white southerners who embraced the economic and material benefits of Sunbelt prosperity while remaining skeptical and sometimes resentful of some of the social and political changes that accompanied these gains.

Born in Fort Benning on October 20, 1946, Lewis McDonald Grizzard Jr. grew up in Moreland, where he moved with his schoolteacher mother, Christine, after his father, army captain Lewis McDonald Grizzard Sr., left them. (Grizzard later memorialized his parents in his books *My Daddy Was a Pistol and I'm a Son of a Gun* [1986] and *Don't Forget to Call Your Mama — I Wish I Could Call Mine* [1991].) While a student at the University of Georgia (UGA), he served as sports editor of the *Athens Daily News* and went on to become the executive sports editor of the *Atlanta Journal* at age twenty-three. He endured an unhappy stint with the *Chicago Sun Times*, which he chronicled in *If I Ever Get Back to Georgia, I'm Gonna Nail My Feet to the Ground* (1990). In 1977 he returned to his home state and soon began to write a regional color column for the *Atlanta Constitution* that was eventually syndicated in about 450 newspapers. Compilations of those columns formed the basis for many of his twenty-five books on a variety of subjects, from women and religion to golf and UGA football. Many of these were best sellers, including *Elvis Is Dead and I Don't Feel So Good Myself* (1984), *Chili Dawgs Always Bark at Night* (1989), and the posthumously published *Southern by the Grace of God* (1996).

In the self-deprecatory tradition of southern humorists, Grizzard often called himself a redneck, but as journalist Peter Applebome has observed, he was actually "the patron saint of the new suburban South, where you could have both the values of the old general store and the designer label wares of the mega-malls." He lived in Atlanta's exclusive Ansley Park, his footwear of choice was Gucci loafers (worn without socks), he was partial to Geoffrey Beene cologne, and he used the gun rack behind the seat of his truck to hold his golf clubs. Although he protested that he liked pork barbecue much better, he owned up to eating caviar at Maxim's in Paris and even to visiting the Louvre Museum.

Grizzard was at his best regaling audiences with stories of "rat-killings" in Moreland or discussing the subtleties of the southern pronunciation of "nekkid," but his country-boy perspective shaped his reaction to all of his personal experiences even as he became a national and international celebrity. In a humorous story entitled "There Ain't No Toilet Paper in Russia," he described Peter the Great's palace as "fifteen times bigger than Opryland."

If Grizzard's humor revealed the ambivalence amid affluence of the Sunbelt South, it reflected its conservative and increasingly angry politics as well. He was fond of reminding fault-finding Yankee immigrants that "Delta is ready when you are," and, tired of assaults on the Confederate flag, he suggested sarcastically that white southerners should destroy every relic and reminder of the Civil War, swear off molasses and grits, drop all references to the South, and begin instead to refer to their region as the "Lower East." Grizzard also wore his homophobia and hatred for feminists on his sleeve, and one of the last of his books summed up his reaction to contemporary trends in its title, *Haven't Understood Anything since 1962 and Other Nekkid Truths* (1992).

In the end, which came in 1994, when he was only forty-seven, the lonely, insecure, oft-divorced, hard-drinking Grizzard proved to be the archetypal comic who could make everyone laugh but himself. He chronicled this decline and his various heart surgeries in *I Took a Lickin' and Kept on Tickin', and Now I Believe in Miracles* (1993), published just before his final, fatal heart failure.

Ironically, Moreland now boasts museums honoring both him and native son Erskine Caldwell, whose darkly critical vision of the South helped to bring on the changes that Grizzard and his generation of white southerners both embraced and bemoaned.

JAMES C. COBB, *University of Georgia*

SUGGESTED READING

Peter Applebome, *Dixie Rising: How the South Is Shaping American Values, Politics, and Culture* (New York: Times Books, 1996).

Charles R. Wilson, "Lewis Grizzard," *Encyclopedia of Southern Culture* (Chapel Hill: University of North Carolina Press, 1989).

ANTHONY GROOMS
(b. 1955)

Anthony "Tony" M. Grooms is a writer and arts adminis-
trator who is well known in the Atlanta area for his work in
organizing arts events and for his support and encouragement
of other writers.

Born January 15, 1955, Grooms was raised and educated in
rural Louisa County, Virginia, 120 miles south of Washington,
D.C. The eldest of six children, he grew up among an extended
African American family that also claimed Native American and
European heritage.

His parents — Robert E. Grooms, a refrigeration mechanic,
and Dellaphine Scott, a textile worker and housewife — encouraged his education. In 1967, as a preface to the forced racial integration of Virginia's public school system, his parents enrolled
him in the Freedom of Choice plan that brought about limited
integration of the white public schools. Though he notes that
many of his attitudes about race and class in the United States
were formed before 1967, the school integration experience was,
nonetheless, a landmark event in his life, contributing to a perspective that is evident in many of his writings.

Grooms graduated from the College of William and Mary in
1978 with a B.A. degree in theatre and speech. His focus was
playwriting, and student theater groups produced several of his
plays. Later he studied at George Mason University, where he
developed a professional interest in creative writing, and graduated in 1984 with an M.F.A. degree in English. After graduate
school, he married Pamela B. Jackson, an administrative judge,
and moved to Atlanta in 1988 to teach, where he found a subject for his writings in the American civil rights movement of the
1960s.

Grooms is the author of a collection of poetry, *Ice Poems*
(1988), a collection of stories, *Trouble No More* (1995), and

a novel, *Bombingham* (2001). His stories and poems also have been published in *Callaloo*, *African American Review*, *Crab Orchard Review*, *George Washington Review*, and other literary journals. He is the recipient of the Lillian Smith Prize for Fiction, the Sokolov Scholarship from the Breadloaf Writing Conference, the Lamar lectureship from Wesleyan College, and an Arts Administration Fellowship from the National Endowment for the Arts.

Reviewing *Trouble No More* for *MELUS*, a critical journal of multiethnic literature, Diptiranjan Pattanaik writes that Grooms demonstrates "the insider's profound knowledge of the history and struggles of African Americans, while consistently managing to circumscribe his breadth of understanding with a tender story-telling art."

Though the subject matter of his work varies, Grooms's most notable writing focuses on characters struggling with the uncertainty of the civil rights movement. His novel, *Bombingham*, takes place in Birmingham in 1963, during the height of the tumult.

JUNE AKERS SEESE, *Atlanta*

SUGGESTED READING

Jabari Asim, "Homegrown Terrorism," review of *Bombingham*, by Anthony Grooms, *Washington Post Book World*, 9 October 2001, C11.

Don O'Briant, "The Practice of Writing: For Anthony Grooms, Putting Words on Paper Is Daily Habit," *Atlanta Journal-Constitution*, 19 July 1992.

Diptiranjan Pattanaik, review of *Trouble No More*, by Anthony Grooms, *MELUS: The Journal of the Society for the Study of the Multi-Ethnic Literature of the United States* 24, no. 3 (1999): 193–95.

EVELYN HANNA
(1900–1982)

Evelyn Hanna was one of a number of southern women whose writing became known as one of Georgia's new "money crops." Like her contemporary Margaret Mitchell, Hanna used the American Civil War as a backdrop for her romantic fiction. The *Atlanta Journal* touted her novel *Blackberry Winter* (1938) as "a possible companion for *Gone With the Wind* for screen entertainment" and enlisted Hanna in the literary renaissance of the South, characterized by depictions of "that determination to endure," as critic Medora Field Perkerson expressed it.

Born October 12, probably in 1900, in Thomaston, Evelyn Hanna was the daughter of Jessie King and Jefferson Davis Hannah. Her maternal grandfather, Captain Jacob S. King, fought for the Confederacy during the Civil War. Educated at Agnes Scott College in Atlanta, the University of California at Los Angeles, and Wesleyan College in Macon, Hanna enrolled in Emory University's library course but decided to devote her life to writing after taking a Columbia University correspondence course in writing.

Hanna and Carolyn Walker Nottingham coauthored *History of Upson County, Georgia*, which was published in April 1930. The project, sponsored by the Daughters of the American Revolution, inspired Hanna to dramatize the lives of those embroiled in the Civil War. While promoting *Blackberry Winter* in London, she fell in love with her literary agent, Robert L. Sommerville, who later became her husband. In 1942 she published her second novel, *Sugar in the Gourd*, which portrays the struggle to uphold southern tradition in a modern world. Hanna was one of the founders of the Roswell Public Library in 1956 and in the 1960s and 1970s served on the board of trustees of the Atlanta Public Library. Hanna died on May 7, 1982, in Roswell.

VALERIE D. LEVY, *University of Georgia*

SUGGESTED READING

Frank Daniel, "Hollywood Isn't a Suburb of Atlanta," *Atlanta Journal Sunday Magazine*, October 9, 1938.

Evelyn Hanna to Margaret Mitchell, 1936, Margaret Mitchell Collection, Special Collections Department, Robert W. Woodruff, Emory University.

Medora Field Perkerson, "A Novel Written in Automobile," *Atlanta Journal Sunday Magazine*, September 25, 1938.

WILL HARBEN
(1858–1919)

Considered a minor author today, Will Harben was one of the most popular novelists in America during the first two decades of the twentieth century. Although in his thirty books and numerous short stories Harben portrays the mountaineers of his native north Georgia with authenticity and color, the sentimental romanticism demanded by readers of his day mars his novels, consequently diminishing his position in the world of letters. However his sharp, sincere observations of the speech, manners, wisdom, and morality of north Georgia mountaineers are a significant contribution to the literature of the American South.

William Nathaniel Harben was born on July 5, 1858, of well-to-do parents, Myra Richardson and Nathaniel Parks Harben, in the small town of Dalton. Harben was a bright, fun-loving youth who showed an interest in writing at an early age. He became familiar with the rustic people he would later glorify by working for many years as a merchant in Dalton (fictionalized as "Darley" in his works). At the age of thirty, encouraged by both Joel Chandler Harris and Henry Grady, he decided to take his chances on writing as a profession. After several successful short stories, he made his first mark on the literary scene in 1889 with a melodramatic but extremely popular novel entitled *White Marie*, about a white girl brought up as a slave. The novel's success prompted him to move to New York City, although he always spent part of every summer in Dalton. He married the South Carolina socialite Maybelle Chandler in 1896, and the couple eventually had three children.

The 1890s were Harben's experimental years. *Almost Persuaded* (1890), a religious novel, was so well received that Queen Victoria of England requested an autographed copy. It was followed by a moderately successful romance, *A Mute Confessor* (1892). In 1894 *Land of the Changing Sun*, his only science fiction novel, appeared. The story concerns a voyage to the center of the earth and was obviously influenced by Jules Verne's popular novel *Journey to the Center of the Earth* (1864). Using Arthur Conan Doyle's Sherlock Holmes as a model, Harben also created the supersleuth Minard Hendricks in three detective novels. During this decade he continued to write short stories about his native region, all published in leading magazines of the day.

The turning point for Harben occurred in 1900, when he published *Northern Georgia Sketches*, a collection of ten of his best local-color stories. The book brought him renewed national attention as well as the high regard of William Dean Howells, known as the "dean of American letters," who became Harben's mentor and friend. For the next nineteen years Harben published at least one novel a year and many short stories, most of them featuring the picturesque Georgia hillbillies for which he became well known.

Harben excelled in creating memorable characters of older backwoods men and women, including Abner Daniel, a cracker-box philosopher noted for such witticisms as "The wust things I ever seed was sometimes at the root o' the best. Manure is a bad thing, but a cake of it will produce a daisy bigger'n any in the field." Pole Baker, a younger, cruder version of Abner, also has a way with words: "Well, boys, ef I had to go, I'd like to be melted up into puore corn whiskey an' poured through my throat tell thar wasn't a drap left of me." Ann Boyd is one of Harben's strongest characters. She is an honest, perceptive, but bitter recluse who admits that she has "done more hating in my life than loving." All three are title characters in their own books, but Abner and Pole appear in several other novels as well.

Besides *Abner Daniel* (1902), *Pole Baker* (1905), and *Ann Boyd* (1906), other noteworthy works include *Westerfelt* (1901), *The Georgians* (1904), *Dixie Hart* (1910), *The New Clarion* (1914), and *The Triumph* (1917), a Civil War epic that could have been Harben's masterpiece had he refined it further. Although Harben often tackled worthwhile, interesting, and controversial themes (racism and equal rights, antiwar beliefs, isolation, religion), he allowed sentimentality to overshadow such themes and weaken their effectiveness.

Harben wrote until his death in New York City on August 7, 1919, and was buried in his beloved Dalton.

JAMES K. MURPHY, *University of West Georgia*

SUGGESTED READING

Robert Bush, "Will N. Harben's Northern Georgia Fiction," *Mississippi Quarterly* 20 (spring 1967).

William Dean Howells, "Mr. Harben's Georgia Fiction," *North American Review* 191 (March 1910).

James K. Murphy, *Will N. Harben* (Boston: Twayne, 1979).

CORRA HARRIS
(1869–1935)

Novelist Corra White Harris was one of the most celebrated women from Georgia for nearly three decades in the early twentieth century. She is best known for her first novel, *A Circuit Rider's Wife* (1910), though she gained a national audience a decade before its publication. From 1899 through the 1920s, she published hundreds of essays and short stories and more than a thousand book reviews in such magazines as the *Saturday Evening Post, Harper's, Good Housekeeping, Ladies Home Journal*, and especially the *Independent*, a highly reputable New York-based periodical known for its political, social, and literary critiques.

Harris established a reputation as a humorist, southern apologist, polemicist, and upholder of premodern agrarian values. At the same time she criticized southern writers who sentimentalized a past that never existed. Most of Harris's nineteen books were novels, though she also published two autobiographies, a travel journal, and a coauthored book of fictional letters. Two of her works became feature-length movies. Of these, the best known is *I'd Climb the Highest Mountain* (1951), inspired by *A Circuit Rider's Wife*. She was the first female war correspondent to go abroad in World War I (1917–18).

Born Corra Mae White on March 17, 1869, on Farmhill Plantation in the foothills of Elbert County, she was the daughter of Tinsley Rucker White and Mary Elizabeth Mathews White. Like many southern women of her day, she did not have an extensive education. She attended Elberton Female Academy but never graduated and, as a writer, was largely self-taught. In 1887 she married Methodist minister and educator Lundy Howard Harris. They had three children, only one of whom — a daughter named Faith — lived beyond infancy.

Harris's career developed out of financial necessity. Her husband's life in the Methodist ministry and in ministerial education was punctuated by incapacities from bouts of alcoholism and depression. Before and after Lundy Harris's death in 1910, Corra Harris assumed responsibility for her immediate and extended family's financial survival. She remained a widow, spending the last two decades of her life at the place she named "In the Valley" just outside Cartersville in Bartow County. There she died in 1935, having outlived her daughter by sixteen years.

Harris's prolific writing career began in 1899 with an impassioned letter to the editor of the *Independent*. William Hayes Ward wrote a searing editorial about the lynching in Georgia on April 23, 1899, of Sam Horse, a black man accused of killing a white farmer and raping his wife. Harris replied with a conventional defense of lynching, yet she so impressed the editors with her disarming expression of homespun politics that the *Independent* encouraged further submissions.

Of all Harris's works, the most acclaimed was *A Circuit Rider's Wife*, the first of a trilogy in the Circuit Rider series. *A Circuit Rider's Widow* (1916) and *My Son* (1921) followed. Semiautobiographical, *A Circuit Rider's Wife* is the story of itinerant Methodist minister William Thompson and his wife, Mary, and their life together on a church circuit in the north Georgia mountains. The novel received much attention when first published because Harris alleged that itinerants and their families suffered needless hardships from the unfair distribution of resources to urban clerics. The book has been noted since that time for its portrayal of rural mountain folk in their earthiness and simplicity. It was reprinted in 1998 by the University of Georgia Press.

Less well known, though not less relevant for its social critique, is *The Recording Angel* (1912). This novel, set in an inert little town called Ruckersville in the hills of north Georgia, depicts a place where residents are so devoted to the legacy of their Confederate heroes that they have isolated themselves and become culturally barren. Harris mocks the Lost Cause mythology, and again she reveals the excesses and limitations of evangelical religion. This book, along with Harris's first novel, reflects her efforts to come to terms with modernity.

One of her works, *The Co-Citizens* (1915), illustrates especially well the paradoxical nature of Harris's personality and politics. The protagonist is loosely based on Rebecca Latimer Felton, a fellow Georgian, and Harris purportedly wrote the novel to illustrate support for the woman suffrage movement, though she was actually more ambivalent about than supportive of the movement. Although many (including Felton) accepted *The Co-Citizens* as a pro-suffrage statement, others read it as a barely veiled attack on feminism, a way of life Harris lived in practice yet rejected in theory.

Harris's two autobiographies were quite acclaimed in their day. *My Book and Heart* (1924) was more popular with the public, though Harris felt that *As a Woman Thinks* (1925) was her best and most satisfying work. During the 1930s her publishing career was largely limited to the locally popular "Candlelit Column," a tri-weekly article in the *Atlanta Journal*. Harris died of heart-related illness on February 7, 1935.

CATHERINE BADURA, *Valdosta State University*

SUGGESTED READING

Catherine Badura, "Reluctant Suffragist / Unwitting Feminist: The Ambivalent Political Voice of Corra Harris," *Southeastern Political Review: Women in Southern United States Politics* 28 (September 2000): 397–426.

Walter Blackstock, "Corra Harris: An Analytical Study of Her Novels," *Florida State University Studies* 19 (1955): 39–92.

Karen Coffing, "Corra Harris and the *Saturday Evening Post*: Southern Domesticity Conveyed to a National Audience, 1900–1930," *Georgia Historical Quarterly* 79 (summer 1995): 367–93.

Wayne Mixon, "Traditionalist and Iconoclast: Corra Harris and Southern Writing 1900–1920," in *Developing Dixie: Modernization in a Traditional Society*, ed. Winfred B. Moore Jr., et al. (Westport: Greenwood Press, 1988).

Ruby Reeves, "Corra Harris: Her Life and Works" (master's thesis, University of Georgia, 1937).

John E. Talmadge, *Corra Harris: Lady of Purpose* (Athens: University of Georgia Press, 1968).

JOEL CHANDLER HARRIS
(1845–1908)

One of the South's most treasured authors, Joel Chandler Harris gained national prominence for his numerous volumes of Uncle Remus folktales. Harris's long-standing legacy as a "progressive conservative" New South journalist, folklorist, fiction writer, and children's author continues to influence our society today.

Harris was born in Eatonton on December 9, 1845 (not 1848, as traditionally believed). His mother, Mary Ann Harris, had left Richmond County to live in Eatonton — the original hometown of her maternal grandmother, Tabitha Turman — with her lover. Harris's father, however, whose identity is uncertain, deserted his young family shortly after his son's birth. Leading Eatonton citizen Dr. Andrew Reid befriended Mary and Joel, giving them a small cottage to live in behind his own mansion.

To make herself financially independent, Mary Harris took in sewing and helped neighbors with gardening. She also gave young Joel constant attention, reciting middle Georgia pioneer stories and reading Oliver Goldsmith's *Vicar of Wakefield* aloud so regularly that he memorized whole passages. When Harris reached school age, Andrew Reid stepped forward again and paid his tuition at Kate Davidson's local academy for boys and girls. Harris later attended the Eatonton Academy for boys. One of his teachers recalled his excellent memory and writing ability. He also devoured newspapers and as many books as he could find. His classmates remembered that the undersized, carrot-topped, freckled-faced boy had a robust sense of humor and was an inveterate practical joker. In part, his joking and pranking may have been a way of masking a slight stammer, which was a lifelong affliction.

Gifted with a strong memory and a love of books, writing skills and a mischievous sense of humor, Harris was hired in

March 1862 at age sixteen as a printing compositor for Joseph Addison Turner, the owner of the one-thousand-acre Turnwold Plantation. The semirestored plantation house and the historical marker commemorating Turnwold and Harris's years there are located nine miles northeast of Eatonton on Old Phoenix Road. A country squire of the Thomas Jefferson mold, Turner aimed "to cultivate corn, cotton, and literature." He had installed an old Washington hand press in a building behind the main house and was ready to publish what was probably America's only plantation newspaper, *The Countryman*.

Harris's four years at Turnwold (1862–66) shaped his career in profound ways. Like Benjamin Franklin a century earlier, and like contemporaries Mark Twain and Walt Whitman, Harris learned to write by hand-setting newspaper type as a young man. He began composing lines of type at Turner's elbow. Turner soon obtained a draft exemption for Harris because of his undersized build — and because his work for a paper loyal to the Southern cause aided the war effort. Turner gave Harris fatherly advice and expanded his education in the liberal arts by recommending books from his vast personal library. An avid sectionalist, Turner endorsed Edgar Allan Poe and Henry Timrod but also stressed Dickens and Shakespeare. He encouraged Harris to write creatively and critically. Harris published at least thirty poems and book reviews for *The Countryman*, along with numerous comic paragraphs over the byline "The Countryman's Devil."

Harris also had full access to Turnwold's slave quarters and to the kitchen, where he listened to African American animal stories told by Uncle George Terrell, Old Harbert, and Aunt Crissy. These slaves became models for Uncle Remus, Aunt Tempy, and other figures in the African American animal tales Harris began writing a decade later. Harris's fictionalized autobiography, *On the Plantation* (1892), chronicles the influence of the Turnwold years on his development. The people he met and the stories he heard, the literary sensibility he began to cultivate there, and several physical features of the extensive middle Georgia plantation property itself informed Harris's writing.

General William T. Sherman's March to the Sea left Turnwold unscathed, but on May 8, 1866, Turner reluctantly had to suspend operations. Harris found himself a published author at age twenty, and he had also learned that writing was in his blood. After a brief homecoming in Eatonton, Harris took a typesetting job in 1866 for the *Macon Telegraph*, some forty miles south, but he found that writing only routine journalism did not satisfy his expanding literary ambitions. After serving briefly as personal secretary to William Evelyn, publisher of the *New Orleans Crescent Monthly*, Harris returned home to accept the job of editor with the *Monroe Advertiser* of Forsyth, forty miles southwest of Eatonton. Harris enjoyed his years (1867–70) on the staff of this lively weekly owned by James P. Harrison, who had worked for Turner and also knew Harris. His sketches of rural Georgia life and character, book reviews, puns, and humorous paragraphs were widely reprinted and soon gained him a statewide reputation. In the fall of 1870 he was offered the position of associate editor on the highly respected *Savannah Morning News*. William Tappan Thompson, whose "Major Jones" sketches were second only in popularity to Augustus Baldwin Longstreet's *Georgia Scenes*, was the founder and editor of the paper. In Savannah, Harris returned to a heritage of Georgia humor at its best.

Harris's comic and human-interest paragraphs in his "Affairs of Georgia" column for the *Morning News* were regularly reprinted around the state as "Hot shots from Red Hair-is," "Harris Sparks," and "Red-Top Flashes." Harris also wrote editorials for the *Morning News* about compromised morality and "shifty" politicians that revealed the humane and democratic philosophy he espoused throughout his personal and professional life. While he was living at the Florida House (later part of the Marshall House) in Savannah, he courted and fell in love with a fellow resident, French Canadian Esther LaRose, the daughter of a steamer captain who plied the Georgia-Florida coast. They married in April 1873.

When a deadly yellow fever epidemic hit Savannah in August 1876, the Harris family, which now included two children, moved to higher ground in Atlanta to wait out the epidemic. In September 1876 *Atlanta Constitution* editor Evan Howell and his outspoken new associate editor Henry W. Grady hired the young journalist whose paragraphs they had already been reprinting. He was soon named associate editor. Harris quickly discovered that Atlanta had become not only the fastest-growing city in the Southeast but also the very center of what Grady, a decade later, famously described as the New South. Harris soon was recognized as one of the country's most important chroniclers of the changing face of the Old South become New.

Harris's *Constitution* editorials expanded on the social, political, and literary themes he had begun exploring in Forsyth and Savannah — themes he would also treat both directly and indirectly in his folktales and fiction to come. When he was asked to fill in for absent dialect-writer Sam Small, he invented an engaging black character named Uncle Remus, who liked dropping by the *Constitution* offices to share humorous anecdotes and sardonic insights about life on the streets of bustling postwar Atlanta. But an article Harris read on African American folklore in *Lippincott's*, which included a transcribed story of "Buh Rabbit and the Tar Baby," reminded him of the Brer Rabbit trickster stories he had heard from the slaves at Turnwold Plantation. His Uncle Remus character now began to tell old plantation folktales, back-home aphorisms, and slave songs, and newspapers around the country eagerly reprinted his rural legends and sayings. Before long, Harris had composed enough material for a book. *Uncle Remus: His Songs and His Sayings — the Folklore of the Old Plantation* was published by Appleton in November 1880. Within four months it had sold ten thousand copies and was quickly reprinted. Harris eventually wrote 185 of the tales.

For the next quarter-century, Harris lived a double life professionally. He was one of two associate editors of the premier newspaper in the Southeast, helping readers interpret the complex New South movement. He was also the creative writer, the "other fellow," as he termed himself: a prolific, committed, and ambitious re-creator of folk stories, a literary comedian, fiction writer, and author of children's books. Harris published thirty-five books in his lifetime, in addition to writing thousands of articles for the *Constitution* over a twenty-four-year period. Along with his first book, *Uncle Remus: His Songs and His Sayings*, the most ambitious of the Uncle Remus volumes is *Nights with Uncle Remus: Myths and Legends of the Old Plantation* (1883). This book comprises seventy-one tales that feature stories told by four different black narrators, including Uncle Remus.

Harris published five other collections of Uncle Remus tales in his lifetime, the most accomplished of which is *Told by Uncle Remus: New Stories of the Old Plantation* (1905). In this volume, a seemingly ageless Uncle Remus tells his complex allegorical tales to the son of the little boy from the first stories. This frail, citified, and "unduly repressed" child is sent by Miss Sally, his grandmother, to Remus's knee to learn how to be a real boy in a complex, competitive, and even predatory world. Three shorter volumes of previously uncollected Uncle Remus stories appeared after Harris's death.

The Uncle Remus volumes assured Harris's reputation, which became international almost overnight. Professional folklorists praised his work in popularizing black storytelling traditions. In 1888 Harris was named a charter member, with Mark Twain, of the American Folklore Society. Before long, in fact, publishing local dialect tales became an international phenomenon: Harris helped spawn a whole industry. Twain had been so impressed by Harris's dialect-writing skills that he had invited Harris in 1882 to meet him and George Washington Cable in New Orleans, Louisiana, to plan an ambitious series of platform readings around the country. Because of his persistent stammer, however, Harris turned down the lucrative offer. The future author of *Huckleberry Finn* took some of Harris's material on the road with him, and Twain reported later that the tar baby story was always one of his most popular stage-readings.

Harris also left his impact on major literary figures to come. Rudyard Kipling, Zora Neale Hurston, William Faulkner, Flannery O'Connor, Ralph Ellison, and Toni Morrison all responded to the legacy of Brer Rabbit and the tar baby that Harris had helped popularize. Fellow Eatonton writer Alice Walker protested, however, that Harris had stolen her African American folklore heritage and had made it a white man's publishing commodity.

Harris was a much more ambitious writer than he implied in his typically self-effacing public statements about being "an accidental author." He had been writing literary reviews for two decades before he moved to Atlanta, and he had published his first attempt at extended fiction — a somewhat clumsy episodic love story, *The Romance of Rockville* — as a serialized novel in the *Constitution* in 1878. Yet Harris took his work as a fiction writer seriously, and he honed his craft considerably in the course of publishing seven volumes of short stories (in addition to the Uncle Remus tales) and three more novels. In his local-color short fiction and novels, Harris explored the lighter and the darker sides of conflicts in race, class, and gender in the South.

Harris published his first collection of short stories, *Mingo and Other Sketches in Black and White*, in 1884, followed by *Free Joe and Other Georgian Sketches* (1887), *Balaam and His Master and Other Sketches and Stories* (1891), and an interlocking set of narratives, *The Chronicles of Aunt Minervy Ann* (1899). Among the best of Harris's local-color stories are "Free Joe and the Rest of the World," a poignant and regularly anthologized story about an isolated black freedman scorned by black slaves and resented by poor whites; "Mingo," a study in prejudice and resentment between upper-class and lower-class white families; "At Teague Poteet's," a Georgia moonshiner tale that also influenced *Huckleberry Finn*; and several of the energetic and highly engaging Minervy Ann narratives. The title story of *The Making of a Statesman and Other Stories* (1902) is a modern narrative about the personal sacrifices a ghostwriter makes in order to help a politician be successful.

Harris's Uncle Remus volumes are simultaneously adult folktales and children's literature because the Brer Rabbit trickster tales work on multiple levels, as voluminous scholarship on these stories confirms. But Harris also wrote six volumes of stories primarily for children: *Little Mr. Thimblefinger and His Queer Country* (1894) and its sequel, *Mr. Rabbit at Home* (1895); *The Story of Aaron* (1896) and its companion volume, *Aaron in the Wildwoods* (1897); and another tandem set of stories, *Plantation Pageants* (1899) and *Wally Wanderoon and His Story-Telling Machine* (1903). Harris's recreation of believable and engaging critters, particularly in his Brer Rabbit tales, virtually revolutionized the modern children's story. Beatrix Potter's Peter Rabbit, Howard Garis's Uncle Wiggly, and A. A. Milne's Pooh Bear — not to mention a whole herd of film and television reincarnations of trickster Brer Rabbit and his gullible adversaries — are all reinventions of Harris's highly animated creatures that talk and behave "de same ez folks."

Harris retired from the *Atlanta Constitution* in 1900, free at last of what he termed the "newspaper grind" but leaving an influential legacy as a "progressive conservative" — a New South journalist who actively promoted socioeconomic, sectional, and racial reconciliation. In addition to publishing the final volumes of Uncle Remus stories, children's books, and adult fiction, he founded *Uncle Remus's Magazine*, was honored by President Theodore Roosevelt in Atlanta and at the White House, and was named to the American Academy of Arts and Letters.

Harris died on July 3, 1908, of acute nephritis and was buried in Westview Cemetery, West End, Atlanta. Obituary writers were not exaggerating when they eulogized this celebrated middle Georgia writer as "the most beloved man in America." Only Harris's friend and admirer, Mark Twain, who died two years later, surpassed Harris in popular reputation at the beginning of the twentieth century. Harris's retelling of the story of Brer Rabbit and the tar baby remains one of the world's best-known folktales, and his complex legacy as a literary comedian, New South journalist, folklorist, fiction writer, and children's author continues to influence modern culture in a surprising number of ways.

Harris's fully restored Victorian home and museum house in Atlanta, the Wren's Nest, located off I-20 at 1050 Ralph David Abernathy Boulevard sw, has served as the headquarters for the Joel Chandler Harris Association (previously called the Uncle Remus Memorial Association) since 1913. The Uncle Remus Museum on 214 Oak Street in Eatonton, comprising two authentic mid-nineteenth-century hewn-log slave cabins, contains Harris memorabilia and a diorama of scenes from the folktales.

R. BRUCE BICKLEY JR., *Florida State University, Tallahassee*

SUGGESTED READING

R. Bruce Bickley Jr., *Critical Essays on Joel Chandler Harris* (Boston: G. K. Hall, 1981).

R. Bruce Bickley Jr., *Joel Chandler Harris: A Biography and Critical Study* (Athens: University of Georgia Press, 1987).

Walter M. Brasch, *Brer Rabbit, Uncle Remus, and the 'Cornfield Journalist': The Tale of Joel Chandler Harris* (Macon, Ga.: Mercer University Press, 2000).

Paul M. Cousins, *Joel Chandler Harris: A Biography* (Baton Rouge: Louisiana State University Press, 1968).

Hugh T. Keenan, ed., *Dearest Chums and Partners: Joel Chandler Harris's Letters to His Children — A Domestic Biography* (Athens: University of Georgia Press, 1993).

THE HEART IS A LONELY HUNTER

The first novel by Georgia writer Carson McCullers (1917–67), *The Heart Is a Lonely Hunter* is commonly treated as a coming-of-age story by readers and critics alike. Many of the characters in the novel are *grotesques*, a term in southern literature for those who are known for their exaggerated attributes, unusual characteristics, or obsessive-compulsive thought processes or behaviors. *The Heart Is a Lonely Hunter* is a compelling portrait of isolated characters and of their longing for self-expression, human connection, and spiritual integration.

Born Lula Carson Smith in Columbus, McCullers was in her early twenties when she wrote *The Heart Is a Lonely Hunter*. Like many southern writers, including William Faulkner, McCullers was conflicted about her birthplace. She dreamed of the snow, excitement, and diversity of New York, and much of that longing is reflected in her first novel. McCullers is best known for her novels *The Heart Is a Lonely Hunter* (1940), *Reflections in a Golden Eye* (1941), *The Member of the Wedding* (1946), and *The Ballad of the Sad Café* (1951).

Critics disagree about whether Mick Kelly, an adolescent girl, or John Singer, a deaf mute, is the protagonist of *The Heart Is a Lonely Hunter*. McCullers said Singer is the hub of a wheel around which the other characters move like spokes. No matter which protagonist the reader selects, however, there is little doubt that Mick represents McCullers herself or that she serves as a lens for the reader. Like McCullers, Mick is androgynous, often wearing what is considered boy's clothing; is dissatisfied with life in a small southern town; is a musician; lives in a place replete with factories, mills, and churches; develops a series of crushes and intense relationships; is determined to learn about Jewish, Catholic, and other religious and cultural perspectives in the predominantly Protestant South; is left out of many activities enjoyed by her peers; and is fearful that she will spend the rest of her life trapped in a job she despises.

In the novel, Singer becomes an ironic and ineffectual Christ figure. Mick, Dr. Benedict Mady Copeland, and Jake Blount make Singer the savior they need him to be. Copeland believes Singer is a Jew. Blount insists he's Irish. Mick finds in Singer the nurturing and tenderness she desires and compares him to what she believes God might be.

In McCullers's fictional world, human communication is inadequate and unsatisfying, and the isolation of her characters represents a universal longing for human connection. Mick, Blount, Biff Brannon, Copeland, and Singer himself seek those who will listen to them and understand their needs. Although her characters often fail to find solace, McCullers's world is not bleak and empty, nor are her characters fated. McCullers celebrates the power of human communication as the only avenue to love, to God, and to one's dreams, even as she acknowledges the near impossibility of attaining it.

In April 2004 the novel was chosen by the talk-show host Oprah Winfrey to be featured in her book club, spiking sales and public awareness of the classic in the twenty-first century.

In 1968 *The Heart Is a Lonely Hunter* became the third of McCullers's novels to be adapted to the screen, following *A Member of the Wedding* (1952) and *Reflections in a Golden Eye* (1967). Filmed on location in Selma, Alabama, and directed by first-time director Robert Ellis Miller, the movie is a relatively faithful adaptation of the novel and was well received by critics both for its sensitivity in dealing with the themes of loneliness and alienation and for its moving performances.

Alan Arkin starred as John Singer, and his speechless performance earned him the New York Film Critics Award as best actor of 1968, as well as an Academy Award nomination. Twenty-one-year-old Tennessee native Sondra Locke, in her film debut, also gave an Oscar-nominated performance as the fifteen-year-old Mick Kelly. Others in the cast included Stacy Keach, in his film debut, as Jake Blount; Percy Rodriguez as Dr. Copeland; Cicely Tyson as Copeland's daughter Portia; and comic actor Chuck McCann as Spiros Antonapoulos, Singer's simpleminded fellow mute.

In spring 2005 the Alliance Theater in Atlanta presented the first stage adaptaton of *The Heart Is a Lonely Hunter*. Written by Alabama native Rebecca Gilman and directed by Doug Hughes, the play was commissioned and produced by the Acting Company of New York City. Although staged on a stark, minimalist set, the Atlanta production made sophisticated use of sound and light to convey the late-1930s working-class, mill-town setting and places even more emphasis on time and place than does the film. Reviews of the Atlanta production were mixed, but the play continued to tour in other cities.

JAN WHITT, *University of Colorado, Boulder*

SUGGESTED READING

Virginia Spencer Carr, *The Lonely Hunter* (Garden City, N.Y.: Doubleday, 1975; reprint, Athens: University of Georgia Press, 2003).

Virginia Spencer Carr, *Understanding Carson McCullers* (Columbia: University of South Carolina Press, 1990).

Richard M. Cook, *Carson McCullers* (New York: Ungar, 1975).

Margaret B. McDowell, *Carson McCullers* (Boston: Twayne Publishers, 1980).

Mary Hood is best known for her work as a short-story writer, although she regularly publishes reviews and essays in popular and literary magazines. Hood's first collection of stories, *How Far She Went* (1984), won the Flannery O'Connor Award for Short Fiction and the *Southern Review* / Louisiana State University Short Fiction Award. Two years later *And Venus Is Blue* (1986), Hood's second collection, won the Townsend Prize for Fiction and the Dixie Council of Authors and Journalists Author-of-the-Year Award. The stories in these two collections have been chosen for twenty-two anthologies in the "best and new" categories and have been reprinted in textbooks. Hood sets her stories in her native Georgia, a terrain she knows from the southeastern coast to the northern Blue Ridge Mountains.

Mary Hood was born on September 16, 1946, in Brunswick. Her father, William Charles Hood, was an aircraft worker who hailed from New York City; her mother, Mary Adella Katherine Rogers Hood, was a teacher of Latin and a native of Cherokee County. When Hood was two years old her family moved to Bartow County. They lived in the Methodist parsonage in the town of White, where her maternal grandfather was a Methodist minister. When their family's house was built, they moved to Douglas County, living at various times in Worth and Dougherty counties. The Hood family settled in 1976 in Cherokee County in Woodstock, a small community in the foothills of the Appalachians, north of Atlanta. Hood lived in Woodstock for thirty years before moving to Commerce, where she continues to reside.

To the fiction writer in the South, place is everything. It is the literal ground, the red clay, and the dogwood trees; it is the metaphor for identity and love; and it is where one's family and community are. Mary Hood's dedication of her first book, *How Far*

She Went, "For Little Victoria, big enough," stands as a memorial to her small rural neighborhood, now surrounded by nearly 1,000 houses built on as many acres. Seven of the nine stories in this book are set in rural north Georgia. The plight of many of the characters is that connections to home and family are shorted or severed, some irretrievably broken. Cut off from the source of life that has sustained them, they enter the modern world of isolation.

Hood's characters see the land they have lived on for generations disappear before their very eyes. The theme of isolation Hood developed in *How Far She Went* is expanded in her second volume of stories, *And Venus Is Blue*. The belief nurtured in Hood by her parents, and rendered in her fiction as truth, is that connection to the land gives spiritual sustenance. But even as Hood was writing in the 1980s Cherokee County was fast becoming an exurb of Atlanta.

Routed out by land-clearing for subdivisions and golf courses, the humans and animals in *And Venus Is Blue* struggle to survive their dying world. The gradual destruction of Hood's own rural neighborhood is mirrored in these stories, where new shopping centers, trailers, rental homes, and junkyards take over the countryside. But in her art Hood has preserved the old folk who were disappearing, being taxed off their land. She honors the people who worked with their hands.

Mary Hood continues to be acknowledged as one of the finest writers of fiction today. Since her novel *Familiar Heat* was published in 1995, she was the John and Renée Grisham Southern Writer-in-Residence at the University of Mississippi (1996). She was also the first writer-in-residence at Berry College (1997–98), and at Reinhardt College (2001). During the winter short term of 1999 she was visiting writer at Centre College in Danville, Kentucky. Kennesaw State University named Hood the Writer of the Decade in honor of the tenth anniversary of the Contemporary Literature and Writing Conference.

DEDE YOW, *Kennesaw State University*

David Aiken, "Mary Hood: The Dark Side of the Moon," in *Southern Writers at Century's End*, ed. Jeffrey J. Folks and James A. Perkins (Lexington: University Press of Kentucky, 1997).

Joy A. Farmer, "Mary Hood and the Speed of Grace: Catching Up with Flannery O'Connor," *Studies in Short Fiction* 33 (winter 1996): 91–99.

Dede Yow, "Mary Hood," *Dictionary of Literary Biography*, vol. 234, ed. Patrick Meanor and Richard E. Lee (Detroit: Gale, 2001).

MAC HYMAN

(1923–1963)

Mac Hyman published only one book before he died at the age of thirty-nine. He secured international fame, however, with that novel, *No Time for Sergeants*.

Hyman was born August 25, 1923, in Cordele. He discovered his passion for writing when he was a student at Cordele High School, and he first displayed his skill in a humorous article published in the school newspaper. Although Hyman frequently lived away from his hometown, he always returned to it; he once said that he felt more at home in Cordele than anywhere else. After graduating from high school Hyman studied for a year at North Georgia College and State University in Dahlonega and then attended Duke University in Durham, North Carolina, in 1941. He interrupted his studies in 1943 to serve in the Army Air Corps as a photo navigator during World War II. He returned to Duke in 1946. His talent was recognized by his creative writing professor, William Blackburn, who became his mentor and lifelong friend, and who eventually edited his collected letters.

Just before graduating from Duke in February 1947, Hyman married his high school sweetheart, Gwendolyn Holt. For the next two years he worked in a variety of jobs, including selling ice cream in a stand at the beach. In 1949, after the first of his three children was born, he reenlisted in the air force and served until 1952.

Between 1947 and 1954 Hyman, drawing from his own military experience, worked on the comic novel that would give him literary success. Several publishing houses rejected the manuscript before it was accepted by Random House. *No Time for Sergeants*, published in 1954, centers on the mishaps of a country bumpkin from south Georgia who is drafted into the air force. Will Stockdale, a good-natured farm boy whose hometown of Callville closely resembles Cordele, narrates his own story in an uneducated southern dialect. The book enjoyed immediate popularity. Within a year of its publication it was adapted by author and screenwriter Ira Levin as a play, first produced for television; then as a Broadway production, where it ran for two years (1955–57); and then as a film in 1958. It made a star out of North Carolina native Andy Griffith, who played Will Stockdale in all three versions. *No Time for Sergeants* was later adapted into a television comedy series that lasted only a single season (1964–65), though it loosely served as the basis of a much more successful series, *Gomer Pyle, USMC*, which ironically derived from a popular country-bumpkin character played by Jim Nabors on *The Andy Griffith Show*.

Income from his novel and these various productions provided Hyman and his family with financial security, but he struggled with writing after his early success. *No Time for Sergeants* and three short stories constitute the only work Hyman published during his lifetime. In 1963, a month before his fortieth birthday, he died unexpectedly of a heart attack. In 1965 Random House published *Take Now Thy Son*, a novel that Hyman began before the publication of *No Time for Sergeants* and continued working on until his death. Although *Take Now Thy Son* is also set in Hyman's fictional version of Cordele, it is a much darker novel than *No Time for Sergeants*. A volume of collected letters, published in 1969, is entitled *Love, Boy*, from Hyman's habit of signing his letters to his parents with his childhood nickname, "Boy." The letters reveal his literary talent as well as his love of people, keen sense of humor, and passion for writing.

CHARLOTTE PFEIFFER, *Abraham Baldwin Agricultural College*

SUGGESTED READING

William Blackburn, ed., *Love, Boy: The Letters of Mac Hyman* (Baton Rouge: Louisiana State University Press, 1969).

I AM A FUGITIVE FROM
A GEORGIA CHAIN GANG!

I *Am a Fugitive from a Georgia Chain Gang!* was a sensational best-selling book by Robert Elliott Burns. Published in 1932, it recounts the dramatic story of the author's imprisonment in Georgia and his two successful escapes, eight years apart, with seven years of freedom, business success, and emotional intrigue in between. It was also the basis of a popular movie entitled *I Am a Fugitive from a Chain Gang*, produced later that year by Warner Brothers.

A native of Brooklyn, New York, Burns was a drifter and a battle-scarred World War I (1917–18) veteran who found himself living in a cheap hotel in Atlanta in 1922. In February of that year Burns and an accomplice stole $5.80 from a local grocer, Samuel Bernstein. They were arrested instantly; Burns was swiftly tried, convicted, and sentenced to six to ten years on the Campbell County (later Fulton County) chain gang. It did not take the stunned northerner long to comprehend that ten years on the chain gang was practically a death sentence. Southern chain gangs, notorious across the rest of the nation, had their origins in the scandalous convict-lease system of the late nineteenth century. When convict leasing was abolished in 1908, with the demand for convict labor still growing, the chain gang took its place.

Burns's book is full of sensational, lurid, yet mostly verifiable descriptions of mistreatment, brutality, disgusting food, and labor so unrelenting and exhausting that it left men in a stupor. As he soon learned from his wretched fellow prisoners that to leave the chain gang a man had to "work out, pay out, die out, or run out," Burns decided to run out. He did so in June 1922, after serving only a few months' time. Burns's dramatic escape to Chicago was crowned by brilliant success in the publishing business, social recognition, and marriage. But years later when he proved an unfaithful husband, his wife, Emily, turned him in to the authorities. His arrest on May 22, 1929, caused a sensation in Chicago. Burns had never told Emily about his past, but she discovered his secret by opening letters from his brother, the Reverend Vincent Burns, an Episcopal priest.

In negotiations with officials from Georgia, Burns arranged to return to Georgia, take a soft job in the prison system, and receive a pardon after one year — or so he believed. But the state of Georgia was unrelenting, and Burns once more faced the hardships of the chain gang, this time at a prison in Troup County. In September 1930 he escaped a second time and made his way to Newark, New Jersey. There he wrote, "Georgia cannot win! ... I have decided to write the true story, while in hiding, of my entire case." Burns's memoir, first serialized in *True Detective Mysteries* magazine, was published in January 1932 and was an instant success. "It would be hard to find a more thrilling story in either truth or fiction," a *New York Times* reviewer wrote.

Some critics and scholars believe Burns's brother ghostwrote the book. Vincent Burns, who was known mostly for his patriotic and religious poetry, served as the poet laureate for the state of Maryland from 1962 until his death in 1970. He also wrote *Out of These Chains* (1942), a sequel to *I Am a Fugitive from a Georgia Chain Gang!*, and *The Man Who Broke a Thousand Chains; The Story of Social Reformation of the Prisons of the South* (1968), a memoir of Robert Burns. Vincent Burns later sued his brother for a greater share of the profits received from the book and the film.

A motion picture version was put into production shortly after the book's publication, directed by Mervyn LeRoy and starring one of Hollywood's finest actors, Paul Muni, in the title role. Burns himself went incognito to serve as a consultant on the film. As indignant as Georgia officials were over the book's publication, they were even more upset over the movie, and they insisted that Warner Brothers drop "Georgia" from the film's title. Upon the movie's release in late 1932 — during one of the darkest periods of the Depression and days after the election of President

Franklin D. Roosevelt — the theaters could not screen it often enough. A telegram to Warner Brothers in Hollywood told the tale: "fugitive biggest broadway sensation in last three years stop thousands turned away from box office tonight with lobby delay held four hours stop."

In spite of its rather stilted script, the film was one of the major achievements of 1930s Hollywood. LeRoy had just completed *Little Caesar*, the first great work in a new genre, the gangster film, while Muni himself had just completed another classic gangster picture, *Scarface*. Thus, both star and director were moving from the founding of one genre toward establishing a second, the southern prison adventure. *Fugitive* was named Best Picture of the Year by the National Board of Review of Motion Pictures. Muni and the film received three Oscar nominations. It was remade in 1987 under the title *The Man Who Broke 1,000 Chains* (HBO Films, directed by Daniel Mann). Scenes, themes, and motifs from the 1932 LeRoy picture also abound in *Cool Hand Luke* (Warner Brothers, 1967, directed by Stuart Rosenberg).

Burns was apprehended yet again in December 1932 in Newark, but the state of New Jersey refused to extradite him, despite the insistence of Georgia officials. After two other failed attempts to bring him back to Georgia, Burns met newly elected Georgia governor Ellis Arnall in New York in 1943 and requested a pardon. Arnall arranged to have Burns return to Georgia in November 1945 to face the parole board, where he stood by Burns's side as his counsel. The board commuted Burns's sentence to time served. Governor Arnall's gesture capped an administration devoted to prison reform, including the abolition of chain gangs. Burns died on June 5, 1955, at his home in Union, New Jersey, where he had worked as a tax consultant.

MATTHEW J. MANCINI, *St. Louis University, St. Louis, Missouri*

SUGGESTED READING

Robert Elliott Burns, *I Am a Fugitive from a Georgia Chain Gang!* (1932; reprint, Athens: University of Georgia Press, 1997).

Vincent Godfrey Burns, *The Man Who Broke a Thousand Chains; The Story of Social Reformation of the Prisons of the South* (Washington: Acropolis Books, 1968).

I Am a Fugitive from a Chain Gang [screenplay], ed., with an introduction, John E. O'Connor (Madison: University of Wisconsin Press, 1997).

ARTHUR CREW INMAN
(1895–1963)

Arthur Crew Inman was a reclusive and unsuccessful poet whose seventeen-million-word diary, extending from 1919 to 1963, provides a panoramic record of people, events, and observations from more than four decades of the twentieth century.

Inman was born in 1895 into one of the most powerful and affluent families in Atlanta. His grandfather was Samuel Martin Inman, a wealthy cotton magnate and philanthropist who owned a portion of the *Atlanta Constitution* and was an early director for the Georgia Institute of Technology. Inman felt close to neither of his parents, Roberta Sutherland Crew and Henry Arthur Inman, and expressed relief at his father's death. He began his elementary schooling in Atlanta, but in 1908 he left Georgia to attend Haverford School (where he was miserable) and then Haverford College, both in Haverford, Pennsylvania. After two years of college, he suffered a nervous breakdown in 1916 that left him mentally and physically impaired. He did not return to the South after 1915 and lived in Boston for the rest of his life.

After failing to win acclaim with several volumes of undistinguished poetry, Inman decided that he might find fame by writing a diary. By the end of his life he had filled some 155 handwritten volumes. Inman wrote the diary in Garrison Hall, a residential hotel in Boston, where he rented five apartments and lived for most of his adult life. To avoid light, to which he claimed unusual sensitivity, he often kept the interior of his apartment darkened, and when he did occasionally go out into the city, it was to ride around in a 1919 Cadillac, painted black.

Despite his numerous eccentricities, Inman in 1923 married Evelyn Yates, who remained with him for the rest of his life. She occupies a prominent if not always hallowed place in the diary: "She is homely as a stump fence built in the dark," he wrote of her in the diary, "but she doesn't giggle all the time." Inman suffered from various ailments throughout his life. He committed suicide in 1963.

The 155 volumes of the diary remain mostly unpublished, but in 1985 Harvard professor of English and American literature Daniel Aaron published a two-volume abridged edition that includes many highlights. Aaron suggested that Inman would have called his diary "both a history of my times and the story of my self-discovery." On the one hand it is an account of Inman's day-to-day thoughts and activities. On the other it is a record of his recollections of his early life in Atlanta, his family, his life in Boston, contemporary events in America and the world, and his many eccentricities, opinions, and prejudices.

Virtually everyone Inman knew or encountered became the victim of his criticism. He advertised in a Boston newspaper for people to come discuss their lives with him; many of their stories and letters are preserved in his diary. A number of the women who came to talk to him he also seduced, and he wrote about this, too. His wit was fiercely unrelenting and pitiless.

Whether it is an epical literary reflection of the man and the age or the product of a demented mind, Inman's diary remains one of the most unusual literary products of the twentieth century.

HUGH RUPPERSBURG, *University of Georgia*

SUGGESTED READING

Daniel Aaron, ed., *From a Darkened Room: The Inman Diary* (Cambridge, Mass.: Harvard University Press, 1996).

Daniel Aaron, ed., *The Inman Diary: A Public and Private Confession,* 2 vols. (Cambridge, Mass.: Harvard University Press, 1985).

Lewis P. Simpson, "The Last Casualty of the Civil War: Arthur Crew Inman," *The Fable of the Southern Writer* (Baton Rouge: Louisiana State University Press, 1994), 155–82.

Bob Summer, "An Inman's Private Life Becomes Public," *Atlanta Journal-Constitution*, October 13, 1985.

Philip Zaleski, "The Inman Diary," *Atlanta Journal-Constitution*, October 27, 1985.

HA JIN
(b. 1956)

A widely acclaimed author of novels, short stories, and poetry, Ha Jin launched his writing career in 1990 — just three years before joining the creative writing faculty of Emory University — with the publication of a collection of poems entitled *Between Silences: A Voice from China*. Since that first book, he has produced several other works, including two additional volumes of poetry: *Facing Shadows* (1996) and *Wreckage* (2001); three short-story collections: *Ocean of Words: Army Stories* (1996), which won the PEN/Hemingway Award, *Under the Red Flag* (1997), which garnered the Flannery O'Connor Award for Short Fiction, and *The Bridegroom: Stories* (2001); and four novels: *In the Pond* (1998), *Waiting* (1999), which won both the National Book Award for Fiction and the PEN/Faulkner Award, *The Crazed* (2002), and *War Trash* (2004), which also won the PEN/Faulkner Award.

Ha Jin is the pen name of Xuefei Jin, born February 21, 1956, in China's Liaoning Province. He grew up during the turbulent years of the Cultural Revolution, served in the army, and completed bachelor's and master's degrees in his home country before coming to the United States in 1985 to pursue his doctorate in English at Brandeis University in Waltham, Massachusetts. The Tiananmen Square massacre of 1989, which roughly coincided with the completion of his Ph.D., convinced Jin not to return to China; he soon began writing in English and searching for an academic job in the United States. In 1993 Jin joined the creative writing faculty at Emory University in Atlanta as an assistant professor of poetry. After spending a decade at Emory, Jin returned as a full professor to the creative writing program at Boston University, where he had previously studied writing.

In 1990 Jin, who had only recently begun writing in English, published his first volume of poetry. This effort, *Between Silences*, and his two subsequent books of poetry, *Facing Shadows* and *Wreckage*, offer a sweeping panorama of Chinese history, from the excesses of the emperors to the public enthusiasm and private suffering attending the Cultural Revolution. Often narrative in form, Jin's poems likewise offer a glimpse into the family background and cultural antecedents that color his own writing: his verses trace a path from his home province in China to Georgia and beyond.

Though he was hired by Emory as a professor of poetry, Jin became well known for his fiction. His first story collection, *Ocean of Words: Army Stories*, is set on the border between China and the Soviet Union in the 1970s. The stories focus on the human experience at the front: they tell of love and longing ("Love in the Air"), the dynamic between leaders and followers ("Dragon Head"), and the shame that can arise from the constraints of Chinese and military culture ("Miss Jee"). *Under the Red Flag*, Jin's second collection, is perhaps even more brutal in the truths it reveals about China and human nature. The first story in the volume, "In Broad Daylight," which earned a Pushcart Prize, chronicles the public punishment of a married woman who has performed sexual acts for money.

More recently, in the title story of *The Bridegroom*, Jin has written about a homosexual man who, having taken a homely bride as a cover, is nonetheless found at a gay men's club and subsequently assigned by the courts to be "rehabilitated" through the use of electroshock therapy.

Jin's first novel, *In the Pond*, is a comic tale about a low-ranking worker at a Chinese fertilizer plant who publishes satiric cartoons about the Communist Party and company officials who have passed him over for a housing upgrade. *The Crazed*, Jin's third novel, concerns a graduate student's academic coming-of-age at the bedside of his mentor and future father-in-law, an esteemed professor whose "crazed" rants while recovering from a stroke reveal far more about himself and the oppressive life of a Chinese academician than the professor intends.

Jin's second and most celebrated novel, *Waiting*, is the story of Lin Kong, a doctor in the Chinese army torn between his responsibilities to his wife, Shuyu, and daughter in the countryside — unwelcome reminders of a loveless arranged marriage — and his girlfriend in the city, an army nurse with whom he has only a platonic relationship because of strict military regulations about fraternization. Chinese law prevents him from divorcing Shuyu without her consent until the couple has been separated for eighteen years. When Lin Kong is finally granted a divorce, he marries the nurse only to find that the long years of waiting have permanently damaged their relationship.

War Trash, Jin's fourth novel, is the first-person account of a Chinese army officer's struggle to survive a prisoner-of-war camp after he is captured by Americans during the Korean War (1951–53). Published in fall 2004, *War Trash* is considered by many critics to be Jin's most ambitious and incendiary novel yet. While the central character is purely fictional, the mistreatment of the Korean prisoners at the hands of their captors is, according to Jin, a historical reality. The author's representation of these events draws upon his own experience in the Chinese army and his memory that "most of the soldiers were afraid of captivity more than death."

Ha Jin continues to write and teach at Boston University. He is married to Lisha Bian, and they have one son, Wen.

SANDRA S. HUGHES, *University of Georgia*

SUGGESTED READING

Dwight Garner, "Ha Jin's Cultural Revolution," *New York Times Magazine*, February 6, 2000.

Paula E. Geyh, "Ha Jin," in *The Dictionary of Literary Biography*, vol. 244, *American Short-Story Writers since World War II*, 4th ser., ed. Patrick Meanor and Joseph McNicholas (Detroit: Gale, 2001).

Paula E. Geyh, "An Interview with Ha Jin," *Boulevard* 51 (2002): 127–40.

Jocelyn Lieu, "Beating the Odds," *Chicago Tribune*, November 24, 1996.

GEORGIA DOUGLAS JOHNSON
(ca. 1877–1966)

Georgia Douglas Johnson was an important figure of the Harlem Renaissance, the literary and cultural movement that flourished in the predominantly black Harlem neighborhood of New York City after World War I (1917–18). Johnson's four volumes of poetry, *The Heart of a Woman* (1918), *Bronze* (1922), *An Autumn Love Cycle* (1928), and *Share My World* (1962), established her as one of the most accomplished African American woman poets of the literary movement.

Johnson was born in Atlanta on September 10, around the year 1877, to Laura Jackson and George Camp. Johnson graduated from Atlanta University Normal College in 1896. She also studied music at Oberlin Conservatory and at the Cleveland College of Music, both in Ohio. She met her husband, Henry Lincoln Johnson, a lawyer and government employee, while at Atlanta University. With her husband she moved in 1910 to Washington, D.C., where she remained for the rest of her life. After the death of her husband in 1925, Johnson was forced to support herself and her two sons through a series of temporary jobs. She worked as a substitute teacher and a file clerk for the civil service, ultimately securing a position with the Department of Labor, where she worked for a number of years.

Johnson called her home at 1461 S Street Northwest in Washington the Half-Way House, in the spirit of her willingness to provide shelter for those in need. On Saturday nights she hosted open houses attended by such Harlem Renaissance writers as Louis Alexander, Gwendolyn Bennett, Marita Bonner, Countee Cullen, Clarissa Scott Delaney, Jessie Redmon Fauset, Angelina Weld Grimke, Langston Hughes, Alain Locke, Kelly Miller, May Miller, Bruce Nugent, Willis Richardson, Anne Spencer, Jean Toomer, and E. C. Williams. The gathering became known as the S Street Salon, and prominent writers often debuted new works at the gatherings. The writer Zora Neale Hurston was a regular at the salon as well.

Johnson's first collection of poems, *The Heart of a Woman and Other Poems*, established her as one of the notable African American woman poets of her time. Built on themes of loneliness, isolation, and the confining aspects of the roles of women, the title poem substitutes the metaphor of "a lone bird, soft winging, so restlessly on" for "the heart of a woman," which ultimately "falls back with the night / And enters some alien cage in its plight, / And tries to forget it has dreamed of the stars." Although some critics have praised the richly penned, emotional content, others see a need for something more than the picture of helplessness presented in such poems as "Smothered Fires," "When I Am Dead," and "Foredoom."

Johnson's second collection of poems, *Bronze: A Book of Verse*, deals primarily with the issue of race, while her third collection, *An Autumn Love Cycle*, returns to the feminine themes explored in her first collection. From this collection the poem "I Want to Die While You Love Me" is the most often anthologized of her work. It was read at her funeral.

In addition to poetry, Johnson wrote several plays. During the fall of 1926, her play *Blue Blood* was performed by the Krigwa Players in New York City and was published the following year. In 1927 *Plumes*, a folk tragedy set in the rural South, won first prize in a literary contest sponsored by the National Urban League's African American magazine *Opportunity*. Johnson also submitted plays to the Federal Theatre Project, but none were ever produced. Johnson wrote a number of plays dealing with the subject of lynching, including "Blue-Eyed Black Boy," "Safe," and "A Sunday Morning in the South." According to the "Catalogue of Writings" that she produced in 1962–63, Johnson wrote twenty-eight dramatic works, but few were ever published or produced, and most have been lost.

The catalog also lists a manuscript dealing with her literary salon, a collection of short stories, and a novel — all have been lost as well. Workers may have unknowingly thrown away some of these unpublished works when they cleaned out her house after her death in 1966.

Johnson accepted an honorary doctorate in literature from Atlanta University in 1965. W. E. B. Du Bois wrote in his foreword to her poetry volume *Bronze*, "Her word is simple. . . . It is singularly sincere and true, and as a revelation of the soul struggle of the women of a race it is invaluable."

CARMINE D. PALUMBO, *Middle Georgia College*

SUGGESTED READING

Harold Bloom, ed., *Black American Women Poets and Dramatists* (New York: Chelsea House, 1996).

Countee Cullen, ed., *Caroling Dusk: An Anthology of Verse by Negro Poets* (New York: Harper and Brothers, 1927).

Gloria T. Hull, *Color, Sex, and Poetry: Three Women Writers of the Harlem Renaissance* (Bloomington: Indiana University Press, 1987).

Judith Stephens, "'And Yet They Paused' and 'A Bill to Be Passed': Newly Recovered Lynching Dramas by Georgia Douglas Johnson," *African American Review* 33 (autumn 1999): 519–22.

GREG JOHNSON
(b. 1953)

An award-winning short-story writer, novelist, poet, biographer, and scholar, Greg Johnson is a professor of English and a faculty member in the graduate writing program at Kennesaw State University. A frequent reviewer for such publications as the *New York Times Book Review*, *Georgia Review*, and *Atlanta Journal-Constitution*, Johnson has published two novels, a study of Emily Dickinson, three critical works on Joyce Carol Oates, a book of poems, and three collections of short fiction.

Born July 13, 1953, in San Francisco, Johnson moved with his family to Liverpool, England, for three years and then to Tyler, Texas. He received B.A. and M.A. degrees from Southern Methodist University in Dallas, and a Ph.D. from Emory University in Atlanta in 1980. His dissertation was published as *Emily Dickinson: Perception and the Poet's Quest* (1985). He taught briefly at Emory, Widener University in Chester, Pennsylvania, and the University of Mississippi, and has been at Kennesaw State since 1989.

Of Johnson's numerous short stories, fifty-two are collected in *Distant Friends* (1990), *A Friendly Deceit* (1992), *I Am Dangerous* (1996), and *Last Encounter with the Enemy* (2004). Reviewers see in Johnson's well-crafted prose keen observations of the contemporary world, where the protagonists lead their quietly desperate lives in a traditional Southern Gothic landscape. Many of his stories are set in the modern South, with familiar Atlanta landmarks as their setting. Family conflict, unresolved issues, and marital discord are a few of Johnson's themes, and he portrays many of his characters at decisive moments in their lives. Some characters are obsessed with violence, deceit, secrets, and undeveloped love, as the titles of his collections suggest. There are often telling moments when the characters cannot avoid their fates, but there are also moments when the painful truth becomes redemptive.

In his collection of poetry, *Aid and Comfort* (1993), Johnson deals with the issues of AIDS, dying, suicide, violence, and aging. The same year he published *Pagan Babies*, his first novel. Set largely in Atlanta, the novel explores growing up Catholic and homosexual in the age of AIDS, issues Johnson says he identifies with. The poignant and frankly sexual novel follows the intertwining, stormy relationship between Janice Rungren and her friend Clifford Bannon, who first meet as third-graders in a Catholic school in Texas. As adults, Janice and Clifford must confront serious personal issues.

In his second novel, *Sticky Kisses* (2001), Johnson again uses Atlanta as the setting where his characters struggle with the complex rules of society and family in the South. Abby Sadler has returned to be with her estranged brother, Thom, recently diagnosed with HIV. The novel explores the irrevocable stories of family and the healing power of love.

Johnson has won prizes from the Academy of American Poets and the PEN Syndicated Fiction Project. He was named Georgia Author of the Year for 1990 and 1997, and his stories have been published in *Prize Stories: The O. Henry Awards* (1986) and *New Stories from the South: The Year's Best* (1990). As the authorized biographer of Joyce Carol Oates, Johnson followed his critical studies of the author in 1987 and 1994 with the publication of *Invisible Writer: A Biography of Joyce Carol Oates* in 1998.

In both his stories and his novels, Johnson is an astute, honest observer of the emotional damage we do to ourselves. Though his characters' lives are often failures in one way or another, he sees in their struggle the "language of survival."

GARY KERLEY, *North Hall High School*

SUGGESTED READING

Contemporary Authors, vol. 140 (Detroit: Gale, 1993), s.v. "Johnson, Greg."

Rebecca Ransom, "Writer's Profile," *Southern Voice*, February 11, 1993.

Michael Upchurch, "Greg Johnson," in *Dictionary of Literary Biography*, vol. 234, *American Short-Story Writers since World War II* (Detroit: Gale, 2001).

Teresa Weaver, "Atlanta-Set 'Sticky Kisses' Navigates the Shoals of Family," *Atlanta Journal-Constitution*, January 27, 2002.

NUNNALLY JOHNSON
(1897–1977)

After an early career as a journalist and short-story writer, Georgia native Nunnally Johnson emerged as one of Hollywood's most accomplished screenwriters and producers from the 1930s through the 1950s, when he began to direct motion pictures as well.

Nunnally Johnson was born on December 5, 1897, in Columbus to Johnnie Pearl Patrick and James Nunnally Johnson. His father worked as a superintendent for the Central of Georgia Railway, and his mother was an activist on the local school board. An avid reader with an acute sense of humor, Johnson grew up and attended school in Columbus, his mother's hometown. In later life he remembered fondly his youthful days delivering on his bicycle the *Columbus Enquirer-Sun,* attending theatrical productions at the Springer Opera House, and playing first base on the high school baseball team. Johnson later recalled the YMCA building, an ornate marble structure built in 1903 with funds donated by George Foster Peabody, as his "social club."

After graduating from Columbus High School in 1915, Johnson worked briefly as a reporter for the *Columbus Enquirer-Sun* before moving to Savannah to work for the *Savannah Press.* He continued to visit Columbus annually until his father's death in 1953.

In 1919 Johnson moved to New York City and by the mid-1920s had emerged as one of the city's leading newspapermen, reporting major national events for the *Brooklyn Daily Eagle* (1919–25), the *New York Herald Tribune* (1926), and the *New York Evening Post* (1927–30). At the *Evening Post,* he also penned a weekly column of humorous social commentary under the heading "Roving Reporter." From 1925 to 1932 he published some fifty short stories in the *Saturday Evening Post* and several stories in the *New Yorker.* These writings were mostly light satirical pieces depicting contemporary manners and mores in New York City and in a fictionalized version of Columbus that he called Riverside. Three of his stories won O. Henry Memorial Awards in the late 1920s. In 1931 he published a collection of his stories, *There Ought to Be a Law*.

In 1932 Johnson moved to Los Angeles, California, where he worked as a screenwriter for Twentieth Century Fox. Among the dozens of scripts he wrote, he excelled at converting novels into screenplays. His most successful efforts included screenplays for John Steinbeck's *The Grapes of Wrath* (1940) and *The Moon Is Down* (1943); *The Keys of the Kingdom* (1944) and *The Man in the Grey Flannel Suit* (1956), both of which starred Gregory Peck; Daphne du Maurier's *My Cousin Rachel* (1952); and his final screenplay, *The Dirty Dozen* (1967). He worked in other genres as well. Among his most popular productions were the musical *Rose of Washington Square* (1939) and the comedy *How to Marry a Millionaire* (1953), one of actress Marilyn Monroe's earliest films. By the 1950s he was the highest-paid screenwriter in Hollywood.

Two of Johnson's most important adaptations were of Georgia-based stories: Erskine Caldwell's *Tobacco Road* (1941), his third partnership with the director John Ford, and *The Three Faces of Eve* (1957), based on a true case of a Georgia woman with multiple personality disorder. That film, which Johnson also produced and directed, earned an Academy Award for actress Joanne Woodward, a Thomasville native, in her first starring role.

Johnson was married three times. His first wife was Alice Mason, whom he married in 1919 and with whom he had a daughter. They divorced in 1920. Johnson married Marion Byrnes in 1927, and they also had a daughter. The couple divorced in 1938. In 1940 Johnson married Dorris Bowdon, an actress he met while both were working on *The Grapes of Wrath*; they had three children. Johnson died on March 25, 1977, in Hollywood. A collection of his correspondence with famous friends and colleagues was published in 1981.

CRAIG LLOYD, *Columbus State University*

Nora Johnson, *Flashback: Nora Johnson on Nunnally Johnson* (Garden City, N.Y.: Doubleday, 1979).

Nunnally Johnson, *The Letters of Nunnally Johnson* (New York: Knopf, 1981).

Craig Lloyd, "Nunnally Johnson in Columbus," *Muscogiana* 9 (summer 1998): 29–36.

Tom Stempel, *Screenwriter: The Life and Times of Nunnally Johnson* (San Diego: A. S. Barnes, 1980).

RICHARD MALCOLM JOHNSTON
(1822–1898)

Richard Malcolm Johnston was a lawyer, teacher, and dialect humorist from Hancock County. A disciple of Augustus Baldwin Longstreet, he called his first book *Georgia Sketches* (1864) in honor of Longstreet's *Georgia Scenes* (1835). In an enlarged form, this collection was renamed *Dukesborough Tales* (1871); the second edition of *Dukesborough Tales*, published in 1883, launched his national literary career.

Johnston's writing has been called a bridge between antebellum humor and postbellum local color traditions. In his four novels and six other collections of stories, he never strayed far from the themes he explored in *Dukesborough Tales*, which included schooling, law, marriage, death, religion, paternalism, and the psychological conflict within rural families over such issues as land greed. His biographer, Bert Hitchcock, argued that the unchanging focus of his work was the life of the common people between the 1820s and 1840s. In an essay entitled "Middle Georgia Rural Life," which appeared in *Century Magazine* in March 1892, Johnston defined the common people as those who owned between 200 and 1,000 acres and between one and fifty slaves.

Johnston was born on March 8, 1822, near Powelton, to Catherine Davenport and Malcolm Johnston, a planter and Baptist minister. His formal education included field schools, the Powelton Academy, and Mercer University in Penfield, where he graduated in 1841. Before the Civil War, he vacillated between law and teaching, an experience that provided material for his literary endeavors later in life. For sixteen years, beginning in 1841, Johnston was a law partner of Linton Stephens, Alexander Stephens's younger half brother. When he was defeated for a circuit judgeship in 1857, Johnston accepted a University of Georgia professorship, which he held until 1862. Returning to his plantation in Hancock County, Johnston opened Rockby, a select boarding school for boys. From May to July 1864 he served on the staff of Governor Joseph E. Brown. As the war drew to a close, he helped to hide Robert Toombs and assisted his efforts to escape from Union forces. Johnston moved to Baltimore after the war, where his friend Sidney Lanier encouraged his literary ambitions.

Johnston's most famous story is "The Goosepond School," the lead story in the 1871 edition of *Dukesborough Tales*. In it Johnston makes his case for humane and liberal education by describing the downfall of Israel Meadows, an unschooled and sadistic master of a plantation field school. The rest of the stories examine other aspects of life in Dukesborough, such as the workings of the superior court, the trials of a poor widow and her children, and the courtship of an old bachelor. Like Powelton, Dukesborough was a village that had grown gradually, without direction, and had suffered "the most absolute decay that I have known ever to befall any village."

Johnston's novels *Old Mark Langston: A Tale of Duke's Creek* (1884), *Ogeechee Cross-Firings* (1889), and *Widow Guthrie* (1890) continue the paternalistic themes of *Dukesborough Tales* and sentimentally portray the Middle Georgia frontier before the Civil War as devoid of poverty and class conflict. Two other collections of tales are *Mr. Absalom Billingslea and Other Georgia Folk* (1888) and *The Primes and Their Neighbors: Ten Tales of Middle Georgia* (1891). Johnston's *Autobiography* appeared in 1900. He remained in Baltimore until his death on September 23, 1898.

MICHAEL E. PRICE, *Armstrong Atlantic State University*
CAROL M. ANDREWS, *Armstrong Atlantic State University*

SUGGESTED READING

Bert Hitchcock, *Richard Malcolm Johnston* (Boston: Twayne, 1978).

Robert L. Phillips Jr., "The Novel and the Romance in Middle Georgia Humor and Local Color: A Study of Narrative Method in the Works of Augustus Baldwin Longstreet, William Tappan Thompson, Richard Malcolm Johnston, and Joel Chandler Harris" (Ph.D. diss., University of North Carolina, 1971).

Michael E. Price, *Stories with a Moral: Literature and Society in Nineteenth-Century Georgia* (Athens: University of Georgia Press, 2000).

TAYARI JONES
(b. 1970)

Tayari Jones, born and raised in Atlanta, Georgia, has written a number of short stories and articles and is best known for her two novels, *Leaving Atlanta* (2002), about the Atlanta child murders in 1979–81, and *The Untelling* (2005). Although she has not lived in her hometown for almost a decade, her stories and literary imagination center on Georgia and its capital city.

Born to Mack and Barbara Jones in 1970, Jones spent most of her childhood in southwest Atlanta, with the exception of 1983, when her father, a Clark Atlanta University professor on a Fulbright Scholarship, took the family to Nigeria, West Africa. Jones received her bachelor's in English in 1991 from Spelman, a master's in English from the University of Iowa (1994), and an M.F.A. in creative writing from Arizona State University (2000). Since then she has received fellowships from the Bread Loaf Writers' Conference, the Corporation of Yaddo, the MacDowell Colony, the Arizona Commission on the Arts, and Le Château de Lavigny (Switzerland).

Leaving Atlanta, a story told primarily from a child's perspective, centers on Atlanta's infamous child murders of 1979–81. Jones was in fifth grade at Oglethorpe Elementary when thirty African American children from the neighborhoods near her home and school were murdered. In interviews, she has described the novel as a documentation of that particular moment of her childhood. Her character's point of view contrasts the sweetness of a recollected girlhood with the terror of facing an unknown killer. *Leaving Atlanta* is, as Jones herself puts it, her effort to "record the events of [her] generation," focusing particularly on the Atlanta child murders, while highlighting Atlanta neighborhoods and considering the urban South and rising black middle class. The book won many awards, including the Zora Neale Hurston / Richard Wright Foundation Legacy Award for Debut Fiction, and was named "Novel of the Year" by *Atlanta Magazine* and "Best Southern Novel of the Year" by *Creative Loafing Atlanta*. Both the *Atlanta Journal-Constitution* and the *Washington Post* listed it as one of the best novels of 2002.

In *The Untelling* Jones presents a black family split by a tragedy that isolates the surviving members from each other and disrupts their secure middle-class life. The novel's main character, Aria, a twenty-five-year-old literacy advocate working and living among Atlanta's poor, helps to reveal the city's fault lines of race, class, and gender through her individual struggle with her personal tragedy. Much of the novel is set in places familiar to Atlantans: Mosley Park, Spelman College, Windy Hill Road. By presenting her characters through several eras of Atlanta development, Jones underscores the level of change the city has undergone through time and how black life in the urban South has changed for the post–civil rights era generation. *The Untelling* won the 2005 Lillian Smith Award in fiction.

Jones's works have received excellent reviews. The *Boston Globe* has commented on her ability to characterize in a vivid and memorable way, being literary but not so much so as to obscure the narrative. The *Washington Globe* has remarked on her wry, poignant, honest characters. The *Atlanta Journal-Constitution* called *Leaving Atlanta* an "impressive first novel to explore one of the most hateful periods in the recent history of the City Too Busy to Hate." *Publisher's Weekly* proclaimed the novel a "strongly grounded tale [that] hums with the rhythms of schoolyard life." Reviewers also complimented her ability to render the child's perspective.

Jones has published in a variety of periodicals and anthologies, including *Sou'wester, Crab Orchard Review, Gumbo, Proverbs for the People, 64, Figdust, Catalyst,* and the *Langston Hughes Review*. Quietly negotiating the complicated social and political landscape of Atlanta, Jones also has become a voice for her generation, expressing, as she says in interviews, a sense of "entitlement and empowerment" her generation has inherited from the civil rights movement. Jones taught and coordinated a developmental reading program at Prairie View A&M University and was the Geier Writer in Residence at East Tennessee State University. She is currently an assistant professor of English at the University of Illinois, Urbana-Champaign, where she teaches creative writing.

ELIZABETE VASCONCELOS, *University of Georgia*

JUBILEE

Margaret Walker's novel *Jubilee*, the 1966 winner of Houghton Mifflin's Literary Fellowship Award, is one of the first novels to present the nineteenth-century African American historical experience in the South from a black and female point of view. The novel is a fictionalized account of the life of Walker's great-grandmother, Margaret Duggans Ware Brown, who was born a slave in Dawson in Terrell County and lived through Reconstruction in southwest Georgia. It is based on stories told to Walker by her maternal grandmother. Walker herself was not a Georgian by birth. Born in Alabama, she spent most of her teaching career in Mississippi and earned her doctorate at the University of Iowa, where she wrote most of *Jubilee*, which served as her dissertation.

Walker also learned much about the life of her great-grandfather, a free man from birth. While on a speaking engagement in nearby Albany in 1947, Walker visited Dawson, where she found a man who had known her great-grandfather, Randall Ware, who worked as a blacksmith and operated a grist mill, which she was able to visit. Walker based the description of the Dutton plantation, where most of her story is set, on an antebellum house that she discovered while visiting Bainbridge.

Walker's narrative is divided equally into sections on the antebellum era, the Civil War (1861–65), and Reconstruction. Each section contains eighteen to twenty-two chapters. Despite the lengthy narrative passages and the demands on the reader imposed by the various dialects, *Jubilee* moves its heroine, Vyry, from the slave cabin to the "Big House," and from slavery to freedom.

Jubilee draws on both history and folk traditions. The treatment of the slaves is based on numerous slave narratives Walker researched in archives and libraries in Georgia, North Carolina, and the National Archives. The Civil War section of *Jubilee* traces the battles, historically, from Tennessee to Sherman's march through Georgia. The African American male characters Randall Ware and Brother Zeke, who are both literate, function in dual roles as spies for the Union army and foot soldiers in the Confederate army. As the Union soldiers storm and destroy the plantations, including the Dutton place, Vyry's role changes from that of chattel slave to primary protector of the property and caretaker of her master's daughter and two grandchildren.

The book's final section begins with the war's end. It does not bring immediate freedom for Vyry. In addition to her caretaking duties, she, along with a "contraband" freedman named Innis Brown, must work the crops, as she anxiously awaits word from Randall Ware, her husband. When she receives news that Ware is dead, her heart will not allow her to believe it. Innis Brown, however, expresses interest in Vyry, befriends her children, "Minna" and Jim, and asks Vyry to marry him. His hard work and his dream of owning his home and farm persuade her to do so. They leave the Dutton plantation and move to Alabama. After several temporary homes, including one burned by the Ku Klux Klan, Vyry and her family settle in Greenville, Alabama. The building of the new house is a community effort. Vyry's midwifery and the marketing of her vegetables establish a bond between blacks and whites in the community. The house-building celebration concludes with quilting bees, plenty of food, and the solidarity of the "neighborhood watch."

With a home and a farm in place, Randall Ware, who survived the Civil War after all, fulfills Vyry's dream of schooling for her children. After seven years of military duty, work in his smithy and grist mill in Dawson, and service as a charter member of the Georgia Equal Rights Association, Ware traces Vyry and her family to Greenville. He knows of her marriage to Innis Brown, but his mission is to take his son, Jim, to a training school in Selma, Alabama. The final section of *Jubilee* thus shifts its focus to the education of blacks during and after Reconstruction.

The ending of *Jubilee* suggests a connection between the events the novel has described during Reconstruction and the civil rights movement of the 1960s. The narrative ends on a train bound for Selma. As Jim and his father board the train, the conductor announces the seating order — colored up front and whites in the rear.

JACQUELINE MILLER CARMICHAEL, *Georgia State University*

SUGGESTED READING

Kay Bonetti, *An Interview with Margaret Walker* (Columbia, Mo.: American Audio Prose Library, 1991).

Jacqueline Miller Carmichael, *Trumpeting a Fiery Sound: History and Folklore in Margaret Walker's "Jubilee"* (Athens: University of Georgia Press, 1998).

Margaret Walker, *How I Wrote "Jubilee"* (Chicago: Third World, 1972).

TERRY KAY
(b. 1938)

Terry Kay is the author of nine novels, a children's book, a collection of nonfiction prose, and several screenplays. His novel *To Dance with the White Dog* became a best-seller that was dramatized by the Hallmark Hall of Fame in a televised production.

Terry Winter Kay was born February 10, 1938, in Hart County, the eleventh of twelve children of T. H. Kay, a farmer and nurseryman, and Viola Winn Kay. He grew up on a farm, played football for Royston High School, and earned his B.A. degree in social science from LaGrange College in 1959. In August of that year, he married Tommie Duncan.

In 1959, after a brief, unsuccessful career as an insurance salesman, Kay began working as a copy boy and then a reporter for the *Decatur-DeKalb News*. From 1962 to 1973 he worked as a sportswriter and a film and theater critic for the *Atlanta Journal*. Kay left the newspaper for the corporate world, working as creative director and account executive for various advertising firms between 1973 and 1977. At the Oglethorpe Power Corporation in Chamblee, where he worked from 1977 until he left in 1989 to devote his full time to writing, Kay rose to the level of senior vice president.

Kay's first novel, *The Year the Lights Came On* (1976), began as a magazine piece that his friend Pat Conroy encouraged him to turn into a novel. The novel draws on Kay's boyhood in Royston. A nostalgic coming-of-age story set in the 1940s, the novel describes the effects of rural electrification on two rival gangs in the fictional county of Eden, Georgia.

Kay set his second novel, *After Eli* (1981), in a remote Appalachian village in the Great Smoky Mountains during the late 1930s. Michael O'Rear, an itinerant and charismatic Irishman, attempts to win the hearts of Rachel Pettit, her daughter, and her sister, in order to find a legendary fortune left by Eli Pettit. A drama of unfolding terror and psychological horror, the novel is a disturbing ghost story. *Dark Thirty* (1984), set also in the hills of north Georgia, continues the theme of violence.

In 1990 Kay published his breakthrough novel, *To Dance with the White Dog*. The work made him internationally famous. The Hallmark Hall of Fame dramatization of the novel in 1993 won an Emmy. The novel began as a nonfiction work to celebrate Kay's parents' long marriage and to recount how his father, who died of cancer in 1980, was visited by a white dog after his wife's death in 1973. The eighty-one-year-old protagonist, Sam Peek, has just lost his wife, Cora, after fifty-seven years of marriage. A phantom-like white dog appears soon afterward, and Sam is convinced that it is the soul of Cora. The dog accompanies Sam on a journey, literally and symbolically, to his high school reunion in Madison. This touching novel explores universal themes of love, loss, and coming to terms with mortality.

Kay followed this best-seller with *Shadow Song* (1994), drawn from three summers spent working in the Catskill Mountains in New York to save money for college. *Shadow Song*, like Kay's first novel, began as a magazine piece, and once again Pat Conroy urged him to turn the story into a longer work. In 1997 Kay published *The Runaway*, a novel set in the small town of Crossover, Georgia, shortly after World War II. Son Jesus and Tom, both twelve years old, lead a kind of Tom Sawyer and Huck Finn life of adventure until they discover human bones in an old sawmill.

The plot of *The Kidnapping of Aaron Greene* (1999) was conceived by Kay more than twenty-five years before its publication, when he worked for the *Atlanta Journal*. Aaron Greene is kidnapped on his way to his job as a mail clerk at an Atlanta bank. The kidnappers ask for $10 million, not from his family but from the bank. The manager, seeing Aaron as a "nobody," refuses to pay the ransom, and Aaron is left frightened and alone, waiting for the life-or-death outcome.

Kay's novel *Taking Lottie Home* (2000) is set in northeast Georgia and is the story of a woman named Lottie Barton, "something of an amateur prostitute," who, leaving her shanty home in Augusta, meets two failed minor league ballplayers on a train. Despite her trials and failures, Lottie "never loses her innocence."

The Valley of Light (2003) is Kay's ninth novel. The story concerns a young fisherman in the north Georgia mountains and has some similarities with *To Dance with the White Dog*. Kay says, "Both have very strong metaphors — the white dog and the fish. *The Valley of Light* is about someone who has some incapacities, but who has a great gift in other ways." In 2004 the novel won the Townsend Prize for Fiction.

Among the other awards that Kay has received are the Georgia Author of the Year Award in 1981 for *After Eli* and the Southeastern Library Association Outstanding Author of the Year Award in 1991 for *To Dance with the White Dog*, which was twice nominated for the American Booksellers Association's Book of the Year. Kay also won an Emmy in 1990 for his original teleplay *Run Down the Rabbit*. In addition to his eight novels, he has also written *To Whom the Angels Spoke: A Story of the Christmas* (1991) and a collection of columns and essays, *Special K: The Wisdom of Terry Kay* (2000).

Kay lives with his wife in Athens, Georgia; the couple has four children and four grandchildren. In 1999 LaGrange College awarded him an Honorary Doctor of Humane Letters.

GARY KERLEY, *North Hall High School*

SUGGESTED READING

Contemporary Authors, vol. 110 (Detroit: Gale, 1984), s.v. "Terry Kay."

Contemporary Southern Men Fiction Writers: An Annotated Bibliography (Lanham, Md.: Scarecrow, 1998), s.v. "Terry Kay."

Contemporary Southern Writers (Detroit: St. James, 1999), s.v. "Terry Kay."

Bob Summer, "PW Interviews: Terry Kay," *Publishers Weekly*, October 10, 1994.

JAMES KILGO
(1941–2002)

James Patrick Kilgo, an essayist and novelist, wrote with a reverence for the natural world and a deep and abiding sense of family and history. His essays on hunting, nature, family, and personal introspection won him national attention, and his novel, *Daughter of My People*, earned him the Townsend Prize for Fiction.

The son of John and Caroline Kilgo, he was born and grew up in Darlington, South Carolina. He received his undergraduate degree from Wofford College in Spartanburg, South Carolina, and earned M.A. and Ph.D. degrees in English from Tulane University in New Orleans, Louisiana. Kilgo joined the faculty at the University of Georgia in 1967, where he received five Outstanding Honors Professor awards and the Honoratus Award for Excellence in Teaching. He directed the creative writing program from 1994 to 1996 and retired from teaching in 1999. Kilgo, who battled cancer for more than ten years, died in 2002 at the age of 61.

Trained as a scholar in American literature, Kilgo wrote his doctoral dissertation on novels about World War II and taught courses in American and southern literature. From an early point in his life he tried his hand at wood carving, sketching, and other creative activities; his friends also knew him as an able storyteller. Dissatisfied with scholarly writing, Kilgo began to write creative essays in the late 1970s, at first in the form of hunting columns for a local newspaper.

Pleased with these early efforts, he began to write longer essays. Though many of them seem to concern his experiences as a hunter, they actually chronicle his gradual disenchantment with hunting. What attracted his interest instead was the comradeship he enjoyed with friends he made while hunting and the experience of nature itself. Kilgo organized these essays into his first book, *Deep Enough for Ivorybills* (1988), in which he uses hunting to discuss how certain experiences in the natural world have enriched his life. Hunting deer in the swamps of South Carolina allows Kilgo to know animals in nature not as an abstraction or an idea, but as an experience: "Their attractive force clapped me to them." Hunting also offers rituals of manhood that bind fathers and sons in a reverential sacrament: "the spilled blood" on hand and face "a baptism with all the rights and privileges thereunto pertaining." Hopes of seeing and hearing the nearly extinct ivorybilled woodpecker in the South Carolina swamps become in this book a metaphor for the powerful and persistent tug that the natural world, despite its vulnerability and fragility, exerts on us.

In his second essay collection, *Inheritance of Horses* (1994), Kilgo focuses on the relationship between nature and the rest of his life. What empowers this book is his dawning awareness that he is not a man of the wilderness but a professor, a writer, and a family man, and it is to his family that he must turn if he is to claim his full inheritance. Significantly, he leaves his hunting buddies behind in the essay "According to Hemingway" and goes fishing instead with his family. We still have the manly drama, in which Kilgo catches a marlin, but with him now he also has Jane, his wife, and Sarah Jane, his daughter, as he learns, before landing the catch, that there is more than fish to this story: his daughter is getting married. What this volume lacks in the unity of the first collection it gains in diversity and breadth. Some of the essays focus on natural subjects, such as bird-watching or a hornet building a nest outside his living room window. Others, however, reveal broader concerns: a tall-tale encounter with moonshiners in north Georgia, hunting for arrowheads, a hair-raising plunge in a jeep down Brasstown Bald, or a moving account of the close friendship of his grandfathers. The essays display a writer of considerable range and talent, at home in the natural as well as the domestic world.

Devotion to family gains full voice in Kilgo's 1998 novel, *Daughter of My People*, based on a story from his own family history. In the novel the protagonist Hart Bonner falls in love with Jennie Grant, a beautiful mixed-race woman who is the descendant of a union between Bonner's grandfather and a slave. When Hart's brother Tison also falls in love with and attempts to force himself on Jennie, the stage is set for the novel's primary conflict. In this novel Kilgo explores the deep paradoxes and ironies of the heritage of race in the South and of the United States — a history whose very divisions are built on connections and kinship. In a world of racial bigotry, cruelty, and family struggle, Kilgo creates in Jennie a character who defies human categories. He describes her in a way that emphasizes the meaninglessness of racial divisions: "[Jennie] has many colors. It depends on the light and on her temperature and mood and what part of her body. She is the color of pears and ribbon cane molasses and rye whiskey in a glass." In Hart Bonner he creates a character whose conflicts with family history, his own prejudices, and the racism of his region are emblematic of southern and national history. In recognition for this book, Kilgo received the Townsend Prize for Fiction in 1998.

Kilgo's final book, *The Colors of Africa*, was published in 2003, shortly after his death. This narrative of a hunting trip to Africa in 2000 combines his interests in hunting, the natural world, and family and friends with his concern over the developing illness that would eventually take his life. As a travel journal, natural history, and meditative autobiography, the result is a distinctive work. Neither endorsing nor criticizing the concept of the white hunter in Africa, it describes in straightforward and candid detail Kilgo's experiences and sensations. He notes early in the book that travel to Africa had always been his dream. In accepting a friend's invitation to accompany him on a safari, Kilgo did so planning to go only as a photographer. Once there he is offered the opportunity to shoot a kudu, the animal at the center of Ernest Hemingway's *The Green Hills of Africa*, one of Kilgo's favorite books. This becomes a test of his own physical sense of himself as a man who once could hunt with skill and confidence but who now is not so sure of his energies.

Kilgo wrote about the remote and wild areas of the southern mountains in *The Blue Wall: Wilderness of the Carolinas and Georgia* (1996), a book done in collaboration with the photographer Thomas Wyche. His memoir, *The Hand-Carved Creche and Other Christmas Stories* (1999), recalls memories of Christmas with his family in Darlington. In all of his books, he suggests that we are a product of two shaping forces: our families and the natural world. Meaning, his books tell us, resides there.

HUGH RUPPERSBURG, *University of Georgia*
STEVE HARVEY, *Young Harris College*

SUGGESTED READING

David Miller, "Out Far and Deep," *Sewanee Review* 96, no. 4 (1988): 684–87.

Paul Schullery, "The Sporting Life," review of *Deep Enough for Ivorybills*, by James Kilgo, *New York Times*, April 24, 1988.

JOHN OLIVER KILLENS

(1916–1987)

The African American writer John Oliver Killens, a native of Macon, drew on his own encounters with racism to compose such works as *Youngblood*, a classic of social protest fiction. Working within a tradition that coupled art with activism, Killens said, "There is no such thing as art for art's sake. All art is propaganda, although there is much propaganda that is not art." The founding chairman of the celebrated Harlem Writers Guild, Killens became a spiritual father of the Black Arts Movement of the 1960s. Like the writer Richard Wright, whom he greatly admired, Killens inspired a subsequent generation of African Americans through writings charged with strong social and political messages.

Killens was born on January 14, 1916, to Charles Myles Killens Sr., a restaurant manager, and Willie Lee Coleman, an insurance company clerk. His parents were well read and kept abreast of trends and events important to African Americans. Along with Killens's great-grandmother, his parents instilled in him a pride in black culture and a belief in the power of the arts to effect social change.

Killens graduated in 1933 from Ballard Normal School in Macon, a private institution run by the American Missionary Association and, at the time, one of the few secondary schools for blacks in Georgia. With the aim of becoming a lawyer, Killens did his undergraduate coursework at Edward Waters College in Jacksonville, Florida; Morris Brown College in Atlanta; and Howard University in Washington, D.C. He then attended the Robert H. Terrell Law School in Washington, D.C., but quit before his final year to study creative writing at Columbia University in New York.

His college years encompassed other formative experiences: a stint at the National Labor Relations Board (NLRB), military service, and marriage. His work with the NLRB turned him into a lifetime advocate for organized labor. During World War II Killens served from 1942 to 1945 in a U.S. Army amphibious unit. He spent more than two years in the South Pacific, and rose to the rank of master sergeant. In 1943 Killens married Grace Ward Jones, with whom he had two children: a son, John Charles, and a daughter, Barbara.

In the early 1950s Killens, who had settled in New York, joined three of his friends to form the Harlem Writers Guild. Killens polished his first novel, *Youngblood* (1954), at meetings in members' homes. Spanning the Jim Crow era through the Great Depression, it portrays ordinary black people in the fictional rural community of Crossroads, Georgia, as they struggle to maintain their dignity and secure their rights.

His second novel, *And Then We Heard the Thunder* (1963), is about a law school student who, just as Killens did, interrupts his education to serve in an all-black amphibious regiment in World War II. As an officer, the main character endures not only the hardships of war but also the bigotry of his white fellow officers. Critic Jonathan Yardley of the *Washington Post* wrote that it was "one of the few distinguished novels about World War II" and a "powerful — though regrettably little-known — examination of the lives of black servicemen." Another of Killens's important works is the novel *The Cotillion; or, One Good Bull Is Half the Herd* (1971). Satirizing class pretensions, *The Cotillion* uproariously portrays the conflicts between militants and social climbers within black society in the 1960s.

Killens wrote six novels for adults. Additional book-length works include *Black Man's Burden* (1965), essays on race in America; *Great Black Russian* (1989), a biographical work on the poet Alexander Pushkin; and two books for young readers, *Great Gittin' Up Morning* (1972), a biography of Denmark Vesey, and *A Man Ain't Nothin' but a Man* (1975), which recounts the adventures of John Henry. Killens also wrote plays, screenplays, and numerous articles and short stories that appeared in publications ranging from *Black Scholar* and the *New York Times* to

Ebony and *Redbook*. His works have been published in some fifteen countries, and a representative sampling remains in print today.

When Killens was not writing, he worked for social causes and racial equality. A man whose low-key manner belied his hard-edged activist beliefs, Killens knew both Martin Luther King Jr. and Malcolm X — but identified more closely with the latter. Killens once wrote, "My fight is not to be a white man in a black skin, but to inject some black blood, some black intelligence into the pallid mainstream of American life." As a writer-in-residence at Howard University; Fisk University in Nashville, Tennessee; and Medgar Evers College in New York, Killens was known as a generous, encouraging mentor. He was instrumental in establishing black writers' conferences at each of the schools.

Killens's many honors include the vice presidency of the Black Academy of Arts and Letters, a National Endowment for the Arts fellowship (1980), and a Distinguished Writer Award from the Middle Atlantic Writers Association (1984). The Before Columbus Foundation, which sponsors the American Book Awards, cited Killens for lifetime achievement in 1985. He is also a member of the Georgia Writers Hall of Fame.

Killens died on October 27, 1987.

DAVID E. DES JARDINES, *University of Georgia Press*

SUGGESTED READING

C. Gerald Fraser, "John Oliver Killens, 71, Author and Founder of Writers' Group," obituary, *New York Times*, October 30, 1987.

John Oliver Killens, "Speaking Out: Negroes Have a Right to Fight Back," *Saturday Evening Post*, July 2, 1966.

Adele Sarkissian, ed., "The Half Ain't Never Been Told," *Contemporary Authors Autobiography Series*, vol. 2 (Detroit: Gale, 1985), s.v. "John Oliver Killens."

No southerner was more outspoken in expressing moral indignation about the region's injustices and inequities during the pre–civil rights era than the writer Lillian Smith, and in no work did she articulate that indignation more fully than in *Killers of the Dream*. First published in 1949, and revised and expanded in 1961, it is arguably the most influential and enduring of the many writings this self-described "tortured southern liberal" produced over her three-decade career.

Smith had already established a national reputation as an unrelenting critic of southern racism with the publication of her controversial novel *Strange Fruit* in 1944 as well as in numerous essays and articles. In the wake of *Strange Fruit*'s success, she decided to elaborate on its themes in nonfiction and in 1947 began writing the book that would become *Killers of the Dream*. The title alludes to those human forces — racism, violence, poverty, ignorance, and oppression — that destroy mankind's "dreams" of freedom and human dignity.

Upon its publication by W. W. Norton in the fall of 1949, *Killers of the Dream* garnered widely varying reactions. Enthusiastic reviews appeared in the New York and Boston press, whose critics admired Smith's hard-hitting and insightful analysis as well as the sheer courage of a southerner in publishing so unsparing an indictment of her native region. Far more of the response was hostile, however, and criticized the book's poor organization, repetitious and elliptical arguments, and strident tone.

Smith was most disappointed, even angered, by the reaction of other so-called southern liberals to the book. *Atlanta Constitution* editor Ralph McGill claimed to admire her honesty and eloquence but concluded that her writing was "too crowded with her own Freudian interpretations and emotions to be of real value." Sales of the book proved disappointing as well. *Killers* sold twenty-eight thousand copies in its first year of publication, well below the performance of her more sensationalistic novel five years earlier. Smith felt scorned, and then ignored, by southern moderates and conservatives and silenced by the literary establishment nationwide.

Killers of the Dream consists of a mix of genres and reads more like a series of disparate essays than like a coherent narrative. Although Smith once labeled the work a memoir, its autobiographical passages are fleeting and anecdotal. *Killers* also consists of sociological and historical analysis, editorial commentary, and allegory. Smith's interest in Jim Crow and its effects were more psychological than political. She later stated that she wrote the book "because I had to find out what life in a segregated culture had done to me, one person." She drew from certain traumas of her own childhood to examine the psyches of children, black and white, and how their early inculcation into a racially oppressive society warped their sense of values and stifled any prospects of challenging the social and economic shortcomings of their elders. Her opening sentence — "Even its children knew that the South was in trouble" — suggests her preoccupation not only with youth but also with guilt and shame, both individual and collective, all of which remain constant themes throughout the book.

Smith was explicit in her attacks on all manifestations of southern racism, including the Ku Klux Klan, lynch mobs, sharecropping, and segregation. She was also interested in gender and class oppression as by-products of racial attitudes and was particularly effective in probing the effects of race on southern womanhood and on the exploitation of poor whites. In a chapter called "Three Ghost Stories," Smith analyzes the extent to which relationships between white men and black women, white fathers and their mulatto children, and white children and their black nurses had long haunted southern society. In a parable entitled "Two Men and a Bargain," she illustrates the conscious conspiracy between Mr. Rich White and Mr. Poor White to subjugate blacks economically by shutting them out of lowly employment opportunities, thus allowing a fuller exploitation of a poor white labor force — who were grateful not to have to compete with blacks for jobs.

A book too far ahead of its time in 1949 to resonate with most readers, *Killers of the Dream* had become far more relevant by 1961, as Americans sought to understand a South then in the midst of a social and political revolution. Smith persuaded her publisher to issue a revised edition of the book to take advantage of the national and international attention focused on the region during the civil rights movement. She rewrote the book's last two chapters to address the movement in progress and its implications for the South's future. She also wrote a lengthy foreword in which she explains the new relevance of the book's original message and condemns the continued apathy of many well-meaning Americans to the racial injustices of the South, which she found much more disturbing than the fanatical resistance of die-hard segregationists.

Smith was gratified by the far more positive reception of the revised edition of *Killers* and took full advantage of the celebrity status it brought her among a new generation of college students and other young activists in the movement. The black college students who staged the first sit-in in Greensboro, North Carolina, in 1960 stated that they were most influenced by the ideas of the economist and sociologist Gunnar Myrdal, the leader of India and proponent of nonviolent protest Mahatma Gandhi, and Smith.

Smith succumbed to cancer in 1966; thus she did not live long enough to see *Killers of the Dream* emerge as a classic of twentieth-century southern literature. The work continues to be standard reading in college courses covering southern history, race relations, and women's studies.

JOHN C. INSCOE, *University of Georgia*

SUGGESTED READING

Fred Hobson, *Tell about the South: The Southern Rage to Explain* (Baton Rouge: Louisiana State University Press, 1983).

Anne C. Loveland, *Lillian Smith, a Southern Confronting the South: A Biography* (Baton Rouge: Louisiana State University Press, 1986).

Randall Patton, "Lillian Smith and the Transformation of American Liberalism, 1945–1950," *Georgia Historical Quarterly* 76 (summer 1992): 373–92.

Morton Sosna, *In Search of the Silent South: Southern Liberals and the Race Issue* (New York: Columbia University Press, 1977).

MARTIN LUTHER KING JR.

(1929–1968)

Martin Luther King Jr., Baptist minister and president of the Southern Christian Leadership Conference, was the most prominent African American leader in the civil rights movement of the 1950s and 1960s.

Family, church, and education were the central forces shaping King's early life. Michael Luther King Jr. was born in Atlanta on January 15, 1929, the son of Alberta Williams and Michael Luther King Sr. In 1934, after visiting Europe, Michael King Sr. changed his and his son's name in honor of the sixteenth-century German church reformer Martin Luther. King spent his early years in the family home at 501 Auburn Avenue, about a block from Ebenezer Baptist Church. His maternal grandfather, A. D. Williams, was pastor at Ebenezer from 1894 until 1931. After Williams's death, the elder King succeeded his father-in-law at the pulpit.

King was educated in Atlanta, graduating from Booker T. Washington High School in 1944. He then followed in the path of his maternal grandfather and father and enrolled at Morehouse College. King first considered studying medicine or law but decided to major in sociology. He ultimately found the call to the ministry irresistible, however. He served as assistant to his father at Ebenezer while studying at Morehouse. In February 1948 King Sr. ordained his son as a Baptist minister.

After graduating from Morehouse in June 1948 King studied for a divinity degree at Crozer Theological Seminary in Upland, Pennsylvania, graduating in May 1951. The following September King enrolled at Boston University in the Ph.D. program in systematic theology. There he met his future wife, Coretta Scott. King's father preferred that his son marry an Atlanta woman and initially opposed King's plans to marry Coretta. When King refused to back down, his father relented, and on June 18, 1953, he performed the marriage ceremony at the Scott family home in rural Perry County, Alabama.

During his last year of residential studies at Boston University, King sought employment while he finished his dissertation. Through a family friend he learned of a vacant position at Dexter Avenue Baptist Church in Montgomery, Alabama. Desiring a pulpit in a southern city and wanting to escape Atlanta and gain independence from his father, King arranged a trial sermon. He was offered the position, and in 1954 he moved to Montgomery with Coretta. In June 1955 King received his Ph.D. The Kings' first child, Yolanda Denise, was born November 17, 1955.

On December 1, 1955, Rosa Parks, a respected member of Montgomery's black community, refused to surrender her bus seat to a white passenger when asked to do so. She was arrested for violating a city segregation statute. Community activists proposed a bus boycott in protest. They asked King if his church could be used as a meeting place to discuss the boycott. Although he supported the plan to boycott, King hesitated to become involved because of his existing commitments. After some persuasion, however, he agreed.

At the meeting black leaders agreed on a one-day boycott. When this was successful, they agreed to extend the action. King was asked to head the Montgomery Improvement Association (MIA), a new organization formed to run the bus boycott. He had not planned to take a leading role, but he agreed to serve. The boycott ran for 381 days. Throughout, whites in Montgomery tried to stymie it. King and other MIA members were arrested. Segregationists even bombed King's home.

The intimidation strengthened the resolve of the black community. The initial demands of the MIA for a modified system of segregation on city buses evolved into a lawsuit that called for its total abolishment. The case went all the way to the U.S. Supreme Court, which ruled segregation on Montgomery buses unconstitutional. On December 21, 1956, King was among the first passengers to board an integrated bus.

The bus boycott made King a national symbol of black protest.

In the next few years he spoke alongside other national black leaders and met with U.S. president Dwight D. Eisenhower and a host of foreign dignitaries. In 1958 King published *Stride toward Freedom*, his account of the Montgomery boycott. But his new-found recognition came at a price. In September 1958 a mentally ill black woman, Izola Ware Curry, stabbed King in the chest at a book signing in New York. King barely survived that injury. Earlier that month, police in Montgomery had again arrested King. The Federal Bureau of Investigation (FBI) began to take an interest in him, starting a covert surveillance of his activities that continued for the rest of his life.

All the while King looked to capitalize on the success of the Montgomery boycott. In August 1957 the Southern Christian Leadership Conference (SCLC), an organization comprising religious, civic, and political affiliate groups, was launched with King as president. The SCLC, with headquarters in Atlanta, initially focused on supporting bus boycotts and instituting drives to register black voters. These campaigns made little impression. At the end of 1959 King resigned from his position at Dexter and in early 1960 moved back to Atlanta, sharing the pastorate at Ebenezer with his father. There he could maintain closer contact with SCLC headquarters, in the hope of launching more effective campaigns in the future. Though his work kept him away much of the time, Atlanta remained his home base, and that of Coretta and his children, for the final eight years of his life.

Events quickly overtook King and the SCLC. In February 1960 four black students staged a sit-in at a segregated lunch counter in Greensboro, North Carolina. The sit-in movement rapidly expanded to other cities, where it met with some success in persuading local communities to desegregate facilities. In April 1960 the Student Nonviolent Coordinating Committee (SNCC), based in Atlanta, was formed to support student protest. In 1961 the Chicago-based Congress of Racial Equality (CORE) held interracial "freedom rides" to test the court-ordered desegregation of southern bus terminals. The freedom rides ultimately led to federal action in upholding the court order.

The success of sit-ins and freedom rides demonstrated the relevance of nonviolent direct action to the civil rights movement. During the Montgomery boycott, two of King's close advisors, white pacifist Glenn E. Smiley and black activist Bayard Rustin, tutored King in nonviolence. King's interest in nonviolence continued to develop and became a central tenet of his leadership. King joined student sit-ins in Atlanta, though he declined an invitation to participate in the freedom rides.

King and the SCLC embarked upon their first nonviolent direct-action campaign in 1961 in Albany, at the invitation of local blacks. The Albany Movement encountered numerous problems. King and the SCLC lacked specific goals and a coherent strategy. Divisions in the black community hampered demonstrations. Albany police chief Laurie Pritchett refused to engage protestors and instead made mass arrests that quickly depleted the movement's resources. Without dramatic points of conflict, the tactic of nonviolence lacked potency. The federal government refused to intervene, and the local white business community refused to enter into substantive negotiations. The campaign dissolved without gaining any significant concessions.

Learning the lessons of Albany, in 1963 King and the SCLC carefully chose their next target. In Birmingham, the Alabama Christian Movement for Human Rights (ACMHR) under the leadership of the Reverend Fred Shuttlesworth provided an established local base for protest. Specific goals and a movement strategy were drawn up in advance. As expected, Birmingham police chief Eugene "Bull" Connor met protestors with force, using police dogs and high-power fire hoses to break up demonstrations. The conflict brought national news headlines and federal intervention, and pulled local white businessmen to the negotiating table. The campaign won significant gains in desegregating downtown facilities and in opening up black employment opportunities, although segregationist violence in the city remained a serious problem.

The years between 1963 and 1965 represented the high point of King's career. In August 1963 the civil rights movement staged its largest gathering ever, with as many as 250,000 participants at the March on Washington for Jobs and Freedom. King's "I Have a Dream" speech was the most memorable event of the day and confirmed him as black America's most prominent spokesperson. In 1964 King was awarded the Nobel Peace Prize in Oslo, Norway. The same year, Congress passed the 1964 Civil Rights Act, outlawing segregation in public facilities. In 1965 King and the SCLC campaigned in Selma, Alabama, for black voting rights. The campaign led to the passage of the 1965 Voting Rights Act, which abolished legal impediments to voting rights for African Americans and initiated greater federal protection for blacks at the polls.

Not everything went King's way. Attempts to renew demonstrations in Birmingham after a surge in white violence met with stiff opposition and failed to make much headway. U.S. president John F. Kennedy's assassination in November 1963 lost King a carefully cultivated federal ally, although the new president, Lyndon B. Johnson, proved equally if not more sympathetic with the civil rights movement. A new SCLC campaign launched in St. Augustine, Florida, in 1964 failed to win meaningful concessions for local blacks. King's attempts to mediate the seating of the Mississippi Freedom Democratic Party delegation at the 1964 Democratic Party convention failed. The FBI stepped up its campaign of harassment and intimidation against King.

As was often the case in King's relatively short public career, victory and defeat, advancement and setback, were never far apart.

In the last few years of King's life, important changes were taking place in his thinking, in the civil rights struggle, and in American society. Between 1965 and 1967 blacks rioted in several U.S. cities. In 1966 some activists adopted the slogan "Black Power," which represented a new wave of militancy that, frustrated with persistent racism in American society, questioned the relevance and efficacy of nonviolence in addressing racial problems. The escalation of the Vietnam War shifted public debate, material resources, and political will away from the civil rights movement. Conservative politicians, playing to a white backlash against black gains, were increasingly successful in advocating a tougher law-and-order stance to subdue protest.

King responded to these developments in a variety of ways. He took the SCLC into the northern ghettos in an attempt to alleviate the conditions that caused the urban riots. He opposed much of the angry rhetoric of Black Power and continued to stress the importance of nonviolence. He spoke out ever more stridently in opposition to American involvement in the Vietnam War. He opposed conservative politicians who sought to exploit white racial fears. He also gained new insight about black problems in the United States as the movement shifted from tackling segregation to confronting the problem of racial discrimination.

In 1965–66 the SCLC launched its first northern campaign in Chicago. King felt that the urban riots in northern cities underlined the need for SCLC assistance, focusing on such issues as black employment, housing, and education opportunities. The Chicago campaign highlighted the difficulties of fighting entrenched racism. The city was much bigger than previous communities in which the SCLC had worked. Discrimination was much more difficult to dramatize than segregation. SCLC funds declined, making operations even more problematic. Despite some successes, the SCLC failed to make the desired impact on black advancement in Chicago.

The Chicago campaign convinced King that many of the problems faced by African Americans were due to fundamental economic inequalities in American society. Consequently, he called for a redistribution of wealth and resources, advocating a move away from the harsher aspects of capitalism toward a society modeled on some form of democratic socialism. The last campaign King planned with the SCLC was a Poor People's March to Washington to dramatize the problem of poverty in the United States. But on April 4, 1968, before the march took place, King was assassinated in Memphis, Tennessee, where he was supporting striking sanitation workers. King was survived by his wife and four children, Yolanda Denise, Martin Luther III, Dexter Scott, and Bernice Albertine.

In 1983 Congress passed legislation to make the third Monday in January a national holiday in honor of King. The first Martin Luther King Jr. holiday was observed on January 20, 1986. King remains the only African American to be commemorated in this way.

JOHN A. KIRK, *Royal Holloway, University of London, United Kingdom*

SUGGESTED READING

Taylor B. Branch, *Parting the Waters: America in the King Years, 1954–1963* (New York: Simon and Schuster, 1988).

Taylor B. Branch, *Pillar of Fire: America in the King Years, 1963–65* (New York: Simon and Schuster, 1998).

Clayborne Carson, ed., *The Autobiography of Martin Luther King, Jr.* (New York: Warner Books, 1998).

Michael Eric Dyson, *I May Not Get There with You: The True Martin Luther King, Jr.* (New York: Free Press, 2000).

Adam Fairclough, *To Redeem the Soul of America: The Southern Christian Leadership Conference and Martin Luther King, Jr.* (Athens: University of Georgia Press, 1987).

David J. Garrow, *Bearing the Cross: Martin Luther King, Jr., and the Southern Christian Leadership Conference* (New York: Morrow, 1986).

David J. Garrow, *The FBI and Martin Luther King, Jr.: From "Solo" to Memphis* (New York: Norton, 1981).

John A. Kirk, *Martin Luther King Jr.: Profiles in Power* (New York: Longman, 2004).

SIDNEY LANIER
(1842–1881)

Sidney Lanier contributed significantly to the arts in nineteenth-century America. His accomplishments as a poet, novelist, composer, and critic reflect his eclectic interests, and his melodic celebrations of Georgia's terrain are among his most widely read poems. His works reflect a love of the land, as well as his concern over declining values and commercial culture in the Reconstruction South. Some of his writings extol the rhythmic natural world and the religious vision it evokes. Lake Lanier was dedicated to him in 1955 in recognition of his life and accomplishments.

Sidney Lanier was born in Macon on February 3, 1842. He graduated from Oglethorpe College near Milledgeville in 1860 with high honors. When the Civil War began, he volunteered to serve in the Confederate army. In 1864 he was captured and held as a prisoner of war for four months in Maryland, during which time he contracted the debilitating tuberculosis that plagued him for the rest of his life. His marriage to Mary Day in 1867 led to the births of four sons. Rarely fully focused on one occupational pursuit, Lanier had difficulty maintaining steady employment and providing for his family; he worked in Georgia, Alabama, and Texas as a tutor, teacher, and law clerk. He was frequently impoverished and sometimes ill with the ever-present tuberculosis, which was exacerbated by stress and worry. For one school year he was principal of an academy in Prattville, Alabama, but it closed in 1868 in the face of economic depression. From 1868 to 1873, he studied law and worked in his father's legal office in Macon. Lanier then moved to Baltimore, where he accepted a position as first flutist for the Peabody Orchestra. During his years in Baltimore, he studied English literature and eventually became a lecturer at the Peabody Institute and then at Johns Hopkins University. Lanier's health continued to worsen. He died on September 7, 1881, in Lynn, North Carolina, where he had traveled in the hope that the climate might cure him.

Lanier's works reflect his education, his love of literature and music, and his concerns for the Reconstruction South. His first major publication was his only novel, *Tiger-Lilies* (1867). Depicting the moral and actual tension between devilish Yankee materialist John Cranston and Southern Rebel humanist Philip Sterling before and during the Civil War, the novel balances romantic views of good and evil with realistically portrayed battle scenes. While the novel was unsuccessful, it mirrored some of the painful struggles of the war-torn South. As his focus shifted from poetry to music with his acceptance of the Peabody Orchestra position, he composed his *Danse des Moucherons (Midge Dance)* (1873) for the flute.

Following this success, Lanier returned to poetry, writing his most memorable poems in a relatively brief period of time. They reflect his accomplished infusion of music into poetic lines. For example, "The Symphony" (1875), thematically an assault upon materialism, is a work of technical virtuosity. Employing remarkable shifts in meter and tone, Lanier structured the poem like the parts of a symphony orchestra. Violins describe the poverty and oppression caused by trade. They are followed by the flute's description of transcendent nature, the clarinet's admonition against prostitution, the horn's celebration of chivalry, and the final plea by "ancient wise bassoons" for a return to innocence. The final lines of the poem reflect Lanier's desire to spare the postbellum South its suffering, but they also illustrate his artistic vision:

> And yet shall Love himself be heard,
> Though long deferred, though long deferred:
> O'er the modern waste a dove hath whirred:
> Music is Love in search of a word.

Today Sidney Lanier is most noted for his experimental musical renderings of Georgia's fields, rivers, and shores in such poems as "Corn" (1875), "The Song of the Chattahoochee" (1877), and "The Marshes of Glynn" (1879). In "Corn," the narrator wanders to the edge of a field of corn stalks that stand in rows like soldiers, born in the field and soon to die there honorably. He recalls how a previous farmer, now fled west, had succumbed to commercialism and King Cotton and had suffered great loss. Now the narrator sees the field as returning to its rightful task in producing the older crop. Lanier regarded traditional southern agriculture, rather than commerce from the North, as offering the best hope for the South. In the alliterative and fast-flowing lines of "The Song of the Chattahoochee," the river speaks of its rush through the northeast Georgia counties of Habersham and Hall. Despite the call to "abide" made by the luxurious native laurels, ferns, grasses, oaks, chestnuts, and pines, as well as the "friendly brawl" of stones and jewels on the river's bottom, the Chattahoochee insists upon its duty. It must water the fields and turn waterwheels on the plains as it makes its way toward the Gulf of Mexico.

Lanier found his purest voice in the religious vision of "The Marshes of Glynn." Set in southeastern Glynn County, the poem begins with a rhythmic description of the thick marsh as the narrator feels himself growing and connecting with the sinews of the marsh itself. Then as his vision expands seaward, he recognizes in an epiphanal moment that the marshes and sea, in their vastness, are the expression of "the greatness of God" and are filled with power and mystery.

Sidney Lanier wrote three texts of literary criticism, two of which were published posthumously. *The Science of English Verse* (1880), a systematic study of verse forms and methods of versifying, seeks to construct a scientific basis for the writing of verse, and hence, the writing of music. *The English Novel and the Principle of Its Development* (1883) delineates the development of the Western human personality and its manifestations in music, literature, and science through the course of Western history. Throughout the text Lanier argues that growth in these fields occurs concurrently. *Shakspere and His Forerunners: Studies in Elizabethan Poetry and Its Development from Early English* (two volumes, 1902) was an outgrowth of his scholarly work as a lecturer at Johns Hopkins University.

SUSAN COPELAND HENRY, *Clayton College and State University*

SUGGESTED READING

Jack De Bellis, *Sidney Lanier* (New York: Twayne Publishers, 1972).
Jane S. Gabin, *A Living Minstrelsy: The Poetry and Music of Sidney Lanier* (Macon, Ga.: Mercer University Press, 1985).

STANLEY LINDBERG

(1939–2000)

As editor of the *Georgia Review* from 1977 until his death, Stanley Lindberg was nationally and internationally recognized for transforming a good regional literary magazine into one of the best magazines of its time, a handsome and colorful quarterly filled with excellent essays, poetry, fiction, and artwork created by distinguished artists from the state, the South, the nation, and abroad. In addition, he conceived and produced, or shared responsibility for, some of the most daring and stimulating cultural events the state of Georgia has hosted, including a celebration of Georgia's own heritage in creative writing — the "Roots in Georgia" Literary Symposium of 1985 — and a remarkable international gathering of recipients of the Nobel Prize in Literature held in conjunction with the 1996 Summer Olympic Games in Atlanta.

Stanley W. Lindberg was born on November 18, 1939, in Warren, Pennsylvania. He wrote his Ph.D. dissertation at the University of Pennsylvania on the eighteenth-century essayist and dictionary maker Samuel Johnson, a model of the clear, intelligent, strong expression that he later sought in the writers he published in the *Georgia Review*. Lindberg had achieved distinction as a scholar and editor before he came to the University of Georgia Department of English in 1977 from Ohio University, where he had already raised a regional literary magazine, the *Ohio Review*, to national prominence.

The success of the *Georgia Review* during Lindberg's more than twenty years as editor marks his greatest achievement. Under his direction the *Georgia Review* received increasing praise and won a number of state and national awards for its editorial excellence. In 1986, outshining such well-financed commercial magazines as the *New Yorker*, *Atlantic Monthly*, and *Harper's*, the *Georgia Review* won a prestigious National Magazine Award in Fiction.

In recommending Lindberg for a University Professorship at the University of Georgia, which he received in 1999, a committee of scholars and writers observed that Lindberg had made the *Georgia Review* "the single most widely respected and sought after literary review published in the United States." Competing against commercial magazines with enormous budgets, Lindberg repeatedly attracted into the pages of the *Georgia Review* such notable writers as Rita Dove, Shelby Foote, Henry Louis Gates Jr., Seamus Heaney, Joyce Carol Oates, John Updike, Robert Penn Warren, and Eudora Welty.

Recognition of Lindberg's editorial role in the development of the *Georgia Review* made him widely sought after as a speaker and consultant on editing, publishing, and writing. He collaborated with L. Ray Patterson, a University of Georgia colleague, to write a valuable book on American copyright law, *The Nature of Copyright: A Law of Users' Rights* (1991). He also edited or coedited a number of books, including two anthologies of the best poetry (*Keener Sounds*, 1987) and fiction (*Necessary Fictions*, 1986) from the *Georgia Review* and a volume containing selections from a famous American textbook series known as McGuffey's Readers (*The Annotated McGuffey*, 1976).

Lindberg's high regard for clarity and precision extended to a love for music and a dedication to the humanistic enterprises of the University of Georgia and its Department of English, both of which he served in important capacities. His greatest legacy to the state of Georgia remains, however, his tenure with the *Georgia Review*. He not only attracted writers who were well established and sought after, but he also discovered, nurtured, and promoted many new talents.

Lindberg died in Atlanta on January 18, 2000.

THOMAS L. McHANEY, *Georgia State University*

SUGGESTED READING

Stephen Corey, ed., "Remembering Stanley Lindberg: A Festschrift," special issue, *Georgia Review* 54 (summer 2000).

AUGUSTUS BALDWIN LONGSTREET

(1790–1870)

In 1835 Augustus Baldwin Longstreet published Georgia's first important literary work, *Georgia Scenes, Characters, Incidents, Etc. in the First Half Century of the Republic*. Because of this book he is remembered most often as a literary figure. Longstreet, however, only dabbled in fiction writing, just as he dabbled in many other careers, including roles as a lawyer, judge, state senator, newspaper editor, minister, political propagandist, and college president.

Augustus Baldwin Longstreet was born in Augusta in September 1790 to Hannah Randolph and William Longstreet. His father was a sometime politician and failed inventor. His mother was the driving force behind his education. He received his early schooling at Richmond Academy in Augusta and Hickory Gum Academy in Edgefield District, South Carolina. In 1808 he enrolled in Moses Waddel's famous academy in Willington, South Carolina, and in 1811 he matriculated at Yale University in New Haven, Connecticut. While in college Longstreet regaled his teachers and fellow students with stories that he would later publish in *Georgia Scenes*. In 1813 he began his legal studies at Tapping Reeve's law school in Litchfield, Connecticut.

In 1814 Longstreet returned to Georgia, where he passed the bar exam the following year. While tending to legal business in Greensboro, he met Frances Eliza Parke. They married in 1817 and remained married, by Longstreet's count, for "fifty years, seven months, and ten days." Of their eight children, only two — daughters Frances Eliza and Virginia Lafayette — lived to adulthood.

In 1821 Longstreet began a term in the Georgia General Assembly as a representative from Greene County. This term was cut short the following year when the assembly appointed him to serve for three years as the judge of the Superior Court of the

Ocmulgee Circuit. Two years later, however, in 1824, Longstreet was campaigning for the U.S. Congress when the death of his first-born child, Alfred Emsley, prompted him to withdraw from the race.

Longstreet had never been religious, but his acute grief over the death of his son led to a conversion. He began earnestly to read the Bible and to pray, and soon he was "a thorough believer in Christianity."

After the term of Longstreet's judgeship ended, he and his family moved to Augusta. He joined the Methodist church in 1827 and felt called to preach the following year. In the fall of 1828 he was licensed to preach locally. His full-time ministerial career began nearly a decade later in December 1838, when he became a traveling Methodist minister.

Longstreet's earliest publications have been lost. His first was a hoax letter to a newspaper, supposedly written by two escaped convicts who were awaiting death. The date of this publication is unknown. Lost as well is "Review of the Decision of the Supreme Court of the United States in the Case of *McCulloch vs. the State of Maryland*" (1819). Longstreet's earliest surviving publication, *An Oration, Delivered before the Demosthenian and Phi Kappa Societies of the University of Georgia*, did not appear until 1831.

By the time of the oration, Longstreet had probably begun to commit his "Georgia Scenes" to paper. The first to appear in print was "The Dance," published in the *Milledgeville Southern Recorder* in 1833. Seven additional scenes appeared in the *Southern Recorder* before Longstreet purchased the federalist *North American Gazette*, which he renamed the *Augusta State Rights Sentinel*. Scenes began to appear in the *Sentinel* in January 1834; the last was published in March 1835.

Longstreet's literary sketches would probably have been forgotten had he not collected them into a book. In September 1835 he published *Georgia Scenes, Characters, Incidents, Etc. in the First Half Century of the Republic* from the *Sentinel* office. The poet Edgar Allan Poe gave it a rave review, and in 1840 the book was reissued by a New York publisher, Harper and Brothers. Longstreet hoped that his book would not be forgotten, as his purpose in writing it was to preserve Georgia's social history. In his words, he wanted "to supply a chasm in history which has always been overlooked — the manners, customs, amusements, wit, dialect as they appear in all grades of society to an ear and eye witness of them."

Between 1838 and 1843 Longstreet published eight more "Georgia Scenes," and in 1864 he published his only novel, the poorly received *Master William Mitten; or, A Youth of Brilliant Talents, Who Was Ruined by Bad Luck.* Most of Longstreet's later writings were political, including two lengthy defenses of slavery, *Letters on the Epistle of Paul to Philemon* (1845) and *A Voice from the South* (1847). Shortly before his death, Longstreet completed a work of biblical scholarship, *A Correction of the Canonized Errors in Biblical Interpretation.* Unfortunately, this manuscript was lost in a fire at the home of his literary executor.

Longstreet's brief career as a full-time minister ended when he became president of Emory College in Oxford in January 1840. In 1844 he came to national prominence when he played a central role in the division of the Methodist Episcopal Church. Four years later, in 1848, he resigned his post at Emory, and the following year he served briefly as president of Centenary College in Jackson, Louisiana. He was president of the University of Mississippi from 1849 to 1856. After resigning his post in Mississippi, the sixty-five-year-old Longstreet considered himself retired. He left retirement in 1857, however, when he was offered the presidency of South Carolina College (later the University of South Carolina).

Longstreet served South Carolina College until late 1861, by which time most of his students had left school to join the Confederate effort in the Civil War (1861–65). Longstreet then moved to Oxford, Mississippi, where his ill wife had been living with one of their daughters. In December 1862 Federal troops reached Oxford and, using Longstreet's papers as kindling, burned his house. The Longstreets relocated to Oxford, Georgia, and then to Columbus. Longstreet served the Confederacy as he could with his pen. His efforts included a leaflet of encouragement for Confederate soldiers and letters of advice to his nephew, the Confederate General James Longstreet. After the war Longstreet returned to Oxford, Mississippi, where he died on July 9, 1870.

DAVID RACHELS, *Virginia Military Institute, Lexington, Virginia*

SUGGESTED READING

Augustus Baldwin Longstreet, *Augustus Baldwin Longstreet's Georgia Scenes Completed: A Scholarly Text,* ed. David Rachels (Athens: University of Georgia Press, 1998).

Augustus Baldwin Longstreet, "The Letters of Augustus Baldwin Longstreet," ed. James R. Scafidel (Ph.D. diss., University of South Carolina, 1977).

James B. Meriwether, "Augustus Baldwin Longstreet: Realist and Artist," *Mississippi Quarterly* 35 (1982): 351–64.

Ahmed Nimeiri, "Play in Augustus Baldwin Longstreet's *Georgia Scenes,*" *Southern Literary Journal* 33 (2001): 44–61.

David Rachels, "A Biographical Reading of A. B. Longstreet's *Georgia Scenes,*" in *The Humor of the Old South,* ed. M. Thomas Inge and Edward J. Piacentino (Lexington: University Press of Kentucky, 2001): 113–29.

John Donald Wade, *Augustus Baldwin Longstreet: A Study of the Development of Culture in the South* (New York: Macmillan, 1924).

Jessica Wegmann, "'Playing in the Dark' with Longstreet's *Georgia Scenes*: Critical Reception and Reader Response to Treatments of Race and Gender," *Southern Literary Journal* (fall 1997): 13–26.

GRACE LUMPKIN

(1891–1980)

The radical novels that Grace Lumpkin wrote in the 1930s, *To Make My Bread* and *A Sign for Cain*, represent two of the best examples of literary social realism produced in response to the economic and social turmoil of the Great Depression. Lumpkin used the Loray Mill strike, which took place in Gastonia, North Carolina, in 1929, and the Scottsboro case, which erupted in Alabama in 1931, as the historical and social backdrops for her novels. She proudly answered the call made in 1929 by Mike Gold, a prominent literary critic with ties to the Communist Party, for socially conscious young writers to "go left." Like other writers of her generation, Lumpkin was convinced that a new, revolutionary form of writing could not only record the hardships and heroic struggles of the American working class but also mark a welcome return of social consciousness to American literature.

Born in Milledgeville on March 3, 1891, Lumpkin later moved with her family (including her older sister, Katharine Du Pre Lumpkin, who grew up to become a well-known sociologist) to South Carolina, where she witnessed firsthand the suffering of black and white sharecroppers and laborers. She returned briefly to Georgia, where she trained to be a teacher at Brenau College in Gainesville and eventually organized an adult night school for farmers and their wives. During most summers she lived in the mountains of North Carolina, staying with mill workers, share-croppers, and other laborers, and as she would describe it later, she became "convinced . . . that the workers could better their lives only by means of unions." Her stay in the mountains intro-duced her to the families that she wrote about in her first novel.

In the mid-1920s Lumpkin moved to New York City, where she enrolled in evening courses in creative writing and journal-ism at Columbia University. She also became fully immersed in the radical culture around her, attending demonstrations, joining picket lines, speaking at conferences and meetings, and generally supporting pacifist, socialist, and radical causes. After witnessing the brutal tactics used against workers in the recurrently violent textile strike in Passaic, New Jersey, Lumpkin joined the Communist Party.

The publication of *To Make My Bread* in 1932 launched Lumpkin's career as a writer and gave her prominence on the literary left. She counted among her many friends and acquaintances Sherwood Anderson, Whittaker Chambers, John Dos Passos, Josephine Herbst, Granville Hicks, Scott Nearing, Mary Heaton Vorse, and Edmund Wilson. First lady Eleanor Roosevelt was among those who attended a theatrical adaptation of *To Make My Bread*; her presence was a sign of the extent to which a radical agenda had made its way into the political mainstream of America. After the publication of *A Sign for Cain* in 1935 Lumpkin went on to publish two more novels, *The Wedding* (1939) and *Full Circle* (1962).

Lumpkin's life and writing were dramatically influenced by cultural radicalism, with its links to U.S. communism in the 1930s, and the ferreting out of Communists and Communist sympathizers in the 1950s. Although she was a Communist during the 1920s and 1930s, Lumpkin became aggressively reactionary twenty years later — during U.S. senator Joseph McCarthy's witch hunts for former radicals Lumpkin gave the names of her radical acquaintances to a Senate subcommittee. Soon after her testimony she returned to the South, eventually moving to Columbia, South Carolina. Her later writing was devoted to exposing the evils of communism and exploring Communist-to-Christian conversion experiences. She died in Columbia in 1980.

SUZANNE SOWINSKA, *Seattle, Washington*

Ronald Eller, *Miners, Millhands, and Mountaineers: Industrialization of the Appalachian South, 1880–1930* (Knoxville: University of Tennessee Press, 1982).

Barbara Foley, *Radical Representations: Politics and Form in U.S. Proletarian Fiction, 1929–1941* (Durham, N.C.: Duke University Press, 1993).

Jacquelyn Dowd Hall, "Women Writers, the 'Southern Front,' and the Dialectical Imagination," *Journal of Southern History* (February 2003): 3–38.

Sherry Linkon and Bill Mullen, eds., *Radical Revisions: Rereading 1930s Culture* (Champaign-Urbana: University of Illinois Press, 1996).

Suzanne Sowinska, introduction to *To Make My Bread*, by Grace Lumpkin (Champaign-Urbana: University of Illinois Press, 1995).

KATHARINE DU PRE LUMPKIN
(1897–1988)

Sociologist, activist, teacher, and writer, Katharine Du Pre Lumpkin spent a lifetime studying and combating economic and racial oppression. She is best known for her autobiography, *The Making of a Southerner.*

Katharine Lumpkin was born in 1897 in Macon, Georgia, to William Lumpkin and Annette Caroline Morris Lumpkin. As a member of a prominent Georgia family and the daughter of a Civil War veteran, she was inculcated in the cultural mythologies of the Lost Cause and white supremacy. The Lumpkin children responded differently to their upbringing: although Katharine's eldest sister, Elizabeth, remained committed to the Lost Cause, another sister, Grace, later wrote a series of leftist novels.

As Lumpkin describes in her autobiography, her racial attitudes slowly but irrevocably changed during her undergraduate and graduate careers. She attended Brenau College in Gainesville, Georgia, from 1912 to 1915 and worked there as a teaching assistant following her graduation. In 1918 she moved on to Columbia University in New York, where she received an M.A. in sociology the following year. Between 1920 and 1925 Lumpkin worked as the national student secretary for the YWCA's southern region. In 1925 she entered the sociology program at the University of Wisconsin, where she earned a Ph.D. in 1928.

After year-long appointments as an instructor at Mount Holyoke College in South Hadley, Massachusetts, and a post-doctoral fellow at the Social Sciences Research Council in New York City, Lumpkin spent the next two decades as a director of research, first at Smith College's Council of Industrial Studies (1932–39), then at the Institute of Labor Studies (1940–53), both in Northampton, Massachusetts. During this time, her scholarly output was prodigious. She published *The Family: A Study of Member Roles* (1933), *Shutdowns in the Connecticut*

Valley: A Study of Worker Displacement in the Small Industrial Community (1934), *Child Workers in America* (with Dorothy W. Douglas, 1937), and *The South in Progress* (1940). This last work saw a return to Lumpkin's southern roots that continued in her next work, *The Making of a Southerner* (1947). Part family history, part autobiography, and part sociological study, *The Making of a Southerner* describes Lumpkin's transition from passive inheritance of white supremacy to conscious rejection of the racial values of a segregated South.

After a year as a lecturer at Mills College in Oakland, California, (1956–57), Lumpkin took a position in 1957 as professor of sociology at Wells College in Aurora, New York. For the next decade she remained at Wells, where she taught a course, "The Negro Minority in American Life," that often focused on contemporary events in the civil rights struggle. In 1967 she retired to Charlottesville, Virginia, where she taught extension courses at the University of Virginia and was active in the League of Women Voters. She continued to lecture and write and in 1974 published *The Emancipation of Angelina Grimké*, a study of the important nineteenth-century abolitionist from South Carolina. In 1979 she moved to Chapel Hill, North Carolina, where she died in 1988.

Although Lumpkin's long, rich career was marked by achievement in several areas, it is for her autobiography that she will be remembered. In *The Making of a Southerner*, she left a classic testament of her conflict as a white southerner committed to racial justice in a culture where little was to be found.

SCOTT ROMINE, *University of North Carolina, Greensboro*

Jacquelyn Dowd Hall, "Open Secrets: Memory, Imagination, and the Refashioning of Southern Identity," *American Quarterly* 50, no. 1 (1998).

Fred Hobson, *But Now I See: The White Southern Racial Conversion Narrative* (Baton Rouge: Louisiana State University Press, 1999).

Fred Hobson, "The Sins of the Fathers: Lillian Smith and Katharine Du Pre Lumpkin," *Southern Review* 34, no. 4 (1998).

Katharine Du Pre Lumpkin, *The Making of a Southerner*, forward by Darlene Clark Hine (Athens: University of Georgia Press, 1991).

Darlene O'Dell, *Sites of Southern Memory: The Autobiographies of Katharine Du Pre Lumpkin, Lillian Smith, and Pauli Murray* (Charlottesville: University Press of Virginia, 2001).

A MAN IN FULL

The publication in 1998 of *A Man in Full*, Tom Wolfe's mammoth novel about the making of modern Atlanta, became the biggest single event in the city's cultural life since the world premiere in 1939 of *Gone With the Wind* at Loew's Grand Theater. Wolfe's impact on Atlanta has been compared with General William T. Sherman's in 1864, and his judgments were given the same weight as International Olympic Committee President Juan Antonio Samaranch's critical assessment of Atlanta's Olympic Games of 1996.

Wolfe, born and raised in Richmond, Virginia, is a former newspaper reporter and the best-selling author of such works as *The Kandy-Kolored Tangerine-Flake Streamline Baby* (1965), *The Right Stuff* (1979), and *The Bonfire of the Vanities* (1987).

Two weeks before the novel's publication, the November 2 cover of *Time* magazine featured Wolfe's portrait and the announcement "Tom Wolfe Writes Again." Cover stories and lavish photo layouts also appeared in *American Spectator, Vanity Fair, Harper's, Biblio: Exploring the World of Books, Book: The Magazine for the Reading Life*, and even Delta Air Lines's in-flight periodical *Sky*. Eleven years in the works, Wolfe's much-anticipated second novel was eminently newsworthy — his first fictional effort since *The Bonfire of the Vanities*, the satire set in New York City, which had sold 750,000 copies in hard cover. *A Man in Full* immediately topped best-seller lists, was nominated for a National Book Award, and became target for controversy — especially in Atlanta. The fact that Wolfe, a New Yorker since the early 1960s, was an outsider only exasperated the issue.

In anticipation of Wolfe's arrival in Atlanta in mid-November 1998, timed to coincide with the official release of his novel, the *Atlanta Journal-Constitution* began issuing a "Wolfe Watch."

The Buckhead Coalition withdrew its invitation for him to speak at its annual meeting because of Wolfe's purported "Buckhead bashing" in the book. The Atlanta Convention and Visitors Bureau, on the other hand, invited the author to its own big-bash breakfast in the hope that the book might do for the tourist trade in Atlanta what *Midnight in the Garden of Good and Evil* had achieved for Savannah. An overflow audience attended a reading from the novel on November 18 at the Atlanta History Center, after which 150 well-heeled admirers paid six hundred dollars each for a dinner in Wolfe's honor that would benefit the Margaret Mitchell House and Museum. The next morning, some 1,100 people crowded a Buckhead bookstore to purchase auto-graphed copies of *A Man in Full*. For its Christmas decorations a few weeks later a downtown clothier presented in the windows of its Peachtree Street store a display entitled "A Christmas in Full": mannequins dressed as characters from Wolfe's novel.

A Man in Full captivated Atlantans because it headlined the city's quintessential mythic hero: the entrepreneur, the booster, the developer, the leader. Such an individual, real or imagined, historical or contemporary, serves as the embodiment of the progress-at-any-price "Atlanta spirit." Since the city possesses no natural advantages — such as access to a harbor or navigable river, proximity to mineral deposits, or dominance over an agri-cultural hinterland — Atlanta's sole reason for being has always been its potential for development. The Atlanta spirit is governed not by the city's past but by its purportedly boundless future. Margaret Mitchell's Scarlett O'Hara embodies that expansionist ethos for the nineteenth-century city; Tom Wolfe's hero, Charlie Croker, does the same for the twentieth-century megalopolis.

Early in the novel the sixty-year-old developer seems to have accumulated all the markers of turn-of-the-century achievement: a twenty-nine-thousand-acre "show plantation" in his native south Georgia, an English manor house in suburban Buckhead, a wife half his age to grace them, flights of corporate jets and fleets of company limos, and his own "edge city" — a massive multiuse mall on the northern frontier of an exploding Greater

Atlanta. Croker Concourse, the crown jewel in his economic empire, stands more as a monument to "Cap'm" Charlie's ego than to his business acumen. Ignoring the three cardinal rules of real-estate development — location, location, location — Croker gambles that the next wave of suburban expansion will wash up against his distant development; instead, the wave crests and then recedes. Croker Concourse is left high and dry — and empty. The builder's bubble on which it was erected quivers, then bursts.

The central plot of *A Man in Full* involves its hero's abortive attempts to save both his financial empire and his sense of self-worth. Croker's efforts are quickly compromised by the politics of race in the self-proclaimed "City Too Busy to Hate." A sexual incident between a Georgia Tech football star and the daughter of a major power broker — consensual sex according to the black athlete, date rape according to the white debutante — threatens to widen the already considerable fissure that marks the city's racial fault line. The threat of bad publicity, a challenge to Atlanta's claims for being the nation's (according to some of its boosters, the world's) civil rights capital, calls for problem solving "the Atlanta way." As lines are drawn between the races, as well as between classes on each side of the city's color line, negotiations between Atlanta's two major power groups — black politicians and white businessmen — are set in place for behind-the-scenes, back-door, Atlanta-style politics. The designated spokesman for the Atlanta way this time around, both factions agree, will be Charlie Croker, legendary Tech football star and edge-city entrepreneur. How well he performs in this role would seem to determine his fate, both financial and personal.

The subplots of *A Man in Full* detail the machinations of investment bankers in recouping corporate losses while guaranteeing their own personal gain; where and how the city's elite — on both sides of its racial divide — live, play, and create their own distinctive communities and subcultures; the creation of new immigrant enclaves (from California to Georgia) under the pressures of economic globalization; as well as the language and inner dynamics of a multiracial, coast-to-coast jailhouse culture.

For page after page Wolfe's Atlanta novel provides detail after detail of numerous slices of the city's life. Its satiric narrative, responsible for much of the local controversy surrounding the novel, faults Atlanta for its obsession with boosterism, expansion, and hollow social platitudes about racial harmony. In socioscientific terms, its reach is both anthropological and sociological. As much as any sprawling social novel can, *A Man in Full* captures wide swatches and many levels of today's Atlanta in full.

DANA F. WHITE, *Emory University*

SUGGESTED READING

William McKeen, *Tom Wolfe* (New York: Twayne, 1995).

Dana F. White, "Cities in Full: The Urban South during the Final Century of the Past Millennium," *Atlanta History* 44 (winter 2001): 49–57.

FRANK MANLEY
(b. 1930)

The author of poems, plays, novels, and short stories, Frank Manley writes mostly about southern characters in marginal encounters that force them to engage spiritual questions or dilemmas of faith and reason. Moving easily between academic and literary careers, Manley has produced a wide-ranging body of work, with critical editions of John Donne and Sir Thomas More, poems about Roman emperors, and violent tales involving trailer parks and mountain cockfighting arenas. Manley grew up in pre–World War II Atlanta, yet he emerged as a southern writer much later, midway through what could be considered his first career, as professor of Renaissance English literature at Emory University. His various awards for creative writing — which include two Georgia Author of the Year awards (one for fiction and one for short stories / anthologies), a National Endowment for the Arts fellowship, and first prize at the 1985 Humana Festival of New American Plays — have contributed to a list of already impressive achievements.

Manley was born in Scranton, Pennsylvania, on November 13, 1930, the son of Kathryn L. Needham and Aloysius F. Manley. Reared a Roman Catholic, he attended the Marist School in Atlanta, then studied English literature at Emory (B.A., 1952; M.A., 1953). In 1952 he married Carolyn Holliday of Decatur, Georgia, with whom he has two daughters, Evelyn and Mary. After serving as an enlisted man in the U.S. Army (1952–55), Manley earned his Ph.D. from Johns Hopkins University in Baltimore (1959) and then taught English at Yale University in New Haven, Connecticut (1959–64). After the publication of his first book, a critical edition of Donne's *The Anniversaries* (1963), he returned to Emory as an associate professor of English literature in 1964. Twice a Guggenheim fellow, he remained at Emory until his retirement in 2000. He was named Charles Howard

Candler Professor of Renaissance Literature in 1982, and he directed Emory's creative writing program from its inception in 1990 until his retirement.

In the late 1960s and early 1970s Manley began composing poems about family, the historical figures he had studied, and the Gilmer County mountain community where he had built a home. He published his poetry in literary quarterlies and ultimately in a volume entitled *Resultances* (1980), which won the University of Missouri Press's Devins Award. A book-length discussion of his poems, *Some Poems and Some Talk about Poetry* (with fellow Emory professor Floyd Watkins), appeared in 1985.

In a 1985 interview with the *Atlanta Constitution*, Manley said that he began writing plays simply by chance. He wrote his first play at the suggestion of a colleague in Emory's theater studies department, who noted the narrative emphasis of Manley's early attempts at short fiction. Manley has continued to publish many of his stories both as dramas and as fictional narratives. "The Rain of Terror," "An Errand of Mercy," and "The Baptism of Water" appeared initially as parts of his first two plays, *Two Masters* (1985) and *Prior Engagements* (1987). He subsequently published them as short stories and included them in his short-story collection *Within the Ribbons* (1989). His second collection, *Among Prisoners* (2000), includes several stories that appear as all or part of his plays *The Evidence* (1990), *Married Life* (1996), and *Learning to Dance* (1998). Manley's coming-of-age-novel, *The Cockfighter* (1998), was subsequently adapted for the stage as well.

Manley's fiction typically features characters who are imprisoned in some way and for whom chance encounters offer the possibility of liberation. *The Evidence* turns on a mountain man's interpretation of a "Bigfoot" encounter. *The Trap* (1993) tells the story of a committee of university professors investigating an allegation of sexual harassment. *Two Masters*, *Prior Engagements*, and *Married Life* all include multiple one-act "miniplays" in which characters wrestle to escape physical and spiritual prisons.

Manley's *The Emperors* (2001) is a combination of memoir and poetry. *The Emperors* emerged from Manley's contemplation of emperors he was led to consider while editing St. Thomas More's *Dialogue of Comfort against Tribulation*.

KEITH HULETT, *University of Georgia Libraries*

SUGGESTED READING

"Emory to Ellijay, Playwright Follows His Star," *Atlanta Constitution*, September 27, 1985.

"A Play for Outrage," *Atlanta Journal-Constitution*, January 27, 1993.

"To Build a Poem: The Work of Twelve Emory Poets and Some Talk about Poetry," *Emory Magazine* (autumn 1991).

Who's Who in America, 55th ed. (Chicago: A. N. Marquis, 2001), s.v. "Manley, Frank."

FRANCES MAYES

(b. ca. 1940)

Frances Mayes has achieved wide recognition for two best-selling books about her life and her second home in Italy: *Under the Tuscan Sun: At Home in Italy* and *Bella Tuscany: The Sweet Life in Italy*.

Mayes was born in Fitzgerald to Garbert and Frankye Davis Mayes. Her exact birth date is unknown. She attended Randolph-Macon Woman's College in Virginia and obtained her B.A. from the University of Florida and her M.A. from San Francisco State University in 1975. She taught creative writing at San Francisco State University until 2001. She married her second husband, poet Ed Kleinschmidt in 1998.

Mayes published six books of poetry from 1977 to 1995: *Climbing Aconcagua* (1977), *Sunday in Another Country* (1977), *After Such Pleasures* (1979), *The Arts of Fire* (1982), *Hours* (1984), and *Ex Voto* (1995). Many of her poems explore the rich, complex landscape of her childhood home in south Georgia, a hierarchical world where class, race, and gender determine roles in small-town life. In other works Mayes writes about landscapes far removed from the South, sometimes fusing the two seemingly disparate worlds. She moves easily from exterior to interior landscapes, examining issues of identity, relationships, death, and loneliness. For Mayes, memory creates another landscape that colors the present.

Mayes brings her poetic voice to her two most popular works, *Under the Tuscan Sun* (1996) and *Bella Tuscany* (1999). The former opens with the purchase of an Italian villa outside the town of Cortona, Italy, and details its renovation and the discovery of a vibrant new culture. The work began as a blank book entitled "Italy," where Mayes included lists of wildflowers, words, sketches, and planting advice. *Under the Tuscan Sun* thus became a memoir / cookbook / travel guide / renovation and gardening manual. Mayes writes in the preface that the transformation of the house and garden became a metaphor for transformations in her own life. She learned "to live another kind of life," one far removed from the breakneck speed of her academic job and life in a modern American city. In Italy, friends and family, the beauty of a garden, and a good meal are savored. A movie version of *Under the Tuscan Sun*, starring Diane Lane, was released in 2003.

In *Bella Tuscany*, the renovation of the villa nearly complete, Mayes writes about explorations around Tuscany and growing connections to this new/old world. She also connects the process of writing to the process of living, claiming that "living in Italy, I'm especially aware of *storing* what I experience and see. If I ever end up rocking on the porch of a dogtrot house in the backwoods of Georgia, I aim to have plenty to visualize."

At the heart of her work is a preoccupation with a sensual world and a need to live life moment by moment. Mayes writes in *Under the Tuscan Sun*: "Growing up, I absorbed the Southern obsession with place, and place can seem to me somehow an extension of the self. If I am made of red clay and black river water and white sand and moss, that seems natural to me." She recaptures the same feelings in Italy, where she is *"returned* to that primal first awareness of home."

Mayes finally turned her attention back to home with the novel *Swan* (2002), set in the fictitious town of Swan, Georgia, and ripe with allusions to her hometown of Fitzgerald. Her book *A Year in the World* appeared in 2006.

MAE MILLER CLAXTON, *Western Carolina University, Cullowhee, North Carolina*

SUGGESTED READING

Contemporary Authors: New Revision Series, vol. 74 (Detroit: Gale, 1999), s.v. "Mayes, Frances."

CARSON McCULLERS
(1917–1967)

With a collection of work including five novels, two plays, twenty short stories, more than two dozen nonfiction pieces, a book of children's verse, a small number of poems, and an unfinished autobiography, Carson McCullers is considered to be among the most significant American writers of the twentieth century. She is best known for her novels *The Heart Is a Lonely Hunter*, *The Ballad of the Sad Café*, *Reflections in a Golden Eye*, and *The Member of the Wedding*, all published between 1940 and 1946. At least four of her works have been made into films.

Born Lula Carson Smith on February 19, 1917, in Columbus, McCullers was the daughter of Lamar Smith, a jewelry store owner, and Vera Marguerite Waters. Lula Carson, as she was called until age fourteen, attended public schools and graduated from Columbus High School at sixteen. An unremarkable student, she preferred the more solitary study of the piano. Encouraged by her mother, who was convinced that her daughter was destined for greatness, McCullers began formal piano study at age ten. She was forced to give up her dream of a career as a concert pianist after rheumatic fever left her without the stamina for the rigors of practice or a concert career. While recuperating from this illness, McCullers began to read voraciously and to consider writing as a vocation.

In 1934, at age seventeen, McCullers sailed from Savannah to New York City, ostensibly to study piano at the Juilliard School of Music but actually to pursue her secret ambition to write. Working various jobs to support herself, she studied creative writing at New York's Columbia University and at Washington Square College of New York University. Back in Columbus in the fall of 1936 to recover from a respiratory infection, McCullers was bedridden several months, during which time she began work on her first novel, *The Heart Is a Lonely Hunter*. Her first short story, "Wunderkind," was published in the December 1936 issue of *Story* magazine, edited by Whit Burnett, her former teacher at Columbia.

In September 1937 she married James Reeves McCullers Jr., a native of Wetumpka, Alabama, whom she met when Reeves was in the army stationed at Fort Benning, near her hometown. The marriage was simultaneously the most supportive and destructive relationship in her life. From the beginning it was plagued by alcoholism, sexual ambivalence (both were bisexual), and Reeves's envy of McCullers's writing abilities. Moving to New York in 1940 when *The Heart Is a Lonely Hunter* was published, McCullers and Reeves divorced in 1941, only to reconcile and remarry in 1945.

During a separation from Reeves in 1940, McCullers moved into a house in Brooklyn Heights owned by George Davis (literary editor of *Harper's Bazaar*) and shared with the British poet W. H. Auden. This house, located at 7 Middagh Street, became the center of a bohemian literary and artistic constellation including Gypsy Rose Lee, Benjamin Britten, Peter Pears, Richard Wright, and Oliver Smith. In spring 1941 McCullers and Reeves, who were temporarily reconciled, both fell in love with the American composer David Diamond. This complicated love triangle led to a second separation and found expression in the love-triangle theme found in McCullers's short novel *The Ballad of the Sad Café* and her novel and play *The Member of the Wedding*. Following her father's sudden death in August 1944, McCullers moved with her mother and sister to Nyack, New York, where Mrs. Smith purchased a house. McCullers spent most of the rest of her life in this house on the Hudson River.

While living near Paris in the early 1950s, Reeves tried to convince McCullers to commit suicide with him. Fearing for her life, she fled to the United States. Remaining behind, Reeves committed suicide in a Paris hotel room in November 1953.

In April 1938 Carson McCullers submitted an outline and six chapters of *The Heart Is a Lonely Hunter* to Houghton Mifflin and was offered a contract and $500 advance. The book was published in June 1940. The story of a deaf mute to whom the lonely and isolated people of a southern town turn for silent solace, the novel includes the themes of loneliness and isolation that recur in much of McCullers's work. It was an immediate success. Rose Feld's *New York Times Book Review* was typical of the positive critical response: "No matter what the age of its author, 'The Heart Is a Lonely Hunter' would be a remarkable book. When one reads that Carson McCullers is a girl of 22 it becomes more than that. Maturity does not cover the quality of her work. It is something beyond that, something more akin to the vocation of pain to which a great poet is born."

Reflections in a Golden Eye, McCullers's second novel, first appeared in *Harper's Bazaar* in October and November 1940 and was published in book form by Houghton Mifflin in 1941. Readers who expected a book like the author's first novel were shocked by the troubling story of voyeurism, obsession, repressed homosexuality, and infidelity set on a peacetime army base. *Reflections in a Golden Eye* received a mixed critical reception, and its author faced ridicule from the people of her hometown who saw negative reflections of themselves in the maladjusted characters of the novel.

During the years 1943 to 1950 McCullers published what many consider her finest creative work. *The Ballad of the Sad Café*, set in a small southern town, is the lyrical story of jealousy and obsession in a triangular love relationship involving an amazon-like Miss Amelia, a hunchbacked midget, Cousin Lymon, and an ex-convict, Marvin Macy. It appeared in the August 1943 issue of *Harper's Bazaar*. The work was later published by Houghton Mifflin in an omnibus edition of the author's work, *"The Ballad of the Sad Café": The Novels and Stories of Carson McCullers* (1951).

March 1946 saw the publication of McCullers's fourth major work, *The Member of the Wedding*, the story of a lonely adolescent girl, Frankie Addams, who wants to find her "we of me" by joining with her older brother and his bride. McCullers's theatrical adaptation of the novel opened on Broadway in 1950 to near-unanimous acclaim and enjoyed a run of 501 performances. This adaptation proved to be her most commercially successful work. It was critically successful as well, winning the 1950 New York Drama Critics Circle Award for best American play of the season and the Donaldson Award for best play and best first play by an author.

During the final fifteen years of her life, McCullers experienced a marked decline in health and creative abilities. Bedridden by paralysis from a series of debilitating strokes, she was devastated by the failure of her second play, *The Square Root of Wonderful*, which closed after only 45 performances on Broadway in 1957, and the mixed reception of her final novel, *Clock Without Hands* (1961). Her final book-length publication was a volume of children's verse, *Sweet as a Pickle and Clean as a Pig* (1964). At the time of her death she was at work on an autobiography, "Illumination and Night Glare." A more encouraging event in her final years was the success of Edward Albee's 1963 adaptation of *The Ballad of the Sad Café*, which enjoyed a Broadway run of 123 performances. On August 15, 1967, she suffered her final cerebral stroke. Comatose for forty-six days, she died in the Nyack Hospital and was buried in Nyack's Oak Hill Cemetery on the banks of the Hudson River.

Assessing McCullers's stature in American arts and letters, biographer Virginia Spencer Carr wrote: "Critics continue to compare and contrast McCullers with Eudora Welty, Flannery O'Connor, and Katherine Anne Porter, whom they generally consider to be better stylists in the short form than McCullers. Yet they tend to rank McCullers above her female contemporaries as a novelist. McCullers herself had a keen appreciation of her own work without regard to the sex of those with whom she was compared." In an appraisal of her life and work accompanying McCullers's front-page obituary in the September 30, 1967, *New York Times*, Eliot Fremont-Smith wrote of the impact of *The Heart Is a Lonely Hunter* in what could also be an assessment of McCullers's lasting influence:

It is not so much that the novel paved the way for what became the American Southern Gothic genre, but that it at once encompassed it and went beyond it. . . . The heart of this remarkable, still powerful book is perhaps best conveyed by its title, with its sense of intensity, concision and mystery, with its terrible juxtaposition of love and aloneness, whose relation was Mrs. McCullers's constant subject. . . . Mrs. McCullers was neither prolific nor varying in her theme. . . . This is no fault or tragedy: to some artists a vision is given only once. And a corollary: only an artist can make others subject to the vision's force. Mrs. McCullers was an artist. She was also in her person, an inspiration and example for other artists who grew close to her. Her books, and particularly "The Heart," will live; she will be missed.

In addition to the New York Drama Critics Circle and Donaldson awards for her play *The Member of the Wedding*, McCullers also received two Guggenheim fellowships (1942, 1946), an Arts and Letters Grant from the American Academy of Arts and Letters and the National Institute of Arts and Letters (1943), and various other awards and honors. She was inducted into the National Institute of Arts and Letters in 1952.

CARLOS DEWS, *Columbus State University*

SUGGESTED READING

Harold Bloom, ed., *Carson McCullers*, Modern Critical Views Series (New York: Chelsea House, 1986).

Virginia Spencer Carr, *The Lonely Hunter: A Biography of Carson McCullers* (Garden City, N.Y.: Doubleday, 1975; reprint, Athens: University of Georgia Press, 2003).

Virginia Spencer Carr, *Understanding Carson McCullers* (Columbia: University of South Carolina Press, 1990).

Beverly Lyon Clark and Melvin J. Friedman, eds., *Critical Essays on Carson McCullers* (New York: G. K. Hall, 1996).

Richard Cook, *Carson McCullers* (New York: Ungar, 1975).

Dale Edmonds, *Carson McCullers* (Austin, Texas: Steck-Vaughn, 1969).

Oliver Evans, *The Ballad of Carson McCullers* (New York: Coward-McCann, 1966).

Lawrence Graver, *Carson McCullers* (Minneapolis: University of Minnesota Press, 1969).

Judith Giblin James, *Wunderkind: The Reputation of Carson McCullers, 1940–1990* (Columbia, S.C.: Camden House, 1995).

Margaret B. McDowell, *Carson McCullers* (Boston: Twayne, 1980).

Josyane Savigneau, *Carson McCullers: A Life*, trans. Joan E. Howard (Boston: Houghton Mifflin, 2001).

Adrian M. Shapiro et al., *Carson McCullers: A Descriptive Listing and Annotated Bibliography* (New York: Garland, 1980).

Louise Westling, *Sacred Groves and Ravaged Gardens: The Fiction of Eudora Welty, Carson McCullers, and Flannery O'Connor* (Athens: University of Georgia Press, 1985).

RALPH McGILL
(1898–1969)

Ralph McGill, as editor and publisher of the *Atlanta Constitution*, was a leading voice for racial and ethnic tolerance in the South from the 1940s through the 1960s. As an influential daily columnist, he broke the code of silence on the subject of segregation, chastising a generation of demagogues, timid journalists, and ministers who feared change. When the U.S. Supreme Court outlawed segregated schools in 1954 and southern demagogues led defiance of the court, segregationists vilified McGill as a traitor to his region for urging white southerners to accept the end of segregation. In 1959, at the age of sixty-one, he was awarded the Pulitzer Prize for editorial writing.

Ralph Emerson McGill was born on February 5, 1898, in the remote farming community of Igou's Ferry, about twenty miles north of Chattanooga, Tennessee. He was the second son (the first died as an infant) of Mary Lou Skillern and Benjamin Franklin McGill. McGill graduated from the McCallie School in Chattanooga and between 1917 and 1922 (with time out for service in the U.S. Marines in 1918–19) attended Vanderbilt University in Nashville, Tennessee, but he did not graduate. In his senior year he was suspended after writing a column in the student newspaper that suggested wrongdoing because Vanderbilt had not erected a student lounge, as stipulated in the will of a professor who had bequeathed the school $20,000. McGill might have appealed to return to graduate, but he had found a full-time job as a reporter for the *Nashville Banner*, and as a colleague noted, "the degree didn't mean that much to him."

During the 1920s McGill became the *Banner*'s sports editor and sports columnist, but he eagerly looked for opportunities to break away from the seasonal sports routine to cover murder trials and political campaigns. Friendships with other southern sportswriters led him in 1929 to the *Atlanta Constitution*, as assistant sports editor and later sports editor and columnist. Also in 1929 McGill married Mary Elizabeth Leonard, the daughter of a dentist, whom he met when he interviewed her brother, a Vanderbilt football star. They had a daughter, who died days after her birth. Shortly thereafter the couple adopted a baby girl, and she died a few years later from leukemia. A son, Ralph Jr., was born in 1945. McGill's wife died in 1962, and in 1967 McGill married Mary Lynn Morgan, an Atlanta children's dentist.

McGill's distinct writing voice established him as a popular talent, giving the morning *Constitution* an edge over the two afternoon papers, the *Atlanta Georgian*, owned by the William Randolph Hearst chain, and the *Atlanta Journal*. As in Nashville, his enormous energy and sense of timing secured him opportunities to write on serious subjects. In 1933 he got his first break in international journalism, persuading the *Constitution* to send him to cover the Cuban revolution. His datelined stories, including an exclusive interview with dictator Gerardo Machado days before he fled, were displayed on the front page of the paper, establishing McGill as a serious journalist.

McGill completed his transformation to serious journalism after he won a Rosenwald Fellowship, freeing him to study and write from Europe during the first six months of 1938. From Vienna, Austria, his front-page accounts of Adolf Hitler's seizure of that country earned him a promotion to editor of the editorial page when he returned to Atlanta.

From June 1938 until his death in February 1969, McGill wrote daily, more than ten thousand columns. In 1942 he was promoted to editor-in-chief of the *Constitution*, and in 1960 to publisher. For much of his career he was a lone voice in Atlanta journalism, breaking the white code of polite silence about social and educational segregation and political disfranchisement — the so-called situation, or "sitch."

Between 1938 and 1954 McGill courageously portrayed the South's failure to live up to the "separate but equal" ruling by the U.S. Supreme Court in 1896. Without advocating integration, he described the deplorable conditions of Georgia's black schools, comparing their budgets for books and buildings with those of white schools. In the political arena he noted that one day African American voters would have considerable influence.

McGill understood that he could not write unrelentingly about civil rights and still keep his audience. In sportswriting he had chronicled pitchers who cleverly mixed their pitches, and he adopted that pattern: he mixed his columns, writing one day about barbecue, then about a charity, then about a newsworthy Atlanta citizen, then a sports column, and then, again, the "sitch." A notable column in 1953, "One Day It Will Be Monday," presaged the Supreme Court's ruling that would outlaw the system of dual societies: "So, somebody, especially those who have a duty so to do, ought to be talking about it calmly, and informatively."

For such comments segregationists vilified him. They telephoned his home and wrote letters, often with misspelled words, which he found somewhat humorous and shared with his small group of likeminded "brethren" editors across the South, among them Harry Ashmore at the *Arkansas Gazette* and William C. "Bill" Baggs at the *Miami News*. Segregationists branded McGill as "Rastus," a Communist, a traitor. His colleague Jack Tarver noted that the *Constitution*'s polls showed readers were evenly divided between those who loved him and those who reviled him, that some could not eat breakfast without reading McGill and others could not eat breakfast after reading him.

All these emotions erupted after the *Brown v. Board of Education* decision in 1954. The U.S. Supreme Court ruling and southern governors' resistance forced the issue of segregation out of the sanctuary of silence. McGill sided with the law of the land, which meant a radical reorientation of a society that for generations nurtured legal segregation from the rest of the nation.

During the late 1950s and 1960s McGill made another career transformation, becoming a national voice as a syndicate circulated his column to hundreds of newspapers. With his national audience in mind, McGill traveled frequently to Washington, D.C. As a lifelong Democrat, he gained an inside political track during the administrations of U.S. presidents John F. Kennedy and Lyndon B. Johnson. Both presidents sent him on cold war ambassadorial trips to newly independent nations in Africa to persuade leaders that the United States was working to solve its civil rights problems.

Intimacy with the presidency had a downside. McGill, as a loyal Democrat and a former marine, was unwilling to criticize America's war in Vietnam. In general, he was more likely to be correct about what was closest to his heart and soul — the South — than about the other worlds he reached out to — distant cultures where he was not a citizen but a sojourner.

Two things were clear to McGill's appreciative contemporaries. The first was that he spoke and wrote unfalteringly what he thought and felt, and in doing so he inspired others to break the silence. He had a poet's facility with language and a journalist's ease with the medium. In the last months of his life, he repeated a central article of faith — that "the desire for individual dignity and freedom . . . is in the genes of all mankind."

The second reality was his bedrock intellectualism — a never-ending appetite for scholarship. Few public men read so ravenously as McGill, and few understood as much and communicated it to so large an audience — an audience that was often unready and frequently hostile. McGill consciously employed his mind methodically, he developed habits that made him work his mind tirelessly, and he found the conditions that encouraged him to study, to write, and to publish daily.

McGill published four books over the course of his career. The first three consisted primarily of compilations of his newspaper columns. One of these three, *A Church, a School* (1959), comprised his editorials on the Temple bombing in Atlanta and on hate crimes by the Ku Klux Klan. It was these editorials for which McGill won the Pulitzer Prize in 1959.

His most notable book was the *The South and the Southerner*, first published in 1963. A selective memoir of his East Tennessee upbringing and various facets of his journalistic career, it is also a much broader social commentary on and sharp critique of the South, past and present, though it also reflected his optimism for the region's capacity for progressive change.

McGill died suddenly of a heart attack in Atlanta on February 3, 1969, just two days before his seventy-first birthday. In 2005 he was inducted into the Georgia Writers Hall of Fame.

LEONARD RAY TEEL, *Georgia State University*

SUGGESTED READING

Barbara Barksdale Clowse, *Ralph McGill: A Biography* (Macon, Ga.: Mercer University Press, 1998).

Calvin M. Logue, ed., *Ralph McGill: Editor and Publisher* (Durham, N.C.: Moore, 1969).

Harold Martin, *Ralph McGill, Reporter* (Boston: Little, Brown, 1973).

Ralph McGill, *The South and the Southerner* (Athens: University of Georgia Press, 1992).

Leonard Ray Teel, *Ralph Emerson McGill: Voice of the Southern Conscience* (Knoxville: University of Tennessee Press, 2001).

JAMES ALAN McPHERSON
(b. 1943)

Essayist, short-story writer, and critic, James Alan McPherson is among that generation of African American writers and intellectuals, including Charles Johnson and Stanley Crouch, who were inspired and mentored by Ralph Ellison. McPherson's early short story "Gold Coast" won the 1965 *Atlantic Monthly* Firsts award. In 1978 he was the first African American recipient of the Pulitzer Prize in fiction for his 1977 story collection, *Elbow Room*. Frequently anthologized, McPherson has received such prestigious honors as a Guggenheim Fellowship (1972–73), the MacArthur Fellowship (1981), several Pushcart Prizes, and induction into the American Academy of Arts and Sciences (1995).

Born in Savannah on September 16, 1943, before integration, McPherson recollects playing hooky from school in order to read in the "colored branch" of the local Carnegie Library. In 1962 he worked as a dining-car waiter for the Great Northern Railroad. He attended Morgan State University in Baltimore, Maryland, from 1963 to 1964 and earned a B.A. degree at Morris Brown College in Atlanta in 1965. Subsequently he attended Harvard University Law School (LL.B., 1968) in Cambridge, Massachusetts, the Writers Workshop at the University of Iowa, and the Yale University Law School in New Haven, Connecticut. With his M.F.A. degree in creative writing from the University of Iowa (1969), he has taught at a variety of institutions, including the University of California, Santa Cruz; Harvard University; the University of Virginia; and the University of Iowa, where he is currently professor of English. He has also lectured in Japan.

As a writer McPherson sees himself most fully as a practitioner of the short story. His stories have appeared in many different magazines, including popularly oriented periodicals like the *Atlantic Monthly* and *Playboy* and small-press journals like the

Harvard Review and *Ploughshares*. The best of his work has been collected in *Hue and Cry* (1968) and *Elbow Room* (1977). His memoir, *Crabcakes* (1998), which records his life from 1976 through his experiences teaching in Japan, is also very much in the mode of a series of stories.

Like Ralph Ellison, McPherson sees African American culture as integrally connected with the "white" culture. He doesn't consider himself a "black writer" but rather thinks of himself in relation to other practitioners of the American tradition of short fiction. Although he writes on topics drawn from his experiences as a black man, he rejects the notion that black or white fiction must necessarily concern certain black or white topics. Indeed, his concern is to record stories that might be lost because of such conformity.

As an editor and critic, McPherson has produced several books. *Railroad: Trains and Train People* (1976), coedited with poet Miller Williams, grew out of his experiences working on the railroad. In association with DeWitt Henry, founding editor of *Ploughshares*, McPherson compiled and edited *Confronting Racial Difference* (1990) and *Fathering Daughters: Reflections by Men* (1998). In 2000 he published *A Region Not Home: Reflections from Exile*, a collection of twelve essays and reviews. It includes his classic "On Becoming an American Writer" and "Gravitas," his appreciation of Ralph Ellison on the occasion of the posthumous publication of Ellison's novel *Juneteenth* in 1999.

THOMAS COOKSEY, *Armstrong Atlantic State University*

SUGGESTED READING

Herman Beavers, *Wrestling Angels into Song: The Fictions of Ernest J. Gaines and James Alan McPherson* (Philadelphia: University of Pennsylvania Press, 1995).

Joseph Cox, "James Alan McPherson," in *Contemporary Fiction Writers of the South: A Bio-Bibliographical Source Book*, ed. Joseph M. Flora and Robert Bain (Westport, Conn.: Greenwood Press, 1993).

ADDITIONAL RESOURCES

James Alan McPherson, Writer's Workshop Series (Alexandria, Va.: PBS, 1980), video.

THE MEMBER OF THE WEDDING

Along with her first novel, *The Heart Is a Lonely Hunter*, Carson McCullers's third novel, *The Member of the Wedding*, and the play adapted from it remain her most enduring literary achievements. Born in 1917 in Columbus, Carson McCullers revealed at a young age the creative genius that would distinguish her as one of the South's most talented writers. After publishing *The Heart Is a Lonely Hunter* in 1940 at age twenty-three, McCullers began writing *The Member of the Wedding*.

Like her first novel, *The Member of the Wedding* (1946) evokes the solitude and uncertainty of a young outcast in the Deep South. Its central focus falls on the shifting emotions of twelve-year-old Frankie Addams, a precocious, sensitive, gangly girl in the midst of a summer of boredom and loneliness in a small Georgia mill town. Frankie feels desperately left out of everything — the social life of her peers, the goings-on of the town, the faraway war raging in other parts of the world, and especially her brother's wedding. Ostracized by her peers yet too old for child's play, Frankie spends most of her time with the family's black housekeeper, Berenice, and her six-year-old cousin, John Henry. In their many evenings spent together in the sweltering Addams kitchen, Berenice and John Henry act as sensible foils to Frankie's restless histrionics.

Frankie feels haunted by the news that her brother, who is in the military and has been stationed in Alaska, is returning home to marry. The upcoming wedding deeply affects her as yet one more glamorous and exciting event in a world full of glamour and excitement that does not include her. She longs for the wedding to happen and imagines that afterward she will go away with the wedding couple, never to return to her hometown. Frankie builds all her fantasies around the event, imagining that she can begin a new and exciting life with the couple and erase the disappointment of her life thus far. This thought becomes her solace throughout the summer as she repeats over and over to herself that her brother and his bride "are the we of me" — the *we* of companionship and belonging that Frankie feels unable to find. Anticipating her new life of belonging and worldliness, she assumes the sophisticated persona of "F. Jasmine." Walking around town as "F. Jasmine," she finds the attention and inclusion she desires but with tragicomic results.

Frankie Addams remains one of McCullers's most memorable protagonists. Her frustration, loneliness, and restlessness resonate with anyone who has ever felt unknown and misunderstood. McCullers's triumph is her ability to portray the awkwardness of the misfit Frankie, whose alternating sullenness and mania frustrate both herself and those around her. Using the semi-autobiographical character of Frankie as a vehicle, McCullers masterfully explores the grotesqueries, poignancy, pathos, and banality of life, especially through Frankie's marginalization by her own sense of difference and alienation in her town.

McCullers adapted her novel for the stage, and it opened to critical acclaim as a play on Broadway in 1950, starring Ethel Waters as Berenice, Julie Harris as Frankie, and Brandon de Wilde as John Henry. It won the New York Drama Critics Circle Award as the best play of the season. All three actors re-created their roles for a film version produced in 1952. *The Member of the Wedding* continues to be a popular play for regional and college theater productions and has been filmed twice more, both times for television, the latest version appearing in 1997 with Alfre Woodard and Anna Paquin in the lead roles.

LESA C. SHAUL, *University of Alabama, Tuscaloosa*

SUGGESTED READING

Harold Bloom, ed., *Carson McCullers* (New York: Chelsea House, 1986).

Virginia Spencer Carr, *The Lonely Hunter: A Biography of Carson McCullers* (Garden City, N.Y.: Doubleday, 1975; reprint, Athens: University of Georgia Press, 2003).

Virginia Spencer Carr, *Understanding Carson McCullers* (Columbia: University of South Carolina Press, 1990).

Louise Westling, *Sacred Groves and Ravaged Gardens: The Fiction of Eudora Welty, Carson McCullers, and Flannery O'Connor* (Athens: University of Georgia Press, 1985).

MIDNIGHT IN THE GARDEN
OF GOOD AND EVIL

The impact of *Midnight in the Garden of Good and Evil* on Savannah has been greater than that of any other book in the city's history. Written by John Berendt and published by Random House in January 1994, the nonfiction narrative quickly became known locally as simply "The Book." Since that time it has sold more than three million copies in 101 printings, has been translated into twenty-three languages and appeared in twenty-four foreign editions, and has brought hundreds of thousands of tourists to Savannah to visit this loveliest of crime scenes. The one point on which both critics and admirers agree is that, after *Midnight in the Garden*, Savannah's clock will never be turned back.

Author John Berendt was born in 1939 and grew up in Syracuse, New York; attended Harvard University, where he wrote and edited for the *Harvard Lampoon*; and was an associate editor at *Esquire* and editor of *New York* magazine before moving to Savannah in 1985 to research *Midnight in the Garden*. He took an apartment and for eight years lived off and on in the city, interviewing locals and gathering material.

The book is constructed loosely around the shooting of male hustler Danny Hansford by internationally known antiques dealer Jim Williams in May 1981 and the subsequent four murder trials that lasted more than eight years. Williams was finally acquitted, but the main interest of the story for many readers has been the wealth of exquisitely drawn incidental characters from every level of society and the artfully woven anecdotes that create a tapestry of Savannah.

Among memorable Savannahians depicted are singer/pianist Emma Kelly, "The Lady of 6,000 Songs" (so dubbed by Savannah songwriter Johnny Mercer); Joe Odom, a southern gentleman/lawyer who covers his bad checks with charm; an inventor (named Luther Driggers in the book) who possesses a vial of poison strong enough to kill the whole city if it were to infiltrate the water supply; Minerva, the Lowcountry "root doctor" who works spells for Jim Williams; Sonny Seiler, Williams's defense attorney and owner of Uga, the University of Georgia's renowned mascot; and The Lady Chablis, a drag queen who gleefully crashes an annual African American debutante ball.

Reviews of the book almost unanimously praised the quality of the writing. The *Savannah Morning News* called it "a compelling, mordbidly fascinating, beautifully written book," though the reviewer found the profusion of characters and anecdotes — however masterfully rendered — "overwhelming and overindulgent." The same reviewer also lamented the lack of a "strong plot" to propel the action, as in "a conventional murder mystery," and felt let down by the final ambiguity of whether the killing was murder or self-defense.

The *Washington Post* described *Midnight in the Garden* as "one of the most unusual books to come this way in a long time, and one of the best," and the *Los Angeles Times* claimed that Berendt "seems congenitally unable to write a dull paragraph." Of Berendt's portrayal of Savannah, *Newsweek* stated, "Few cities have been introduced more seductively." The *New York Times Book Review* agreed: "Mr. Berendt's writing is elegant and wickedly funny, and his eye for telling details is superb. . . . *Midnight in the Garden of Good and Evil* might be the first true crime book that makes the reader want to call a travel agent and book a bed and breakfast for an extended weekend at the scene of the crime."

Tourists from all over the world have done just that, dispelling unequivocally a *Savannah Morning News* columnist's early skepticism. Hotel-motel tax revenues rose about twenty-five percent in the two years following publication of the book, and cottage industries related to *Midnight in the Garden* sprang up like morning glories: trolley tours of the main sites; candles in the shape of the Bird Girl (photographed by Jack Leigh for the dust jacket); T-shirts, mugs, postcards, a newsletter, even a gift shop devoted specifically to Midnightabilia. On April 22, 1996, the Savannah Economic Development Authority honored Berendt with a special award, and Mayor Floyd Adams declared April 26 of that year "John Berendt Day."

The book won the Southern Book Award and was a finalist for the Pulitzer Prize in nonfiction, but without doubt its most significant achievement was the record number of weeks (216) it spent on the *New York Times* best-seller list. It also spawned a jazz concert based on Johnny Mercer songs, which toured the country in 1996, an eight-episode series on *This Old House* in 1996, and a two-hour A&E documentary titled *Midnight in Savannah* in 1997.

Warner Brothers bought the rights to the movie, and John Lee Hancock wrote the script. He showed it to Clint Eastwood, who had directed and starred in Hancock's *Perfect World* (but who had not read Berendt's book). On May 5, 1997, shooting began on Monterey Square in Savannah. The cast included Kevin Spacey as Jim Williams, Jude Law as Danny Hansford, John Cusack as the John Berendt character (renamed John Kelso), Paul Hipp as Joe Odom, Jack Thompson as Sonny Seiler (Seiler himself played the judge in the trial), Irma P. Hall as Minerva, and Eastwood's daughter Alison as Mandy Nichols (a romantic interest of Odom in the book, of Kelso in the movie). Playing themselves in the film were Emma Kelly and The Lady Chablis, and Uga V, the University of Georgia's bulldog mascot, played his sire.

Savannahians filled many minor roles and rounded out crowd and party scenes. Eastwood made good use of the tree-lined streets and historic squares, and several scenes were shot at Mercer House itself (Williams's mansion). The movie premiered in Savannah at the Johnny Mercer Theater on November 20, 1997, with Kevin Spacey, Paul Hipp, The Lady Chablis, and local actors attending, and it opened nationwide the following day.

Reviews of the movie were generally lukewarm. Roger Ebert, after commending Eastwood's "determined attempt to be faithful to the book's spirit" and conceding "something ineffable is lost just by turning on the camera," concluded that "the movie never reached takeoff speed." Liz Smith (*New York Post*) found it "very long. . . . Judicious editing would help this movie a lot." Desson Howe (*Washington Post*) observed, "You're thinking about a graceful exit long before Eastwood even thinks to send you home." Kenneth Turan (*Los Angeles Times*): "Listless, disjointed, and disconnected, this meandering, two-hour, 32-minute exercise in futility will fascinate no one who doesn't have a blood relation among the cast or crew." Performances by Spacey and Cusack were generally deemed good, considering the script's flat lines, but only Jack Thompson's Sonny Seiler was cited as Oscarworthy. Even The Lady Chablis, ad-libbing most of her lines, seemed not quite herself.

Fortunately, the A&E documentary *Midnight in Savannah*, originally aired at the time of the movie's release, succeeds resoundingly in portraying the city, the book, and its impact.

CARL SOLANA WEEKS, *Savannah*

SUGGESTED READING

Susan Sully, *Savannah Style: Mystery and Manners*, photographs by Steven Brooke, foreword by John Berendt (New York: Rizzoli, 2001).

ADDITIONAL RESOURCES

Midnight in Savannah, A&E Television Networks, 1997, cat. no. AAE-17037, film.

This Old House, Savannah, Georgia, programs 1519–1526, WGBH, Boston, video.

CAROLINE MILLER

(1903–1992)

Caroline Miller published her first novel, *Lamb in His Bosom*, in 1933 and became the first Georgian to win the Pulitzer Prize for fiction. The thirty-year-old housewife and author produced one of the most critically acclaimed first novels of the Southern Renaissance period. In addition to the Pulitzer, the novel earned France's Prix Femina in 1934 and became an immediate best-seller.

Miller, the youngest of seven children, was born August 26, 1903, in Waycross to Elias Pafford, a schoolteacher and Methodist minister, and his wife, Levy Zan Hall Pafford. Miller's father died while she was in junior high school; her mother died in her junior year of high school. She demonstrated an early interest in writing and acting and performed in several high school plays. Shortly after graduation she married her high school English teacher, William D. Miller, and the couple moved to Baxley. In 1927, after six years of marriage, a son, William Dews Miller Jr., was born. Miller gave birth again in 1929 to twin boys, George and Harvey. In addition to her domestic duties, Miller continued to write short stories to supplement the family income.

Described by literary critics as a work of regional historical realism, *Lamb in His Bosom* depicts the struggle and hardships of nineteenth-century pioneer life on the south Georgia frontier, known as the Wiregrass region. The story begins with the marriage of sixteen-year-old Tillitha Cean Carver to Lonzo Smith, a neighboring yeoman farmer several years her senior. By the time Cean is forty-three, she has borne fourteen children, buried five of them and a husband, and survived civil war, a venomous snakebite, a ferocious panther attack, and a deadly house fire. She perseveres to find contentment in a second marriage to a New Light preacher named Dermid O'Connor. Miller centers the story of the Carver and Smith families around the experiences

of Cean and her sister-in-law Margot Kimbrough, an indepen-
dent-minded girl from the coast. Childbirth, the central theme of
novel, represents both religious rebirth and feminine fulfillment.

With characters named after Miller's own family members,
Lamb in His Bosom grew out of her interest in local research
and genealogy. While traveling around the south Georgia countryside, she collected in a notebook the folktales and idiomatic
expressions that became the basis for her simple and direct style
of writing. The author, who had no formal training, received
high praise from literary critics for her faithful representation of
Wiregrass dialect and culture.

The stress of sudden fame and attention strained the Millers'
marriage, and in 1936 the couple divorced. In 1937 Caroline
Miller married a florist and antique dealer, Clyde H. Ray Jr. The
couple made their home in Waynesville, North Carolina, where
Caroline helped her husband in his business and gave birth to a
fourth son, Clyde H. III, and a daughter, Caroline Patience.

After moving to North Carolina, Miller continued to write
features and short stories for newspapers and magazines. Her
second novel, *Lebanon* (1944), received a lukewarm reception
from critics, and Miller herself was not satisfied with it. Trying
to recreate the success of her first book, Miller once again placed
her heroine, Lebanon Fairgale, in the backwoods of Georgia.
For this novel, however, Miller formulated an awkward romantic
plot, garnering criticism that *Lebanon* lacked the realistic cred-
ibility of *Lamb in His Bosom*.

During the following decades Miller wrote prolifically and
completed several manuscripts. Uncomfortable in the glare of the
public spotlight so many years earlier, Miller chose not to publish any additional work. She remained in her mountain home
in western North Carolina, cherishing her privacy and solitude.
Lamb in His Bosom enjoyed a resurgence of popularity a year after Miller's death, when Peachtree Publishers reprinted the novel
with an afterword by historian Elizabeth Fox-Genovese. This sig-
naled a new attention to her work by both literary scholars and
historians. Caroline Miller died on July 12, 1992, knowing that

she had received what she once declared to be the true reward of a novelist — "the knowledge that after he dies he will leave the best part of himself behind."

CAREY O. SHELLMAN, *University of Florida, Gainesville*

SUGGESTED READING

Dictionary of Literary Biography, vol. 9, pt. 2, *American Novelists, 1910–1945* (Detroit: Gale, 1981), s.v. "Caroline Miller."

JUDSON MITCHAM
(b. 1948)

Examining basic human themes within the specific landscape of Georgia, Judson Mitcham's writing is both poignant and powerful. His poetry has been widely published, appearing in such journals as *Harper's*, *Georgia Review*, *Chattahoochee Review*, *Gettysburg Review*, *Poetry*, *Southern Poetry Review*, and *Southern Review*. His poetry collection *Somewhere in Ecclesiastes* earned him both the Devins Award and recognition as Georgia Author of the Year. His first novel, *The Sweet Everlasting*, won him the Townsend Prize for Fiction and a second Georgia Author of the Year award. *Sabbath Creek*, his second novel, also won the Townsend Prize, making Mitcham the first writer to receive the award twice.

Mitcham was born in 1948 in Monroe, where he grew up and where much of his work is centered. His parents, Myrtle and Wilson Mitcham, figure prominently in his poetry. Mitcham was not formally trained as a writer. Instead he studied psychology at the University of Georgia, where he earned his undergraduate and graduate degrees. He received his Ph.D. in 1974. From then he taught in the psychology department at Fort Valley State University until his retirement in 2004 with the rank of associate professor. He has also served as adjunct professor of creative writing at the University of Georgia and at Emory University, where he has directed the Summer Writers' Institute. He resides in Macon with his wife, Jean. They are the parents of two children.

Somewhere in Ecclesiastes (1991) offers a moving sequence of poems, written throughout the 1980s, about youth, family, mortality, and the southern cultural scene. Most of the poems are first-person narratives. In "Night Ride 1965" Mitcham narrates the memory of sneaking out of the house at night and riding with a friend through the darkness, talking and gazing at the dark landscape:

> we cruise all night down narrow country roads
> talking as though we could say it all, could tell
> what it means to grow quiet at the first light,
> while the stars all fail, what it means
> finally to turn home.

Mitcham writes the poem as a man in middle age, looking back on his youth with longing and regret. "Notes for a Prayer in June" also uses memories to illuminate the poet's struggle to understand the meaning of life and mortality. Mitcham celebrates life's mystery and joy even as he refuses to ignore the tragedies that strike, "the unbelievable sadness of chance," the deaths of children and of friends. In the collection's title poem, he describes a young boy's death as "a piece of deep blue in the puzzle / his mother hasn't yet put together." He wonders whether "we are blessed / only by accident, only by chance," and asks whether proof of immortality would lessen the impact of life's sadness:

> What if it were true, after all,
> that the body is a garment, a light cotton shirt,
> we will easily do without?
>
> If we knew this beyond any question
> would it alter the funerals of children?

In "Sunday" Mitcham interweaves memories of his father and his family in a poignant meditation on time and mortality. Such themes continue to develop in poetry he has written during the 1990s, focusing on his mother and his awareness of mortality as it is driven home through the deaths of other family members. This intensely felt, elegiac sense of loss is the central feeling in many of Mitcham's poems. The later poems, many of them collected in the 2003 volume *This April Day*, are tinged with a deepening pessimism and despair over the disappearance of the people who played a crucial role in his early life and in the formation of his identity.

Mitcham's 1996 novel *The Sweet Everlasting* offers an eloquent elegy for a vanished past. Narrated by Ellis Burt, a seventy-four-year-old ex-convict, the novel recounts the life of a sharecropper's son in south Georgia and his marriage to a beautiful young woman. Separated from her for decades by tragic circumstances that lie at the novel's heart, Burt tells how he comes to be reunited with his wife, who is suffering from late-stage Alzheimer's disease and is unable to remember him. *The Sweet Everlasting* is not so much a southern novel as a book about a man attempting in old age to come to terms with his life, his mistakes, and the people he has known. At the same time, it takes a hard look at class conflict and racial prejudice in the rural South of the early twentieth century. A reviewer for the *Atlanta Journal-Constitution* writes, "Mitcham has an affinity for people on the margins of life and an ability to look at their lives and see the threads common to us all. The simple words of Ellis Burt suffuse 'The Sweet Everlasting' with a tenderness and depth of feeling that will haunt you long after the reading."

In 2004 Mitcham published his second novel, *Sabbath Creek*, which follows Charlene Pope and her son, Lewis, on a road trip through south Georgia. The *New York Times* described the book as a "spare, lovely novel" that is "generous in humor [yet] anchored by sorrow and interspersed with portents of tragedy."

In both his novels and his poetry, Mitcham's elegiac voice looks backwards with fondness and discernment on a personal and regional past slipping rapidly beyond reach.

HUGH RUPPERSBURG, *University of Georgia*

SUGGESTED READING

Cathy High, "A Simple Georgia Man Comes to Grips with Life," review of *The Sweet Everlasting*, by Judson Mitcham, *Atlanta Journal-Constitution*, 7 July 1996: Arts, p. 8.

MARGARET MITCHELL

(1900–1949)

Margaret Mitchell was the author of *Gone With the Wind*, one of the most popular books of all time. The novel was published in 1936 and sold more than a million copies in the first six months, a phenomenal feat considering it was the depression era. More than 30 million copies of this Civil War–era masterpiece have been sold worldwide in thirty-eight countries. It has been translated into twenty-seven languages. Approximately 250,000 copies are still sold each year. Shortly after the book's publication the movie rights were sold to David O. Selznick for $50,000, the highest amount ever paid for a manuscript up to that time. In 1937 Margaret Mitchell was awarded the Pulitzer Prize.

Margaret Munnerlyn Mitchell was born on November 8, 1900, in Atlanta. Her great-great-great-grandfather Thomas Mitchell fought in the American Revolution, and his son William Mitchell took part in the War of 1812. Her great-grandfather Isaac Green Mitchell was a circuit-riding Methodist minister who settled in Marthasville, which later was named Atlanta. Mitchell was thus a fourth-generation Atlantan. Her grandfather Russell Mitchell fought in the Civil War and suffered two bullet wounds to the head during the fighting at Antietam. Twice married, he had twelve children, the oldest of whom was Mitchell's father, Eugene.

Mitchell's mother's family was Irish Catholic. Her great-grandfather Phillip Fitzgerald came to America from Ireland and eventually settled on a plantation near Jonesboro in Clayton County. The Fitzgeralds had seven daughters. Annie Fitzgerald, Mitchell's grandmother, married John Stephens, who had emigrated from Ireland and settled in Atlanta. Stephens amassed large real-estate properties and helped found a trolley-car system in the city. The Stephenses had twelve children; Mary Isobel (May Belle), Mitchell's mother, was the seventh. May Belle married Eugene

Muse Mitchell on November 8, 1892. Eugene was a noted Atlanta attorney, and May Belle was a staunch supporter of woman suffrage. They had a son, Stephens, followed four years later by a daughter, Margaret Munnerlyn.

Mitchell began making up stories before she could write, dictating them to her mother. Later she made her own books with cardboard covers and filled them with adventure stories using her friends, relatives, and herself as characters. As she grew older she switched to copybooks, which her mother stored in inexpensive enamel bread boxes. A few of the hundreds of tales that she wrote have survived, including two Civil War tales. When the family moved to Peachtree Street, the young Mitchell attended the Tenth Street School and later Woodberry School, a private school. She branched out to writing, directing, and starring in plays, coercing the neighborhood children to take part.

From 1914 to 1918 Mitchell attended the Washington Seminary, a prestigious Atlanta finishing school, where she was a founding member and officer of the drama club. She was also the literary editor of *Facts and Fancies*, the high school yearbook, in which two of her stories were featured. She was president of the Washington Literary Society.

When America entered World War I in 1917, the seminary girls were in demand at dances for the young servicemen stationed at Camp Gordon and Fort McPherson. At one such dance in the summer of 1918 Mitchell met twenty-two-year-old Clifford Henry, a wealthy and socially prominent New Yorker who was a bayonet instructor at Camp Gordon. The two fell in love and became engaged shortly before he was shipped overseas. He was killed in October 1918 while fighting in France.

In September 1918 Mitchell entered Smith College in Northampton, Massachusetts, where she began using the nickname "Peggy." Her freshman year at college was disrupted when an influenza epidemic forced the cancellation of classes. In January her mother contracted influenza and died the day before her daughter reached home. Mitchell completed her freshman year at Smith, then returned to Atlanta to take her place as mistress of the household and to enter the upcoming debutante season. During the last charity ball of the season, Mitchell created a scandal by performing a sensuous dance popular in the nightclubs of Paris, France.

Soon Mitchell met Berrien Kinnard Upshaw, who was from a prominent Raleigh, North Carolina, family. They were wed in 1922, but the marriage was brief. After four months Upshaw left Atlanta for the Midwest and never returned. The marriage was annulled two years later.

In the same year that she married, Mitchell landed a job with the *Atlanta Journal Sunday Magazine*. She used "Peggy Mitchell" as her byline. Her interviews, profiles, and sketches of life in Georgia were well received. During her four years with the *Sunday Magazine*, Mitchell wrote 129 articles, worked as a proofreader, substituted for the advice columnist, reviewed books, and occasionally did hard news stories for the paper. Complications from a broken ankle led her to end her career as a journalist.

Mitchell's second marriage was to John Robert Marsh on July 4, 1925, and the couple set up housekeeping in a small apartment affectionately called "the Dump." They entertained the newspaper crowd and other friends on a regular basis. Marsh, originally from Maysville, Kentucky, worked for the Georgia Power and Light Company as director of the publicity department.

In 1926, to relieve the boredom of being cooped up with a broken ankle, Mitchell began to write *Gone With the Wind*. Setting up her Remington typewriter on an old sewing table, she completed the majority of the book in three years. She wrote the last chapter first and the other chapters in no particular order. Stuffing the chapters into manila envelopes, she eventually accumulated almost seventy chapters. When visitors appeared, she covered her work with a towel, keeping her novel a secret. There has been much speculation on whether the characters were based on real people, but Mitchell claimed they were her own creations.

In April 1935 Harold Latham, an editor for the Macmillan publishing company in New York City, toured the South looking for new manuscripts. Latham heard that Mitchell had been working on a manuscript and asked her if he could see it, but she denied having one. When a friend commented that Mitchell was not serious enough to write a novel, Mitchell gathered up many of the envelopes and took them to Latham at his hotel. He had to purchase a suitcase to carry them. He read part of the manuscript on the train to New Orleans, Louisiana, and sent it straight to New York. By July Macmillan had offered her a contract. She received a $500 advance and 10 percent of the royalties.

As she revised the manuscript, Mitchell cut and rearranged chapters, confirmed details, wrote a new first chapter, changed the name of the main character (originally called Pansy), and struggled to think of a title that suited her. Titles considered included *Tomorrow Is Another Day, Another Day, Tote the Weary Load, Milestones, Ba! Ba! Blacksheep, Not in Our Stars*, and *Bugles Sang True*. Finally she settled on a phrase from a favorite poem by Ernest Dowson: "I have forgot much, Cynara! gone with the wind, / Flung roses, roses riotously with the throng." Published in 1936, *Gone With the Wind* was 1,037 pages long and sold for three dollars.

Gone With the Wind was a phenomenal success and received rave reviews. Overnight, Mitchell became a celebrity and remained very much in the public spotlight through the production and premiere of the film based on her novel in 1939. She was in constant demand for speaking engagements and interviews. At first she complied, but later, pleading poor health, she usually declined these requests and stopped autographing copies of her book. She said she wanted to remain simply Mrs. John Marsh.

Gone With the Wind was Mitchell's only published novel. At her request, the original manuscript (except for a few pages retained to validate her authorship) and all other writings were destroyed. These included a novella in the Gothic style, a ghost story set in an old plantation home left vacant after the Civil War. According to the recollections of Lois Cole, a friend of Mitchell's and a Macmillan employee, three people had read this tale (written before *Gone With the Wind*) and thought it was worth publishing by one of the bigger publishing houses. Cole suggested that Mitchell enter it in the Little, Brown novelette contest.

Possibly one of the reasons that Mitchell never wrote another novel was that she spent so much time working with her brother and her husband to protect the copyright of her book abroad. Up until the publication of *Gone With the Wind*, international copyright laws were ambiguous and varied from country to country. Correspondence also took much of her time. During the years following publication, she personally answered every letter she received about her book. With the outbreak of World War II in 1941, she worked tirelessly for the American Red Cross, even outfitting a hospital ship. She also set up scholarships for black medical students.

On August 11, 1949, Mitchell and her husband decided to go to a movie, *A Canterbury Tale*, at the Peachtree Art Theatre. Just as they started to cross Peachtree Street, near 13th Street, a speeding taxi crested the hill. Mitchell stepped back; Marsh stepped forward. The driver applied the brakes, skidded, and hit Mitchell. She was rushed to Grady Hospital but never regained consciousness. During the five days before she died, crowds waited outside for news. U.S. president Harry Truman, Georgia governor Herman Talmadge, and Atlanta mayor William B. Hartsfield all asked to be kept informed of her condition. Special phone lines were installed at Grady Hospital, and friends manned the lines in four-hour shifts. Mitchell died on August 16, 1949, and was buried in Oakland Cemetery in Atlanta.

JANE THOMAS, *Greensboro, North Carolina*

SUGGESTED READING

Patrick Allen, ed., *Margaret Mitchell, Reporter* (Athens, Ga.: Hill Street Press, 2000).

Anne Edwards, *Road to Tara: The Life of Margaret Mitchell* (New Haven, Conn.: Ticknor and Fields, 1983).

Jane Eskridge, ed., *Before Scarlett: Girlhood Writings of Margaret Mitchell* (Athens, Ga.: Hill Street Press, 2000).

Finis Farr, *Margaret Mitchell of Atlanta, the Author of "Gone With the Wind"* (New York: William Morrow, 1965).

Richard Harwell, ed., *Margaret Mitchell's "Gone With the Wind" Letters, 1936–1949* (New York: Macmillan, 1976).

Darden Asbury Pyron, *Southern Daughter: The Life of Margaret Mitchell* (New York: Oxford University Press, 1991).

Marianne Walker, *Margaret Mitchell and John Marsh: The Love Story behind "Gone With the Wind"* (Atlanta: Peachtree, 1993).

MARION MONTGOMERY
(b. 1925)

Poet, novelist, intellectual, and literary critic, Marion Hoyt Montgomery taught composition, literature, and creative writing at the University of Georgia for thirty-three years. He also wrote hundreds of poems, twenty-seven short stories, three novels, and one novella. Montgomery has published seventeen books of literary and cultural criticism. He received numerous awards for his fiction and verse in the 1960s and early 1970s. In 2001 he received the Stanley W. Lindberg Award for outstanding contributions to Georgia's literary heritage.

Montgomery was born in Thomaston, the son of Lottie May Jenkins and Marion H. Montgomery. He served in the U.S. Army from 1943 to 1946 and married Dorothy Carlisle in 1951. They have five children. He received his B.A. (1950) and M.A. (1953) at the University of Georgia and did postgraduate work in creative writing at the University of Iowa (1956–58).

Montgomery's three novels, all set in twentieth-century Georgia, focus on conflicts between the Old and the New South. *The Wandering of Desire* (1962) takes its title from Ecclesiastes as well as its themes: "all is vanity" and "that which has been will be again." Two ambitious men, a self-made yeoman farmer and a progressive farmer, fight for control of "the Hill," a tract of land in northeast Waring County. Both ultimately are defeated by the forces of nature and human depravity. Faulknerian in style and scope, *The Wandering of Desire* powerfully captures the history, geography, and culture of the region.

His second novel, *Darrell* (1964), combines comedy, satire, and tragedy in its depiction of the misadventures of a country-born boy and his grandmother as they attempt to adjust to life in an Athens neighborhood. Darrell's longing for an even more exciting life in Atlanta is counterbalanced by his grandmother's common sense and longing for the country.

Montgomery's most ambitious and experimental novel is *Fugitive* (1974). In it country music writer Walt Mason flees from Vanderbilt University in Nashville, Tennessee, to a small village in northeast Georgia, where he seeks "the good life" in the country. Hugh Akers, his guide to genuine country ways, and other residents in the community envelop the narrative with bawdy, comic, tragic, and wise stories and sayings. Authentic country wit and idiom is one of the strongest features of the novel.

Several of Montgomery's short stories have been anthologized: two notable ones are the comic "I Got a Gal" and the poignant "The Decline and Fall of Officer Fergerson," which appeared in *Southern Writing in the Sixties* (1966) and *The Best American Short Stories: 1971*.

Montgomery's verse has been collected in three volumes: *Dry Lightning* (1960), *Stones from the Rubble* (1965), and *The Gull and Other Georgia Scenes* (1969). The culture of the South and the roles he has played in his own life — poet, teacher, husband, father — form the bedrock for traditional and free-verse poems illuminating universal human experiences and human nature. Lyrical, ironic, satirical, and reflective, Montgomery is also occasionally philosophical, as in his long poem "At Al Johnson's Lake," a tense, engaging celebration of the mystery of being.

With the exception of a few poems, most of Montgomery's writing in the last twenty-five years has been critical. Yet the poet's insights and language illuminate the theological, philosophical, and literary issues he examines in his criticism. In *The Prophetic Poet and the Spirit of the Age* (1981–84), a three-volume study of Western modernism, Montgomery calls his readers back to traditional and orthodox truths that are central in all of his work: namely, that spiritual concerns are compatible with realism in literature; that reason and imagination are gifts that should be carefully exercised in life, faith, and art; that ideas have consequences; that intellectual errors should be traced to their root in time and place; that being should be celebrated rather than subjugated; that piety and openness to creation are the proper responses to existence; and that mind and heart, reason and feeling are companionable faculties. The trilogy and such later works as *Possum and Other Receits for the Recovery of "Southern" Being* (1987), *Liberal Arts and Community* (1990), and *Romantic Confusions of the Good* (1997) defend a Christian vision of the world. Montgomery's antagonist is modernity, an intellectual attitude, he contends, that divorces man from both tradition and transcendence.

In both poetry and fiction Montgomery makes his subjects palpable, giving the reader a keen sense of the flora, fauna, geography, and human culture of his region. His work, both creative and critical, is informed by his intellectual heritage. Like Flannery O'Connor, among other writers, Montgomery was influenced by the Southern Agrarians. In theology and philosophy he is a neo-Thomist (advocating the thought of thirteenth-century philosopher Thomas Aquinas). This combination is a distinctive feature of his traditional conservatism. The starting point in all of his work is piety: a reverent awareness of the physical creation, moral and spiritual realities, individual gifts such as reason and imagination, and cultural life (values, customs, and traditions inherited from the past). Piety and a recovery of reason are constant themes in his writing.

MICHAEL M. JORDAN, *Hillsdale College, Hillsdale, Michigan*

SUGGESTED READING

Robert H. Brinkmeyer Jr., "The Southern Temper and the Modern Mind," *Southern Review* 24 (winter 1988).

The Hillsdale Review: A Symposium on Marion Montgomery's Trilogy 8, no. 1–2 (spring/summer 1986).

Thomas Landess, "Marion Montgomery," in *Dictionary of Literary Biography*, vol. 6, *American Novelists since World War II*, 2d ser., ed. James E. Kibler Jr. (Detroit: Gale, 1980).

Simone Vauthier, "The 'Fundamental Dialogue': Listening In to Marion Montgomery's *Fugitive*," *Recherches Anglaises et Americaines* 9 (1976).

William Walsh, "An Interview with Marion Montgomery," *Webster Review* 13 (fall 1988).

Frances Newman was a novelist, translator, critic, book reviewer, and librarian. Writing within a feminist tradition of southern fiction that has been nearly forgotten, Newman differed from her feminist contemporaries Ellen Glasgow, Mary Johnston, and Isa Glenn in her playful humor and stylistic experimentation. Her novels portrayed the widely acclaimed social change in the South at the turn of the century as superficial rather than substantial for women, who continued to have restrictive roles in marriage and limited educational and career opportunities. Her modernist novels *The Hard-Boiled Virgin* (1926) and *Dead Lovers Are Faithful Lovers* (1928) stunned her native Atlanta with their satire of southern culture and were banned in Boston for their allusions to sexuality.

Newman was the youngest daughter in a prominent Atlanta family. Her father, Judge William T. Newman, was a Confederate war hero who became a U.S. district judge. Her mother, Fanny Percy Alexander Newman, was a direct descendant of the founder of Knoxville, Tennessee. Newman attended the Calhoun Street School and Washington Seminar in Atlanta and finishing schools in Washington, D.C., and New York City. She briefly enrolled in Agnes Scott College in Decatur, Georgia, and completed a library science degree at the Atlanta Carnegie Library in 1912.

Newman worked for a year as a librarian at Florida State College for Women in Tallahassee but returned to Atlanta in 1914, after a Mediterranean tour, to work at the Atlanta Carnegie Library. Here she began her writing career with witty reviews for the *Atlanta Journal* and the *Atlanta Constitution*, attracting the attention of Virginia novelist James Branch Cabell and critic H. L. Mencken. She also wrote her first novel, *The Gold-Fish Bowl* (1921), but was unable to find a publisher. Newman continued at Carnegie Library until 1923, when she left to study at the

Sorbonne and to complete *The Short Story's Mutations*, a collection of stories she translated from five languages. Upon her return in 1924 she accepted a position as librarian at the Georgia Institute of Technology.

Desiring more time to devote to writing, Newman took a year's leave of absence from Georgia Tech in August 1925. She was accepted at the MacDowell Colony in Peterborough, New Hampshire, for the next summer with recommendations from Sherwood Anderson and Mencken. There she was able to complete *The Hard-Boiled Virgin* in two months. An immediate best-seller, the novel enabled her to continue writing full-time. Newman returned to Peterborough the following summer and began work on *Dead Lovers Are Faithful Lovers*. Despite frequent illnesses, she completed the novel by the end of January 1928 and left for Europe before it was released.

In Europe, Newman's research for her work on a translation of Jules LaForgue's short fiction was interrupted by a serious eye problem. She returned to the United States for medical treatment but was unable to get relief from the intense pain or to see well enough to write. Nevertheless, by September she had finished her translation by dictation, while maintaining her characteristically good humor. Between scheduled appointments with neurologists in New York, she was found unconscious in her hotel room on October 19 and died three days later, apparently of a cerebral hemorrhage, although later reports blamed an overdose of a barbiturate. She was buried on October 24, 1928, in the Westview Cemetery in Atlanta.

In her novels Newman reveals, often hilariously, how the thoughts of her characters conflict with the socially imposed façade of behavior expected of the southern lady. *The Gold-Fish Bowl* is a lighthearted comedy of manners written in the style of her beloved Jane Austen. Although this book was not published in Newman's lifetime, it was edited as a dissertation by Margaret M. Duggan in 1985.

In Newman's epigrammatic novel *The Hard-Boiled Virgin*, Katharine Faraday must unlearn the rigid social codes of her upbringing to envision becoming a writer herself rather than being validated by the attention of celebrated male writers. Embedded in this novel are subtle references to sexual arousal, menstruation, and birth control, taboo topics that young Katharine ponders but cannot discuss openly.

Dead Lovers Are Faithful Lovers blurs distinctions between two literary stereotypes, the selfless angel of the house and the other woman, suggesting that actual women do not fit such limiting literary conventions. The novel also cleverly exposes the misogyny and racism underlying the image of the southern lady.

Newman's premature death at the height of her literary powers precluded the writing of several planned novels. Denounced by the influential Southern Agrarians because she unveiled the pervasive sexism and racism of the patriarchal South, Newman was excluded from the canon of southern literature and has only recently been rediscovered.

BARBARA ANN WADE, *Berea College, Berea, Kentucky*

SUGGESTED READING

Emory Reginald Abbott, "A Southern Lady Still: A Reinterpretation of Frances Percy Newman's *The Hard-Boiled Virgin*," *Southern Quarterly* 27 (summer 1989).

Anne Goodwyn Jones, "Frances Newman: The World's Lessons," *Tomorrow Is Another Day: The Woman Writer in the South, 1859–1936* (Baton Rouge: Louisiana State University Press, 1981).

Barbara Ann Wade, *Frances Newman: Southern Satirist and Literary Rebel* (Tuscaloosa: University of Alabama Press, 1998).

FLANNERY O'CONNOR

(1925–1964)

Flannery O'Connor is considered one of America's greatest fiction writers and one of the strongest apologists for Roman Catholicism in the twentieth century. Born of the marriage of two of Georgia's oldest Catholic families, O'Connor was a devout believer whose small but impressive body of fiction presents the soul's struggle with what she called the "stinking mad shadow of Jesus."

Born in Savannah on March 25, 1925, Mary Flannery O'Connor began her education in the city's parochial schools. After the family's move to Milledgeville in 1938, she continued her schooling at the Peabody Laboratory School associated with Georgia State College for Women (GSCW), now Georgia College and State University. When she was fifteen, O'Connor, an only child, lost her father to systemic lupus erythematosus, the disease that would eventually take her own life at age thirty-nine. Devastated by the loss of this close relationship, O'Connor elected to remain in Milledgeville and attend GSCW as a day student in an accelerated three-year program.

An avid reader and artist, she served as editor of the *Corinthian*, GSCW's college literary magazine, and as unofficial campus cartoonist. O'Connor provided cartoons for nearly every issue of the campus newspaper, for the college yearbook, and for the *Corinthian*, as well as for the walls of the student lounge. Most significant, she contributed fiction, essays, and occasional poems to the *Corinthian*, demonstrating early on her penchant for satire and comedy. A social science major with a number of courses in English, O'Connor is remembered by her classmates as obviously gifted but extremely shy. Her closest friends recall her sly humor, her disdain for mediocrity, and her often merciless attacks on affectation and triviality.

In 1945 O'Connor received a scholarship in journalism from

the State University of Iowa (now the University of Iowa). In her first term, she decided that journalism was not her metier and sought out Paul Engle, head of the now world-famous Writers' Workshop, to ask if she might enter the master's program in creative writing. Engle agreed, and O'Connor is now numbered among the many fine American writers who are graduates of the Iowa program. While there she got to know several important writers and critics who lectured or taught in the program, among them Robert Penn Warren, John Crowe Ransom, Austin Warren, and Andrew Lytle. Lytle, for many years editor of the *Sewanee Review*, was one of the earliest admirers of O'Connor's fiction. He later published several of her stories in the *Sewanee Review*, as well as critical essays on her work. Engle years after declared that O'Connor was so intensely shy and possessed such a nasal southern drawl that he himself read her stories aloud to workshop classes. He also asserted that O'Connor was one of the most gifted writers he had ever taught. Engle was the first to read and comment on the initial drafts of what would become *Wise Blood*, her first novel, published in 1952.

O'Connor's master's thesis was a collection of short stories entitled *The Geranium*, the title work having already become her first published story (*Accent*, 1946). Most stories in this collection, however, are the work of an apprentice in search of her own territory and voice; they suggest only faintly the sharp wit, finely honed style, and spiritual scope of O'Connor's mature work. "The Turkey" most genuinely represents the significant connection between language and belief that came to pervade O'Connor's work. This story also reveals her ear for southern dialect and marks one of her first attempts at the literary irony for which she later became famous.

Following the completion of her M.F.A. in 1947, O'Connor won the Rinehart-Iowa Fiction Award for a first novel (for her submission of a portion of *Wise Blood*) and was accepted at Yaddo, an artists' retreat in Saratoga Springs, New York. There she continued to work on the novel and became friends with the poet Robert Lowell. In 1949, after several months at Yaddo and some time in New York City and Milledgeville, O'Connor moved into the garage apartment of Sally and Robert Fitzgerald in Ridgefield, Connecticut, where she boarded for nearly two years. In the Fitzgeralds, O'Connor found devout Catholics who provided her with the balance of solitude and communion necessary to her creativity and her intellectual and spiritual life.

This stabilizing and productive time was interrupted in 1950, however, when O'Connor was stricken with lupus, the incurable, autoimmune disease that was then treated only by the use of steroid drugs. O'Connor survived the first life-threatening attack, but she was forced to return to Milledgeville permanently. Remaining in this historic central Georgia town for the rest of her life, from 1951 until 1964, O'Connor lived quietly at Andalusia, the family farm just outside town. In spite of the debilitating effects of the drugs used for treating lupus, O'Connor managed to devote a good part of every day to writing, and she even took a surprising number of trips to lecture and read from her works.

A prolific and devoted correspondent, O'Connor stayed in touch with the literary world through letters to the Fitzgeralds, Robert Lowell, Caroline Gordon, and others. It was, in fact, through letters that O'Connor came to know Gordon, who offered invaluable suggestions about her writing, especially about *Wise Blood*. O'Connor also took time to respond to letters from younger writers, to review works of theology for the *Georgia Bulletin* (a publication of the diocese of Atlanta), to tend her growing number of peacocks, and to receive visitors seeking advice on matters both literary and spiritual. During this time, O'Connor won numerous awards, among them grants from the National Institute of Arts and Letters and the Ford Foundation, a fellowship from the *Kenyon Review*, and several O. Henry awards.

An early 1964 surgery for a fibroid tumor reactivated O'Connor's lupus, which had been in remission, and her health worsened during the following months. On August 3, 1964, after several days in a coma, she died in the Baldwin County Hospital. She is buried beside her father in Memory Hill Cemetery in

Milledgeville. At the time of her death, the *Atlanta Journal* observed that O'Connor's "deep spirituality qualified her to speak with a forcefulness not often matched in American literature."

In 1972 the posthumous collection *The Complete Stories* received the National Book Award, usually given to a living writer. The judges deemed O'Connor's work so deserving that an exception was made to honor her lifetime achievement. In 1979 *The Habit of Being: Letters*, edited by Sally Fitzgerald, was published to rave reviews. These letters reveal a great deal about O'Connor's life in Milledgeville, her writing habits, and most important, her profound religious convictions. For the first time readers were able to see — beyond the shocking stories — the warm and witty personality and the incisive intellect of the writer. The collection of letters received a number of awards, and *Christian Century* magazine named *The Habit of Being* one of the twelve most influential religious books of the decade.

O'Connor's first novel, *Wise Blood*, received mixed reviews. Even some of the strongest commentators on southern literature seemed to be at a loss to describe this dark novel. While working on the novel in the early years, O'Connor had defied an insistent and authoritative editor at Rinehart by stating that *Wise Blood* was not "a conventional novel," so confident was she in her intent. Scholars who have spent time in the O'Connor Collection in the Georgia College and State University library know that even O'Connor's juvenilia anticipate the relentlessly stark vision that became the mature writer's trademark. The closest literary "kin" of *Wise Blood* in American letters arguably is Nathanael West's *Miss Lonelyhearts*; both novels are filled with black humor and written in a sharply honed style. A novel of spiritual quest, *Wise Blood* presents the male "pilgrim," Hazel Motes, as inhabiting a sterile and ugly modern landscape derivative of T. S. Eliot's *Waste Land*.

The publication of her first short-story collection, *A Good Man Is Hard to Find* (1955), made O'Connor's Christian vision and darkly comic intent somewhat clearer to readers and allowed them to more easily grasp the intent of her 1960 novel, *The Violent Bear It Away*. A second collection of stories, *Everything That Rises Must Converge*, published posthumously in 1965, contains some of O'Connor's most popular short fiction, including the title story and "Revelation."

The body of O'Connor's work resists conventional description. Although many of her narratives begin in the familiar quotidian world — on a family vacation or in a doctor's waiting room, for example — they are not, finally, realistic and certainly not in the sense of the southern realism of William Faulkner or Erskine Caldwell. Furthermore, although O'Connor's work was written during a time of great social change in the South, those changes — and the relationships among blacks and whites — were not at the center of her fiction. O'Connor made frequent use of violence and shock tactics. She argued that she wrote for an audience who, for all its Sunday piety, did not share her belief in the fall of humanity and its need for redemption. "To the hard of hearing," she explained, "[Christian writers] shout, and for the . . . almost-blind [they] draw large and startling figures" — a statement that has become a succinct and popular explanation of O'Connor's conscious intent as a writer.

O'Connor had read Faulkner and Caldwell, as well as Eudora Welty, Caroline Gordon, and Katherine Anne Porter, among southern writers. Faulkner and Porter were strong influences, as were Nathaniel Hawthorne, Joseph Conrad, and the French writers Georges Bernanos and François Mauriac. These last four reinforced O'Connor's emphasis on original sin, guilt, and alienation, especially as she focused on the twentieth-century tendency to find in technology and in the idea of "progress" the panacea to life's ills. Although O'Connor knew that she — like her early model T. S. Eliot — was in the minority in her disdain for the increasing secularism of her time, she refused to back down.

Flannery O'Connor was a painstaking and disciplined writer, devoting each morning to her work and making great demands of herself even in her last years as she struggled with lupus. She possessed a keen ear for southern dialect and a fine sense of irony and comic timing; with the combination of these skills, she produced some of the finest comedy in American literature. Like the comedy of Dante, O'Connor's dark humor consciously intends to underscore boldly our common human sinfulness and need for divine grace. Even her characters' names (Tom T. Shiflet, Mary Grace, Joy/Hulga Hopewell, Mrs. Cope) are often ironic clues to their spiritual deficiencies. O'Connor's recurrent characters, from Hazel Motes in *Wise Blood* to O. E. Parker of "Parker's Back," are spiritually lean and hungry figures who reject mere lip service to Christianity and the bland certainty of rationalism in their pursuit of salvation. These same characters, usually deprived economically, emotionally, or both, inhabit a world in which, in O'Connor's words, "the good is under construction."

O'Connor was a Roman Catholic in the Bible Belt South; her fiction, though, is largely concerned with fundamentalist Protestants, many of whom she admired for the integrity of their search for Truth. The publication of her essays and lectures, *Mystery and Manners* (1969), and the publication ten years later of *The Habit of Being* confirmed the strong connection between O'Connor's fictional treatment of the search for God and the quest for the holy in her own life. Indeed, her life and work were of a piece. She attained in her brief life what Sally Fitzgerald called (after St. Thomas Aquinas) "the habit of being," which Fitzgerald describes as "an excellence not only of action but of interior disposition and activity" that struggled to reflect the goodness and love of God.

SARAH GORDON, *Georgia College and State University*

Jon Lance Bacon, *Flannery O'Connor and Cold War Culture* (New York: Cambridge University Press, 1993).

Robert Brinkmeyer, *The Art and Vision of Flannery O'Connor* (Baton Rouge: Louisiana State University Press, 1989).

John Desmond, *Risen Sons: Flannery O'Connor's Vision of History* (Athens: University of Georgia Press, 1987).

The Flannery O'Connor Bulletin, vols. 1–26/27(1972–2000), and *The Flannery O'Connor Review*, vols. 1– (2001–), Georgia College and State University.

Melvin J. Friedman and Beverly Lyon Clark, eds., *Critical Essays on Flannery O'Connor* (Boston: Hall, 1985).

Richard Giannone, *Flannery O'Connor: Hermit Novelist* (Urbana: University of Illinois Press, 2000).5

Sarah Gordon, *Flannery O'Connor: The Obedient Imagination* (Athens: University of Georgia Press, 2000).

Louise Westling, *Sacred Groves and Ravaged Gardens: The Fiction of Eudora Welty, Carson McCullers, and Flannery O'Connor* (Athens: University of Georgia Press, 1985).

FLANNERY O'CONNOR'S SHORT FICTION

Economy of form, biting satire, vivid characterizations, and a stern moral vision are the defining characteristics of Flannery O'Connor's short fiction. Her reputation as a short-story writer rests on two volumes, only the first of which appeared in her lifetime: *A Good Man Is Hard to Find* (1955). *Everything That Rises Must Converge* was published in 1965, a year after her death from lupus.

O'Connor began writing fiction in earnest at the Iowa Writers' Workshop in the late 1940s. During her apprentice years there, she enjoyed the advice of such older writers as Paul Engle, Caroline Gordon, Robert Lowell, Andrew Lytle, Allen Tate, and Robert Penn Warren. Shortly after completing her master's thesis, a group of stories entitled "The Geranium," she won the Rinehart-Iowa Fiction Award for her unpublished first novel: *Wise Blood* was published in 1952, and soon after, she began to write the stories for which she is renowned.

O'Connor's stories are set in the modern South, more often in the country than in the city. Many are placed on farms similar to the one on which she herself lived. The main character is often a middle-aged, middle-class woman living on her own, with responsibility for a farm. Less often the protagonist is a child, usually a young girl, or a young man. All her protagonists have well-established views of themselves, of human nature, and of the world. They attempt to order their lives in accordance with their views of the world. The pattern of action in the stories moves toward a moment in which the main characters recognize the falseness of their views.

Often the catalyst for this recognition is another character, either an outright antagonist, such as the Misfit in "A Good Man Is Hard to Find" or the Bible salesman Manley Pointer in "Good Country People," or a lower-class woman whose opinions clash with the protagonist's, serving as a foil to her. In "A Circle in the Fire" Mrs. Pritchard, who works for the main character, Mrs. Cope, serves this function. Her fascination with a woman in an iron lung who died in childbirth irritates Mrs. Cope and her desire to run an orderly, upright farm. O'Connor typically works to deflate social and intellectual pretensions — as she does in "Everything That Rises Must Converge" and "The Enduring Chill" — or even to portray them as evil.

O'Connor's stories typically set opposing forces against one another — the modern secular world with its emphasis on science, social programs, humanism, and progress, and the God-centered spiritual world, with its emphasis on sin and salvation. This pattern is almost always present, but the stories are not formulaic, and they vary considerably in situation and in character.

O'Connor examines other concerns as well. She is especially effective in portraying the consciousness of a character on the verge of enlightenment, change, or transformation, as in "A Temple of the Holy Ghost," "A Stroke of Good Fortune," and "Parker's Back." She also wrote several successful stories about race, the best-known of which is "The Artificial Nigger," in which two inhabitants of the north Georgia mountains visit Atlanta, encounter African Americans for the first time, and discover the meaning of racism in a lawn ornament.

Most of the stories in *A Good Man Is Hard to Find* had been published in literary journals by the time the collection appeared. The title story is about a middle-class Atlanta family murdered by a criminal known as the Misfit on their way to a Florida vacation. The story pays much attention to the banal details of the family's existence: the bickering children, the irritable father, the bland mother, and the manipulative grandmother, whose unreliable memories lead to the final disaster. Underneath the ordinary surfaces of modern life, O'Connor suggests, is a real and menacing evil that can intrude without warning.

In "Good Country People" evil appears in the form of a Bible salesman. The main character, Hulga, an amputee with a Ph.D. in philosophy, decides to seduce the salesman to show him the truth about life's meaninglessness. He instead opens his hollowed-out Bible, shows her pornographic pictures, steals her wooden leg, and leaves her trapped in a hayloft.

In "The Life You Save May Be Your Own" a tramp marries a retarded girl in order to steal her mother's car. After abandoning the girl at a roadside diner, he picks up a boy who has run away from home and tries to talk him into returning to his family by telling his own story, "My mother was a angel of Gawd. . . . He took her from heaven and giver to me and I left her." The boy retorts, "My old woman is a flea bag and yours is a stinking pole cat." The story ends with the tramp's prayer, "Break forth and wash the slime from this earth!" Many of O'Connor's stories end with similar redemptive moments; "Revelation" is an example.

O'Connor slowly and arduously wrote the nine stories of *Everything That Rises Must Converge* during the final years of her illness. In comparison with those in her first volume, they are darker in tone and more directly contend with contemporary issues. In the title story a young man named Julian, recently graduated from college, wants to embarrass his old-fashioned mother by forming friendships with black people. He wants to force her to accept the reality of the modern world and abandon her romantic illusions, yet he is caught up in his own illusions — he wants to be a writer but sells typewriters instead, and he lives with his mother, rather than making his own way. The story's setting and central symbol is a public bus, an emblem of the civil rights movement through its association with the Montgomery bus boycott in 1955–56 and the Freedom Riders of 1961. When Julian accompanies his mother on the bus to the local "Y," their encounter with several black passengers leads to a crisis that reveals his essential hollowness. The story ridicules Julian's intellectual pretensions and his lack of compassion for his mother. This final moment of self-discovery is reminiscent of the epiphany used by James Joyce in his short-story collection *Dubliners* (1914).

When O'Connor died in 1964, she left unpublished three other short stories, along with an unfinished novel. Her portraiture of characters, her evocation of mystery, her descriptions of the regional culture of the modern South, and her trenchant humor imbue her stories with a unique distinctiveness. Her view of the modern world is bleak. Many of her characters suffer terrible fates. What she offers as consolation is the possibility of spiritual redemption that lies at the heart of her view of the world: in a letter to a friend, she referred to this philosophical position as "Christian realism." The nineteen stories in her two volumes of short fiction make her one of the most highly regarded writers of short fiction in the twentieth century.

HUGH RUPPERSBURG, *University of Georgia*

SUGGESTED READING

Robert Brinkmeyer, *The Art and Vision of Flannery O'Connor* (Baton Rouge: Louisiana State University Press, 1989).

Sally Fitzgerald, ed., *The Habit of Being: Letters of Flannery O'Connor* (New York: Farrar, Straus, and Giroux, 1979).

Sarah Gordon, *Flannery O'Connor: The Obedient Imagination* (Athens: University of Georgia Press, 2000).

Alice Walker, "Beyond the Peacock: The Reconstruction of Flannery O'Connor," in *In Search of Our Mothers' Gardens* (New York: Harcourt Brace Jovanovich, 1983), 42–59.

Margaret Earley Whitt, *Understanding Flannery O'Connor* (Columbia: University of South Carolina Press, 1995).

EUGENIA PRICE
(1916–1996)

Eugenia Price is known for her best-selling historical fiction, much of which is set in Georgia. At the time of her death in 1996, Price had written fourteen novels, twenty-two inspirational books, and three autobiographies. Her books have sold more than forty million copies. Most of her novels appeared on the *New York Times* best-seller list, including her last novel, *The Waiting Time*, published after her death.

Eugenia Price was born on June 22, 1916, in Charleston, West Virginia, to Anna Davidson and Walter Wesley Price, an upper-middle-class couple of German, Scottish, and Welsh ancestry. Price often credited her mother with nurturing her passions for writing, music, and history.

At the age of sixteen, Price left her Charleston home for Ohio University in Athens, Ohio. She began as an English major but changed to dentistry in her junior year and transferred to Northwestern University in Evanston, Illinois. Three years later, she transferred to the University of Chicago, where she listed philosophy as her major.

Price never earned a college degree, but when she was twenty-three years old, the National Broadcasting Company, better known as NBC, hired her to write for daytime serials. A few years later, she began working for Procter and Gamble in Cincinnati, Ohio, writing the serial *Joyce Jordan, M.D.* In 1945 she started her own company, Eugenia Price Productions, which produced daytime serials. She also broadcast daily radio commentary, and over the next few years she hosted or cohosted radio programs in Chicago.

By the late 1940s Price was well known in the radio broadcast business, having successfully tackled the roles of writer, director, producer, and host. Her popularity grew in the Midwest when she started cohosting *Unshackled*, a Christian radio show. Soon she was receiving invitations to speak at church and civic meetings, leading to her next career as an inspirational speaker and author. By 1962 Price had written eleven nonfiction books and traveled to nearly every state in the country, talking to standing-room-only audiences.

In late 1961, while en route from West Virginia to Florida for a book signing, Price visited St. Simons Island in Georgia for the first time. She had read about the island in a Southeastern American Automobile Association guidebook, which mentioned the story of a young minister, Anson Greene Phelps Dodge Jr., who in 1884 had rebuilt Christ Church in memory of his bride, Ellen, who died of cholera on their honeymoon in India. The church had been severely damaged by Union soldiers during the Civil War (1861–65).

For three years Price and her friend and fellow writer Joyce Blackburn researched the lives of Dodge, his first wife, and his second wife, Anna Gould Dodge. The writers spent hundreds of hours interviewing descendants of the Dodge and Gould families, as well as longtime St. Simons residents who remembered life on the island at the end of the nineteenth century. "Research for my earliest St. Simons stories came out of the brains of the oldest people I could find and out of people's dresser drawers," Price said in a 1982 newspaper interview.

The author used available resources — including eyewitness recordings, aging photographs, and the research of regional historians — and then maintained a chronology of key events during the period covered in her first novels, 1790s–1920s. What was to be one novel, *The Beloved Invader*, turned into three, and with the St. Simons trilogy — her first fiction — Price defined herself as a historical novelist who devoted months, sometimes years, to researching her subjects and the era in which they lived.

The St. Simons trilogy, written between 1962 and 1969, renewed interest in the history of the Golden Isles of Georgia — St. Simons, Jekyll, Sea Island, Cumberland, and Little St. Simons — and this interest resulted in the founding of the Coastal Georgia Historical Society, based in St. Simons, in 1965.

Eugenia Price **351**

In 1965 Price and Blackburn moved from Chicago to St. Simons, where both continued to write. During her thirty-one years on the island, Price demonstrated a steadfast commitment to the community. She fought to ensure that the island's marshes, beaches, indigenous flora, and wildlife would not be harmed by advancing industry and a growing coastal population; she supported, both vocally and financially, its historic sites, including the Lighthouse Museum and the Fort Frederica National Monument, as well as the Coastal Georgia Historical Society and the Georgia Sea Island Festival.

Price and Blackburn, an award-winning biographer and author of children's books, established the Eugenia Price–Joyce Blackburn Foundation, a nonprofit organization whose proceeds fund grants and scholarships, support charitable organizations, and create programs that promote excellence in writing.

Price, who often traveled across the country to do promotional tours for her novels, always told her audiences about the two conversions that changed her life: one to Jesus Christ in October 1949 and the other to the American South in November 1961. The second conversion, she said, led to her three-decade career as a writer of historical fiction, which began with the St. Simons trilogy. Through her novels and her community activism, Price helped preserve the history of coastal Georgia. She died of congestive heart failure on May 28, 1996.

Price's fiction includes *The Beloved Invader* (1965), *New Moon Rising* (1969), and *The Lighthouse* (1971), which make up the St. Simons trilogy; *Don Juan McQueen* (1974), *Maria* (1977), and *Margaret's Story* (1980), the Florida trilogy; *Savannah* (1983), *To See Your Face Again* (1985), *Before the Darkness Falls* (1987), and *Stranger in Savannah* (1989), the Savannah quartet; *Bright Captivity* (1991), *Where Shadows Go* (1993), and *Beauty from Ashes* (1995), the Georgia trilogy; and *The Waiting Time*, published in 1997.

Although her early books focused on real people who lived in coastal Georgia during the eighteenth and nineteenth centuries — James Gould, Horace Gould, John Couper, Mary Gould,

Anna Gould Dodge, and Anson Greene Phelps Dodge Jr. — her later novels featured fictional characters. It is the earlier novels that bring tourists to St. Simons year after year, where they walk among the moss-draped oaks in Christ Church Cemetery, searching for the graves of the islanders brought back to life in Price's books.

In 2001 the Georgia Center for the Book, which promotes and celebrates Georgia literature, composed a list of twenty-five books every Georgian should read. Price's *The Lighthouse*, the final installment in the St. Simons trilogy, was among the books.

RENEE PEARMAN, *Macon State College*

SUGGESTED READING

Contemporary Authors: New Revision Series, vol. 18 (Detroit: Gale, 1986), s.v. "Eugenia Price."

Historic Glimpses of St. Simons Island, Georgia, 1736–1924 (Brunswick, Ga.: Coastal Georgia Historical Society, 1973).

Mary Bray Wheeler, *Eugenia Price's South: A Guide to the People and Places of Her Beloved South* (Atlanta: Longstreet Press, 1993).

WYATT PRUNTY

(b. 1947)

Wyatt Prunty is identified with a widely based movement among poets sometimes called the New Formalism. Such poets use form (verse and meter) and narrative as a way of exploring and expressing meaning. Prunty does not restrict his poetry to preestablished forms but employs control and order as liberating means of expression. He writes about domestic subjects — his parents, family, personal experiences, and modern life. He is the author of six collections of poetry and one book of criticism and is a frequent reviewer or essayist for poetry and literary journals.

Eugene Wyatt Prunty was born on May 15, 1947, in Humboldt, Tennessee, the son of Eugenia Wyatt and Merle Prunty. His family moved early in his life to Athens, where his father organized the Department of Geography at the University of Georgia. He received his undergraduate education at the University of the South (B.A., 1969) in Sewanee, Tennessee, where Allen Tate was one of his teachers, and where his first poems were published in the *Sewanee Review* under the editorship of Andrew Lytle. After three years in the navy, Prunty enrolled in the Johns Hopkins University writing seminars in Baltimore, Maryland, and received his M.A. in 1973. He earned his Ph.D. from Louisiana State University in Baton Rouge and counted among his mentors there Donald Stanford and Lewis P. Simpson. He has taught at Louisiana State University, Virginia Polytechnic Institute and State University, and since 1989, the University of the South, where he is Ogden D. Carlton Chair of English and director of the Sewanee Writers' Conference, one of the most successful annual events of its type in the nation.

Writing in the *New York Times Book Review*, Melanie Rehak has observed that Prunty has devoted his career to "examining the ways in which human experience is made up of small traditions bound together into a larger story — the subset of ritual within narrative." Certain themes in Prunty's work are prominent: family life, the connection between past and present, the capricious and inexplicable nature of events, and the link between human action and the outer world. In writing about personal experience and family, as he often does, Prunty is not engaged in self-scrutiny but instead is seeking to connect with a larger set of meanings.

The range of Prunty's poetry in form and subject is impressive. His impulse is usually narrative and ultimately philosophical. His poem "A Winter's Tale" speculates on the birth of his son, which signifies the completion of a cycle of death and resurrection:

> Ian, your birth was my close land
> Turned green, the stone rolled back for leaving,
> My father dead and you returned.

His poem "Blood" meditates on the rhythmic participation of human life in an ancient process. It does so in a way that is characteristic of Prunty's approach to a subject: he begins with the literal nature of a subject, in this case the fact that the circulation of blood sustains human life:

> . . . it runs between
> The spent asphyxiated blues
> Of time and work and that bright filigree
> Through which the impounding heart pumps back
> Our reddened and ventilated lives.

Blood brings oxygen to the body and keeps it alive. Having established this, the poem moves to symbolic and metaphoric properties:

> Scripted in a secret and minute hand
> That writes itself and signs its origins
> In unrepeated blues and reds
> The blood holds to its systole and diastole.

Blood, in this regard, is a link to our ancient origins, both in fact and in metaphor ("bloodline"). It staves off death, as long as it circulates, and is the stuff of our life and mortality: "Blood surfaces our dust, and something more, / The potent changing earth of us."

Prunty's longer narrative poems are especially impressive. In "The Depression, the War, and Gypsy Rose Lee" he muses over a photograph of his parents taken in 1938, before their children were born. The photo becomes a symbol of the mystery and uncertainty of life. The poet sees in the picture the history of everything that followed the moment it preserved, yet he knows also that the young faces in the picture suspect nothing of their future:

> Locked arms to pose a photograph
> Surviving all these two survived
> No hint of what they saw ahead
> Making them smile.

"Haying" describes a young boy helping farmers gather hay. The poem is reminiscent of the work of poet Robert Frost, in such poems as "Out, Out" and "After Apple Picking," but while Frost usually drives toward a clearly enunciated theme, Prunty allows events to speak for themselves, without mediation. The boy finds the work difficult, but he persists and at the end of the day feels elated about what he has done. He stumbles across a nest of yellow jackets and is stung. The men take care of him, waiting for the doctor, apparently unconcerned, and the boy listens to their talk:

> Lie there, boy,
> And listen to their neutral voices —
> Used for selecting seed, planting, calving,
> Used when wringing necks or cutting calves to steers,
> Used for harvest, slaughter, funerals, drought —
> And August always turns to drought,

One baking gust that cures the grass
Like a breath inhaled and held
So long that light turns colors.

In some narratives Prunty more aggressively questions the meaning of events: "Falling through the Ice" describes how people tell and retell the story of a boy who drowns in a frozen pond. They do so:

Because it pulls us back again
This side of what no man
Has ever laddered over with a name . . .
A riddle, a story, a children's game.

They know the event signifies something about human life, its capricious unpredictability; they are fascinated by their own powerlessness to understand or explain. It is this interest and fascination with life's mystery, the question of what lies beneath or above it all, that Prunty searches for in his poetry.

Prunty's poetry collections include *The Times Between* (1982), *What Women Know, What Men Believe* (1986), *Balance as Belief* (1989), *The Run of the House* (1993), *Since the Noon Mail Stopped* (1997), and *Unarmed and Dangerous: New and Selected Poems* (2000). His book of essays about modern poetry, *Fallen from the Symboled World: Precedents for the New Formalism*, was published in 1990. He has also edited or coedited several literary anthologies.

HUGH RUPPERSBURG, *University of Georgia*

SUGGESTED READING

Contemporary Authors: New Revision Series, vol. 99 (Detroit: Gale, 2002), s.v. "Prunty, (Eugene) Wyatt."

Roger Matuz, ed., *Contemporary Southern Writers* (Detroit: St. James Press, 1999), 302–4.

Melanie Rehak, "The Small Stuff," review of *Unarmed and Dangerous, New York Times Book Review*, March 19, 2000, p. 4.

JANISSE RAY
(b. 1962)

J anisse Ray, an environmental activist and poet, is the award-winning author of *Ecology of a Cracker Childhood*, a highly praised book that combines elements of ecology and autobiography into a multifaceted work. As activist and memoirist, Ray alternates chapters between her childhood in rural southern Georgia and the ecological history of that region — an effective switch that shows the delicate symbiotic nature of the landscape and the people who are irrevocably connected with the land.

Ray was born on February 2, 1962, and grew up near Baxley in rural Appling County on land that she has described as "about as ugly as a place gets." Raised in her father's junkyard, Ray was surrounded by a pop-impressionistic landscape of junkyards, wiregrass, and mobile homes adjacent to U.S. Highway 1. Living in rural isolation, she was further suppressed by an evangelical father with a religious fervor matched only by his passion for wildlife. Franklin Ray was a fatherly conundrum, depriving his children of such luxuries as television and inspiring them to preserve nature while junking up the landscape with old cars and blown-up tires. In order to survive the clutter, Ray found solace in a growing passion for the longleaf ecosystem that had all but vanished long before her time.

Along with the longleaf pine forests, the Ray family had barely survived. Descendants of a Celtic race called "Borderlanders," the Rays were among the original "Crackers," forefathers who migrated to the Georgia coastal area in the mid- to late 1800s and then promptly destroyed the longleaf forests — a heritage that later included rampant mental illness and poverty. Ray's father and grandfather both struggled with mental illness, exemplifying the "critically endangered" people who were slowly deteriorating along with their natural counterpart.

Determined to save herself from a "legacy of ruination," Ray left home at eighteen to attend North Georgia College (later North Georgia College and State University) in Dahlonega. After discovering environmentalism at North Georgia, Ray became a dedicated naturalist and environmental activist, specializing in issues of critically endangered species. After two years at North Georgia College, she transferred to Florida State University, from which she later graduated. Ray's passion for literature and the environment eventually led her to attend graduate school at the University of Montana, where she received an M.F.A. in creative writing in 1997. During this period she received the 1996 Merriam-Frontier Award for *Naming the Unseen*, a chapbook of poetry about biology and place, and the Writer's Conferences and Festivals' Nonfiction Award. Ultimately, however, her passion for the longleaf pines led her back home.

In 1999 Ray published her first book, *Ecology of a Cracker Childhood*, a work of literary nonfiction that examines the vanishing cracker culture in relation to its diminishing longleaf pine forest. Ray takes a critical look at her less than perfect lineage, not only showing human culpability for the destruction, but also explaining how a dying ecosystem can negatively affect a rural community. Ray's book successfully turns a tough look at family, poverty, and a dying ecosystem into a passionate indictment of a "lost forest" that is not a lost cause. The book ends with a list of endangered species and longleaf resources, as well as comprehensive lists of southeastern organizations dedicated to preserving and restoring the longleaf pines.

Ray's unique and inspiring work became an instant success, winning the Southeastern Booksellers Award for Nonfiction in 1999 and the Southern Environmental Law Center Award for Outstanding Writing on the Southern Environment, the Southern Book Critics Circle Award for Nonfiction, and the American Book Award in 2000.

Ray had returned to Baxley by the time *Ecology of a Cracker Childhood* was published, seventeen years after she had left home. She continued chronicling her legacy in a second autobiography, *Wild Card Quilt: Taking a Chance on Home*, which was published in 2003. The book discusses her return from Montana to Appling County with her son, Silas, as she once again reclaims her family's past.

In 2005 Ray published a third book, *Pinhook: Finding Wholeness in a Fragmented Land*. *Pinhook* chronicles the restoration of Pinhook Swamp, which joins the Okefenokee Swamp in Georgia with the Osceola National Forest in Florida. Through the efforts of Ray and other environmentalists, the swamp is now a protected wildlife corridor.

As an activist and writer, Ray has published many poems and essays in such magazines and newspapers as *Georgia Wildlife, National Geographic Wildlife,* and *Orion*. A nature commentator for Georgia Public Radio and a founding board member of Altamaha Riverkeeper, Ray also helped to form the Georgia Nature-Based Tourism Association and continues working to preserve the thirty-four-hundred-acre Moody Forest in Appling County.

KIM PURCELL, *Georgia Center for the Book*

SUGGESTED READING

Janisse Ray, *Ecology of a Cracker Childhood* (Minneapolis, Minn.: Milkweed, 1999).

Janisse Ray, *Pinhook: Finding Wholeness in a Fragmented Land* (White River Junction, Vt.: Chelsea Green, 2005).

Janisse Ray, *Wild Card Quilt: Taking a Chance on Home* (Minneapolis, Minn.: Milkweed, 2003).

BYRON HERBERT REECE
(1917–1958)

Byron Herbert Reece was the author of four books of poetry and two novels. During his short career he received attention throughout the United States for his poems. He was nominated for a Pulitzer Prize, earned two Guggenheim awards, and served as writer-in-residence at the University of California at Los Angeles, Emory University, and Young Harris College. He never achieved wide recognition, however, and is known today as the poet whose old-fashioned, finely crafted ballads and lyrics celebrate the life and heritage of the north Georgia mountains.

Born near Blood Mountain above Dahlonega on September 14, 1917, Reece entered a family that had a long connection to the rural mountain world. The Reeces had lived in the area since the early 1800s and were firmly rooted in the mountain culture. The young Reece, nicknamed "Hub," showed his talents early. By the first grade he had read the Bible and John Bunyan's *Pilgrim's Progress* (1678), texts that would influence his writing. By the age of fifteen, he was publishing poems in the local Blairsville newspaper. After high school he attended nearby Young Harris College, a small, private two-year school, where he found a coterie of friends who encouraged his poetic development.

Reece's first try at college was short-lived because he needed to devote his time to farming. After working on the family farm for three years, he was able to return with a scholarship and permission to alternate quarters between farm work and schoolwork. Despite these accommodations, he never finished his two-year degree.

In 1943 Reece's poetic endeavors took a major step forward when Jesse Stuart, a well-known writer from Kentucky, "discovered" him. When Reece's poem "Lest the Lonesome Bird" appeared in the *Prairie Schooner* journal, Stuart was intrigued by the ballad skills of the young poet. Stuart asked Reece to show him more poems and persuaded his publisher, E. P. Dutton, to publish the young Georgian's work. In 1945 Reece's first collection of poems, *Ballad of the Bones and Other Poems*, appeared to critical praise.

The next ten years proved fruitful for Reece. While *Ballad of the Bones* attracted national attention, *Bow Down in Jericho* (1950) earned Reece a nomination for the Pulitzer Prize. *Newsweek* magazine featured him in its January 1, 1951, issue. Also during this period Ralph McGill, the executive editor (and later, publisher) of the *Atlanta Constitution*, became a friend of Reece's and an advocate of his work.

The first of Reece's two novels, *Better a Dinner of Herbs*, was published in 1950. This book and *The Hawk and the Sun* (1955) constitute all of Reece's published fiction, though he apparently was planning to write a trilogy of novels about the settlement of north Georgia — plans thwarted by his final illness. *Better a Dinner of Herbs* narrates the journey of two brothers down from the mountains to the lowlands. Its Old Testament story of love, murder, and retribution takes on the basic tone of the ballad form that dominates Reece's verse. *The Hawk and the Sun* narrates events leading up to a lynching in a small Georgia town. Both novels are distinctive and highly original.

Although Reece's final two volumes of poetry, *A Song of Joy* (1952) and *The Season of Flesh* (1955), were also praised, his traditional style was out of step with the Beat and confessional poets who dominated the literary world. Unlike the work of most writers, Reece's poetry showed little change or development in his four volumes; his poetic forms (most notably the ballad and the lyric), his themes, and his point of view seem to have been fully formed by the time he reached the age of twenty.

Nearly all of Reece's poetry deals with one of four themes — nature, death, love, and religion. In form the poems vary from short lyrics, sequences of couplets or quatrains, to sonnets and longer ballads. "A Song of Sorrow" summons farmers from their fields to help a woman mourn the loss of her daughter:

O men, come in from the field and the lane
And pray over Sarah's one daughter again
For she is possessed of a terrible pain.

O men, come in and softly abide
In reverent silence with your knees spread wide
For Sarah's one daughter has suffered and died.

O men, come in from the field and the plow
And pick at your teeth with the tip of a bough,
And say to her kindly brave words for tomorrow
For Sarah's possessed of a pitiful sorrow.

"I Go by Ways of Rust and Flame" describes the solitude of the individual in nature. Its speaker "walk[s] alone as all men must / Upon the roads of flame and rust." Some longer poems concern the traditional content of folk ballads: murder, jealousy, disappointment in love. "Lest the Lonesome Bird," "Ballad of the Rider," and "Ballad of the Weaver" are examples. Other long poems retell biblical stories: "Ballad of the Bones" recasts the tale of Ezekiel, and a sequence of poems in *Bow Down in Jericho* is about the Old Testament figures of David and Jonathan.

One of Reece's most effective expressions of allegiance to his north Georgia region was his poem "Roads," which compares the relative virtues of life in the city and the country. The poem comments on the "roofs of iron" and "sheer perpendiculars of steel" that characterize the architecture of the city, along with the hard "streets that bruise the country heel." In the city, Reece writes,

My heart's contracted to a stone.
Therefore whatever roads repair
To cities on the plain, my own
Lead upward to the peaks; and there
I feel, pushing my ribs apart,
The wide sky entering my heart.

Reece keeps a narrow focus on the solitary individual's relationship to the world. The individual, whether looking at nature, death, love, or religion, removes the veil of community to see with his eyes alone; the narrator is not a farmer or a mountaineer or a poet, just a private man alone to face the world, a world that can be beautiful and horrific.

Reece's professional successes were offset by personal strife — farm life was hard; his mother, Emma, died of tuberculosis; and his father, Juan, fell ill with the disease. Reece contracted tuberculosis while caring for his parents. During his final years Reece also taught classes at Young Harris College to earn extra money. On June 3, 1958, he committed suicide. He was found in his office, with Wolfgang Amadeus Mozart playing on the record player and his final set of student papers graded and neatly stacked in the desk drawer.

ALAN JACKSON, *Georgia Perimeter College*

SUGGESTED READING

"Byron Herbert Reece, In Memoriam, I-IV," *Georgia Review* 12 (winter 1958): 357–75.

Jim Clark, ed., *Fables in the Blood: The Selected Poems of Byron Herbert Reece* (University of Georgia Press, 2002).

Raymond Cook, *The Mountain Singer: The Life and Legacy of Byron Herbert Reece*, 2d ed. (Atlanta: Cherokee, 1995).

Mildred Greear, "Meeting Byron Herbert Reece," *Chattahoochee Review* 15 (winter 1995): 39–43.

Alan Jackson, *Byron Herbert Reece (1917–1958) and the Southern Poetry Tradition* (Lewiston, N.Y.: Edwin Mellen Press, 2001).

Bettie Sellers, *The Bitter Berry: The Life of Byron Herbert Reece* (Atlanta: Georgia Humanities Council, 1992).

JOHN ROLLIN RIDGE

(1827–1867)

John Rollin Ridge (also known as Cheesquatalawny and Yellow Bird), considered the first Native American novelist, was born near New Echota (near the present city of Rome) on March 19, 1827. His grandfather Major Ridge, his father, John Ridge, and his uncles Elias Boudinot (Buck Watie) and Stand Watie led the Cherokee "Treaty Party," which signed a removal agreement at New Echota in 1835. The four leaders were marked for execution by members of the John Ross party in 1839. All but Stand Watie were killed, and twelve-year-old John Rollin Ridge witnessed his father's murder.

Publicly, the Ridge-Watie-Boudinot family embraced assimilation. Major Ridge adopted his first name from his rank in the Red Stick Creek War and sent his children to local missionary and New England boarding schools. In New England, Buck Watie adopted the name of his benefactor, Elias Boudinot. After John Ridge and Elias Boudinot married white brides in Cornwall, Connecticut, the two couples fled mobs and took refuge in the Cherokee Nation. After they returned to Georgia, the brothers established successful plantations. The family held slaves, yet educated the children of slaves; it was led by patriarchs, yet often driven by strong women.

By the time of John Rollin Ridge's birth, Elias Boudinot could rightly claim that the Cherokee Nation had a far greater literacy rate and a more highly developed political structure than did the white population of Georgia. By 1828 Boudinot had begun publishing the bilingual *Cherokee Phoenix*, which he edited until 1832. John Rollin Ridge studied with Sophia Sawyer, a missionary teacher who strongly opposed the boarding school method of "civilizing" Native American students. During Ridge's childhood, tension grew within the Cherokee Nation over the question of accommodation or resistance to white settlers' encroachments on Cherokee territory. The 1828 Jackson election and Indian Removal Act of 1830 laid the groundwork for Georgia confiscation of Cherokee land and deepened the split between the Ross and Ridge parties.

After the 1835 Treaty of New Echota, the Ridge family settled comfortably in present-day Missouri. The mass removal of 1838 (the Trail of Tears) brought the Ross party into power, and the 1839 executions of Ridge's father, uncle, and grandfather forecast further violence. John Rollin Ridge then moved to Fayetteville, Arkansas, with his widowed mother and in the 1840s read the law; married Elizabeth Wilson, a white woman; and wrote anti-Ross essays. In 1849 Ross sympathizer David Kell took and gelded a stallion that belonged to Ridge, who confronted and killed the man. Ridge then fled to Missouri and on to California in 1850 to join the gold rush. There his pen primarily served the Democratic Party, producing conventional poetry, acerbic essays, and what many consider the first Native American novel and the first novel written in California, *The Life and Adventures of Joaquin Murieta, the Celebrated California Bandit* (1854).

Set at a time when California was a cultural palimpsest reinscribed by a flood of would-be gold miners, *Murieta* tells the tale not of a displaced Cherokee but of a Sonoran, "born . . . of respectable parents." He is "remarkable for a very mild and peaceable disposition" but encounters an outrage very much akin to what Ridge must have experienced at his father's murder: "A band of these lawless men, having the brute power to do as they pleased, visited Joaquin's house and peremptorily bade him leave his claim, as they would allow no Mexicans to work in that region. . . . Not content with this, they . . . ravished his mistress before his eyes." In a curious inversion of the "Indian hater" motif, the peaceable youth remakes himself into a machine of revenge: "He had contracted a hatred to the whole American race, and was determined to shed their blood, whenever and wherever an opportunity occurred."

Ridge's preference for assimilation colors his narrator's view of other Native Americans, contrasting the lowly Diggers and the "poor miserable, cowardly Tejons" to the effective "Cherokee half-breeds" who aid in the final hunt for Joaquin. Among the Americans, only those possessing "nobility" have any luck in pursuing the bandit, particularly "a chivalrous son of the South," who "had grown up under a discipline which taught him that honor was a thing to be maintained at the sacrifice of blood or of life itself." The book ends with "the important lesson that there is nothing so dangerous in its consequences as *injustice to individuals* — whether it arise from prejudice of color or from any other source; that a wrong done to one man is a wrong to society and to the world."

Ridge, who contributed to a number of antiabolitionist papers before and during the Civil War, spent the last seventeen years of his life working as a newspaper editor and writer for the *Sacramento Bee* and the *San Francisco Herald*, among other publications. Significant later poems include "Poem," "The Atlantic Cable," and "California." He died on October 5, 1867.

DAVID H. PAYNE, *University of Georgia*

SUGGESTED READING

John Lowe, "'I Am Joaquin!': Space and Freedom in Yellow Bird's *The Life and Adventures of Joaquin Murieta, the Celebrated California Bandit,*" in *Early Native American Writing: New Critical Essays*, ed. Helen Jaskoski (Cambridge: Cambridge University Press, 1996).

Louis Owens, *Other Destinies: Understanding the American Indian Novel* (Norman: University of Oklahoma Press, 1992).

James W. Parins, *John Rollin Ridge: His Life and Works* (Lincoln: University of Nebraska Press, 1991).

John Rollin Ridge, *Poems, by a Cherokee Indian, with an Account of the Assassination of His Father, John Ridge* (San Francisco: H. Payot, 1868).

Yellow Bird [John Rollin Ridge], *The Life and Adventures of Joaquin Murieta, the Celebrated California Bandit* (1854; reprint, with an introduction by Joseph H. Jackson, Norman: University of Oklahoma Press, 1955).

Larry Jerome Rubin has published hundreds of poems in literary magazines and four volumes of selected verse since he came to Atlanta in 1950 and began his long academic career as an English professor at the Georgia Institute of Technology in 1956. Though Rubin has appeared in several collections of contemporary southern poets, his poems characteristically focus on ahistorical images and the interior self rather than on any particular time or place. Rubin is a self-described romantic poet whose inspirations include Emily Dickinson and whose writing includes several articles on American romantic literature.

Rubin was born in 1930 in Bayonne, New Jersey, the son of Lillian Strongin and Abraham Joseph Rubin. Reared in Miami Beach, Florida, he studied briefly at New York's Columbia University (1949–50) and earned degrees in journalism (B.A., 1951; M.A., 1952) and English (Ph.D., 1956) at Emory University in Atlanta. Immediately after receiving his doctorate he became an instructor at Georgia Tech and eventually rose to full professor. Having received a Smith-Mundt Award from the U.S. State Department, Rubin taught American literature during the 1961–62 academic year at the Jagiellonian University of Kraków in Poland. He also spent three years overseas as a visiting Fulbright scholar — at the University of Bergen in Norway in 1966–67, at the Free University of West Berlin in 1969–70, and at the University of Innsbruck in 1971–72.

Rubin had already published numerous poems in literary magazines when "Instructions for Dying" won the Poetry Society of America's Reynolds Lyric Award in 1961. His first volume of poetry, *The World's Old Way*, appeared in 1962. Its introductory poem, "The Bachelor," introduces Rubin's signature persona, the bachelor-poet. In a Faustian vow to the solitary artist's life, he trades the prospect of immortality through one's children for a childless life spent conjuring magic from words. *The World's Old Way* won the Georgia Writers Association's Literary Achievement Award and Oglethorpe College's Sidney Lanier Award for a first book of poems.

In 1965 the Poetry Society of New Hampshire presented its John Holmes Memorial Award to Rubin for the poem "For Parents, Out of Sight," a line of which provided the title for his next collection. *Lanced in Light* (1967) explores the theme of time and its transformation of life and love. The Dixie Council of Authors and Journalists named him Georgia Poet of the Year in 1967 for *Lanced in Light* and again in 1975 for *All My Mirrors Lie*, his third book.

All My Mirrors Lie represents the bachelor-poet at middle age, his eye ranging the various "mirrors" of self reflected in his relationships with the living and the dead. The collection includes "The Bachelor, as Professor," for which Rubin received an annual lyric award from the Poetry Society of America in 1973. *Unanswered Calls*, Rubin's fourth book, appeared in 1997. In it he expands the territory he surveyed in the chapbook *All My Mirrors Lie* to include the vistas of an aging poet facing his accumulated memories and ghosts and looking forward to decay and death.

Since his retirement from Georgia Tech in 1999, Rubin continues to travel and write. A career member of the College English Association, a professional organization of teacher-scholars, he directs the association's annual poetry workshop. In 2001, the CEA presented Rubin its Life Membership Award.

KEITH HULETT, *University of Georgia Libraries*

SUGGESTED READING

Contemporary Authors: New Revision Series, vol. 47, ed. Pamela S. Dear (Detroit: Gale, 1995), s.v. "Larry (Jerome) Rubin."

Shawn Jenkins, "A Man of Letters," *Georgia Tech Alumni Magazine* 76 (summer 1999), 70–71.

John D. Thomas, "To Build a Poem: Emory Writers Discuss Poetry in Process," *Emory Magazine* (fall 1991), 6–8.

FERROL SAMS
(b. 1922)

A physician, humorist, storyteller, and best-selling novelist, Ferrol Sams is the author of seven books. Most notable is his trilogy of novels in which an eccentric and quixotic hero, Porter Osborne Jr., mirrors Sams's own Georgia boyhood. All of his works are rooted in the oral traditions of southern humor and folklore. With engaging and graceful prose, Sams's fiction celebrates love of the land, the changing southern landscape, and what he calls "being raised right" in the rural South.

One of four children born to Mildred Matthews and Ferrol Sams Sr., the Fayette County school superintendent, Ferrol Sams Jr. (nicknamed "Sambo" by his father) was born on September 26, 1922, in Fayetteville, in the house built by his great-grandfather in 1848. Sams traces his family back six generations, to James Sams, who settled in rural Fayette County in 1820. Ferrol Sams Jr. graduated from Mercer University in Macon in 1942 and attended Emory University School of Medicine for two quarters before joining the U.S. Army Medical Corps. After serving from 1943 to 1947 and seeing action in France, Sams returned to Emory to continue his medical studies. He received his M.D. in 1949.

It was at Emory that he met his future wife, Helen Fletcher, also a physician. They married on July 18, 1948. Sams and his wife have been in private practice together in Fayetteville since 1951, and in 1987 they established the Fayette Medical Center. They have four children. Sams has also been an instructor in creative writing at Emory University since 1991 and has taught at Emory Medical School.

In 1982, at age sixty, Sams published *Run with the Horsemen*, the first of the semiautobiographical adventures of his antihero Porter "Sambo" Osborne Jr. He began writing the novel in September 1978, as notes for a family history, so he could tell his four children and ten grandchildren what it was like to grow up in rural Georgia between the two world wars. The novel, which became a national best-seller, is a boy's account of growing up on an ancestral farm in Georgia. Porter is a prank-playing farm boy and aspiring doctor whose misadventures make up a comic memoir of childhood in the South. *The Whisper of the River*, published in 1984, continues Porter's adventures during the 1930s, as he enrolls at Willingham University, a Baptist college in Macon. There a young and self-righteous Porter reexamines his own beliefs. *The Whisper of the River*, a collection of humorous anecdotes and tall tales, is a picaresque tale of a young man's coming of age that also examines serious moral issues.

Faced with writer's block about how to continue with Porter's story, Sams followed his first two novels with *The Widow's Mite and Other Stories* (1987) and two nonfiction works, *The Passing: Perspectives of Rural America* (1988) and *Christmas Gift!* (1989).

The Widow's Mite is a collection of eight first-person stories that highlight the social problems of a small southern town. These dramatically ironic stories are sometimes autobiographical, as in "Saba (An Affirmation)," or they are biblical parables that teach moral lessons and offer insights into human behavior and motivation. Two of the collection's stories, "The Widow's Mite" and "Judgment," were adapted as one-act plays in 1993 for the ART Station Theatre in Stone Mountain. *The Passing*, sixteen vignettes about the vanished ways of rural life told with Sams's characteristic humor and detail, is illustrated with paintings by Jim Harrison, a South Carolina artist. (The book was reprinted in 1990 without illustrations.) *Christmas Gift!* is an account of one family's celebration of Christmas in Fayette County. It evokes nostalgia, southern hospitality, and family traditions.

Sams returned to Porter Osborne Jr. in 1991 with the publication of *When All the World Was Young*, which won the Townsend Prize for Fiction that year and was performed in 1992 for American Public Radio's *Radio Reader*. The novel begins in June 1942, during World War II, with Pfc. Osborne working as a surgical technician for the army during the invasion of Normandy, France. This final volume of the trilogy finds the self-indulgent, practical joker Osborne, obsessed with sex and dating, returning home a wiser man, having maintained his code of honor and compassion.

Epiphany: Stories (1994) is a volume of three philosophical novellas. As the title implies, each of the stories is preoccupied with the sudden revelations of characters and their search for meaning in their lives. One of the stories, "Harmony Ain't Easy," dramatized by the ART Station Theatre for the 1996 Olympic Arts Festival, is an autobiographical misadventure.

With wit, humor, and old-fashioned moralizing, Sams's stories are about unlikely encounters and what people learn from them. A natural storyteller whose works have made him a popular writer in the South and garnered favorable national attention, Ferrol Sams was honored in 2001 for fifty years of commitment and service to the people of Fayette County.

GARY KERLEY, *North Hall High School*

SUGGESTED READING

Contemporary Authors, vol. 186 (Detroit: Gale, 1995), s.v. "Sams, Ferrol."

Contemporary Novelists, ed. Neil Schlager and Josh Lauer (Detroit: St. James Press, 2001), s.v. "Sams, Ferrol."

Bob Summer, "PW Interviews: Ferrol Sams," *Publishers Weekly*, November 22, 1991.

William J. Walsh, "Ferrol Sams," *Speak So I Shall Know Thee: Interviews with Southern Writers* (Jefferson, N.C.: McFarland, 1990).

Linda Welden, "Ferrol Sams," *Contemporary Fiction Writers of the South: A Bio-Bibliographical Sourcebook*, ed. Joseph Flora and Robert Bain (Westport, Conn.: Greenwood Press, 1993).

Bettie Sellers lives and writes poetry in Young Harris, a small college town in the mountains of north Georgia. She is best known for her poems about life in southern Appalachia. Although Sellers was reared in the Piedmont region, near Griffin, her grandmother grew up in north Georgia's Nacoochee Valley. This heritage stimulated Sellers's interest in Appalachia. After earning a B.A. from LaGrange College in 1958 and an M.A. from the University of Georgia in 1966, she accepted a position as professor of English at Young Harris College. After thirty-two years of service to the college, Sellers retired in 1997.

Nature figures prominently in much of Bettie Sellers's verse. Many of her poems observe the passing of seasons and paint vivid pictures of regional plants and animals. They also portray the named world of north Georgia. Her poems frequently celebrate the complex beauty that she observes around her, but they also consider how the land influences people. "Moment at Dusk," probes that issue:

> When September's quarter moon tips down
> toward Sunset rock cool and distant at dusk,
> the mountains darken blue in solid shapes
> quieting the valley for the coming of the night.
> Crickets scratch in the grass; a catbird whines.
> The dome fills up with darkness, reveals
> the Dippers, great and small. My eyes
> trace the distance to the farthest star —
> but the mountain holds my feet in place.

From a rocky perch, the speaker quietly watches evening advance and realizes that the mountains provide strength and stability to those who live in their shadow.

Concern for the preservation of north Georgia's natural places also pervades Sellers's poetry. She recognizes that development and modern technology threaten to destroy wild places, and her poems often lament their passing. In "Wild Ginger," for example, she describes the tower on Brasstown Bald, Georgia's highest peak, as an "inept" intruder. Similarly, "Complaint to Betelgeuse" laments the loss of once-clear night skies in which constellations stood out against the blackness of the heavens:

> Now satellites invade the ridge —
> the star I thought was Venus rising
> keeps on rising out of sight
> to bring the morning's news — and wars
> are instantaneously played on beams
> that tear Orion's belt, divide Andromeda.

A sense of irreparable destruction pervades the poem, and the violent, martial imagery underscores the threat that pristine places face for their survival.

Sellers writes not only of the land but also of the people and families who live on it. Her poetry shows that communal and familial relationships provide part of the continuity of Appalachian life. Birth, death, marriage, divorce, and the dynamics of relationships are all subjects of her poems. "Writing is a terrible, awesome responsibility," Sellers says; thus, she does not shy away from the pain that is sometimes part of life. "Sarah's Quilts," for example, relates the story of a mother gathering stones to mark the grave of one son who has been killed by the other:

> She stands, barefoot, in the creek, homespun dress,
> rich brown with walnut dye, tucked up almost
> to knees that feel the rush, the chilling press
> of Corn Creek's water even in the heat
>
> of August. Now her sons are far away:
> one running over hills his footsteps beat
> on forest trails she never saw. Laurel
> thickets tear his clothes, snatch hands

that picked up stones to end the quarrel
once too often, left his brother dead,
buried beneath the oak that tops the rise
just steps behind the cabin. She sees his head

rest on patchwork squares she sewed; a quilt
she made to warm his bed serves as a shroud
to line his grave. His brother's fear, his guilt
have made him run without a warp to warm

him in the cold of mountain nights, no bright-
patched "Star of Bethlehem" to ward off harm
lurking behind great pines. She prays for brothers
as she picks up stones, piles them along the bank.

One stone, now clean of blood, joins others
she will use to lay around a space,
an outline like the rope-strung attic bed
where he can sleep, her quilt across his face.

An intricately rhymed narrative poem based on the story of Cain and Abel, "Sarah's Quilts" reflects the inspiration that Sellers regularly draws from biblical stories and names. Her verses often portray a region steeped in Christian belief.

Sellers has published four volumes of poetry, including *Spring Onions and Cornbread* (1978), *Morning of the Red-Tailed Hawk* (1981), *Liza's Monday and Other Poems* (1986), and *Wild Ginger* (1989). She has also published three chapbooks and *The Bitter Berry: The Life of Byron Herbert Reece* (1992), a study of another north Georgia poet who lived and taught in Young Harris before his death in 1958.

Sellers was named Author of the Year in 1979 by the Dixie Council of Authors and Journalists. She received the Governor's Award in the Humanities in 1987, and in 1992 was named Poet of the Year by the American Pen Women. In 1997 Governor Zell Miller named her Poet Laureate of Georgia, a position she held for three years, and in 2003 Sellers received the Stanley W. Lindberg Award, which recognizes outstanding contributions to Georgia's literary culture.

ROBIN O. WARREN, *University of Georgia*

SUGGESTED READING

Bettie Sellers, "Westward from Bald Mountain," *Bloodroot: Reflections on Place by Appalachian Women Writers*, ed. Joyce Dyer (Lexington: University Press of Kentucky, 1998), 233–42.

CELESTINE SIBLEY
(1914–1999)

Celestine Sibley, a renowned southern author, journalist, and syndicated columnist, reported for the Atlanta Constitution from 1941 to 1999. Over her long career, she wrote more than ten thousand columns and many news stories of astonishing range, dealing with such varied topics as politics and key lime pie. Sibley was one of the most popular and long-running columnists for the *Constitution*, and her well-written and poignant essays on southern culture made her an icon in the South. Regarded by her colleagues as a reporting legend, Sibley was also the accomplished author of nearly thirty books published between 1958 and 1997.

Celestine Sibley was born in Holley, Florida, on May 23, 1914, to Evelyn Barber and Henry Colley. Sibley's mother, later known as "Muv" in Sibley's column, left her father (though she never officially divorced him) and married Wesley Reeder Sibley, a lumberman from Creola, Alabama. Adopted by her stepfather at the age of seven, the young Celestine was given his last name and spent her childhood in Creola, a small town on the outskirts of Mobile. At age fifteen, Sibley, an ambitious student reporter at Murphy High School's *Hi Times*, was hired as a weekend cub reporter at the *Mobile Press Register*. When she graduated in 1933, Sibley was offered her first full-time paid position at the *Press*. Covering everything from welfare to murder, the young journalist earned priceless experience at the *Press*, while her natural talent and attention to detail established her as a solid writer from the beginning of her career.

In 1936 she and her husband, *Press* colleague and journalist James W. Little, moved to Pensacola, Florida. Sibley began writing for the *Pensacola News-Journal* and continued to cover all aspects of local news. In the summer of 1941, her husband accepted a position with the Associated Press in Atlanta and moved the family there.

Sibley began working at the *Atlanta Constitution* on July 21, 1941, assigned to the federal beat. Less than six months later, Pearl Harbor was attacked, and the United States entered World War II. The resulting staff depletion provided an unprecedented opportunity for Sibley — she became one of the first female editors at the *Constitution*, working under the tutelage of Ralph McGill, whom she later described as her mentor. Competent yet restless in her newly assigned desk position, Sibley still preferred to be a "member of the ground troops" with a natural inclination to cover the stories on the street.

Sibley was given her first column in 1944, which allowed her more time to be with her children. Both full-time reporter and mother, Sibley was still able to become a front-page news and courtroom reporter, covering the three governors controversy in 1946 as well as many high-profile trials. In 1947 her investigative coverage of police and political corruption surrounding a murder case resulted in the acquittal of convicted murderer Floyd Woodward, and she later received the Pall Mall Big Story award, given by NBC for the best story of the week, for her coverage of the case. The following year she covered the murder trial of John Wallace, which later became nationally known through the publication of Margaret Anne Barnes's best-selling book *Murder in Coweta County* (1976), as well as through the adaptation of the book into a television movie in 1983 starring Johnny Cash and Andy Griffith.

In the early 1950s, Sibley worked for five years as the Hollywood correspondent for the Sunday *Atlanta Journal and Constitution Magazine*, traveling to Los Angeles, California, and interviewing movie stars and filmmakers. Her profiles, which she later called "fluff stories," included such celebrities as Clark Gable, Walt Disney, and Jane Russell. "Pulp stories" also became an infamous part of Sibley's versatile writing career during this time. As another creative way to support her family, Sibley moonlighted as a *True Confession* and *True Detective* reporter, selling stories with such shocking headlines as "I Wanted to Die" and "I Was a Junkie."

Her short-lived pulp career was eventually replaced by a long-term book career, beginning with the publication of *The Malignant Heart* (1958), the first book in the Kate Mulcay mystery series. For nearly forty years, Sibley continued to publish books in a variety of genres, including *Peachtree Street, U.S.A.* (1963), a portrait of Atlanta; *Dear Store* (1967), a history of Rich's Department Store; *A Place Called Sweet Apple* (1967), reflections on restoring her log cabin home in Roswell; *Jincey* (1978), her first novel; *Turned Funny* (1988), her memoir; and additional installments in the Kate Mulcay series. In 1982 her novel *Children, My Children* won the first Townsend Prize for children's fiction.

From 1958 to 1978 Sibley covered politics, courts, and the Georgia legislature, including the annual forty-day Georgia General Assembly, which became one of her favorite assignments. Sibley's legislative reporting was considered fair, unbiased, and accessible to the general public. During these years she also reported on the trial of James Earl Ray, who was convicted of assassinating Martin Luther King Jr. in 1968, and on the 1976 presidential election, in which Jimmy Carter became the first Georgian elected president of the United States. As a gesture of appreciation for her years of excellent political reporting, the House of Representatives voted in 2000 to name its press gallery at the state capitol in Sibley's honor.

Although Sibley spent the bulk of her career as a reporter, she is perhaps best remembered as a syndicated columnist for the *Atlanta Constitution*. Even after she retired from reporting in the late 1990s, Sibley continued to spend the majority of her days writing books, as well as continuing her columns about southern life. In 1990 she received the Ralph McGill Award for Lifetime Achievement in Journalism. She also received two honorary degrees during her career, one in 1993 from Spring Hill College in Mobile, Alabama, and another in 1996 from Emory

University in Atlanta. A few months before her death, Sibley was awarded the National Society of Newspaper Columnists Lifetime Achievement Award.

Sibley died of cancer at the age of eighty-five on August 15, 1999. She continued working until the final weeks before her death, with her last regular *Constitution* column appearing on July 25, 1999. Sibley's first husband died at age forty-five; they had three children together. Her second husband, John C. Strong, died in 1988.

KIM PURCELL, *Georgia Center for the Book*

SUGGESTED READING

Richard L. Eldredge, ed., *Celestine Sibley, Reporter* (Athens, Ga.: Hill Street Press, 2001).

Celestine Sibley, *The Celestine Sibley Sampler: Writings and Photographs with Tributes to the Beloved Author and Journalist*, ed. Sibley Fleming (Atlanta: Peachtree, 1997).

Celestine Sibley, *Turned Funny* (New York: Harper and Row, 1988).

ANNE RIVERS SIDDONS

(b. 1936)

Though all of her eighteen books have been set in Georgia or concern southerners living elsewhere, Anne Rivers Siddons is best known for books about Atlanta and its environs. Two novels, *Homeplace* (1987) and *Nora, Nora* (2000), take place in a fictionalized version of her hometown, Fairburn, southwest of Atlanta. She is also the author of two books of nonfiction, *Go Straight on Peachtree* (1978), a McDonald City Guide to Atlanta, and *John Chancellor Makes Me Cry* (1975), a series of essays patterned around the changing seasons in Atlanta. Most important, her novel *Downtown* (1994) recreates her early career as a writer and editor for *Atlanta* magazine. Her most commercially successful book, *Peachtree Road* (1989), portrays modern Atlanta's white elite on the eve of the civil rights era.

Siddons was born Sybil Anne Rivers on January 9, 1936, in Atlanta but was reared in Fairburn. She is the daughter of Marvin Rivers, a lawyer, and Katherine, a secretary at Campbell High School. Her education at Auburn University from 1954 to 1958, where she earned a B.A. degree, became the inspiration for her first novel, *Heartbreak Hotel* (1976), which subsequently became the film *Heart of Dixie* in 1989. At Auburn she worked as a writer for the college newspaper. An editorial she wrote favoring integration was recognized nationally but criticized by the school administration and a second similar editorial led to her dismissal from the newspaper. After college Siddons worked as writer and editor at *Atlanta* magazine with its founder Jim Townsend. In 1966 she married author and advertising executive Heyward Siddons.

Siddons's other books include a horror story set in Atlanta, *The House Next Door* (1978), which has been compared by Stephen King to *The Haunting of Hill House* by Shirley Jackson. *Fox's Earth* (1981), among her best books, is the story of several generations of Georgia women. In *King's Oak* (1991) Siddons moves beyond Atlanta to the more traditional rural South and continues to reflect concern for the environment, evident in each of her books. In *Outer Banks* (1991), *Colony* (1992), *Hill Towns* (1993), *Fault Lines* (1995), *Up Island* (1997), and *Low Country* (1998), Siddons portrays southern characters, usually Georgians, but she places them in other parts of the South and the world. In *Nora, Nora* she returns to scenes of her earlier books set near Atlanta. Her two most recent novels, *Islands* (2004) and *Sweetwater Creek* (2005), are both set in the lowcountry of South Carolina.

Siddons resides with her husband in Charleston, South Carolina, where she moved in 1998.

LAMAR YORK, *Atlanta*

SUGGESTED READING

Contemporary Authors: New Revision Series, vol. 81 (Detroit: Gale, 1999), s.v. "Anne Rivers Siddons."

Contemporary Southern Writers, ed. Roger Matuz (Detroit: St. James Press, 1999), s.v. "Anne Rivers Siddons."

William Walsh, "Anne Rivers Siddons," *Speak, So I Shall Know Thee: Interviews with Southern Writers* (Jefferson, N.C.: McFarland, 1990).

CHARLIE SMITH
(b. 1947)

A Georgia-born poet, novelist, and short-story writer, Charlie Smith is a frequent contributor to national literary journals and periodicals, including *Poetry*, the *Paris Review*, and the *New Yorker*. Equally adept at poetry and fiction, Smith is a master of notable lyrical description, sensory detail, and candor. In five novels, three novellas, and five collections of poetry, Smith balances the loneliness and bleakness of his characters' lives with the beauty and transcendence of the natural world.

Charlie Smith, son of Georgia legislator Charlie O. Smith Sr. and Jeanette Early Smith, was born June 27, 1947, in Moultrie, Georgia. Educated at Phillips Exeter Academy in New Hampshire, Smith received a B.A. in English and philosophy from Duke University in Durham, North Carolina, in 1971, and an M.F.A. from the University of Iowa Writers Workshop in 1983. Smith has been a newspaper writer and editor, businessman, farmer, and laborer. From 1968 to 1970 he was a Peace Corps volunteer in Micronesia.

Smith's first marriage, to Kathleen Huber in 1974, ended in divorce three years later. In 1987 he married Gretchen Mattox, a poet and teacher. He has lived, taught, and traveled throughout the world. He and teaches creative writing and lectures at Princeton University and resides in New York City.

He has won numerous honors and awards, including the Aga Khan Prize from the *Paris Review* for his novella *Crystal River*, the National Poetry Series Award in 1987 and the Great Lakes New Poets Award in 1988, both for *Red Roads*. He is a member of PEN and the Academy of American Poets and served on the board of directors for the Poetry Society of America from 1992 to 1996.

In elegant and lyric prose, Smith explores the limits of his characters' endurance in often violent and erotic encounters. At his best when he cuts through the sentiment of life experiences, Smith chronicles the skirmishes that take place in the hearts of the protagonists.

Canaan (1984), set in South Carolina in the 1940s and 1950s, is the tale of Elizabeth Bonnet Burdette, a former belle whose refusal to follow anyone's rules, including those of her husband, J. C., owner of the ancestral home of Canaan, sets up a confrontation between old and new traditions. *Shine Hawk* (1988) is narrated in a series of long flashbacks by Billy Crew, who returns to the Shine Hawk prairie of south Georgia after years of exile in New York to confront Hazel Rance, his former girlfriend. Billy instead gets involved in a journey to bury his buddy Frank's dead brother. Often erotic and violent, the novel deals with loss, love, and the need to persevere. *The Lives of the Dead* (1990) also involves a journey, this one by Buddy Drake, a cult filmmaker traveling to Florida, whose troubles, both real and imagined, blur the lines between madness and murder.

Crystal River: Three Novellas (1991), which includes the award-winning title story first published by the *Paris Review* in 1983, explores similar themes: protagonists searching for answers in their spiritual journeys, a desire for brotherly love, and absent fathers and ineffectual mothers. Smith's fourth novel, *Chimney Rock* (1993), features a modern Hollywood setting that is both Southern Gothic and metaphoric dreamscape. The novel is part murder mystery, part family tragedy, and part exploration of extremes. The novel's narrator, Will Blake, becomes involved in a violent, Oedipal struggle with his father over their shared love for Kate Dunn, Will's wife. In his novel *Cheap Ticket to Heaven* (1996), Smith chronicles the serial killings of Jack and Clare, bank robbers who cut a bloody swath traveling the length of the Mississippi River.

In his collections of poetry — *Red Roads* (1987), *Indistinguishable from the Darkness* (1990), *The Palms* (1993), *Before and After* (1995), *Heroin and Other Poems* (2000), and *Women of America* (2004) — Smith's elegant lyrics and sensory details plunge his characters into extreme situations and private emotions with honesty and intensity. Whether detailing the landscape of his native South or signifying heroin as a metaphor for longing and desire, Smith's poetry speaks to the same themes as his novels: memories, fate, loneliness, brotherhood, failed relationships, desperate and disillusioned voices, and the sadness and defiance of families falling apart.

In a 1993 interview, Smith acknowledges his wild boy past that gives life to the narrators and situations in much of his poetry. Though his characters often seem to have reached the end of the road, their will to survive is evident in their struggle to overcome self-pity and desperation. The haunting tone of Smith's verse reflects a cynical and disillusioned world whose inhabitants desperately seek a hard-won wisdom that is central to Smith's own experience.

GARY KERLEY, *North Hall High School*

SUGGESTED READING

Contemporary Authors, vol. 143, ed. Donna Olendorf (Detroit: Gale, 1994).

Wendy Smith, "pw Interviews: Charlie Smith," *Publishers Weekly*, May 3, 1993.

LILLIAN SMITH

(1897–1966)

Lillian Smith was one of the first prominent white southerners to denounce racial segregation openly and to work actively
against the entrenched and often brutally enforced world of Jim
Crow. From as early as the 1930s, she argued that Jim Crow
was evil ("Segregation is spiritual lynching," she said) and that it
leads to social moral retardation.

Smith gained national recognition — and regional denunci-
ation — by writing *Strange Fruit* (1944), a bold novel of illicit
interracial love. Five years later she hurled another thunderbolt
against racism in *Killers of the Dream* (1949), a brilliant psychological and autobiographical work warning that segregation corrupted the soul; removed any possibility of freedom and
decency in the South; and had serious implications for women
and children in particular in their developing views of sex, their
bodies, and their innermost selves. From her home in Clayton,
atop Old Screamer Mountain, she openly convened interracial
meetings, and she toured the South, talking to people from all
races and classes. She was unsparing in her criticisms of "liberals" and "moderates" like Atlanta's famed Ralph McGill and
refused to join groups such as the Southern Regional Council
until it could oppose segregation as well as racism. In her own
psyche she struggled with intensely conflicting desires: to write
creatively, following her heart's passions, or to respond to her
stern conscience and the intellectual voice of duty.

Smith's writings, her investigative tours of the South, and the
interracial conferences were signs that intellectual and social
change was brewing in the South. By the time the civil rights
movement made its dramatic debut in the Montgomery bus boycott in 1955, Smith had been meeting or corresponding with
many southern blacks and concerned whites for years and was

well informed about the conditions in which African Americans lived, and about their anger and frustration. How do they stand it day by day? she cried out to a friend. She corresponded with civil rights leader Martin Luther King Jr. and publicly admired his work. She remained unflinchingly dedicated to him until her death. Smith greeted the historic 1954 Supreme Court decision outlawing school segregation as "every child's Magna Charta." The following year she wrote *Now Is the Time*, a tract appealing for compliance with the high court's decision. Her other writings were diverse — from *The Journey* (1954), a book on her ordeal with breast cancer, to *One Hour* (1959), an attack on McCarthyism thinly disguised as a novel.

Lillian Eugenia Smith was born into a large, respectable, prosperous family in Jasper, Florida, on December 12, 1897. When the family business collapsed in 1915, her family moved to their cottage in Clayton, Georgia, and started Laurel Falls Girls Camp. Smith studied at Piedmont College in Demorest, Georgia (1915–16) and then left to help run the family camp. Pursuing her great love of music, she also did two stints at Baltimore's Peabody Conservatory (1917, 1919). In 1922 she went to China to offer musical instruction at a Methodist missionary school. When her parents' health began to fail in 1925, she came home and eventually took over the running of the camp, which in time she converted into a place for serious discussion of social issues. Her longtime partner, Paula Snelling, a school counselor, assisted her.

In 1936 the two founded *Pseudopodia*, a small magazine meant to further their ideals and to give southern writers, including blacks, a forum. After several renamings, including *South Today*, Smith closed the successful magazine in 1945 to devote herself to writing. Unfortunately, none of her books achieved the emotional power of her controversial novel *Strange Fruit* or the intellectual and psychological depths of *Killers of the Dream*. She battled cancer from the early 1950s until her death in 1966, but to the end she remained devoted to her dream of a South liberated from the "ghosts" of southern traditions. Her last published work was *Our Faces, Our Words* (1964), which applauded nonviolence in the civil rights movement.

It is arguable that Smith's sojourn in China, where she witnessed prejudice, oppression, and constant violations of her youthful Christian principles, compelled her to become an outspoken social critic. But she was not a churchgoer and did not refer to herself as religious. She read the giants of intellectual modernism (namely, Freud) with great passion and cited modernist writers (Henri Bergson, Carl Jung, and Paul Tillich among others) in her attack on prejudice and narrowmindedness. Her own sexual orientation and personal life gave her a clearly existential understanding (she read most of the main existentialists of her day) of what it meant to be part of a despised minority considered deviant and dangerous by many.

By and large, Smith's neighbors were polite to her, but she knew what many southerners thought of her and could decipher the ugliness of the expression, uttered by Eugene Talmadge, that *Strange Fruit* was a "literary corncob." Fred Hobson has written that Lillian Smith "was not afraid to confront the darkness within Southern, and American, society — racially, sexually, and politically. She was, in the finest sense of that term, a moralist, an absolutist, one of the last of the all-or-nothing voices." Though her fame may have diminished since her death, she was an important early voice in the movement for civil rights in the American South, one of the first white southern writers to confront the evils of racism and injustice in a forthright, uncompromising manner.

BRUCE CLAYTON, *Allegheny College, Meadville, Pennsylvania*

John Egerton, *Speak Now Against the Day: The Generation Before the Civil Rights Movement in the South* (New York: Alfred A. Knopf, 1994).

Margaret Rose Gladney, *How Am I to Be Heard? Letters of Lillian Smith* (Chapel Hill: University of North Carolina Press, 1993).

Fred Hobson, *Tell About the South: The Southern Rage to Explain* (Baton Rouge: Louisiana State: University Press, 1983).

Anne C. Loveland, *Lillian Smith: A Southerner Confronting the South* (Baton Rouge: Louisiana State University Press, 1986).

Darlene O'Dell, *Sites of Southern Memory: The Autobiographies of Katharine Du Pre Lumpkin, Lillian Smith, and Pauli Murray* (Charlottesville: University Press of Virginia, 2001).

Morton Sosna, *In Search of the Silent South: Southern Liberals and the Race Issue* (New York: Columbia University Press, 1977).

STRANGE FRUIT

In hindsight, the controversy that greeted the publication of Lillian Smith's *Strange Fruit* in 1944 seems unusually heated today. This novel of interracial love was denounced in many places for its "obscenity," although sex is barely mentioned. Massachusetts banned it for a short time; so did the U.S. Post Office. But the book has had many admirers in the years since its publication. It was a commercial success — a best-seller, a Broadway play briefly — and it remains in print in many languages. From her home atop Old Screamer Mountain near Clayton, Georgia, Smith knew that many of her neighbors had bought the book, but in public they snubbed her.

In 1949 she unleashed another diatribe against racism in an imaginative autobiography, *Killers of the Dream*, widely considered to be her best book. In *Strange Fruit* and subsequent writings, Smith attempted to untangle and expose the web of white racism, gender, class, religion, and myriad traditions she thought had put a straitjacket on what her contemporary and admirer, W. J. Cash, called "the mind of the South." She was the first white southerner of any prominence to denounce not just racism but segregation.

Strange Fruit is set in the imaginary small south Georgia town of Maxwell, modeled obviously on the town of Jasper, Florida, Smith's birthplace and home for her first seventeen years. The novel's central events, set against a week of religious revival in August, occur immediately after World War I (1917–18). Tracy Deen, son of middle-class but pretentious white parents, has just returned from a stint in the army. He and Nonnie Anderson, a younger, pretty, light-skinned African American who has been in love with him since she was a very young girl, immediately find themselves in each other's arms. When Nonnie learns that she is pregnant, she allows herself to hope that Tracy will be as happy as she is. He isn't. He has been mired in guilt and self-doubt, and her news only heightens his uncertainty about religion and about his mother's constant urgings that he join the church and marry his presumed sweetheart, a pleasant, conventional young girl. The dreamy Tracy tries to buy Nonnie off with money for an abortion — available in nearby Atlanta to white girls — or a marriage to any black man.

Every southern social force — racism, religious fundamental-ism, class conflict — is at war in the dilemma and dreams of the two protagonists, and the consequence is nothing but tragedy for everyone, even Tracy's innocent, simpleminded black boyhood friend. Lillian Smith was earnest and idealistic, more a social critic than a novelist. She never missed a chance to denounce the corrosiveness of traditions, whether expressed by a dimwit-ted racist, such as Preacher Dunwoodie, or by Nonnie's angry older brother, who resorts to murder and brings on unintended tragedy.

Smith always believed her novel had been deliberately under-rated and misunderstood. She deeply resented criticism from prominent white moderates such as *Atlanta Constitution* editor Ralph McGill. She was hurt when black intellectuals complained that she had patronized Nonnie by portraying the intelligent, college-educated young woman as in a perpetual swoon for a marshmallowy lover who could hardly have treated her more shabbily.

Smith's attitude toward the novel also seemed to change over time. In 1961 she rebuked a literary agent who was trying to negotiate a film version. No one admitted that her novel was a masterpiece, Smith said; people erroneously still viewed the book as being simply about race relations. She even suggested that a white actress could play Nonnie's role. She said her novel was not about race (which it surely was) but instead was a fantasy in which she was every character. Whatever else it might be, *Strange Fruit* is about relationships, crossing lines, breaking rules, being different, rejecting prescribed rules, transcending categories, and those "racial abstractions" that Smith often said existed only to divide and conquer and corrupt their victims.

BRUCE CLAYTON, *Allegheny College, Meadville, Pennsylvania*

SUGGESTED READING

Bruce Clayton, "Race, Gender, and Modernism: The Case of Lillian Smith," in *Varieties of Southern History: New Essays on a Region and Its People*, ed. Bruce Clayton and John Salmond (Westport, Conn.: Greenwood Press, 1996).

Margaret Rose Gladney, *How Am I to Be Heard? Letters of Lillian Smith* (Chapel Hill: University of North Carolina Press, 1993).

Fred Hobson, *Tell About the South: The Southern Rage to Explain* (Baton Rouge: Louisiana State University Press, 1983).

Anne C. Loveland, *Lillian Smith: A Southerner Confronting the South* (Baton Rouge: Louisiana State University Press, 1986).

The first novel by Vereen Bell, *Swamp Water* was published initially in serial form in the *Saturday Evening Post* in November and December 1940, and then in book form by Little, Brown in February 1941. It was an immediate sensation in the South and across the nation. Bell, a native of Cairo, Georgia, edited *American Boy-Youth's Companion* during the late 1930s, and returned home in 1940 to write fiction full-time. *Swamp Water* made him a wealthy man. The narrative, which concerns the exploits of a young boy, his hunting dog, and a fugitive hiding out in the Okefenokee Swamp, was so appealing that Bell was able to sell the movie rights to Twentieth Century Fox for $15,000. The studio made the movie in the summer of 1941 and premiered it in October in Waycross, Georgia. *Swamp Water* and its author are often lauded in southern Georgia for bringing recognition to the area and "international fame" to the Okefenokee Swamp.

Swamp Water is the engaging, fast-paced tale of Ben Ragan, a boy on the verge of manhood who chases his hunting dog, Trouble, into the Okefenokee Swamp against his father's orders. While within the depths of the swamp, Ben is captured by Tom Keefer, a notorious hog-stealer who fled to the swamp after killing his brother-in-law a few years back. The two agree to engage in a secret hunting and trapping partnership. This operation works well until the townspeople begin to suspect that the boy could not possibly collect so many skins on his own. The men of the town ultimately discover that it is Keefer who is helping Ben in the Okefenokee (Ben's sweetheart, Mabel, reveals the secret in a petulant moment), and a posse sets out after the fugitive but is unable to find him in the morass.

A series of incidents reveal Keefer's innocence: it turns out that a pair of vicious brothers named Silas and Bud Dorson have been the ones stealing hogs, and Keefer's sister confesses that Tom killed her husband in order to protect her. His name cleared, Keefer almost emerges from the swamp and into society, but the Dorsons and Jesse Wick (the brother of the man Keefer killed) are there to ambush him. In the aftermath of the firefight, Ben leaves Trouble with an injured Keefer and runs out of the swamp for help — and here the novel ends.

Swamp Water was a best-seller in 1941 (its second printing came the same month as its first), and most reviews were positive. Edith Walton, writing for the *New York Times Book Review* on February 23, 1941, lauded Bell's descriptions of the Okefenokee and pronounced the novel "above all a triumph of atmospheric writing." A reviewer for the *New York Herald-Tribune Books* agreed, writing in March 1941 that "Mr. Bell knows his background, and his descriptions are remarkably evocative. He knows the birds and animals by name and by habit; he has an ear for the native vernacular. . . . This is a fine, artistic, and virile first novel." Some reviewers thought that *Swamp Water*'s characters were inarticulate and thus very dull, but most emphasized that Bell's writing style lifted the tale "above the category of the merely thrilling and picturesque."

The dramatic atmosphere of *Swamp Water* and its engaging plot appealed to the producers at Twentieth Century Fox, and they worked quickly to capitalize on the popularity of the novel. The completed screenplay, written by Dudley Nichols from Bell's novel, placed more emphasis on the love story — the middle-class girl Ben falls for in the novel becomes Keefer's daughter in the film — and added "stock" southern characters like the comic sheriff and some slack-jawed yokels. The movie was the first American film to be directed by Jean Renoir, son of Auguste Renoir and an already famous and revered French director. Renoir insisted that he film some scenes in the Okefenokee itself, and traveled to south Georgia with the actor playing Ben (Dana Andrews), the dog playing Trouble and his trainer, a producer, a cameraman, and a small crew in late June 1941. The group stayed in Waycross and fraternized with many of the inhabitants. Vereen Bell visited and watched some of the shooting, and locals were used as doubles for most of the male characters in long shots taken at the edge of the swamp.

After the Hollywood crowd left, Waycross residents began to campaign to host the movie's premiere. They besieged Twentieth Century Fox executives with requests, and even sent Darryl Zanuck and others live baby alligators with tags affixed to their necks saying, "Even the gators in Okefenokee went to the premiere in Waycross." Zanuck gave in and notified Lamar Swift, manager of the two movie theaters in Waycross — the Ritz and the Lyric — that he could have the premiere, slated for October 23, 1941. Georgia Governor Eugene Talmadge declared the day of the premiere "*Swamp Water* Day" in the state, and Waycross merchants decorated the streets and their stores. A parade, special dinner, and wagon-ride preceded the premiere. Vereen Bell was the guest of honor.

Moviegoers flocked to the premiere and then to theaters all over the South when the movie opened in limited release a week later. By the time *Swamp Water* opened in New York City in November, it was well on the way to becoming one of Fox's biggest moneymakers for the year. Film critics were not so enthusiastic, however. The reviewer for the *New York Times* noted acerbically that "the fact that Jean Renoir's initial screen exercise in this country was completed before he learned the ABC's of our language will mitigate somewhat his responsibility for 'Swamp Water.'" Critics found the acting capable but the script insipid, "sentimental bosh" tricked out with "pretentious hokum."

The studio, however, was pleasantly surprised at the response to the movie, particularly in southern markets, and approved a remake of *Swamp Water* ten years later. *The Lure of the Wilderness*, released in June 1952, received similarly dismal reviews from critics, who saw it as a "rather soggy remake" of the original and an obvious vehicle for the buckskin-clad body of Jean Peters, a Hollywood ingenue and wife of Howard Hughes.

Both the novel *Swamp Water* and its film version brought attention to south Georgia and to the Okefenokee Swamp at a critical moment in the region's history. President Franklin Roosevelt had declared the swamp a Federal Wildlife Refuge by executive order in 1937, and local boosters were just beginning to shape an infrastructure and culture of tourism in the area. Vereen Bell's fictional representation of the swamp's allure and the film's visual depictions of it helped to convert the Okefenokee from a place of local use to a site of national consumption.

MEGAN KATE NELSON, *Texas Tech University, Lubbock, Texas*

SUGGESTED READING

Vereen Bell, *Brag Dog and Other Stories: The Best of Vereen Bell* (Belgrade, Mont.: Wilderness Adventures Press, 2000).
Alexander Sesonske, "Jean Renoir in Georgia: *Swamp Water*," *Georgia Review* 26 (spring 1982): 24–66.

WILLIAM TAPPAN THOMPSON

(1812–1882)

During the middle of the nineteenth century, William Tappan Thompson gained national popularity as a writer of humorous stories. He was best known for creating the fictional character Major Joseph Jones, a down-to-earth Georgia planter who wrote dialect letters about his courtship, rural life, and travels. These letters, originally appearing in periodicals that Thompson edited, were published in *Major Jones's Courtship* and *Major Jones's Sketches of Travel*. Thompson was one of a group of nineteenth-century southern writers whose humorous and realistic tales about the backwoods produced a literature that was distinctively American.

Thompson was born August 31, 1812, in Ravenna, Ohio, to David and Catherine Kerney Thompson. At the age of fourteen, he left home to make his own living. He gained his first newspaper experience on the *Philadelphia Daily Chronicle* and later traveled south to work as a secretary with the territorial government of Florida. Thompson based some of his earliest sketches on his Florida experiences, which included at least two trips to the Seminole reservation.

In 1834 Thompson moved to Augusta, Georgia, to study law under Augustus Baldwin Longstreet, the author of *Georgia Scenes* (1835). He worked in the office of the *State Rights Sentinel*, a newspaper owned by Longstreet. After serving briefly as a volunteer in the Second Seminole War during 1836, he returned to Augusta and in 1837 married Caroline Amour Carrie. Thompson and his wife had ten children, but only six lived to maturity.

Many of Thompson's earliest sketches appeared in the *Augusta Mirror*, a literary magazine that he established in 1838. Within the next few years he was editor or coeditor of three literary periodicals: the *Family Companion and Ladies' Mirror* in Macon, Georgia; the *Southern Miscellany* in Madison, Georgia; and the

Western Continent in Baltimore, Maryland. These were his most productive years for literary writing, and he collected his humorous letters and stories in *Major Jones's Courtship* (1843, with enlarged editions in 1844, 1847, and 1872), *Chronicles of Pineville* (1845), *John's Alive; or, The Bride of a Ghost* (1846), and *Major Jones's Sketches of Travel* (1848). Thompson also wrote three plays that were first performed in Baltimore. The only one to be published was *Major Jones's Courtship; or Adventures of a Christmas Eve, a Domestic Comedy, in Two Acts* (1850).

In *Major Jones's Courtship*, Thompson created Major Joseph Jones, one of the most original characters in American humorous literature. The book consists of letters sent by the Major to Thompson. These letters, written in southern backwoods dialect, give Major Jones's unique perspectives on politics, events in the news, fashions, rural life, and courtship. Thompson intended for the Major Jones letters, with their dialect, bad grammar, misspellings, and common-sense views, to serve as an antidote to the sentimental language used in some of the popular literature published in contemporary periodicals.

Major Jones's Courtship is one of the earliest examples in American literature of a fictional narrative written completely in dialect from the down-to-earth narrator's point of view. This was an approach later used by other writers, including Mark Twain in his *Adventures of Huckleberry Finn*. The circus scene in Twain's book was apparently inspired by "Great Attraction! or the Doctor 'most oudaciously tuck In.' A Sketch from Real Life," which Thompson included in *Chronicles of Pineville*, a volume that portrays a small antebellum Georgia community. In the sketches composing the book, Thompson presents eccentric characters and comic situations, along with descriptions of dueling, fire-hunting, drinking, pranks, and clever legal maneuvering. He wrote in the preface that he had attempted to portray the American backwoodsman, "to catch his 'manners living as they rise,'" before the effects of education and progress caused him to disappear.

Major Jones's Sketches of Travel, originally published as humorous letters in the *Western Continent*, describes the Major's adventures on a tour from Georgia to the North and Canada. His naïvete as a rustic in the big city is the source of much of the book's humor, but the Major's comments on slavery give the volume a serious undertone reflecting the growing controversy between the South and the North.

In 1850 Thompson became the founding editor of the *Savannah Daily Morning News*. Except for a short period during the Civil War, he edited this newspaper until his death. When the Civil War erupted, he vigorously championed the Southern cause until he was forced to leave Savannah as General Sherman's army approached. For a while after the war, the *Daily Morning News* was owned and edited by a Northern journalist under whom Thompson worked. Thompson traveled to Europe in 1867 to collect material for a new book, "Major Jones in Europe," but he never finished the manuscript. In 1868 he resumed the editorial chair of the newspaper, now known as the *Savannah Morning News*, and became a leading spokesman for the South during the postwar years. Joel Chandler Harris worked for the paper during the 1870s before accepting a position with the *Atlanta Constitution*. Thompson served as a mentor for Harris as Longstreet had for him many years earlier.

During the last years of his life, Thompson had a significant influence on Georgia politics. He vigorously supported conservative Democratic principles in his editorials for the *Savannah Morning News*. His loyalty to such political figures as John B. Gordon and Alfred Holt Colquitt sometimes resembled blind devotion, but he regarded himself as a defender of Democratic Party unity against the schemes of the Radical Republicans. Although he made some enemies with his outspoken editorials, few people doubted his integrity or sincerity. He died March 24, 1882, at his home in Savannah. His daughter prepared an appropriate memorial by gathering some of his uncollected writings and publishing them in 1883 as *John's Alive; or, The Bride of a Ghost*.

HERBERT SHIPPEY, *Abraham Baldwin Agricultural College*

SUGGESTED READING

American Humorists, 1800–1950, part 2: *Dictionary of Literary Biography*, vol. 11, ed. Stanley Trachtenberg (Detroit: Gale, 1982), s.v. "William Tappan Thompson (Major Joseph Jones)."

Fifty Southern Writers Before 1900: A Bio-bibliographical Sourcebook, ed. Robert Bain and Joseph M. Flora (New York: Greenwood Press, 1987), s.v. "William Tappan Thompson (1812–1882)."

Henry Prentice Miller, "The Background and Significance of *Major Jones's Courtship*," *Georgia Historical Quarterly* 30 (December 1946): 267–95.

Carl R. Osthaus, "From the Old South to the New South: The Editorial Career of William Tappan Thompson of the *Savannah Morning News*," *Southern Quarterly* 14 (April 1976): 237–60.

FRANCIS ORRAY TICKNOR

(1822–1874)

Physician, poet, and horticulturist, Francis "Frank" Ticknor wrote memorable Civil War poetry and earned a lasting literary reputation on the merit of a single poem, "Little Giffen," a ballad about a young Tennessee soldier named Isaac Newton Giffen. The poem describes how during the war Dr. Ticknor treated and befriended the wounded Confederate lad, only to see him return to the ranks and presumably to his battlefield death.

Francis Ticknor, the youngest of Orray and Harriot Coolidge Ticknor's three children, was born in Fortville, Georgia. He earned a medical degree from the Philadelphia College of Medicine in 1842 and began his practice in rural Shell Creek, Georgia. He married Rosalie "Rosa" Nelson in 1847 and settled at Torch Hill, their Columbus, Georgia, home. They had eight children.

The country doctor published poetry and horticultural articles in numerous periodicals, especially the *Southern Cultivator*. "Little Giffen" first appeared in November 1867 in *The Land We Love*, a Charlotte, North Carolina, magazine. Two collections of his poetry were published posthumously. In 1879 Kate Mason Rowland edited and southern poet Paul Hamilton Hayne wrote the introduction for *The Poems of Frank O. Ticknor, M.D.* An expanded edition, *The Poems of Francis Orray Ticknor*, edited by Ticknor's granddaughter, Michelle Cutliff Ticknor, appeared in 1911. In addition to his popular southern martial poetry, the collections include memorial and religious poems, humorous verses, and songs about home and nature.

Dr. Ticknor died in Columbus and was buried in Linwood Cemetery. The Georgia Historical Commission has placed a marker at the site of Torch Hill.

JOY HUGHES MALLARD, *Atlanta*

SUGGESTED READING

Sarah Cheney, "Francis Orray Ticknor," *Georgia Historical Quarterly* 22 (summer 1938): 138–59.

Charles Stephen Gurr, "Social Leadership and the Medical Profession in Antebellum Georgia" (Ph.D. diss., University of Georgia, 1973).

Annie Belle Rodgers, "Francis Orray Ticknor: Georgia Poet" (master's thesis, University of Georgia, 1928).

Michelle Cutliff Ticknor, ed., *The Poems of Francis Orray Ticknor* (New York: Neale Publishing, 1911).

Although Erskine Caldwell wrote more than sixty books, twenty-five novels among them, he is best known for two works of long fiction, *Tobacco Road* (1932) and *God's Little Acre* (1933). *Tobacco Road* was named one of the Modern Library's one hundred best novels of the twentieth century. Along with the less well-known *Journeyman* (1935), these books make up a seriocomic trilogy of Georgia life in the first half of the twentieth century. They detail the ruination of the land, the growth of textile mills, and the abiding influence of fundamentalist religion in the South. They present a radical contrast to the traditionally genteel and romantic views of the region, popularized most notably by Margaret Mitchell in *Gone With the Wind* (1936).

Tobacco Road, published by Charles Scribner and Sons in 1932, was Caldwell's third novel. It was inspired by the terrible poverty he witnessed as a young man growing up in the small east Georgia town of Wrens. His father, Ira Sylvester Caldwell, who was pastor of the local Associate Reformed Presbyterian Church, was also an amateur sociologist and often took his son with him to observe some of the more destitute members of the rural community. Erskine Caldwell's sympathy for these people and his outrage at the conditions in which they lived were real, and his novel was meant to be a work of social protest. But he also refused to sentimentalize their poverty or to cast his characters as inherently noble in their sufferings, as so many other protest works did.

The novel's Lester family, headed by the shiftless patriarch Jeeter, both appall and intrigue readers with their gross sexuality, casual violence, selfishness, and overall lack of decency. Living as squatters on barren land that had once belonged to their more prosperous ancestors, the Lesters have come to represent in the American public's mind the degradation inherent in extreme poverty. That Caldwell also portrays them as often-comic figures further complicates the reader's response. *Tobacco Road* is a call to action, but it offers no easy answers and thus has generated intense debate both in and out of the South. Many southerners denounced the novel as exaggerated and needlessly cruel and even pornographic, an affront to the gentility of the region. Northern critics, however, tended to read the book as a serious indictment of a failed economic system in need of correction. Caldwell later explained that the book was not meant to represent the entire South, but for many this work confirmed demeaning southern stereotypes.

The stage version of *Tobacco Road* was written by Jack Kirkland and opened on December 4, 1933, at the Masque Theatre in New York City. Caldwell had little to do with the play version and initially felt it would fail. First reviews were mixed, and after a month of sporadic attendance, the play moved to the 48th Street Theater, where it slowly became a word-of-mouth success. With Henry Hull as the first of five actors who would play Jeeter Lester, *Tobacco Road* ran for more than seven years, through 3,182 performances. When it closed on May 31, 1941, it had become the longest-running play in the history of the Broadway stage up to that time.

Road shows took the play to cities throughout the nation and later into foreign countries. In 1934 Chicago mayor Edward F. Kelly declared the play obscene and closed it down. The producers sued, and in a major court case, the play was allowed to continue. This was the first of numerous attempts to censor the show, which was often taken to court or banned during its many runs. Caldwell tirelessly defended the play and the book and, in the process, became a leading advocate for artistic freedom and First Amendment rights.

In 1940 Darryl F. Zanuck and Twentieth Century Fox, which had just produced John Ford's classic film version of John Steinbeck's *The Grapes of Wrath*, bought the screen rights to *Tobacco Road*. Ford and screenwriter Nunnally Johnson (a Columbus, Georgia, native) attempted to preserve the caustic comedy and social protest of the book and play, but the studio overruled them on central issues, specifically the tragic ending. The result was a sentimental burlesque that Caldwell himself disavowed. Starring Charley Grapewin, repeating his stage role as Jeeter Lester, the film was released in 1941. It enjoyed initial success but is now considered one of Ford's lesser movies, a poor relative of his great work in *The Grapes of Wrath*.

EDWIN T. ARNOLD, *Appalachian State University, Boone, North Carolina*

SUGGESTED READING

Edwin T. Arnold, ed., *Conversations with Erskine Caldwell* (Jackson: University Press of Mississippi, 1988).

Sylvia Jenkins Cook, *Erskine Caldwell and the Fiction of Poverty: The Flesh and the Spirit* (Baton Rouge: Louisiana State University Press, 1991).

Robert L. McDonald, ed., *The Critical Response to Erskine Caldwell* (Westport, Conn.: Greenwood Press, 1997).

Dan B. Miller, *Erskine Caldwell: The Journey from Tobacco Road. A Biography* (New York: Knopf, 1995).

Wayne Mixon, *The People's Writer: Erskine Caldwell and the South* (Charlottesville: University Press of Virginia, 1995).

JEAN TOOMER
(1894–1967)

Jean Toomer is best known as the author of the 1923 novel *Cane*, an influential work about African American life in which Toomer drew largely on his experiences in Hancock County. Toomer wrote *Cane* after he left his home in Washington, D.C., and worked briefly as a substitute principal at a black industrial school in the middle Georgia town of Sparta. There he experienced a creative outpouring of poetry, drama, stories, and sketches that formed *Cane*, a narrative that begins in the rural South, switches to the urban North, and returns to the South for its conclusion. "Sempter," the southern setting of *Cane*, is modeled on Sparta and the people and places Toomer encountered there in the fall of 1921.

Jean Toomer was the adopted literary name of Nathan Pinchback Toomer, born on December 26, 1894, in Washington, D.C. His parents were Nathan Toomer and Nina Pinchback, the daughter of the Reconstruction-era politician P. B. S. Pinchback. Toomer's father was a freedman farmer from Houston County who had accrued considerable wealth as the widower of a slave-born Georgia plantation heiress, Amanda America Dickson. After Dickson's death in Augusta in 1893, Nathan Toomer traveled frequently to Washington, D.C., where he met and married Nina Pinchback. Soon after young Toomer was born, his father abandoned the family and returned to Georgia, where he died in Macon in 1906. When Toomer's mother died in 1909, Toomer went to live with his maternal grandparents, and in 1914 he graduated from Washington's M Street High School. He then attended colleges in Wisconsin, Massachusetts, Illinois, and New York before he rejected the idea of a college degree in favor of a writing career.

In 1920 Toomer returned to Washington, and in the fall of

1921 he accepted a short-term job as a substitute principal at the Sparta Agricultural and Industrial Institute, in the Oconee River valley of middle Georgia, not far from Perry, Augusta, and Macon — all places where his mysterious father had lived. In Sparta, Toomer claimed he discovered an African American soul, a "seed" of his own blood that had been obscured by his ambiguous racial upbringing, and a part of African American heritage that he believed was generally disappearing in urbanized America. Previously frustrated in his search for a meaningful subject for his writing, Toomer found that he was overflowing with stories and poetry inspired by the Georgia landscape, the African American voices, and the interracial encounters of the southern blacks and whites he met in the Jim Crow–era agricultural town. *Cane* was the result.

When it was published in 1923, *Cane* impressed contemporary writers and critics, who applauded its lyrical sensitivity to African American life and its bold presentation of racial and sexual issues. Writers of the Harlem Renaissance and the Black Arts Movement and such later African American authors as Alice Walker have repeatedly cited *Cane*'s influence on their own writing. After *Cane*, however, Toomer refused to be held up as a "Negro artist." To the disappointment of many of his admirers, by 1924 he had exhausted his interest in African American characters. Critics and editors have often considered Toomer's subsequent creative efforts to be no more than transparent, allegorical vehicles for the theories of the mystic and psychologist G. I. Gurdjieff, to whom Toomer devoted himself as a disciple.

The questions of psychological identity and spiritual harmony that led Toomer to go looking for himself, first in Georgia and then in the teachings of Gurdjieff, also led him to experiment with various other paths — Jungian psychology, the teachings of Edgar Cayce, and Scientology among them. In 1940 Toomer joined the Quakers, who were a sustaining comfort and influence throughout the rest of his life. He lectured for the Religious Society of Friends and wrote extensively for Quaker publications in the 1940s and 1950s. Toomer was married twice: to Margery Latimer in 1931 (she died in childbirth in 1932), with whom he had one daughter, Margery (Argie); and then to Marjorie Content in 1934. A resident of Doylestown, Pennsylvania, from 1934 onward, Toomer died in a Pennsylvania nursing home of arteriosclerosis on March 30, 1967.

Although he wrote throughout his life, Toomer's literary visibility effectively ended in 1936, with the last publication in his lifetime, the long poem "Blue Meridian," which extolled the potential of an "American" race, a "blue" hybrid that would incorporate and extend the spirits of the black, white, and red races. Toomer's subsequent writings — a considerable body of essays, experimental plays, poetry, and short fiction — would remain unpublished until the mid-1960s, when the scholar-writer Arna Bontemps acquired Toomer's papers for Fisk University in Nashville, Tennessee. *Cane* was reissued for the first time in paperback in 1969, and it has become a classic text of African American studies. Recent publications include collections of Toomer's poetry and essays, as well as the republication of his 1931 self-published book of Gurdjieffian aphorisms, *Essentials*.

In 2005 Toomer was inducted into the Georgia Writers Hall of Fame.

KEITH HULETT, *University of Georgia Libraries*

SUGGESTED READING

Barbara Foley, "'In the Land of Cotton': Economics and Violence in Jean Toomer's *Cane*," *African American Review* 32 (summer 1998).

Barbara Foley, "Jean Toomer's Sparta," *American Literature* 67 (December 1995).

Cynthia Earl Kerman and Richard Eldridge, *The Lives of Jean Toomer: A Hunger for Wholeness* (Baton Rouge: Louisiana State University Press, 1987).

Kent Anderson Leslie and Willard B. Gatewood Jr. "'This Father of Mine . . . a Sort of Mystery': Jean Toomer's Georgia Heritage," *Georgia Historical Quarterly* 77 (winter 1993).

Nellie Y. McKay, *Jean Toomer, Artist: A Study of His Literary Life and Work, 1894–1936* (Chapel Hill: University of North Carolina Press, 1984).

TOWNSEND PRIZE FOR FICTION

Every other year a board of judges awards the Townsend Prize for Fiction to an outstanding novel or short-story collection published by a Georgia writer during the past two years. The award is named for Jim Townsend, the founding editor of *Atlanta* magazine, the associate editor of *Atlanta Weekly Magazine* (of the *Atlanta Journal-Constitution*), and an early mentor to such Atlanta writers as Pat Conroy, Terry Kay, Bill Diehl, and Anne Rivers Siddons.

The prize was conceived by a group of Atlanta writers in 1981. From 1981 to 1997 Georgia State University sponsored the award. In 1997 Georgia Perimeter College and the *Chattahoochee Review* assumed sponsorship. In 2000 the Margaret Mitchell House and Museum and *Atlanta* magazine became additional sponsors.

The Townsend Prize consists of a $2,000 award and a silver tray of commemoration. On the occasion of the award's presentation to Ha Jin in 2002, the *Chattahoochee Review* editor Lawrence Hetrick explained that the prize is intended to recognize two accomplishments by a writer: "First, we're looking for excellence and originality in language. Second, we're looking for human insight."

The prize has served an important role in encouraging and promoting Georgia writers. Philip Lee Williams, who received the award in 1986, explains its importance to him: "Winning the Townsend Prize was extremely important for my career because it brought me to the forefront of Georgia media as a writer. . . . The day I won the award is still one of the happiest days of my professional life because my parents and wife were there for the award and because the novel for which I won it, *The Heart of a Distant Forest*, was my first book." Mary Hood, the 1988 winner of the prize, describes it as "a harvest celebration of the whole state's writing, not just the winner's. This is fertile ground, and there is much to celebrate."

The list of Townsend Prize winners reflects a diverse literary community, ranging from internationally known writers Alice Walker and Ha Jin to locally cherished authors Celestine Sibley and Ferrol Sams to established regional writers Pam Durban, Judson Mitcham, and James Kilgo. The most unexpected name on the list may be Ha Jin, who moved to the United States from mainland China in 1985 and taught with the Emory University creative writing faculty for ten years before moving north to teach at Boston University in 2002. Jin's presence on the Townsend Prize list signifies the increasingly international character of Georgia's literary landscape.

WINNERS OF THE TOWNSEND PRIZE

Celestine Sibley, *Children, My Children* (1982)

Alice Walker, *The Color Purple* (1984)

Philip Lee Williams, *The Heart of a Distant Forest* (1986)

Mary Hood, *And Venus Is Blue* (1988)

Sara Flanigan, *Alice* (1989)

Charlie Smith, *The Lives of the Dead* (1990)

Ferrol Sams, *When All the World Was Young* (1991)

Pam Durban, *The Laughing Place* (1994)

JoAllen Bradham, *Some Personal Papers* (1996)

Judson Mitcham, *The Sweet Everlasting* (1998)

James Kilgo, *Daughter of My People* (2000)

Ha Jin, *The Bridegroom: Stories* (2002)

Terry Kay, *The Valley of Light* (2004)

Judson Mitcham, *Sabbath Creek* (2006)

HUGH RUPPERSBURG, *University of Georgia*

LAMAR TROTTI
(1900–1952)

Lamar Trotti was one of the most prolific and respected screen-writers and producers working in Hollywood during the 1930s and 1940s. Although he earned fame and fortune far from his native Georgia, he never relinquished his love for the South and its history. One of the most famous films that Trotti wrote and produced, *I'd Climb the Highest Mountain* (1951), was filmed on location in north Georgia and starred Susan Hayward. Before shooting began, Trotti assured the local people that the "picture would poke no 'Tobacco Road' fun" at them — a statement that could not be made about the film *Deliverance*, which was shot near the same location twenty years later.

Born in Atlanta on October 18, 1900, Trotti began his career as a journalist. He was the first graduate of the University of Georgia's Henry Grady School of Journalism. He was editor of the student paper, *The Red and Black*, and soon after graduation became the youngest city editor working for a Hearst paper, *The Georgian*. In 1925 he moved to New York City to work for the Motion Picture Producers and Distributors of America. In 1928 he married Louise Hall of Macon. While in New York he wrote his only book, *Fragments from the Life of a Lady: Emma Dineen Trotti*, a sentimental memoir of his mother.

Trotti moved in 1932 to Hollywood, where screenwriter Dudley Nichols got him his first screenwriting assignment with Twentieth Century Fox Studios and collaborated with him on a number of early scripts. Trotti remained at Fox for his entire twenty-year career in Hollywood. In his latter years there, he produced several films in addition to writing screenplays.

Trotti wrote films in many different genres: westerns, such as *The Ox-Bow Incident* (1943); historical epics, such as *Drums Along the Mohawk* (1939) and *Captain from Castile* (1947); comedies, such as *Cheaper by the Dozen* (1950); war films, such as *Guadalcanal Diary* (1943) and *A Bell for Adano* (1945); musicals, such as *Alexander's Ragtime Band* (1938) and *With a Song in My Heart* (1952); and biographies, such as *Young Mr. Lincoln* and *The Story of Alexander Graham Bell* (both 1939). He won an Academy Award for his screenplay *Wilson* (1944), a biographical treatment of Woodrow Wilson's presidency, which premiered in Atlanta during World War II. Trotti's films were commercially and critically successful; they are seen often on television, and they are studied as classics in film schools across the country.

Significantly, Trotti was known among his peers and acquaintances as much for his personal characteristics as for his talent. Nichols referred to him as a "quiet, shy man" who was "morally strong." The comedian and filmmaker Charlie Chaplin referred to Trotti as having "warm sympathy for his fellow man." Given these character traits, no one was surprised when Trotti established a scholarship for rural teachers to further their education at the University of Georgia.

In 1950 one of Trotti's sons, Lamar Jr., was killed in an automobile accident. Trotti never recovered from the tragedy, and he died on August 28, 1952, in California. The Writers Guild of America recognized Lamar Trotti posthumously in 1983 with its coveted Screen Laurel Award.

KAY BECK, *Georgia State University*

SUGGESTED READING

Celestine Sibley, "Hunt Is On for Trotti Contacts," *Atlanta Constitution*, April 23, 1986.

Frank Thompson, "Lamar Trotti," *Atlanta Journal-Constitution*, Oct. 26, 1986.

JOSEPH ADDISON TURNER
(1826–1868)

Joseph Addison Turner was a writer, editor, publisher, lawyer, and planter. He is best known for publishing *The Countryman*, a weekly newspaper produced from his Putnam County plantation during the Civil War (1861–65). Despite previous publishing failures, Turner's *Countryman* generated a wide southern readership during its four-year existence.

Born on September 23, 1826, in Putnam County, Turner was the son of William ("Honest Billy") Turner and Lucy Wingfield Butler. At seven years old, he suffered a bone infection that left him crippled for life and kept him homebound for several years. As a result, Turnwold, the Turner family home located nine miles from Eatonton, served as the primary location for his early education. His father tutored him using the family's extensive library. His later education included six years at the Phoenix Academy in Eatonton and one term at Emory College at Oxford in 1845.

After a year at Emory, Turner moved to Eatonton, where he taught for a year at the Phoenix Academy, then prepared for and passed the Georgia bar. In 1850 Turner married Louisa Jane Dennis. They had eight children. In 1855 he entered politics by running for solicitor general of the Ocmulgee circuit. He lost the race but was elected to the Georgia senate two years later.

Throughout the 1840s and 1850s, Turner pursued his literary passions. He published a wide array of poems, book reviews, articles, and essays under a variety of pseudonyms. In 1848 he began his first publication, *Turner's Monthly*, which lasted only three months. In 1854 Turner founded a weekly journal called the *Independent Press*. It was a business failure, and he shut it down within the year. Throughout the rest of the decade, he edited several other publications that failed. He moved back to his plantation, Turnwold, in 1856, and there, only after the outbreak of the Civil War, did Turner achieve publishing success.

On March 4, 1862, Turner published his first issue of *The Countryman*, a unique venture that stands as probably the only newspaper ever published from a plantation. Declaring Turnwold's purpose to be the cultivation of "corn, cotton, and literature," Turner drew on its extensive library and built a full printing shop on the site. Despite difficulties created by shortages in ink, paper, and other materials over the course of the war, *The Countryman* circulated throughout the Confederacy from its inception through its final issue in May 1866.

Turner was a staunch advocate for slavery and the Confederacy. The original motto for *The Countryman* read, "Brevity is the Soul of Wit," but by 1863 Turner had changed it to "Independent in Everything, Neutral in Nothing." He used *The Countryman* to voice his pro-Confederate views through articles and editorials. The venture was also distinguished for launching the journalistic career of yet another distinguished Georgian — Joel Chandler Harris. Turner hired the sixteen-year-old Harris, an Eatonton native, as an apprentice and typesetter for *The Countryman* in March 1862. Under Turner's guidance and stern editing, Harris remained with the paper for its duration. He developed into an excellent literary composer and contributed a number of essays, poems, and book reviews to the paper himself.

In June 1865 Union officials placed Turner under military arrest for "publishing disloyal articles," and publication of *The Countryman* was suspended for several months. After the suspension ended, Turner managed to revive *The Countryman* for four months before, exhausted, he shut down the operation for good in May 1866. Turner died two years later in Eatonton at forty-two years of age.

JARROD ATCHISON, *University of Georgia*

Paul M. Cousins, *Joel Chandler Harris: A Biography* (Baton Rouge: Louisiana State University Press, [1968]).

Bertram Holland Flanders, *Early Georgia Magazines: Literary Periodicals to 1865* (Athens: University of Georgia Press, 1944).

Joel Chandler Harris, *On the Plantation* (New York: D. Appleton and Co., 1892).

Joseph Addison Turner, *Autobiography of "The Countryman,"* ed. Thomas H. English (Atlanta: Emory University Library, [1943]).

ALFRED UHRY
(b. 1936)

Alfred Uhry, a playwright, lyricist, and screenwriter, is best known for his play *Driving Miss Daisy*, which premiered in New York in 1987 and was later adapted into a film. Uhry has received a Pulitzer Prize, an Academy Award, and several Tony Awards for his work — the only playwright to win all three awards.

Alfred Fox Uhry was born in Atlanta on December 3, 1936, to a prosperous family of German-Jewish descent. He attended Druid Hills High School, and after graduation he attended Brown University in Rhode Island, where he received a degree in English and drama in 1958. Uhry then relocated to New York City, where he taught English at the Calhoun School. In 1975, after several failed attempts at writing a successful play, he collaborated with Robert Waldman to adapt Eudora Welty's short novel *The Robber Bridegroom* into a musical. The production received a Tony Award nomination for Best Book of a Musical, and it marked Uhry's first success as a playwright.

After many long years working in theater, Uhry encountered his next big success in 1987. On April 15 *Driving Miss Daisy* opened at the Studio Theater at Playwrights Horizons in New York City. Set in Atlanta, *Driving Miss Daisy* spans a quarter of a century, from 1948 to 1973, with the action taking place before, during, and after the civil rights movement. The plot centers on two characters, an elderly Jewish widow named Miss Daisy Werthan and her African American driver, Hoke Colburn. The characters, inspired by Uhry's grandmother Lena Fox and her chauffeur, Will Coleman, are universal figures that appeal to a wide audience. Miss Daisy and Hoke struggle to determine their personal and social roles as the world they have always known changes before their eyes. The original production featured Atlanta native Dana Ivey as Miss Daisy, Morgan Freeman as Hoke, and Ray Gill as

Miss Daisy's son, Boolie. *Driving Miss Daisy* was an immediate success, and it earned Uhry the 1988 Pulitzer Prize for drama.

In 1989 Uhry wrote the screenplay adaptation of *Driving Miss Daisy* for a film starring Jessica Tandy, Morgan Freeman, and Dan Aykroyd. The movie was filmed in and around the Atlanta area and features Druid Hills, Lullwater Road, Agnes Scott College, and The Temple. The film received an Academy Award for Best Picture, and Uhry received the award for Best Screenplay.

The Last Night of Ballyhoo (1997) and *Parade* (1998) also draw on Uhry's heritage as a southern Jew, and they mesh aspects of both cultures (southern and Jewish) and their literary traditions. *The Last Night of Ballyhoo* was commissioned for the Olympic Arts Festival in 1996 and debuted at the Alliance Theatre in Atlanta. The play chronicles the lives of a close-knit Jewish family with mainstream southern Christian traditions living comfortably in Atlanta. A young Orthodox Jewish man from New York arrives while World War II is breaking out in Europe, and he challenges the family's abandonment of its Jewish heritage. The play moved to Broadway on February 27, 1997, and featured a cast that included Jessica Hecht, Celia Weston, Dana Ivey, Terry Beaver, Paul Rudd, Arija Bareikis, and Stephen Largay. In 1997 *Ballyhoo* received a Tony Award for Best Play as well as the Outer Critics Circle Award.

The musical *Parade* tells the story of Leo Frank, a Jewish factory manager convicted of murdering a young girl in Atlanta in 1913. A mob removed Frank from his jail cell in Milledgeville one night and "paraded" him to Marietta, where they lynched him. In 1986, some seventy years later, the Georgia Board of Pardons reversed Frank's conviction. The play's title refers both to a Confederate Memorial Day parade and to the procession that carried Frank to his death. (Uhry may have been moved to write the play because of personal connections; his great uncle owned the factory where Leo Frank worked, and his grandmother — the model for Miss Daisy — was a friend of the Frank family.) The play opened at the Lincoln Center's Vivian Beaumont

Theater in New York City on December 17, 1998, and featured Brent Carver and Carolee Carmello as Leo and Lucille Frank. *Parade* was nominated for nine Tony Awards in 1999, and it won two.

Uhry's lesser-known theatrical works include contributions to *Swing* (1980), *Little Johnny Jones* (1982), and *America's Sweetheart* (1985). He also wrote the screenplays for several films, including *Mystic Pizza* (1988), which featured Julia Roberts in her first major role, and *Rich in Love* (1993). Uhry is married to Joanna Kellogg. They have four daughters and live in New York.

MIRIAM TERRY, *Macon*

SUGGESTED READING

Ben Brantley, "Theater Review: Southern Jewish Angst as One-Liners," *New York Times*, February 28, 1997.

Michael Taub, "Alfred Uhry," in *Contemporary Jewish-American Dramatists and Poets: A Bio-Critical Sourcebook*, ed. Joel Shatzky and Michael Taub (Westport, Conn.: Greenwood Press, 1999).

Alex Witchel, "Remembering Prejudice, of a Different Sort," *Atlanta Journal-Constitution*, February 23, 1997.

UNCLE REMUS TALES

The Uncle Remus tales are African American trickster stories about the exploits of Brer Rabbit, Brer Fox, and other "creeturs" that were recreated in black regional dialect by Joel Chandler Harris (1845–1908). Harris, a native of Eatonton, was a literary comedian, New South journalist, amateur folklorist, southern local-color writer, and children's author.

Two-thirds of Harris's celebrated trickster tales — which constitute the largest gathering of African American folktales published in the nineteenth century — derive their deep structures and primary motifs from African folktales that were brought to the New World and then retold and elaborated upon by African American slaves living in the southeastern United States. The remaining stories have their roots in European and Native American folklore.

The Brer Rabbit stories have been translated into nearly thirty foreign languages and have had an impressively wide influence on writers and on popular culture generally. Writers indebted to Harris include Mark Twain, Charles Chesnutt, Zora Neale Hurston, Flannery O'Connor, William Faulkner, Ralph Ellison, Toni Morrison, and Van Dyke Parks and Julius Lester (who have retold the Uncle Remus tales in richly illustrated multivolume sets). Eatonton's other famous literary personality, however, Alice Walker, only begrudgingly acknowledges Harris's influence, arguing that he in effect stole a major part of the black folk legacy from its authentic African American creators.

A whole gallery of children's-story heroes, including Kim's animal friends in Rudyard Kipling's *Jungle Books*, Beatrix Potter's Peter Rabbit, Howard Garis's Uncle Wiggily, and A. A. Milne's Winnie-the-Pooh, were influenced by Harris's creation of street-smart, recognizably human animal characters who speak "de same ez folks." Walt Disney's pioneering film that first combined live action and animation, *Song of the South* (1946), Disney World's Splash Mountain theme ride, an endless array of Saturday morning cartoon tricksters, from Bugs Bunny to the Road Runner, and even B&G Foods' Brer Rabbit Molasses were born, bred, or otherwise cooked up in Brer Rabbit's briar patch.

Harris's fictionalized storyteller, Uncle Remus, was a "human syndicate" whom he had admittedly "walloped together" from several black storytellers he had met while working from 1862 to 1866 as a printing compositor on Joseph Addison Turner's Turnwold Plantation, outside Eatonton, in Putnam County. Although Uncle Remus's name has its ultimate origins in Rome's Romulus and Remus legend, its more immediate antecedent was an elderly black gardener Harris met in Forsyth, Georgia, where Harris had served from 1867 to 1870 as an editor for the *Monroe Advertiser*.

From 1876 to 1879, during the first phase of Harris's quarter-century career as associate editor of the *Atlanta Constitution*, he wrote for the newspaper several dialect sketches that portrayed Uncle Remus as a reluctant city dweller who was fond of dropping by the paper's editorial office and sharing comic, philosophical, and sometimes cynical perspectives about city life in what he sometimes called "Atlanta-Ma-Tantrum." The fact was that Remus's heart, like Harris's, was really back in Putnam County.

When Uncle Remus began telling Brer Rabbit tales in rural black dialect, the stories proved to be so popular that they soon outgrew the confines of the *Constitution*. In 1880 Harris published a volume of these folktales, together with old plantation songs, pithy sayings, and Remus's Atlanta street-sketches, as *Uncle Remus: His Songs and His Sayings*. Harris would gather six more volumes of Uncle Remus stories during his lifetime, including, in 1895, a revised edition of his first book, illustrated by A. B. Frost. Two more volumes would appear posthumously, followed in 1955 by *The Complete Tales of Uncle Remus*, a collection of all 185 tales edited by Richard Chase.

Harris embedded the animal folktales he retold in a rhetorically complex narrative frame featuring Uncle Remus and his listener, a little white boy who is the son of the plantation master. In Harris's second volume, *Nights with Uncle Remus* (1883), three other black narrators also tell folktales: Aunt Tempy, the uppity and privileged cook in the Big House; 'Tildy, the often impertinent house maid; and Daddy Jack, a sagacious old Gullah from the Sea Islands who performs stories complexly counterpointed with musical themes. Uncle Remus himself proves, however, to be the most fully developed and gifted vernacular storyteller of the group. Remus's character gradually evolves in the later story collections, even as his young white listener grows up and marries, eventually sending his son to learn at the knee of the seemingly ageless old man, as he himself had done a generation earlier.

On one narrative level Uncle Remus appears to be telling only entertaining, harmless slapstick animal tales, drawn nostalgically from the pre–Civil War Old South plantation tradition, that typically highlight the stupidity of the physically stronger animals. In the introduction to his first volume of Uncle Remus tales, however, Harris acknowledges the allegorical significance of the stories he was retelling. Clearly, Brer Rabbit is the black slave's alter ego and trickster-hero, and the so-called stronger animals represent the white slave owners. On deeper rhetorical, symbolical, and archetypal levels, Uncle Remus's role is to initiate his young white listener into the complex realities of adult life. Yet at the same time, Uncle Remus has been educating entire generations of readers — young and old, white, black, brown, red, and yellow — about the destructive power plays and status struggles among members of the animal kingdom, who clearly represent socially and ethnically different, jealous, contentious, and even openly warring members of the human race itself. The survival strategy that the tricky old shaman counsels, furthermore, is first and foremost to use one's "thinkin' masheen," which almost invariably proves to be a more powerful weapon than brute strength.

Uncle Remus is an accomplished role-player and trickster himself. While humorously and affectionately telling the little boy superficially entertaining tales, he is also narrating double-stories that explore, just below the surface, a violent, predatory world of interracial strife, interclass warfare, and assaults on the human spirit itself. As Uncle Remus once stops to explain, "with unusual emphasis," to the little white boy and to Remus's fellow black raconteurs, 'Tildy, Aunt Tempy, and Daddy Jack, "ef deze yer tales wuz des fun, fun, fun, en giggle, giggle, giggle, I let you know I'd a-done drapt um long ago." Uncle Remus challenges all of his readers and listeners, in his time and our time, to read the complex book of life more compassionately and to find some kind of common ground and common humanity beyond slavery — and beyond terror and violence in any form.

R. BRUCE BICKLEY JR., *Florida State University, Tallahassee*

SUGGESTED READING

Florence E. Baer, *Sources and Analogues of the Uncle Remus Tales* (Helsinki: Folklore Fellows Communications, 1981).

R. Bruce Bickley Jr., *Joel Chandler Harris: A Biography and Critical Study* (Athens: University of Georgia Press, 1987).

R. Bruce Bickley Jr., ed., *Critical Essays on Joel Chandler Harris* (Boston: G. K. Hall, 1981).

Walter M. Brasch, *Brer Rabbit, Uncle Remus, and the "Cornfield Journalist": The Tale of Joel Chandler Harris* (Macon, Ga.: Mercer University Press, 2000).

Peggy A. Russo, "Uncle Walt's Uncle Remus: Disney's Distortion of Harris's Hero," *Southern Literary Journal* 25 (fall 1992): 19–32.

Alice Walker, "The Dummy in the Window: Joel Chandler Harris and the Invention of Uncle Remus," in *Living by the Word: Selected Writings, 1973–1987* (San Diego: Harcourt Brace Jovanovich, 1988).

The *Violent Bear It Away* is a novel written by Flannery O'Connor, one of Georgia's most distinguished writers of the twentieth century. O'Connor was born in Savannah and lived most of her life in the central Georgia town of Milledgeville. When she wrote *The Violent Bear It Away*, O'Connor was living with her mother on a dairy farm called Andalusia, near Milledgeville. She began the novel in the summer of 1952, and it was published in 1960. The book's debut received mixed reviews because critics found it difficult to understand, but it is now considered a classic of American literature.

A devout Catholic, O'Connor drew upon her interest in Christian theology and her rural environment for much of her fiction, including *The Violent Bear It Away*. The title of the novel is taken from Matthew 11:12 in the Bible: "From the days of John the Baptist until now, the kingdom of heaven suffereth violence, and the violent bear it away." The power of violence to effect spiritual awakening and the impact that a conversion of this kind has upon Christian salvation are important themes in *The Violent Bear It Away*. To dramatize these abstract spiritual principles, O'Connor chose to create a world of opposites in conflict.

The backwoods prophet and patriarch of the novel, Old Tarwater, extends his reach beyond the grave in his influence over the lives of his great-nephew, Francis Marion Tarwater (young Tarwater), and his nephew, Rayber. Rayber, a schoolteacher, represents the view of the social scientist, believing that human behavior is shaped by forces of environment and psychology that an aware human being is capable of changing and controlling. Young Tarwater, a teenager raised in rural isolation, is an extension of the personality and religious beliefs of Old Tarwater. Young Tarwater is trenchant in his rejection of the urbane world and struggles internally with the facts of redemption as he has been taught to understand them by his great-uncle.

The novel focuses principally on young Tarwater's conflict with Rayber. These two characters represent the contrast between a sacred and a secular worldview. In one world spiritual salvation is possible, but freedom and individuality bend to God's will. In the other self-actualization is possible, but the life of the spirit has lost significance. This conflict makes *The Violent Bear It Away* an existential novel in which the human condition in a modern, Godless world is examined.

From childhood, young Tarwater has been taught that it is his place to carry on in his great-uncle's footsteps and baptize Rayber's retarded son, Bishop, since Old Tarwater has been unable to do so. In the final chapters the holy rite of baptism becomes a murder scene in which young Tarwater drowns his retarded cousin. During young Tarwater's flight from the murder, he is picked up as a hitchhiker, drugged, assaulted, and left in the woods. The violence he has enacted and that which has been performed upon him ignite a spiritual awakening in which he, not his great-uncle, becomes the prophet of God.

Although O'Connor's two novels, *Wise Blood* (1952) and *The Violent Bear It Away*, are recognized by scholars as valuable and lasting works of American literature, O'Connor is primarily known as a short-story writer. Her two collections of short stories are *A Good Man Is Hard to Find* (1955) and *Everything That Rises Must Converge* (1965).

KELLY S. GERALD, *Arlington, Virginia*

SUGGESTED READING

Sally Fitzgerald, ed., *The Habit of Being: Letters of Flannery O'Connor* (New York: Farrar, Straus, and Giroux, 1979).

Dorothy Tuck McFarland, *Flannery O'Connor* (New York: Frederick Unger, 1976).

JOHN DONALD WADE
(1892–1963)

A noted biographer, essayist, and literary-review editor, John Donald Wade is best remembered for his participation in the Vanderbilt Agrarian movement of the 1930s and especially his contribution to the symposium that was to become that movement's manifesto, *I'll Take My Stand: The South and the Agrarian Tradition* (1930). Wade, a Macon County native who spent much of his life in Georgia, was not as prolific as some of his Agrarian colleagues, notably Donald Davidson, John Crowe Ransom, Allen Tate, and Robert Penn Warren, and as a result did not attain their fame. Still, he exerted an influence over the Agrarian movement, as well as the larger sphere of American letters, that belies his relative obscurity.

A great-great-grandson of John Adam Treutlen, the first governor of Georgia, Wade was born on September 28, 1892, in Marshallville. The son of Dr. John Daniel and Ida Frederick Wade, he spent the first eighteen years of his life in this rural central Georgia town, and its conservative agrarian values were to mark his work throughout his career. After earning a bachelor's degree from the University of Georgia in Athens in 1914 and a master's degree from Harvard University in Cambridge, Massachusetts, a year later, Wade went to New York City to begin work on a doctorate at Columbia University. After two years, his academic progress was deferred while he served as a second lieutenant in World War I (1917–18). He completed his doctorate in 1924.

Beginning in 1919, Wade taught at the University of Georgia while completing his dissertation, a lengthy work that would later be published as *Augustus Baldwin Longstreet: A Study of the Development of Culture in the South* (1924). At a time when philology had not yet relaxed its grip on academic writing, Wade's biography of Longstreet, the author of *Georgia Scenes*, broke new ground by blurring the lines not only between history and literary criticism but also between scholarship and literature. Vigorously researched, the book is nevertheless infused with humor and pathos, and it employs narrative devices verging on the novelistic, including imagined dialogue.

Biography soon became Wade's preferred genre, and he returned to it throughout his career. Sometimes called a modern Plutarch, he found the lives of important persons in the past to be exempla for living a good life. As a Ph.D. advisor, he pioneered the biographical dissertation and in so doing anticipated the interdisciplinary field of American studies.

In 1926 Wade left the University of Georgia. The next year he became assistant editor of the *Dictionary of American Biography* (for which he wrote 116 sketches) and devoted himself to researching a second book. The subject of this new biography was John Wesley, founder of the Methodist Church, to which Wade's family had been devoted for generations. As biography, *John Wesley* (1930) is exemplary, though its literary style and occasional use of irony engendered confusion and even contempt in some Methodist circles.

In 1928 Wade was recruited by Vanderbilt University in Nashville, Tennessee, to direct its newly formed graduate program in American literature. Here he soon fell in with a group of scholars and writers who were enthusiastically engaged in writing and talking about the South and its future in an increasingly modern world. After the Dayton, Tennessee, "Scopes monkey trial" in 1925 provoked the widespread ridicule of traditional southern values, these "Twelve Southerners," as they called themselves, responded with a defiant symposium that extolled the southern agrarian life and the virtues it embodied, while decrying the rapid spread of industrialism and urbanization. It was Wade who titled the book *I'll Take My Stand,* and his contribution, "The Life and Death of Cousin Lucius," is often called the most entertaining and readable piece in the collection.

Predictably taking the form of a biographical sketch, the essay is based on the life of Jacob Walter Frederick, Wade's maternal uncle and a man who embodied the "southern way of life" as defined by many of the book's other contributors. Frederick (fictionalized as "Cousin Lucius") is described as hard working, self-reliant, learned, and tradition bound. As he grows older and times change, Cousin Lucius sees the new generation of young people leaving for the city and recognizes that they desire and expect "without effort, things that have immemorially come as the result of effort only." Wade vividly but dispassionately dramatizes Frederick's life, avoiding the temptation to comment on its lessons until the final two sentences of the essay: "And all who wish to think that he lived insignificantly and that the sum of what he was is negligible, are welcome to think so. And may God have mercy on their souls."

I'll Take My Stand was followed by a sort of sequel, *Who Owns America?* (1936), which sought to combine Agrarian efforts with those of the English Distributists, who articulated a humane vision of social and economic life based upon religious social doctrine. To this volume, Wade contributed "Of the Mean and Sure Estate," a narrative essay illustrating the dangers of rural America's aping of city life. The movement lost momentum soon thereafter, and its various members drifted toward other pursuits. Although the Agrarians were alternately ignored and denounced in their time, their efforts comprise a crucial chapter in the intellectual history of the South, and *I'll Take My Stand* is perhaps the single most influential expression of southern exceptionalism.

In 1934 Wade returned to the University of Georgia, where he served as professor of English and chairman of the Division of Language and Literature. Eight years later he married Julia Floyd Stovall, with whom he had a daughter, Anne. He founded the *Georgia Review* in 1946 and edited it for four years. As stated in his introduction to the inaugural issue, Wade originally envisioned a publication that would "make its contents of special concern to Georgians" and stress the idea "that the dignity and

worth of country life must be reaffirmed for the people who practice it and for people who do not practice it." It soon became
apparent to him, however, that a strictly regional and agrarian
focus was impossibly narrow, and, indeed, by emphasizing quality of writing rather than subject matter, the quarterly became
one of the nation's most prestigious literary reviews. In 1950
Wade retired from the university and returned to the town of his
birth.

In his later years Wade's attention turned to his beloved
Marshallville. His final book to be published in his lifetime was
The Marshallville Methodist Church from Its Beginning to 1950
(1952). As executive of the Marshallville Foundation, Wade spent
twenty years beautifying the town. He died on October 9, 1963,
leaving unfinished a historical novel set in Macon County. In the
years since his death, Wade's admirers have kept his voice alive
through three posthumous publications: *Selected Essays* (1966),
a revised edition of the Longstreet biography (1969), and the
correspondence of Wade and Davidson (2003).

CLAY MORTON, *University of Georgia*

SUGGESTED READING

Robert G. Benson, "The Excellence of John Donald Wade," *Mississippi
Quarterly* 29 (1976): 233–39.

Donald Davidson, "Introduction: The Gardens of John Donald Wade,"
in *Selected Essays and Other Writings of John Donald Wade*, by John
Donald Wade (Athens: University of Georgia Press, [1966]), 1–20.

I'll Take My Stand: The South and the Agrarian Tradition (1930; reprint,
Baton Rouge: Louisiana State University Press, [1977]).

M. Thomas Inge, "The Legacy of John Donald Wade," *Georgia Review*
21 (1967): 287–96.

Michael O'Brien, "Wade: A Turning Inward," *The Idea of the American South, 1920–1941* (Baltimore, Md.: Johns Hopkins University Press, 1979), 97–113.

John Donald Wade, *Agrarian Letters: The Correspondence of John Donald Wade and Donald Davidson, 1930–1939*, ed. Gerald J. Smith (Macon, Ga.: Mercer University Press, 2003).

ALICE WALKER
(b. 1944)

Alice Walker is an African American novelist, short-story writer, poet, essayist, and activist. Her most famous novel, *The Color Purple*, was awarded the Pulitzer Prize and the National Book Award in 1983. Walker's creative vision is rooted in the economic hardship, racial terror, and folk wisdom of African American life and culture, particularly in the rural South. Her writing explores multidimensional kinships among women and embraces the redemptive power of social and political revolution.

Walker began publishing her fiction and poetry during the latter years of the Black Arts movement in the 1960s. Her work, along with that of such writers as Toni Morrison and Gloria Naylor, however, is commonly associated with the post-1970s surge in African American women's literature.

Alice Malsenior Walker was born in Eatonton on February 9, 1944, the eighth and youngest child of Minnie Tallulah Grant and Willie Lee Walker, who were sharecroppers. The precocious spirit that distinguished Walker's personality during her early years vanished at the age of eight, when her brother scarred and blinded her right eye with a BB gun in a game of cowboys and Indians. Teased by her classmates and misunderstood by her family, Walker became a shy, reclusive youth. Much of her embarrassment dwindled after a doctor removed the scar tissue six years later. Although Walker eventually became high school prom queen and class valedictorian, she continued to feel like an outsider, nurturing a passion for reading and writing poetry in solitude.

In 1961 Walker left Eatonton for Spelman College, a prominent school for black women in Atlanta, on a state scholarship. During the two years she attended Spelman she became active in the civil rights movement. After transferring to Sarah Lawrence College in New York, Walker continued her studies as well as her involvement in civil rights. In 1962 she was invited to the home of Martin Luther King Jr. in recognition of her attendance at the Youth World Peace Festival in Finland. Walker also registered black voters in Liberty County, Georgia, and later worked for the New York City Department of Welfare.

Two years after receiving her B.A. degree from Sarah Lawrence in 1965, Walker married Melvyn Rosenman Leventhal, a white civil rights attorney. They lived in Jackson, Mississippi, where Walker worked as the black history consultant for a Head Start program. She also served as the writer-in-residence for Jackson State College (later Jackson State University) and Tougaloo College. She completed her first novel, *The Third Life of Grange Copeland*, in 1969, the same year that her daughter, Rebecca Grant, was born. When her marriage to Leventhal ended in 1977, Walker moved to northern California, where she lives and writes today.

Walker has taught African American women's studies to college students at Wellesley, the University of Massachusetts at Boston, Yale, Brandeis, and the University of California at Berkeley. She supports antinuclear and environmental causes, and her protests against the oppressive rituals of female circumcision in Africa and the Middle East make her a vocal advocate for international women's rights. Walker has served as a contributing editor of *Ms.* magazine, and she is a cofounder of Wild Tree Press.

Walker's appreciation for her matrilineal literary history is evidenced by the numerous reviews and articles she has published to acquaint new generations of readers with writers like Zora Neale Hurston. The anthology she edited, *I Love Myself When I Am Laughing . . . and Then Again When I Am Looking Mean and Impressive: A Zora Neale Hurston Reader* (1979), was particularly instrumental in bringing Hurston's work back into print. In addition to her deep admiration for Hurston, Walker's literary influences include Harlem Renaissance writer Jean Toomer, black Chicago poet Gwendolyn Brooks, South African novelist Bessie Head, and white Georgia writer Flannery O'Connor.

The poems in Walker's first volume, *Once* (1968), are based on her experiences during the civil rights movement and her travels to Africa. Influenced by Japanese haiku and the philosophy of author Albert Camus, *Once* also contains meditations on love and suicide. Indeed, after Walker visited Africa during the summer of 1964, she had struggled with an unwanted pregnancy upon her return to college. She speaks openly in her writing about the mental and physical anguish she experienced before deciding to have an abortion. The poems in *Once* grew not only from the sorrowful period in which Walker contemplated death but also from her triumphant decision to reclaim her life.

Many of the narrative poems of her second volume, *Revolutionary Petunias and Other Poems* (1973), revisit her southern past, while other verses challenge superficial political militancy. *Good Night, Willie Lee, I'll See You in the Morning* (1979) contains tributes to black political leaders and creative writers. In addition to a fourth volume of poetry, *Horses Make a Landscape Look More Beautiful* (1984), Walker has compiled her previously published verses in the collection *Her Blue Body Everything We Know: Earthling Poems 1965–1990 Complete* (1991). In a review of *Absolute Trust in the Goodness of the Earth: New Poems* (2003), *Publishers Weekly* highlighted the volume's spiritual and ecological topics and added that Walker "explor[es] and prais[es] friendship, romantic love, home cooking, the peace movement, ancestors, ethnic diversity, and particularly admirable strong women, among them the primatologist Jane Goodall." Walker's most recent volume of poems, *A Poem Traveled Down My Arm*, was published in 2005.

One of Walker's earliest stories, "To Hell with Dying," captured the attention of poet Langston Hughes, who included it in his 1967 anthology, *The Best Short Stories by Negro Writers*. In the tale, which is based on actual events, the joy and laughter of children rescue an old guitar player named Mr. Sweet from the brink of death year after year. The narrator — a girl at the start of the story — returns home as a young woman to "revive" Mr. Sweet, but with no success. After his death she inherits the bluesman's guitar and his enduring legacy of love.

"To Hell with Dying" was reprinted in Walker's first collection of short fiction, *In Love and Trouble: Stories of Black Women* (1973). The thirteen stories in this volume feature black women struggling to transcend society's narrow definitions of their intelligence and virtue. Her second collection, *You Can't Keep a Good Woman Down: Stories* (1982), continues her vivid portrayal of women's experiences by emphasizing such sensitive issues as rape and abortion. In 2000 Walker published a third collection of stories, *The Way Forward Is with a Broken Heart*. She has also written four children's books, including an illustrated version of *To Hell with Dying* (1988) and *Finding the Green Stone* (1991).

Walker has published several volumes of essays and autobiographical reflections. In the 1983 collection *In Search of Our Mothers' Gardens: Womanist Prose*, she introduced readers to a new ideological approach to feminist thought. Her term *womanist* characterizes black feminists who cherish women's creativity, emotional flexibility, and strength. *Womanism* is further used to suggest new ways of reading silence and subjugation in narratives of male domination. Other essay collections include *The Same River Twice: Honoring the Difficult* (1996), which features Walker's account of her struggle with Lyme disease during the filming of *The Color Purple*, and *Sent by Earth: A Message from the Grandmother Spirit: After the Attacks on the World Trade Center and Pentagon* (2002).

Like her short stories, Walker's six novels place more emphasis on the inner workings of African American life than on the relationships between blacks and whites. Her first book, *The Third Life of Grange Copeland* (1970), details the sorrow and redemption of a rural black family trapped in a multigenerational cycle of violence and economic dependency. Walker also fictionalizes a young civil rights activist's coming-of-age in the novel *Meridian* (1976).

The Color Purple (1982) has generated the most public attention as a book and as a major motion picture, directed by Steven Spielberg in 1985. Narrated through the voice of Celie, *The Color Purple* is an epistolary novel — a work structured through a series of letters. Celie writes about the misery of childhood incest, physical abuse, and loneliness in her "letters to God." After being repeatedly raped by her stepfather, Celie is forced to marry a widowed farmer with three children. Yet her deepest hopes are realized with the help of a loving community of women, including her husband's mistress, Shug Avery, and Celie's sister, Nettie. Celie gradually learns to see herself as a desirable woman, a healthy and valuable part of the universe.

Set in rural Georgia during segregation, *The Color Purple* brings components of nineteenth-century slave autobiography and sentimental fiction together with a confessional narrative of sexual awakening. Walker's harshest critics have condemned her portrayal of black men in the novel as "male-bashing," but others praise her forthright depiction of taboo subjects and her clear rendering of folk idiom and dialect. In 1985 the novel was adapted into a film, directed by Steven Spielberg. The musical stage adaptation premiered at the Alliance Theatre in Atlanta in 2004 and opened on Broadway in 2005.

Literary scholars often link *The Color Purple* with Walker's next two novels in an informal trilogy. Celie's granddaughter, Fanny, is a major character in *The Temple of My Familiar* (1989), and the protagonist of *Possessing the Secret of Joy* (1992) is Tashi, the African wife of Celie's son. In Walker's novel *By the Light of My Father's Smile* (1998), strong sexual and religious themes intersect in a tale narrated from both sides of the grave. The novel features a family of African American anthropologists who journey to Mexico to study a tribe descended from former black slaves and Native Americans. In *Now Is the Time to Open Your Heart* (2004) the main character, Kate, embarks on a literal and spiritual journey to find a way to accept the aging process. Walker says that Kate's search is necessary because the territory is largely "uncharted," and "people seem to lose their imagination about what women's lives can be after, say, 55 or 60."

Reflecting on the unique perspective and versatility of her literary career, Walker says, "One thing I try to have in my life and my fiction is an awareness of and openness to mystery, which, to me, is deeper than any politics, race, or geographical location." With elements of ancestral fable and spirituality, womanist insight, literary realism, and the grotesque, Walker's writing embodies an abundant cultural landscape of its own.

QIANA WHITTED, *Yale University, New Haven, Connecticut*

SUGGESTED READING

Erma Davis Banks and Keith Byerman, *Alice Walker: An Annotated Bibliography, 1968–1986* (New York: Garland, 1989).

Harold Bloom, ed., *Alice Walker's "The Color Purple,"* Modern Critical Interpretations series (New York: Chelsea House, 2000).

Ikenna Dieke, ed., *Critical Essays on Alice Walker* (Westport, Conn.: Greenwood Press, 1999).

Henry Louis Gates and K. A. Appiah, eds., *Alice Walker: Critical Perspectives Past and Present* (New York: Amistad Press, 1993).

Maria Lauret, *Alice Walker*, Modern Novelists series (New York: St. Martin's Press, 2000).

Alice Walker, *The Same River Twice: Honoring the Difficult* (New York: Washington Square Press, 1997).

Evelyn C. White, *Alice Walker: A Life* (New York: Norton, 2004).

Donna Haisty Winchell, *Alice Walker* (New York: Twayne, 1992).

ADDITIONAL RESOURCES

The Color Purple, writ. Alice Walker and Menno Meyjes, dir. Steven Spielberg (Burbank, Calif.: Warner Bros., 1985).

DON WEST
(1906–1992)

A native of north Georgia, Don West achieved success as one of the foremost southern regional poets of the twentieth century. He was at different times a labor organizer, political radical, preacher, progressive educator, and outspoken spokesperson for human equality in the generation before the civil rights movement. Although he is best known for his literary works, West was also an effective proponent of the Social Gospel, embraced by some of the South's most dedicated religious reformers.

Born in 1906 in Devil's Hollow, near Ellijay in Gilmer County, Donald L. West grew to young adulthood in the north Georgia mountains. The eldest son of a farmer, he took pride in the independent spirit that had made his forebears nonconformists who opposed slavery in the antebellum years. This heritage of independence expressed itself in West's career, during which he often found himself at odds with the folkways and beliefs of the communities in which he lived and worked. Throughout his life he remained committed to a progressive view of ethnic and racial harmony, which linked him with his personal family history.

After his family moved to the lowlands as sharecroppers, West enrolled in 1923 at the Berry School in Rome, a school for impoverished children from the north Georgia mountains. During his senior year at Berry, he organized a protest when the racist film *Birth of a Nation* was shown on campus. West was expelled for his part in the protest, and he left the institution without a diploma. After working for a telephone company for a short time, he enrolled at Lincoln Memorial University (LMU) in Tennessee, where he met and married Mabel Constance "Connie" Adams. Expelled from LMU for leading a protest against campus paternalism, the popular West was reinstated and graduated in the class of 1929.

After graduation West enrolled at Vanderbilt University in

Nashville, Tennessee, where he entered the Divinity School to pursue a calling to preach. There he came under the influence of the professors Alva Taylor and Willard Uphaus, both staunch proponents of the Social Gospel, a religious perspective that meshed well with West's own beliefs. During his Vanderbilt years West embraced socialism and began working in the labor movement. He was involved with the 1929 Gastonia, North Carolina, textile strike, and in 1932 he was a labor organizer in the bitter miner's strike at Wilder, Tennessee.

In 1931, the year he received his degree from Vanderbilt, he also published his first volume of poetry, *Crab-Grass*, which celebrated the mountain culture and working people of the South.

As a student West visited the Danish folk schools inspired by N. F. S. Grundtvig, who advocated a curriculum based on folk tradition and cultural heritage. Imbued with the folk school philosophy, in 1932 he collaborated with Myles Horton to establish the Highlander Folk School in Monteagle, Tennessee. After less than a year at Highlander, West broke with Horton and returned to Georgia, where he established the Southern Folk School and Libraries in Kennesaw and immersed himself in political and labor organizing. By now a member of the Communist Party, West assumed a leadership role in the defense of the labor organizer Angelo Herndon, an African American in Atlanta who had been convicted under the Georgia insurrection law in January 1933. Pursued by antilabor authorities, West slipped out of Georgia in 1934 to continue his work as a labor organizer. From 1936 to 1937 he served as organizational director for the Kentucky Workers Alliance, a militant organization for the unemployed.

In the late 1930s and early 1940s West served Congregational churches in Bethel, Ohio, and Meansville, Georgia, where his literary work, often published in radical journals, became controversial and led to his resignation. In 1942 he became a teacher and school superintendent in Lula in Hall County, where he gained a national reputation as a proponent of cooperative, community-based learning. He received a Rosenwald Fellowship and left Lula in 1945. After a year of study, West accepted a position at Oglethorpe University in Atlanta. At Oglethorpe he taught creative writing and continued his own literary work, publishing what is considered to be his finest work, *Clods of Southern Earth*, in 1946. This volume, a strong statement of Appalachian regionalism that emphasized the experience of working people, found a wide audience beyond the intellectual community.

Red-baited ruthlessly by the *Atlanta Constitution* editor Ralph McGill and others, West left Oglethorpe in 1948 after a controversial defense of Rosa Lee Ingram, an African American defendant in a high-profile murder case, and involvement in the presidential campaign of the liberal Henry Wallace. In 1955, while editing a religious newspaper, *The Southerner*, in Dalton, he was again attacked for his labor activism and political affiliations. Subsequently, in 1957 he was forced to testify on his political activities before the Senate Internal Security Subcommittee in Memphis, Tennessee. In 1958 the House Committee on Un-American Activities called him as a witness at their Atlanta hearings, but West left without taking the stand.

By 1960 the Wests were teaching in Baltimore, Maryland, where they saved enough to invest in the establishment of the Appalachian South Folklife Center at Pipestem, West Virginia. Founded in 1964 and dedicated to the preservation of mountain culture and its tradition of self-respecting independence, the new institution attracted college students, activists, folk artists, and other Appalachian residents. At Pipestem in the 1960s and 1970s, West became a mentor for nonsectarian leftists and served as a link between the old and new radicalism. For the remainder of his life, he continued his writing and teaching, emphasizing the preservation of Appalachian values and resistance to the corrosive forces of industrialism. The Folklife Center, together with his poetry, remains as his living legacy to future generations. West died in Charleston, West Virginia, on September 29, 1992.

JAMES J. LORENCE, *Gainesville State College*

Victoria Morris Byerly, "What Shall a Poet Sing? The Living Struggle of the Southern Poet and Revolutionary Don West" (Ph.D. diss., Boston College, 1994).

Robert H. Craig, *Religion and Radical Politics: An Alternative Christian Tradition in the United States* (Philadelphia: Temple University Press, 1992).

Anthony Dunbar, *Against the Grain: Southern Radicals and Prophets, 1929–1959* (Charlottesville: University Press of Virginia, 1981).

John Egerton, *Speak Now against the Day: The Generation before the Civil Rights Movement in the South* (New York: Alfred Knopf, 1994).

Don West, *No Lonesome Road: Selected Prose and Poems*, ed. Jeff Biggers and George Brosi (Urbana: University of Illinois Press, 2004).

Bailey White first achieved popularity reading her local color essays on National Public Radio. Her distinctive, gravelly voice and her gift for portraying eccentric people and unusual situations with a gently self-deprecating wit won her a national following. White has published two essay collections (*Mama Makes Up Her Mind* and *Sleeping at the Starlite Hotel*) and one novel (*Quite a Year for Plums*), and her work has appeared as well in numerous periodicals. Her oral and written stories evoke a vivid picture of life in south Georgia.

White was born in 1950 in Thomasville. Both of her parents influenced her writing. Her father, Robb White, a writer of children's stories and film scripts, left the family to live and work in California while she was still a child. She shared his love of words, however, and began writing as a young teen. Reared by her mother, Rosalie, on a farm in Thomasville, White developed an admiration for the natural environment and for the people who depend on it for their well-being. Both play a central role in her writing.

After graduating from Florida State University, White returned to Thomasville. She taught elementary school for more than twenty years, devoting herself to the children in her classroom during her hours on the job and to her writing in her leisure time. She developed a folksy persona who observed the local townspeople and reported on their activities, opinions, and conversations in her essays, many of which she read on *All Things Considered* for National Public Radio. As a narrator White sounded like anything but the shy elementary-school teacher who actually wrote the pieces.

The oral essays — based on truth and colored with the dialect and dialogue of the area — drew an enthusiastic listening public. As a result, publisher Addison-Wesley collected the essays under the title *Mama Makes Up Her Mind and Other Dangers of Southern Living* and published the volume in 1993. In 1995 a second collection, *Sleeping at the Starlite Motel and Other Adventures on the Way Back Home,* followed. With these books White attracted an appreciative reading audience.

In her next book — *Quite a Year for Plums,* published by Alfred A. Knopf in 1998 — White turned to fiction. She explained her reason for the change in genres: "I liked the idea of starting with just anything . . . and being free to just let the story roll out from there." The novel has a loose plot held together by the character Roger, a plant pathologist who draws the affection and attentions of the women in town. His romance with Della, a bird artist, provides an exciting conversational topic for the community. The episodic novel, which has the same vivid characters and dialogue of the writer's essays, furnishes readers with another look at south Georgia life.

In 1999 White took a break from her teaching position to devote herself to her writing career full time from her family home in Thomasville. She retains close ties with her south Georgia heritage and shares her southern wit and wisdom in oral presentations as well as in her writings.

CHARLOTTE PFEIFFER, *Abraham Baldwin Agricultural College*

A native of Atlanta, Walter White served as chief secretary of the National Association for the Advancement of Colored People (NAACP) from 1929 to 1955. During the twenty-five years preceding the Supreme Court's 1954 *Brown v. Board of Education* decision, White was one of the most prominent African American figures and spokespeople in the country. Upon his death in 1955, the *New York Times* eulogized him as "the nearest approach to a national leader of American Negroes since Booker T. Washington."

White was the fourth of seven children of Madeline Harrison and George White, a teacher and postal worker, respectively. His family belonged to Atlanta's black elite and attended the influential First Congregational Church. Although White was very light-skinned, he chose to identify himself as an African American. If he ever had any reservations about that choice, they were resolved during the Atlanta race riot in 1906, when a white mob threatened to attack his family home. The thirteen-year-old White determined that he could never be part of a race that carried within it such a ghastly hatred.

Upon his graduation from Atlanta University in 1916, White became an official with the Standard Life Insurance Company, one of the largest black-owned businesses of its day. He also took part in civic affairs, helping to found the Atlanta branch of the NAACP that same year. With White as secretary, the branch quickly scored a victory for educational equality by preventing the school board from eliminating seventh grade in the black public schools.

In 1917 James Weldon Johnson, field secretary for the NAACP, visited Atlanta. He was impressed with White's enthusiasm and political skills and persuaded the national board of directors to appoint him the assistant secretary. In January 1918 White moved to New York and joined the NAACP staff.

For the next ten years White's primary responsibility was conducting undercover investigations of lynchings and race riots. Using his fair complexion to his advantage, White approached members of lynch mobs and other whites who had witnessed or were involved in racial violence. He tricked them into giving him candid accounts that the NAACP would then publicize. During these years White investigated forty-one lynchings and eight race riots, including the riots in Elaine, Arkansas, and Chicago, Illinois, during the Red Summer of 1919. On more than one occasion he narrowly escaped vigilantes who discovered his true identity. In the January 1929 issue of *American Mercury*, White published "I Investigate Lynchings," an account of his investigative exploits. His book *Rope and Faggot* (1929) is still considered an authoritative analysis of the extent and causes of lynching.

During the Harlem Renaissance of the 1920s and 1930s White published two novels. The critically acclaimed *Fire in the Flint* (1924) is based on White's experiences investigating lynchings. It tells the story of Kenneth Harper, a black physician in small-town Georgia during the years after World War I (1917–18), who is murdered by whites when he develops a race consciousness. *Flight* (1926) is a novel of the great migration of blacks to the North. It follows the light-skinned African American Mimi Daquin, who hails from New Orleans and Atlanta, as she journeys to Harlem, seeks her fortune by disappearing into white society, and returns once again to her race to seek spiritual fulfillment. More ambitious than *Fire in the Flint* but also more uneven, it received mixed reviews.

White was central in other ways to the flowering of the Harlem Renaissance. He vigorously promoted the work of other artists, including the poets Countee Cullen and Langston Hughes, the novelist Claude McKay, the tenor Roland Hayes (a fellow Georgian), and the singer and actor Paul Robeson. White eagerly vetted manuscripts, introduced writers to publishers, and brought stage and concert performers to the attention of the public.

When James Weldon Johnson retired from the NAACP in 1929, White was elevated to the position of secretary. In this capacity he energetically led the association in its pursuit of full legal equality for African Americans. In 1930 he designed the campaign that successfully blocked President Herbert Hoover's nomination of John J. Parker to the U.S. Supreme Court. As a candidate for governor of North Carolina, Parker had gone on record as favoring the continued disfranchisement of African Americans, and he was known to be hostile to organized labor. The campaign produced enough popular opposition to Parker to defeat his nomination in the Senate. In the 1930 and 1932 elections the NAACP followed up this victory by working to defeat northern senators who had cast votes for Parker. Targeting senators from states with a substantial black minority, the NAACP's efforts met with considerable success. The Parker campaign and its aftermath marked the emergence of the association as a potent force in national politics.

During the administrations of both Franklin Roosevelt and Harry S. Truman, White's trademark style of working for political gain by rallying enlightened elites achieved stunning results. His close friendship with first lady Eleanor Roosevelt gave him direct access to the White House. He orchestrated massive support in Congress for an antilynching law, which was defeated only by a persistent Senate filibuster by southern Democrats. When the popular contralto Marian Anderson, who was black, was refused the use of Constitution Hall, White secured the Lincoln Memorial and assembled a sponsoring committee studded with New Deal officials for her Easter 1939 concert. Two years later, White took a prominent part in A. Philip Randolph's March on Washington Movement, which pressured President Roosevelt into issuing an executive order banning racial discrimination in defense industries. He obtained a promise from President Truman to appoint a commission on civil rights, which in 1947 produced the landmark report *To Secure These Rights*.

During White's tenure as NAACP secretary, the association launched a series of legal suits designed to achieve equality between the races in education. This effort culminated in the Supreme Court's 1954 *Brown v. Board of Education* decision, which declared unconstitutional the doctrine of "separate but equal."

During World War II (1941–45), White traveled to the European and Pacific theaters of war to investigate charges of discrimination against black soldiers and to promote the idea that an Allied victory should lead to the dismantling of European colonialism and to racial equality for African Americans. He pursued these goals in 1945 as one of three NAACP consultants to the U.S. delegation to the founding conference of the United Nations in San Francisco and again in 1948 as a consultant to the U.S. delegation to the United Nations General Assembly meeting in Paris, France.

White soon faced a struggle in the NAACP as a result of his personal life. In 1922 he had married Leah Gladys Powell, a clerical worker in the association's headquarters; they had two children, Jane and Walter. That marriage ended in divorce in 1949, and the same year he married Poppy Cannon, a white woman born in South Africa. Within the NAACP this interracial marriage provoked protests and calls for White's resignation. But White, ever the defender of integration, shrugged off the criticism, maintaining that one's choice of a mate was a private matter. Eleanor Roosevelt, who had joined the association's board of directors after her husband's death, saved White's position by threatening to resign should White be dismissed. Although declining health soon forced him to turn over many of his administrative duties to Roy Wilkins, he remained the NAACP's executive secretary and most important public spokesperson until his death in 1955.

White's importance lay in his organizational skills and leadership style. His ability to cultivate ties with people of influence both in and out of government and to popularize and publicize the association and its program were instrumental in placing civil rights on the national agenda.

KENNETH R. JANKEN, *University of North Carolina, Chapel Hill*

SUGGESTED READING

Poppy Cannon, *A Gentle Knight: My Husband, Walter White* (New York: Rinehart, 1956).

Kenneth R. Janken, "Civil Rights and Socializing in the Harlem Renaissance: Walter White and the Fictionalization of the 'New Negro' in Georgia," *Georgia Historical Quarterly* 80 (winter 1996): 817–34.

Kenneth R. Janken, "From Colonial Liberation to Cold War Liberalism: Walter White, the NAACP, and Foreign Affairs, 1941–1955," *Ethnic and Racial Studies* 21 (November 1998): 1074–95.

Kenneth R. Janken, *White: The Biography of Walter White, Mr. NAACP* (New York: New Press, 2003).

PHILIP LEE WILLIAMS

(b. 1950)

Philip Lee Williams is an award-winning novelist who has spent his entire life in Georgia. He is the author of nine novels, two memoirs, and a children's book. Also a widely published poet, he founded and edited the poetry journal *Ataraxia*.

Born in Madison in 1950, Williams has lived nearly all of his life in and around Athens. He received an A.B. degree in journalism from the University of Georgia in 1972 and began his career working for newspapers. From 1974 to 1978 he served as associate editor of the *Madisonian* and from 1978 to 1985 as managing editor and then editor for the *Athens Observer*. Williams also worked as a science writer for the University of Georgia. Currently he is the director of public information for the Franklin College of Arts and Sciences, as well as an adjunct professor of creative writing, at the University of Georgia. He lives in Watkinsville with his wife, Linda, and his children, Brandon and Megan.

Williams's first novel, *The Heart of a Distant Forest*, won the Townsend Prize for Fiction in 1986. For *The Song of Daniel* he was named Georgia Author of the Year in Fiction in 1991. His work has been translated into Swedish, French, German, and Japanese. In addition, he has written and coproduced several screenplays for documentaries and has composed symphony, choral, and chamber music.

Williams writes about a wide range of themes, genres, and settings. *The Heart of a Distant Forest* (1984) tells of retired history professor Andrew Lachlan, who returns to his family cabin on the shores of a lake in central Georgia. Williams uses another academic setting in *The Song of Daniel* (1989), which takes place on the University of Georgia campus in Athens. In this novel poet Rebecca Gentry uncovers the secrets of a minor Georgia poet (based loosely on Byron Herbert Reece) while beginning a relationship with the mentally and emotionally challenged Daniel Mitchell. In *Perfect Timing* (1991), the musicologist Ford Clayton seeks to mend his broken marriage while tracking down a former college girlfriend he believes is now homeless.

These characters may live in intellectual environments, but emotional conflicts lie at the heart of their stories. Other novels, such as his crime mystery *Slow Dance in Autumn* (1988), derive their emotional impact from drama and action. In *Final Heat* (1992), Williams uses the Southern Gothic mode to relate the story of a depraved rich girl in love with a mechanic and their botched robbery and escape from a small southern town. *Blue Crystal* (1993) takes place mainly in a Kentucky cave, where three former convicts and their tagalong girlfriends mistakenly believe there is a fortune to be stolen from a one-eyed spelunker.

In contrast to these more dramatic offerings, Williams has a comic side that is especially apparent in *All the Western Stars* (1988). Here, Jake Baker, a former construction worker, and washed-up novelist Lucas Kraft form an unlikely duo as they break out of a nursing home in search of adventure. Williams's comic masterpiece is perhaps *The True and Authentic History of Jenny Dorset* (1997). Writing in the voice of Henry Hawthorne, a southern family servant who lived during the American Revolution, Williams tells the tale of the rambunctious and revolutionary Charleston maid Jenny Dorset and also creates an exceptionally realistic memoir (complete with descriptive titles and a dedication to President Washington).

Williams returns to a more dramatic mode with the historical novel *A Distant Flame* (2004), for which he received the 2004 Michael Shaara Award for Civil War Fiction. Told from the perspective of a Confederate sharpshooter, the novel chronicles the Union assault on Atlanta near the end of the Civil War. Alternating chapters reveal the sharpshooter, fifty years later, struggling to prepare a speech about his experiences for his hometown's commemoration of the Atlanta campaign.

Williams's books reflect his strong inclination to meditate as a naturalist, whether from a lake cabin (*The Heart of a Distant*

Forest) or an Appalachian cave (*Blue Crystal*). His attitude toward nature also lies at the center of his memoirs. It is in the woods behind his childhood home where he reaches a final epiphany in the Christmas memoir *The Silent Stars Go By* (1998). *Crossing Wildcat Ridge* (1999) interweaves concerns of his own health following open-heart surgery with a resurgent sensitivity to the landscape around his woodland home. In all his writing, Williams's work illuminates a wide range of human concerns.

BRIAN C. FERGUSON-AVERY, *Georgia Southwestern State University*

SUGGESTED READING

Contemporary Authors: New Revision Series, vol. 65 (Detroit: Gale, 1998), s.v. "Philip Lee Williams."

Don O'Briant, "Writing from the Heart," *Atlanta Journal-Constitution,* May 18, 1997.

Greg S. Rider, "Interview with Philip Lee Williams," *Chattahoochee Review* 12 (fall 1991): 90–109.

CALDER WILLINGHAM
(1922–1995)

Calder Willingham was an accomplished novelist, playwright, and screenwriter who created some of the most memorable characters in the American cinematic and literary canons. Characterized by raw sexual overtones, several of Willingham's novels are set in the South, with Georgia providing the backdrop for two of his novels, *Eternal Fire* and *Rambling Rose*.

Born in Atlanta on December 23, 1922, Calder Baynard Willingham grew up in Rome. Upon graduating from high school, he enrolled briefly at the Citadel, a military college in Charleston, South Carolina. His experience there provided him with fodder for his first novel, *End as a Man*. After completing his education at the University of Virginia, Willingham moved north to New York City, where he associated with many of the era's literary giants, including Truman Capote, Norman Mailer, and Gore Vidal.

When *End as a Man* appeared in 1947, Willingham established himself as a leading author in his own right. The novel presented a scathing and lurid assessment of the overblown machismo Willingham encountered at the Citadel. A reviewer for the *Washington Post Book World*, writing many years later in 1987, called the author "a dangerous sort of writer, mucking about with all sorts of taboos, his dark humor not always covering his tracks." Obscenity charges were filed but later dropped against the book's publisher, Vanguard Press, and in 1953, a theatrical adaptation of the novel enjoyed an off-Broadway success. Willingham wrote the screenplay for a 1957 film version of the work, entitled *The Strange One*, which marked the film debut of actor Ben Gazzara.

Willingham spent the next several years as a screenwriter, working with several prominent actors and producers and co-writing such films as *Paths of Glory* (1957) and *One-Eyed Jacks* (1961). Willingham and Buck Henry collaborated on the screenplay for *The Graduate* (1967), which they adapted from a novel by Charles Webb. The film, starring Dustin Hoffman and Anne Bancroft, became one of the most popular and acclaimed films of 1967, and critics continue to hold it in high esteem. The script earned Henry and Willingham an Academy Award nomination for its fairly ruthless dissection of middle-class hypocrisy, materialism, and lifelessness.

Three years later, Willingham again earned accolades for his screen adaptation of the Thomas Berger novel *Little Big Man* (1970). Also starring Dustin Hoffman, this comedic drama turns the traditional "heroic" tale of the American West on its head by focusing on the apocryphal life and times of Jack Crabb, the lone white survivor of Custer's last stand.

Over the next two decades, Willingham continued to write novels and adapt screenplays for television and Hollywood, although never with the same success he enjoyed with *The Graduate* and *Little Big Man*. In 1972 he published *Rambling Rose*, a semi-autobiographical account of Willingham's adolescence in Rome. The story revolves around the sexual tensions that emerge when a rural Georgia family hires Rose, an alluring housemaid from Birmingham, Alabama. In 1991 Willingham adapted the novel for film. Starring Laura Dern, Robert Duvall, and Diane Ladd, the film received lukewarm reviews but earned Academy Award nominations for both Dern and Ladd.

Despite his years as a screenwriter, Willingham did not see much value in his work for Hollywood and considered his calling to be that of a novelist. His other novels include *Geraldine Bradshaw* (1950), *Reach to the Stars* (1951), *Natural Child* (1952), *To Eat a Peach* (1955), *Eternal Fire* (1963), *Providence Island* (1969), *The Big Nickel* (1975), and *The Building of Venus Four* (1977). He also published a collection of stories and nonfiction, *The Gates of Hell*, in 1951. As a fiction writer, Willingham worked in a variety of genres, spanning conventional coming-of-age plots to science fiction to narratives about sex and family life. *Eternal Fire*, in particular, satirizes the tradition of Southern Gothic fiction.

On February 19, 1995, Willingham died of lung cancer in Laconia, New Hampshire.

ALEX MACAULAY, *Western Carolina University, Cullowhee, North Carolina*

SUGGESTED READING

Contemporary Fiction Writers of the South: A Bio-Bibliographical Sourcebook, ed. Joseph M. Flora and Robert Bain (Westport, Conn.: Greenwood, 1993), s.v. "Calder (Baynard) Willingham Jr."

J. L. Parr, "Calder Willingham: The Forgotten Novelist," *Critique: Studies in Modern Fiction* 11, no. 3 (1969): 57–65.

THE WIND DONE GONE

Few novels have captured the popular American imagination more strongly than Margaret Mitchell's 1936 book, *Gone With the Wind*. Its sweeping, romantic story of the South and the Civil War has entranced readers since the day of its publication. Many readers, however, especially African Americans, have complained that the novel is one-sided. They say that it demeans the role of blacks and that its portrayals of such characters as Mammy and Prissy are racist stereotypes. For them, *Gone With the Wind* has little to tell us about the real experiences of African Americans in the South during and after the Civil War.

In 2001 Alice Randall, a Harvard literature graduate and Nashville, Tennessee, writer of songs and scripts, set out to put the record straight. Her novel *The Wind Done Gone* tells the story of *Gone With the Wind* from the perspective of the daughter of Mammy and Gerald O'Hara and thus the half sister of Scarlett O'Hara. Her name is Cynara (taken from the same Ernest Dowson poem that gave Mitchell her title), and she narrates the novel through diary entries about her life.

Randall loosely based her characters on Mitchell's, though she gave them different names and to some extent redefined them. Gerald O'Hara is Planter, his wife is Lady, Scarlett is Other, and Rhett Butler is R. The plantation Tara becomes Tata. Some of the slaves have altered names as well: Pork becomes Garlic, for instance. Planter is a drunk easily manipulated by Garlic, who in fact runs the plantation. Because his wife is sexually cold, Planter takes Mammy as his mistress. Rhett Butler, in Mitchell's novel a swaggering, virile figure, in Randall's is aging and gray-haired. Scarlett, the strongest character in Mitchell's novel, is weak and given to hysteria in Randall's.

Alice Randall has described her book as a parody, a novel that stands in a long tradition of writing that makes fun of other literary works. Parody is especially important in African American literature. But the estate of Margaret Mitchell and its lawyers interpreted *The Wind Done Gone* differently. They saw it as appropriating without permission the characters and situations of *Gone With the Wind*. Tom Selz, an attorney for the Mitchell estate, argued that Randall's novel commits "wholesale theft" by borrowing characters, scenes, and situations from the Mitchell novel. Mitchell's lawyers sought to suppress publication of the novel on these grounds, and the first court ruling granted their request. Judge Charles Pannell issued the ruling: "When the reader of *Gone With the Wind* turns over the last page, he may well wonder what becomes of Ms. Mitchell's beloved characters and their romantic, but tragic, world. Ms. Randall has offered her vision of how to answer those unanswered questions. . . . The right to answer those questions and to write a sequel or other derivative work, however, legally belong to Ms. Mitchell's heirs, not Ms. Randall."

Randall appealed, and with the support of such well-known writers as Arthur Schlesinger, Harper Lee, Pat Conroy, Charles Johnson, James Alan McPherson, Larry McMurtry, Shelby Foote, and Toni Morrison, she argued that as a parody her book offered a time-honored literary response to another novel. "My book is a parody of *Gone With the Wind*. *Gone With the Wind* in certain ways divides the nation into white and black. My book unites the nation. Ultimately, most of the characters in my book turn out to be black, which is a way to make that line invisible. So, my book is a critique of *Gone With the Wind* in the form of a parody." Randall compared her book to the eighteenth-century English novel *Shamela* by Henry Fielding, which makes light of Samuel Richardson's novel *Pamela*.

On May 25, 2001, the Eleventh Circuit Court of Appeals agreed with Randall's argument and ruled in her favor. *The Wind Done Gone* was published shortly thereafter and quickly became a best-seller, remaining on the *New York Times* list for many weeks. The Mitchell Foundation again appealed, but the Eleventh

Circuit Court upheld its decision in October 2001. Randall and the Mitchell Trusts reached an out-of-court settlement in May 2002 that ended the dispute.

The Wind Done Gone recounts many of the events in *Gone With the Wind*, but from a different point of view and with numerous satiric twists. Behind the fumbling white inhabitants of the plantation are the slaves and former slaves who keep things going and manage to get what they need to survive and prosper by manipulating their owners. Randall shows a deep understanding of Mitchell's novel, and her book is not without compassion for the white characters, whom she sees as victims of their own foibles and weaknesses. At the same time, she demonstrates that *Gone With the Wind* did not accurately portray the historical world of the nineteenth-century South and that Mitchell misunderstood the African American slaves on whom the white plantation owners depended to run their plantations, pick their cotton, work in their homes, and make their lives comfortable.

An important theme in *The Wind Done Gone* is African American self-determination. Many of the black characters actively work to protect themselves and their loved ones, to improve their positions, to provide for the future. While Mitchell presents Mammy as a selfless and devoted servant, Randall presents her as capable of any act that protects the welfare of herself and her loved ones. To maintain control over the household, for example, she has stealthily murdered at birth each of Planter's sons: she wants to remove any male heir who in the future might challenge her authority. Moreover, while Mitchell's novel does not acknowledge the possibility of love in the lives of the slaves at the O'Hara plantation, Randall gives Cynara a full romantic existence, especially in the novel's second half.

In many ways *The Wind Done Gone* moves well beyond the novel it parodies. Rather than surviving to live another day, like Scarlett in Mitchell's story, the Scarlett figure dies. Cynara then follows R to Washington, D.C., where she meets important figures of the Reconstruction era, including Frederick Douglass, author of the famous slave narratives, as well as an African American congressman with whom she falls in love. As the novel concludes, with the end of Reconstruction and the days of Jim Crow laws looming, she takes steps to provide for the future welfare of her own descendants. She thus manages, in the pages of this novel written in the form of her diary, to chart the course of her own history.

As an African American response to *Gone With the Wind*, *The Wind Done Gone* is interesting and sometimes entertaining; however, it is not great literature. Cynthia Tucker, editorial page editor for the *Atlanta Journal-Constitution*, puts it best: "Though clever in places, Randall's book is not that funny. Some reviewers say it does not meet the literary definition of parody, either. (That's probably OK since *Gone With the Wind* doesn't meet the definition of literature.)" Randall leaves too many plot lines undeveloped or incomplete, and most of the characters, including Planter, Other, and Cynara, are hazily indistinct. Randall's own intentions seem unclear — is she writing a parody, as she seems to be doing in the book's first half, or is she writing about a young woman's discovery of her life's purpose? The novel shows the mark of numerous influences, including Alice Walker, Margaret Walker, Frederick Douglass, Toni Morrison, and even William Faulkner, and it never develops its own style and identity. In some ways it substitutes for the myths of Mitchell's Old South another mythology all its own. But as a statement embodying African American reaction to the myths underlying *Gone With the Wind*, it is an important literary and historical document.

HUGH RUPPERSBURG, *University of Georgia*

SUGGESTED READING

Karen Grigsby Bates, "A Through-the-Looking-Glass Version of *Gone With the Wind*," review of *The Wind Done Gone*, by Alice Randall, *Journal of Blacks in Higher Education* 33 (2001): 126–27.

Cynthia Tucker, "'GWTW' Richly Deserves Parody by Black Writer," *Atlanta Journal-Constitution*, May 27, 2001.

Jill Vejnoska, "Author Shakes South to Its Roots," *Atlanta Journal-Constitution*, May 27, 2001.

One of two novels by Georgia writer Flannery O'Connor (1925–64), *Wise Blood* is a masterpiece of allegory and farce (a blending of humor and tragedy). O'Connor takes issue with a world in which Jesus is but another moral man, in which the Incarnation is valid only to the unintellectual, and in which people can — through their own actions or natural goodness — save themselves. Published in 1952, *Wise Blood* is a compelling portrait of isolated characters in their search for spiritual truth. A film adaptation, directed by John Huston and filmed in Georgia, was released in 1979.

The plot of the novel revolves around Hazel Motes, who returns after several years of service in the military to find his family home in ruins and the members of his family either dead or missing. Partially in response to this discovery, he travels to the city of Taulkinham and begins preaching a new gospel, the Church Without Christ, which advocates a humanistic reliance on self rather than on God. Hazel buys a car; meets a number of characters, most notably Enoch Emery and Sabbath Lily Hawks; and becomes increasingly disenchanted with himself and his world. After murdering a preacher who has stolen his identity, he blinds himself and soon thereafter dies.

The characters in *Wise Blood* are representative of the confusion present in the modern world, as O'Connor understood it. For example, Enoch Emery seeks a friend, Onnie Jay Holy deludes himself into selling religion, and Sabbath Lily talks about a dirt road while Hazel Motes tries to discuss spiritual issues with her. Hazel Motes (whose nickname "Haze" represents his own spiritual blindness) both longs for and repudiates Christ; but he also possesses "wise blood," or intuition, that makes it possible for him to understand that salvation comes only as a result of suffering. Many of the novel's characters are *grotesques*, a term in southern literature for those who are known for their exaggerated attributes, unusual characteristics, or obsessive-compulsive thought processes or behaviors. For O'Connor, the grotesque also represents mental or spiritual deformity.

Wise Blood deals with several topics: the way in which people are displaced and marginalized; the arrogance that keeps people from seeing themselves; and the centrality of Christ in the salvation of humankind, with the suggestion that one's awareness of Christ is the mark of one's very character. In the novel O'Connor portrays the moment of grace as an encounter with holiness and as a moment of epiphany and physical and/or emotional violence as an essential part of one's transformation and growth.

Flannery O'Connor, born in Savannah, Georgia, was educated in parochial schools and was devoutly Catholic in both her personal religious sensibilities and her artistic vision. She lived most of her life in Milledgeville, Georgia, where she wrote the short stories, essays, novels, and letters that have defined her spiritual vision. O'Connor believed that rather than blinding her, Christian beliefs made it possible for her to see clearly and perceptively and to respect mystery. She considered her fictional world to be a reflection of the spiritual universe, and she knew that her Christian faith set her apart from an increasingly secular world.

O'Connor creates a fictional world in need of faith. In her work she writes with humor and deep seriousness about characters who — not understanding how much is at stake — gamble with one another and with their very souls. Through violent, perverse, and monstrous images she depicts a landscape characterized by sin, guilt, and judgment. She gazes unflinchingly at evil and shocks readers into seeing with new eyes the injustices and pride they overlook in their daily lives.

The distinguished Hollywood director John Huston considered O'Connor to be one of the great American authors, and in 1979 he made the only feature film to date based on her writings.

A year earlier, Michael Fitzgerald, the son of O'Connor's literary executor, Robert Fitzgerald, mailed a copy of *Wise Blood* to Huston, then in his mid-seventies, and the director immediately expressed interest in adapting it as a film. Huston had already made faithful adaptations of challenging literary works, Stephen Crane's *The Red Badge of Courage* (1951), Herman Melville's *Moby Dick* (1956), and *The Bible . . . In the Beginning* (1966). After *Wise Blood* the director made two more films adapted from literature, Malcolm Lowry's *Under the Volcano* (1984) and James Joyce's *The Dead* (1987).

Due to the novel's odd blend of the mundane and the metaphysical, its grotesque black comedy and unsettling religiosity, many assumed that *Wise Blood* was unfilmable. For Huston, these elements attracted him to the project. "It is both funny and dire," he later explained. "From page to page you don't know whether to laugh or to be appalled."

Huston shot the film almost entirely in and around Macon. Operating on a very limited budget (the smallest ever for Huston), the entire movie was shot in a mere forty-eight days with a minimal crew and much help from Macon's fire and police forces. The screenplay was written by Michael Fitzgerald and his older brother, Benedict, who kept it remarkably true to O'Connor's plot and characters. Rather than trying to recapture the era of the early 1950s, Huston, in his most significant deviation from the novel, decided to set the story in the late 1970s. Thus contemporary cars, buses, and many of downtown Macon's recently built office buildings form the backdrop of the film, and Hazel Motes becomes a veteran of the Vietnam War rather than of World War II.

The film is distinguished by its actors, who were carefully chosen to depict the novel's array of eccentric and unsympathetic characters. Only three cast members were established Hollywood names: Brad Dourif as Hazel Motes, Harry Dean Stanton as the blind preacher Asa Hawks, and Ned Beatty as Hoover Shoates, the promoter who encourages Motes's career as a prophet. Many of the film's supporting cast were Georgia actors, most notably Atlanta stage actress Mary Nell Santacroce, in the role of the lonely landlady who falls in love with Motes. Huston himself played the very small part of Motes's grandfather, a religious fundamentalist.

Wise Blood made its premiere and was enthusiastically received at the New York Film Festival in September 1979. *New York Times* critic Vincent Canby declared it to be "one of John Huston's most original, most stunning movies. It is so funny, so surprising, and so haunting that it is difficult to believe it is not the first film of some enfant terrible instead of the thirty-third feature by a man who is now in his seventies." One of the film's most notable achievements, according to Canby, was that it was "lyrically mad and absolutely compelling even when we don't fully comprehend it." Another critic proclaimed it to be "the best realized religious movie of the decade."

Although the film was not particularly successful at the box office, this daring and dark comedy remains one of the most notable achievements of Huston's late career.

JAN WHITT, *University of Colorado, Boulder*
JOHN C. INSCOE, *University of Georgia*

SUGGESTED READING

Robert H. Brinkmeyer, *The Art and Vision of Flannery O'Connor* (Baton Rouge: Louisiana State University Press, 1989).

Vincent Canby, "Many Try, but *Wise Blood* Succeeds," *New York Times*, March 2, 1980.

Sarah Gordon, *Flannery O'Connor: The Obedient Imagination* (Athens: University of Georgia Press, 2000).

John Huston, *John Huston: Interviews*, ed. Robert Emmet Long (Jackson: University Press of Mississippi, 2001).

John Huston, *An Open Book* (New York: Knopf, 1980).

Michael Kreyling, ed., *New Essays on* Wise Blood (New York: Cambridge University Press, 1995).

Gilbert H. Muller, *Nightmares and Visions: Flannery O'Connor and the Catholic Grotesque* (Athens: University of Georgia Press, 1972).

Miles Orvell, *Invisible Parade: The Fiction of Flannery O'Connor* (Philadelphia: Temple University Press, 1972).

Sura P. Rath and Mary Neff Shaw, eds., *Flannery O'Connor: New Perspectives* (Athens: University of Georgia Press, 1996).

Carol Schloss, *Flannery O'Connor's Dark Comedies: The Limits of Inference* (Baton Rouge: Louisiana State University Press, 1980).

Margaret Earley Whitt, *Understanding Flannery O'Connor* (Columbia: University of South Carolina Press, 1995).

FRANK YERBY
(1916–1991)

Frank Yerby rose to fame as a writer of popular fiction tinged with a distinctive southern flavor. He was the first African American to write a best-selling novel and to have a book purchased by a Hollywood studio for a film adaptation. During his prolific career, Yerby wrote thirty-three novels and sold more than fifty-five million hardback and paperback books worldwide.

Frank Garvin Yerby was born in Augusta on September 5, 1916, to Wilhemenia and Rufus Yerby. His mother was Scots-Irish and his father African American. He graduated from Haines Institute (1933) and Paine College (1937), both located in Augusta. Yerby continued his education at Fisk University in Nashville, Tennessee, where he received an M.A. degree in 1938, and at the University of Chicago, where he began studies toward a doctorate in 1939. For a brief period, Yerby worked as an instructor of English at Florida A&M College (later University) and at Southern University in Baton Rouge, Louisiana. He later migrated north, first to Dearborn, Michigan, where he worked as a technician at Ford Motor Company, and soon thereafter to Jamaica, New York, where he was employed as an inspector at Ranger Aircraft.

Yerby's first literary success came in 1944, when he received the O. Henry Memorial Award for his short story "Health Card," which focuses on the racial inequities faced by an African American soldier and his wife. Prior to this story, Yerby had written a protest novel about racial inequities in the South, but publishers had rejected it. Perhaps in part as a result, he began to write historical novels centering most often on white protagonists. It is from these novels that his literary reputation was built. *The Foxes of Harrow* (1946), in particular, laid the foundation for his career as a popular novelist by becoming the first best-selling novel by an African American author and earning him the title "king of the costume novel." Many of his novels are set in the antebellum South and feature dashing white male protagonists who experience adventures of romance, mystery, and intrigue.

Yerby was often criticized by blacks for the lack of focus on or stereotypical treatment of African American characters in his books. Thus, ironically, while Yerby held the distinction of being the first best-selling black novelist, he also became one of the most disparaged for his lack of racial consciousness. In response to this criticism, Yerby argued that "the novelist hasn't any right to inflict on the public his private ideas on politics, race, or religion." He later amended this stance to a degree, and in the late 1950s and 1960s he wrote novels that touched upon issues of race and southern culture, such as *The Serpent and the Staff* (1958), *The Garfield Honor* (1961), *Griffin's Way* (1962), and *Speak Now* (1969), which features his first African American protagonist. In 1963 Yerby completed a protest novel, *The Tent of Shem*, which was never published. The 1971 publication of his masterpiece, *Dahomean*, which focuses on the life of an enslaved African chief's son who is transported to America, serves as the culmination of Yerby's efforts toward incorporating racial themes into his works.

On November 29, 1991, Yerby died of congestive heart failure. At the time, he was living in Madrid, Spain, his place of residence since his self-imposed exile in 1955. Throughout his career Yerby remained a beloved native son of the South, receiving honorary degrees from Fisk University (1976) and Paine College (1977).

VALERIE FRAZIER, *College of Charleston and The Citadel, Charleston, South Carolina*

SUGGESTED READING

Black Writers: A Selection of Sketches from Contemporary Authors (Detroit: Gale, 1989), s.v. "Frank Yerby."

Contemporary African American Novelists: A Bio-bibliographical Critical Sourcebook (Westport, Conn.: Greenwood Press, 1999), s.v. "Frank Yerby."

James L. Hill, "The Anti-Heroic Hero in Frank Yerby's Historical Novels," *Perspectives of Black Popular Culture* (Bowling Green, Ohio: Popular Press, 1990).

The Oxford Companion to African American Literature (New York: Oxford University Press, 1997), s.v. "Frank Yerby."

CONTRIBUTORS

Edna Acosta-Belén, State University of New York, Albany

Derrick P. Alridge, University of Georgia

Carol M. Andrews, Armstrong Atlantic State University

Edwin T. Arnold, Appalachian State University, Boone,
North Carolina

Jarrod Atchison, University of Georgia

Catherine Badura, Valdosta State University

Kay Beck, Georgia State University

R. Bruce Bickley Jr., Florida State University, Tallahassee

Jacqueline Miller Carmichael, Georgia State University

Mae Miller Claxton, Western Carolina University, Cullowhee,
North Carolina

Bruce Clayton, Allegheny College, Meadville, Pennsylvania

James C. Cobb, University of Georgia

Thomas Cooksey, Armstrong Atlantic State University

Stephen D. Corey, *The Georgia Review*

Herbert W. Denmark, Georgia Poetry Society

David E. Des Jardines, University of Georgia Press

Carlos Dews, Columbus State University

Brian C. Ferguson-Avery, Georgia Southwestern State University

Gary M. Fink, Georgia State University

Valerie Frazier, College of Charleston and The Citadel, Charleston,
South Carolina

Janet Gabler-Hover, Georgia State University

Kelly S. Gerald, Arlington, Virginia

Sarah Gordon, Georgia College and State University

Darren Grem, University of Georgia

Robert W. Hamblin, Southeast Missouri State University, Cape Girardeau

Steve Harvey, Young Harris College

Susan Copeland Henry, Clayton College and State University

Anna R. Holloway, Fort Valley State University

Sandra S. Hughes, University of Georgia

Keith Hulett, University of Georgia Libraries

John C. Inscoe, University of Georgia

Alan Jackson, Georgia Perimeter College

Kenneth R. Janken, University of North Carolina, Chapel Hill

Michael M. Jordan, Hillsdale College, Hillsdale, Michigan

Gary Kerley, North Hall High School

John A. Kirk, Royal Holloway, University of London, United Kingdom

Valerie D. Levy, University of Georgia

Alex Lichtenstein, Rice University, Houston, Texas

Gregory C. Lisby, Georgia State University

Craig Lloyd, Columbus State University

James J. Lorence, Gainesville State College

Alex Macaulay, Western Carolina University, Cullowhee, North Carolina

Joy Hughes Mallard, Atlanta

Matthew J. Mancini, St. Louis University, St. Louis, Missouri

Hubert H. McAlexander, University of Georgia

Thomas L. McHaney, Georgia State University